Jakarta Commons Cookbook™

Other Java™ resources from O'Reilly

Related titles

Programming Jakarta Struts

Jakarta Struts Pocket
    Reference

Tomcat: The Definitive Guide

Ant: The Definitive Guide

Eclipse

Eclipse Cookbook

Java™ Servlet and JSP
    Cookbook

Better, Faster, Lighter Java™

**Java Books
Resource Center**

java.oreilly.com is a complete catalog of O'Reilly's books on Java and related technologies, including sample chapters and code examples.

OnJava.com is a one-stop resource for enterprise Java developers, featuring news, code recipes, interviews, weblogs, and more.

Conferences

O'Reilly brings diverse innovators together to nurture the ideas that spark revolutionary industries. We specialize in documenting the latest tools and systems, translating the innovator's knowledge into useful skills for those in the trenches. Visit *conferences.oreilly.com* for our upcoming events.

The O'Reilly Network Safari® Bookshelf™ (safari.oreilly.com) is the premier online reference library for programmers and IT professionals. Search across thousands of electronic books simultaneously and zero in on the information you need in seconds. Read the books on your Bookshelf from cover to cover or simply flip to the page you need. You can even cut and paste code and download chapters for offline viewing. Try it today for free.

Jakarta Commons Cookbook™

Timothy M. O'Brien

O'REILLY®

Beijing · Cambridge · Farnham · Köln · Paris · Sebastopol · Taipei · Tokyo

Jakarta Commons Cookbook™
by Timothy M. O'Brien

Copyright © 2005 O'Reilly Media, Inc. All rights reserved.
Printed in the United States of America.

Published by O'Reilly Media, Inc., 1005 Gravenstein Highway North, Sebastopol, CA 95472.

O'Reilly books may be purchased for educational, business, or sales promotional use. Online editions are also available for most titles (*safari.oreilly.com*). For more information, contact our corporate/institutional sales department: (800) 998-9938 or *corporate@oreilly.com*.

Editor:	Brett McLaughlin
Production Editor:	Matt Hutchinson
Production Services:	Octal Publishing, Inc.
Cover Designer:	Emma Colby
Interior Designer:	David Futato

Printing History:

November 2004:	First Edition.

RepKover™ This book uses RepKover™, a durable and flexible lay-flat binding.

ISBN: 0-596-00706-X
[M]

Table of Contents

Preface

In this book, you'll find information about a set of libraries developed within the Jakarta Commons (also referred to as "Commons"). Commons (*http://jakarta.apache.org/ commons*) is a set of small, popular components from the Apache Software Foundation's Jakarta project. Ranging from the elementary to the complex, many would consider some of these libraries indispensable to any Java™ project. These components are so widespread, they may already be on your classpath. If you develop an application using Jakarta Struts, Apache Tomcat, or Hibernate, you have Commons BeanUtils and Commons Logging in your classpath. If you just installed Red Hat Enterprise Linux with the default configuration, you've got Commons libraries somewhere in */usr*. If you downloaded Sun's J2EE 1.4 SDK, you will have also downloaded Commons Logging and Commons Launcher. While Jakarta Commons may be everywhere, many are still unaware of the capabilities these components provide.

This book uses Jakarta Commons to focus on tactical implementation details, answering such questions as: How do we parse XML? How do we serialize beans? Is there an easier way to work with Collections? How do we work with HTTP and keep track of cookies? The tactical is often sacrificed for the strategic. Consider a complex J2EE system with a solid, well-conceived architecture. The strategic (or high-level) design appears reasonable from 40,000 feet, but as soon as you drill into the details, you notice that every Servlet or JSP contains pages upon pages of unmaintainable and unnecessary code because the developers were not aware of some valuable timesaver like BeanUtils, Collections, or the Digester. Or, worse, the developer may have spent a week reimplementing most of the capabilities of Commons BeanUtils even though BeanUtils was already in the classpath. Knowing what Jakarta Commons has to offer often helps to inform decisions made at the lowest level.

Few application developers would consider writing a custom XML parser, but developers will frequently write custom components that duplicate freely available libraries. Take, as an example, a set of static utility methods that seems to pop up in almost every complex project. A common process such as reading a file to a String may be refactored into a CommonFileUtils class, or turning a DOM Document into a set of beans may be accomplished with a set of classes in some custom code. Jakarta Commons provides solutions to both of these problems and many more, and reading this book may help you to avoid unnecessary wheel reinvention.

Many people know of these components in a general sense, but few have the months or weeks necessary to sit down and read the relevant tutorials, FAQs, blogs, and archived mailing lists associated with each component. The amount of work involved in keeping up-to-date with an array of open source communities is not trivial. This is why I've tried to compact much of this information into easily accessible recipes. These recipes were written to provide the information you need to start using Commons in a few minutes, but the Discussion and See Also sections give you an opportunity to dig deeper into the motivation behind each Commons component if you need more information.

The tools introduced herein save you serious time and provide you with a set of alternatives you may not currently be aware of. I wish I had read a book like this five years ago; it would have accelerated my learning and helped me to avoid some costly design decisions. Use this text as you will; if you are only interested in Commons Collections, you should be able to quickly familiarize yourself with Collections by browsing Chapter 1. On the other hand, if you are looking for a survey of some of the major projects in Jakarta Commons, read this book from start to finish. Part structured reference, part prose, the cookbook format lets you customize your reading experience, and I hope this book is as interesting to read as it was to write.

What's Inside

This book covers components from Jakarta Commons, a few projects from Jakarta, and one project outside of the Apache Software Foundation. This book covers the following components:

- Jakarta Commons BeanUtils
- Jakarta Commons Betwixt
- Jakarta Commons CLI
- Jakarta Commons Codec
- Jakarta Commons Collections
- Jakarta Commons Configuration
- Jakarta Commons Digester
- Jakarta Commons HttpClient
- Jakarta Commons ID
- Jakarta Commons IO
- Jakarta Commons JEXL
- Jakarta Commons JXPath

- Jakarta Commons Lang
- Jakarta Commons Logging
- Jakarta Commons Math
- Jakarta Commons Net
- Apache Log4J
- Jakarta Velocity
- FreeMarker
- Jakarta Lucene
- Jakarta Slide

All of these projects are covered in detail in the following chapters. Here's what's in each chapter:

Chapter 1, *Supplements to the Java 2 Platform*

This chapter introduces Commons Lang. Automation of `toString()`, working with arrays, formatting and rounding dates, working with enumerations, generating identifiers, and measuring time are some of the topics discussed in this chapter. This chapter also covers the generation of unique identifiers with Commons ID.

Chapter 2, *Manipulating Text*

While Java does not have the extensive text manipulation capabilities of a scripting language like Perl, Commons Lang's `StringUtils` has a number of utility methods that can be used to manipulate text. This chapter deals with `StringUtils`, `WordUtils`, and Commons Codec.

Chapter 3, *JavaBeans*

Beans appear throughout Java; from Jakarta Struts to Hibernate, beans are a unit of information in an object model. This chapter introduces Commons BeanUtils, one of the most widely used components from Jakarta Commons.

Chapter 4, *Functors*

Functors are a fundamental way of thinking about programming as a set of functional objects. Commons Collections introduced predicates, transformers, and closures, and functors, which can be used to model control structures and loops. This chapter demonstrates how one would apply functors to any program.

Chapter 5, *Collections*

Iterators, filtering with predicates, buffers, queues, bidirectional maps, type-safe collections, constraining collections, lazy maps, and set operations are a few of the topics introduced in this chapter. This chapter deals with Commons Collections, new collection types introduced, and the application of functors to various collections.

Chapter 6, *XML*

If you are constantly parsing or creating XML documents, this chapter introduces some alternatives to the standard parser APIs (SAX, DOM, and JDOM). This chapter introduces Commons Digester, Commons Betwixt, and Commons JXPath.

Chapter 7, *Application Infrastructure*

Commons Configuration is introduced as a way to parse properties files and XML configuration files. Other recipes in this chapter show how Commons CLI can be used to parse a complex set of required and optional command-line options. This chapter also details the configuration and use of Commons Logging and Apache Log4J.

Chapter 8, *Math*

This chapter focuses on simple mathematical capabilities in both Commons Lang and Commons Math. This chapter introduces classes to work with fractions, complex numbers, matrices, and simple univariate statistics.

Chapter 9, *Templating*

This chapter deals with simple expression languages such as Commons JEXL to more complex templating engines such as Jakarta Velocity and FreeMarker. This chapter also demonstrates the integration of both Velocity and FreeMarker with a J2EE servlet container such as Jakarta Tomcat.

Chapter 10, *I/O and Networking*

This chapter introduces Commons IO, which contains a number of utilities for working with streams and files, and Commons Net, which contains simple clients for the FTP, POP, and SMTP protocols.

Chapter 11, *HTTP and WebDAV*

If you need to communicate with anything over HTTP, read this chapter, which deals with Jakarta HttpClient and the WebDAV client library from Jakarta Slide.

Chapter 12, *Searching and Filtering*

Commons JXPath can be used to apply XPath expressions to collections and object graphs. Jakarta Lucene is a fully functional search engine that can index any structured document. This chapter demonstrates the use of Lucene with Commons Digester.

Limited time and resources forced me to make some decisions about which projects to include in this text. Projects like Velocity, FreeMarker, and Log4J, while not Commons components, were included because they fit the mold of a small, easily reusable component. Other Commons components were not included in this book because they were still being developed at the time of writing, or because a short recipe would have been impossible without a detailed 30-page introduction. Commons DbUtils, DBCP, Discovery, Jelly, Launcher, Modeler, Pool, Primitives, Chain, and promising sandbox components could fill another entire volume. Some projects, such as Jakarta HiveMind, started as components in the Commons Sandbox only to be promoted directly to subproject status of the Jakarta project. Classification of projects and components in Jakarta can also be somewhat arbitrary; Jakarta ORO and Jakarta RegExp would both seem to be prime candidates for the Jakarta Commons, but they are both subprojects of Jakarta. Other projects, such as Jakarta Commons HttpClient, have recently been promoted to be subprojects of Jakarta, leaving the Commons entirely. Think of this book as focusing on Jakarta Commons with some other projects thrown in to liven up the discussion. I apologize in advance if I left your favorite project out.

Writing a book about a series of frequently released components is reminiscent of a game called whack-a-mole. Just when you finish updating a chapter for a new release, another component has a release. On average, one commons component is released every one or two weeks; therefore, a few of the versions in this book may be obsolete as soon as this book hits the shelves. In general, Jakarta Commons makes a concerted effort to preserve backward compatibility and keep a stable public interface. Lessons learned on Commons BeanUtils 1.6 should remain applicable to Commons BeanUtils 1.7. If you find that a more recent version of a component has been released, you should download that more recent version and check the O'Reilly site for updates related to this book.

Conventions Used in This Book

I'll use a number of conventions you should know about in this book. For example, menu items are separated with an → , like this: File → New → Project. To make them stand out, new lines of code will be displayed highlighted when they're added. Example code is often presented out of context; instead of developing an entire class, only the relevant block of code is presented. Most examples will include the necessary import statements for Commons-relevant classes, and other `import` statements will be implied. When code is omitted or implied, it will be represented by ellipses:

```
import org.apache.commons.digester.Digester;
...
Digester digester = new Digester();
digester.doSomething();
```

In addition, the following typographical conventions are also used in this book:

Italic

> Indicates new terms, URLs, email addresses, filenames, file extensions, pathnames, directories, and Unix utilities.

`Constant width`

> Indicates commands, options, switches, variables, types, classes, namespaces, methods, modules, properties, parameters, values, objects, events, event handlers, and XML tags.

Constant width italic
> Shows text that should be replaced with user-supplied values.

Constant width bold
> Highlights important text within code examples.

 This icon signifies a tip, suggestion, or general note.

 This icon indicates a warning or caution.

What You'll Need

To experiment with the various libraries introduced in this book, you will need the J2SE 1.4 SDK, which can be obtained from *http://www.javasoft.com*. The examples in this book were developed in an IDE named Eclipse, which can be downloaded from the Eclipse project site at *http://www.eclipse.org*. Each chapter contains instructions for downloading the various Jakarta Commons components; to download any component from Jakarta Commons, go to the Jakarta Commons page at *http://jakarta.apache.org/commons* and click on "Binaries" under "Download" in the left menu.

The Jakarta Commons Community

The Jakarta community and the larger community of the Apache Software Foundation is committed to developing open source software. The Apache Software Foundation is a nonprofit corporation registered in Delaware that supports ongoing collaborative software development according to a set of simple ideals: transparency, meritocracy, consensus, and mutual respect. To learn more about the foundation, start at the Frequently Asked Questions page on www.apache.org (*http://www.apache.org/foundation/faq.html*). Jakarta is a project under the Apache Software Foundation, and it is managed by what is known as a Project Management Committee (PMC). This committee manages a number of Jakarta subprojects including the Jakarta Commons.

The Jakarta community and Apache XML community both had tremendous growth spurts from 1999 to 2003, with both projects becoming dominant forces in open source Java. Tomcat, Struts, Xerces, Xalan, Ant, Cocoon, and other projects were embraced by the larger community and Java developed a very strong association with open source because of the influence of Jakarta. Toward the end of this growth spurt, the corporate structure of Apache required a certain level of oversight and accountability, which could not be achieved in an umbrella project like Jakarta with hundreds of committers. A decision was made to encourage Jakarta subprojects to move toward smaller, more focused PMCs. One of the first projects to leave Jakarta was Apache Ant, and other projects such as Maven, Struts, and Log4j followed suit. This new, more nimble approach to the structure of collaborative software development avoids the creation of a management layer between project participants and the PMC. Apache is making way for a new generation of projects that will set the standard for open source Java, including Geronimo, Pluto, Directory, Derby, and Axion. Be aware that the structure of projects and subprojects in Jakarta is somewhat fluid at the moment, and, as the situation evolves, certain components could be split off into separate Apache projects.

If you find the components in this book helpful, I encourage you to take some time to observe the commons-dev developer mailing list. The ASF is (mostly) transparent, and this means that the general public has a window into the collaborative development process that is used to create a large body of great software. I would encourage any developer to take an interest in a piece of software and watch the development process. Follow the decisions, releases, arguments, flame-wars, and evolution of something like Jakarta Commons and you can see for yourself what works and what doesn't work. This is also a great way to keep yourself informed of the changes and direction of certain projects.

I don't intend to speak for this community, and, honestly, no one can speak for a group as diverse as the one that has formed around Jakarta Commons. I wanted to write this book to help attract more people to the concept of Jakarta Commons and to take some time to encourage people to think about how they could contribute to that effort. If there are more people paying attention to the software, Commons components will have higher quality, more bug reports will be filed, and more people might take some time to submit documentation patches. If you find Jakarta Commons (or any other Apache software) useful, you should consider taking a little bit of time to help a fellow user on the user mailing list or submit documentation patches. If you find a typo or a bug, file a report on Apache's Bugzilla installation (*http:// issues.apache.org/bugzilla*) or Jira installation (*http://issues.apache.org/jira*).

There is always a need for greater unit test coverage, and any time you find an inconsistency in code you should file a bug. Contributions can come in many forms— answering user questions, writing documentation, writing unit tests, submitting patches, or providing feedback. All of these contributions help sustain a living community. If you find yourself unable to participate in the community, you can make a small (possibly tax-deductible) donation to the Apache Software Foundation to help offset the cost of infrastructure and bandwidth (*http://www.apache.org/foundation/ contributing.html*).

The Apache Software License

Everything in this book is covered by the Apache Software License 2.0 (except FreeMarker, which is covered by a similar BSD-style license). All developers who touch open source should be familiar with the various licenses and come to their own conclusions; most importantly, you should become familiar with the Apache license (and other BSD-style licenses) and how it differs from the GNU General Public License (GPL) and GNU Lesser General Public License (LGPL). Read the Apache Software License 2.0 at *http://www.apache.org/licenses/*.

I am not a lawyer (IANAL), but I would urge you to learn as much as you can about these licenses before you start to use them. For more information about open source, and for a comprehensive list of licenses, see the Open Source Initiative (OSI) at *http://www.opensource.org*. The Apache license does not place restrictions on people or organizations that wish to redistribute the software it covers, and, in general, the Apache license creates fewer licensing headaches for individuals and organizations that want to incorporate open source software into a commercial product.

Using Code Examples

This book is here to help you get your job done. In general, you may use the code in this book in your programs and documentation. You do not need to contact us for permission unless you're reproducing a significant portion of the code. For example, writing a program that uses several chunks of code from this book does not require permission. Selling or distributing a CD-ROM of examples from O'Reilly books *does* require permission. Answering a question by citing this book and quoting example code does not require permission. Incorporating a significant amount of example code from this book into your product's documentation *does* require permission.

We appreciate, but do not require, attribution. An attribution usually includes the title, author, publisher, and ISBN. For example: "*Jakarta Commons Cookbook*, by Timothy M. O'Brien. Copyright 2005 O'Reilly Media, Inc., 0-596-00706-X."

If you feel your use of code examples falls outside fair use or the permission given above, feel free to contact us at *permissions@oreilly.com*.

We'd Like to Hear from You

Please address comments and questions concerning this book to the publisher:

> O'Reilly Media, Inc.
> 1005 Gravenstein Highway North
> Sebastopol, CA 95472
> (800) 998-9938 (in the United States or Canada)
> (707) 829-0515 (international or local)
> (707) 829-0104 (fax)

O'Reilly maintains a web page for this book, where errata, examples, and any additional information are listed. You can access this page at:

http://www.oreilly.com/catalog/jakartackbk

To comment or ask technical questions about this book, send email to:

bookquestions@oreilly.com

For more information about O'Reilly books, conferences, Resource Centers, and the O'Reilly Network, see the web site:

http://www.oreilly.com

Acknowledgments

This book would have been impossible to write were it not for the support and inspiration of a number of colleagues, friends, and family.

Thanks to Brett McLaughlin, my editor, who had a huge impact on the quality, structure, and content of the book. His feedback and advice over the course of the past year has been immeasurably valuable. Thanks also to Karen Tegtmeyer for reviewing this book.

Primary credit should first go to the Jakarta community and the various individuals who give hours upon hours of time to cut releases and maintain infrastructure. In the face of constant challenge, Jakarta has remained a well spring of innovation.

Thanks to Michael Podrazik, Stefan Winz, Bob Hartlaub, Gautam Guliani, Jarret Rackoff, Robert Sorkin, and Federico Hatoum, and Grassroots Technologies in New York, NY. Stefan originally introduced me to the Commons in the form of the Digester.

Thanks to various colleagues: Tim Beynart, Mike Smith, Felix Sheng, Julian Bleecker, Jim Buswell, Peter Costa, Rich Angeletti, David Winterfeldt, Ray Krueger, Chris Bobbitt, Tom Bergerson, Alex Wolfe, David Navin, Mark Snell, Bill Martens, Sultan Meghji, Daniel Summers, Greg Sandell, Dan Waite, and Benjamin Burton.

Mad props to Dave and Nicola, Rock, Patrick, Kat and Jay, Mike, Kelcey, John, Heather, Nick, Jessica, Marc, Krys, Joan, Jim, Zach, Sarah, and Mickey. Much respect to John Bicknell, Karen Brunssen, Kit Bridges and the Trinity Episcopal Church Choir. Endless thanks to Andrea and Klaus.

Thanks to my family, Chris, Kriste, Charlotte, Lily, Sean, Amy, Lucy, Kathy, Toby, Julie, Taylor, the Gilmores, Janey, all the O'Briens, and my parents Margaret and Michael. Thanks to the Paynes: Becky, James, Heather, Chris, Jeannette, Matt, Susette and Tom, Grandma Barbee and James Sr.

Most of all, I would like to thank my wife, Susan O'Brien, for being perfect. Happy Halloween.

## CHAPTER 1

Supplements to the Java 2 Platform

1.0   Introduction

This chapter introduces utilities that augment the Java 2 Standard Edition (J2SE), providing classes and utilities that make some of the more mundane programming tasks more straightforward. Jakarta Commons Lang is a collection of useful supplements to the J2SE. This package fills gaps present in the standard Java API and provides a number of simple, time-saving utility classes. Sun's Javadoc for the `java.lang` package in the J2SE states that the package "provides classes that are fundamental to the design of the Java programming language." In the same vein, Jakarta Commons Lang provides classes that augment the fundamental design of the Java programming language.

You may be tempted to skip the simple recipes presented in this chapter and continue on to more advanced topics in this text. String manipulation, date truncation, and `toString( )` methods do not inspire the sense of mystery and genius one feels when working with Extensible Markup Language (XML) or an open source text-to-speech engine. But, even if you are the most fluent speaker of Java, there are lessons to be learned from the utilities introduced in this chapter; a simple trick learned here may save you a few minutes every single day. Don't waste your time rewriting and maintaining utilities that already exist in Commons Lang; there are more interesting problems to be solved, and building `hashcode( )` functions is not one of them.

1.1   Obtaining Commons Lang

Problem

You want to use Commons Lang because your program needs to use some of the simple utilities this component provides, such as array manipulation, date manipulation, and enums.

The Advent of Tiger

With the release of Tiger (the codename for Java 1.5), some of these utilities are duplicated or superseded. Those of you who are stuck with 1.4 for a few more months will find some of the supplements in this chapter helpful, regardless of the availability of a new Java Virtual Machine (JVM). Even if you are using Java 1.5, the recipes in this chapter will still be relevant. A few classes in many Jakarta Commons projects have been made obsolete by the release of 1.4, but there are still many vocal users who are using an application that only runs in 1.3 (or even 1.2). The bar for backward compatibility will eventually shift, but for now, most Commons components work with 1.3 or 1.4 at a minimum.

Solution

To download the latest version of Commons Lang, follow these steps:

1. In a web browser, open the URL *http://jakarta.apache.org/site/binindex.cgi*. This URL will select a mirror, and generate a page with links to download binary distributions from an Apache mirror.

2. Find the Commons Lang project section. If you search for the term "Commons Lang," you will find a section that provides a link to download the latest binary release of Commons Lang.

3. Click on either the *2.0 zip* or *2.0 tar.gz* (depending on your platform) to download Commons Lang 2.0.

4. Unzip or untar the binary distribution. This will create a directory named *commons-lang-2.0*. The *commons-lang-2.0* directory should now contain a Java Archive (JAR) file, *commons-lang-2.0.jar*.

5. Copy or add *commons-lang-2.0.jar* to your classpath.

Discussion

Step #5 varies based on your development environment. If you are working with Apache Ant as a build tool, you will need to make sure that your classpath includes the Commons Lang JAR. If you are using an Integrated Development Environment (IDE) like Eclipse, you will need to copy this JAR to a directory in your project, and alter your project's preferences to add Commons Lang 2.0 to the "Java Build Path." If you are using Maven as a build tool, add the following dependency to the dependencies section of your *project.xml*:

```
<dependencies>
 <dependency>
   <id>commons-lang</id>
   <version>2.0</version>
 </dependency>
```

```
...other dependencies...
</dependencies>
```

The Commons Lang library includes utilities for working with dates, exceptions, arrays, enums, and more. It is one of the most widely used libraries in open source Java. To learn more about Commons Lang, visit the Jakarta Commons Lang web site at *http://jakarta.apache.org/commons/lang/*.

 At the time of writing, the most recent version of the Commons Lang component was Version 2.0. If there is a more recent version of Commons Lang available, use the latest version. Although not a guarantee or a promise, most Jakarta Commons components strive for backward compatibility. If an interface has been altered or functionality removed, it will be noted in the release notes for a newer version. If you are going to use a different version of the Commons Lang component with the recipes in this chapter, make sure to read the release notes, which are stored in the file *RELEASE-NOTES.txt*.

See Also

If you are having an issue with one of the utilities in Commons Lang, see Recipe 1.2 on joining the Commons-user mailing list. If you are looking for the source code, see Recipe 1.3 on obtaining the source code for Commons Lang. You can also visit the Commons Lang web site at *http://jakarta.apache.org/commons/lang*.

1.2 Joining the Commons-User Mailing List

Problem

You want to ask a question about a component in Jakarta Commons.

Solution

Join the *commons-user@jakarta.apache.org* mailing list, and ask your question. This mailing list is full of Commons users, and it is a good place to discuss any problems you've had with a particular utility in the Jakarta Commons.

Discussion

Before you join this mailing list, take a moment to familiarize yourself with the mailing list guidelines available at *http://jakarta.apache.org/site/mail.html*. Once you have read these guidelines, you can find information about joining this mailing list at *http://jakarta.apache.org/site/mail2.html#Commons*.

The Jakarta Commons-user mailing list is a place for users of all Commons components to ask questions of other users and Commons developers. This mailing list has a high volume of messages, and subscribers should prefix all subjects with the component you are discussing. In the case of Commons Lang, make sure your email subject starts with [lang] before sending a message to the Commons-user mailing list; otherwise, your email may be ignored.

If you have a question or a comment, you will save yourself time and trouble if you search the archives of the Commons-user mailing list (*http://www.mail-archive.com/ commons-user@jakarta.apache.org/*) for related discussions. The archives of this mailing list are a great place to look if you are having problems with a particular Commons component. Try not to ask a question that has already been asked and answered in a previous discussion, and remember that the Apache Software Foundation (ASF) is a volunteer organization—members of the community will gladly assist you if you provide enough information. And, don't be shy. If you know the answer to someone's question, you don't have to ask for anyone's permission to actively participate.

See Also

The Commons-user mailing list archive is also available from the Eyebrowse list archive at *http://nagoya.apache.org/eyebrowse/SummarizeList?listId=15*.

1.3   Getting the Commons Lang Source Code

Problem

You want to view the source code for the Commons Lang project.

Solution

Download the source code from *http://jakarta.apache.org/site/sourceindex.cgi*. Following the same procedure as outlined in Recipe 1.1, you can download a file named *commons-lang-2.0-src.zip* (or *commons-lang-2.0-src.tar.gz*). Once you unzip this file, you will have the source to Commons Lang in *./commons-lang-2.0-src*.

Discussion

The *commons-lang-2.0-src* directory will contain the following:

build.xml
>   An Apache Ant build file, which you can use to compile the source. If Ant is installed, you can compile or test by running ant `compile` or ant `test`.

src/java
>   This subdirectory contains the source for the classes in Commons Lang.

src/test
>   This subdirectory contains unit tests for the Commons Lang project. Each **Test.java* file is an extension of JUnit `TestCase` class.

See Also

For more information about Apache Ant, see the Ant project page at *http://ant. apache.org*. Also see Chapter 3 in the *Java Extreme Programming Cookbook* by Eric M. Burke and Brian M. Coyner (O'Reilly).

The unit tests in this source distribution use the JUnit testing framework. For more information about JUnit, see the JUnit project page at *http://www.junit.org*. Also see Chapter 4 in the *Java Extreme Programming Cookbook* by Burke and Coyner.

See Recipe 1.1 for information about obtaining the binary distribution for Commons Lang, and see the Commons Lang web site at *http://jakarta.apache.org/commons/lang*.

1.4 Automating the Generation of toString( ) Content

Problem

You want to automate the creation of toString( ) methods.

Solution

Use the Commons Lang `ReflectionToStringBuilder` or `ToStringBuilder` and `ToStringBuilder` to create toString( ) methods. The following code is an example of a toString( ) method, which uses a reflection builder:

```
import org.apache.commons.lang.builder.ToStringBuilder;

public void toString( ) {
    ReflectionToStringBuilder.toString( this );
}
```

Discussion

Assume that you have an object named `PoliticalCandidate`—a bean that represents some information about a presidential candidate. This bean has a set of properties: firstName, lastName, dateOfBirth, moneyRaised, and homeState. Example 1-1 shows the PoliticalCandidate class using a `ReflectionToStringBuilder`; the getter and setter methods have been omitted for brevity.

Example 1-1. The PoliticalCandidate class using ReflectionToStringBuilder

```
import java.math.*;
import java.util.*;
import org.apache.commons.lang.builder.ReflectionToStringBuilder;

public class PoliticalCandidate {

    private String lastName;
    private String firstName;
```

```
    private Date dateOfBirth;
    private BigDecimal moneyRaised;
    private State homeState;

    // get/set methods are omitted for brevity...

    public void toString( ) {
        ReflectionToStringBuilder.toString( this );
    }
}
```

The process of keeping the contents of a toString( ) method synchronized with a changing object model becomes a chore (usually a forgotten one). Commons Lang includes a fairly simple utility designed to automate this chore using reflection. The ToStringBuilder class and its extension, ReflectionToStringBuilder, can condense a large toString( ) method body into one line of code. Most importantly, the ReflectionToStringBuilder reflects any future changes that are made to the object model. The following code demonstrates the output of a string built via reflection:

```
    // Create a State
    State va = new State( "VA", "Virginia");

    // Create a Birth Date
    Calendar calendar = new GregorianCalendar( );
    calendar.set( Calendar.YEAR, 1743 );
    calendar.set( Calendar.MONTH, Calendar.APRIL );
    calendar.set( Calendar.DAY_OF_MONTH, 13 );
    Date dob = calendar.getTime( );

    BigDecimal moneyRaised = new BigDecimal( 293829292.93 );

    // Create a Political Candidate
    PoliticalCandidate candidate =
        new PoliticalCandidate( "Jefferson", "Thomas", dob, moneyRaised, va );

    System.out.println( candidate );
```

Assume that the State object is another bean using the same ReflectionToStringBuilder. The code above sets the properties of a bean and produces the following output:

```
    com.discursive.jccook.lang.builders.PoliticalCandidate@187aeca
        [lastName=Jefferson,\firstName=Thomas,
         dateOfBirth=Sat Apr 13 22:38:42 CST 1743,
         moneyRaised=\293829292.93000007152557373046875,
         state=\com.discursive.jccook.lang.builders.State@87816d
            [abbreviation=VA,name=Virginia]]
```

As in other cases in this book, I've applied a minimal amount of formatting to the output so that it fits on the printed page. Your results will be the same in terms of content but will be all on one long line.

This is not the most readable piece of information in the world, but it *was* automatically generated. Keeping a toString( ) method up-to-date in an object model that contains one hundred entities is next to impossible under the constraints of a deadline and a budget. If your objects have meaningful toString( ) methods, it will be much easier to diagnose problems in your application. If you use the ReflectionToStringBuilder, you are assured that the message printed out will be accurate; the alternative is to have a message that may or may not be relevant—trusting developers to keep toString( ) methods updated manually.

This utility uses the class AccessibleObject in the J2SE reflection package to bypass access modifiers and access private member variables of an object directly. If your system is running under a restrictive SecurityManager, you may need to alter your configuration to allow Commons Lang to bypass these security restrictions. Only use this reflection builder if you are certain that your code will run in an environment without a restrictive security policy. I use this utility in a system that runs on a few servers in a known location, but if I were writing a reusable library, a reflection builder would not be feasible; if someone were to use my library in an environment with a different security policy, calling a toString( ) may cause problems. The relevant permission is the suppressAccessChecks permission target of the java.lang.reflect.ReflectPermission class.

1.5   Customizing Generated toString( ) Content

Problem

You need to automate toString( ) while retaining control over the output, contents, and formatting.

Solution

In addition to the ReflectionToStringBuilder, Commons Lang provides for customization via the ToStringBuilder and ToStringStyle class. From the previous recipe, if you only want the PoliticalCandidate toString( ) method to print lastName and firstName, use the ToStringBuilder class and pass in a ToStringStyle object. The following example demonstrates a toString( ) method implementation that customizes both style and content:

```
import org.apache.commons.lang.builder.ToStringBuilder;
import org.apache.commons.lang.builder.ToStringStyle;
```

```java
public String toString() {
    return new ToStringBuilder(this, ToStringStyle.MULTI_LINE_STYLE)
                    .append("lastName", lastName)
                    .append("firstName", firstName)
                    .toString();
}
```

Calling toString( ) on this object will produce the following output containing only the two properties specified as parameters to append( ):

```
com.discursive.jccook.lang.builders.PoliticalCandidate@1cd2e5f[
  lastName=Jefferson
  firstName=Thomas
]
```

 Unlike the output shown in Recipe 1.4, this output is shown *exactly* as it appears on your screen.

Discussion

Generating toString( ) content using reflection saves time, but the trade-off is that the code using reflection prints out every member variable of a given class. What do you do when the desired behavior is to print out only a few selected variables from a given class? What if your objects are very *wide*, in that they have many properties that you don't want to print out in a toString( ) method? There are situations where an object could have a large number of properties or when a particular property of an object might contain a large amount of textual content. In these situations, it would be counterproductive to use ReflectionToStringBuilder to print out every member variable in a class.

Use a ToStringBuilder and customize the contents of the output with a static member of a ToStringStyle. The constructor of a ToStringBuilder takes an object instance and a ToStringStyle, returning an instance of a ToStringBuilder. This builder is then customized by calling append( ), which lets you specify the properties you want included in the output. To customize the contents of a ToStringBuilder, you must manually add each property to an instance of a builder. The append( ) method accepts all primitives, objects, and arrays. Table 1-1 summarizes the variations of append( ) for integer primitives and objects.

Table 1-1. Variations of ToStringBuilder append( )

ToStringBuilder method	Description
append(int value)	Appends the value of the integer.
append(String n, int value)	Appends the value of the integer and the name of the property.
append(Object value)	Appends the toString( ) of an Object.

Table 1-1. *Variations of ToStringBuilder append( ) (continued)*

ToStringBuilder method	Description
append(String n, Object value)	Appends the toString( ) of an Object and the name of the property.
append(int[] array) append(Object[] array)	Appends the formatted contents of array.
append(String n int[] array) append(String n, Object[] array)	Appends the property name and the size of an array
append(String n, int[] array, boolean detail)	Appends the property name and the full contents of an array.

The ToStringStyle class provides a mechanism to customize the output of a ToStringBuilder, and this class contains a few built-in styles. One example is the ToStringStyle.MULTI_LINE_STYLE, which puts a newline character between every property. Another example is the ToStringStyle.SIMPLE_STYLE, which simply prints the value of every member variable. The following list provides an example of each of these preset styles:

ToStringStyle.DEFAULT_STYLE
    com.discursive.jccook.lang.builders.
    PoliticalCandidate@1cd2e5f[lastName=Jefferson,firstName=Thomas]

ToStringStyle.MULTI_LINE_STYLE
    com.discursive.jccook.lang.builders.PoliticalCandidate@1cd2e5f[
      lastName=Jefferson
      firstName=Thomas
    ]

ToStringStyle.NO_FIELD_NAMES_STYLE
    com.discursive.jccook.lang.builders.PoliticalCandidate@1cd2e5f[Jefferson,Thomas]

ToStringStyle.SIMPLE_STYLE
    Jefferson,Thomas

What's the big deal about toString( ) methods? This is about accuracy and keeping messages relevant in an evolving system. All useful error messages include a string representation of the object involved in the error. If you get an exception, and you print the value of an object, it is usually clear what is causing that exception. In the absence of sensible logging, it is next to impossible to debug a system without diving directly into a debugger. This is especially true if you are trying to diagnose the cause of an infrequent problem that only affects a tiny percentage of users who only encounter a problem if they perform a very specific action in a specific context. In these cases, it is helpful to know the internal state of every object involved in the error, and toString( ) is the easiest way to print this out to a log. Automate your toString( ) method, and your error messages will be more meaningful.

1.6   Automating hashCode( ) and equals( )

Problem

You need a way to automatically implement equals( ) and hashCode( ) methods.

Solution

Commons Lang EqualsBuilder and HashCodeBuilder provide methods to automate both the equals( ) and hashCode( ). Example 1-2 briefly demonstrates these two builders using the PoliticalCandidate bean from the previous two recipes.

Example 1-2. Automating hashCode() and equals()

```java
import org.apache.commons.lang.builder.HashCodeBuilder;
import org.apache.commons.lang.builder.EqualsBuilder;

public class PoliticalCandidate {

    // Member variables - omitted for brevity

    // Constructors - omitted for brevity

    // get/set methods - omitted for brevity

    // A hashCode which creates a hash from the two unique identifiers
    public int hashCode() {
        return new HashCodeBuilder(17, 37)
                    .append(firstName)
                    .append(lastName).toHashCode();
    }

    // An equals which compares two unique identifiers
    public boolean equals(Object o) {
        boolean equals = false;
        if ( o != null &&
            PoliticalCandidate.class.isAssignableFrom(o) ) {
            PoliticalCandidate pc = (PoliticalCandidate) o;
            equals = (new EqualsBuilder()
                        .append(firstName, ps.firstName)
                        .append(lastName, ps.lastName)).isEquals();
        }
        return equals;
    }
}
```

Discussion

HashCodeBuilder has a constructor that takes two integer primitives. These primitives are used as an offset when creating a hash code; both numbers should be odd, nonzero, and prime. The HashCodeBuilder in Example 1-2 is configured to use the firstName and the lastName of the PoliticalCandidate object; therefore, two PoliticalCandidate objects with the same first and last name will have identical hash codes. If a hash code depends on every field in a class, you may use reflection to generate a hash code:

```
public int hashCode( ) {
    return HashCodeBuilder.reflectionHashCode(this);
}
```

Like ToStringBuilder and HashCodeBuilder, the EqualsBuilder is also configured via an append( ) method, which takes two arguments to compare. EqualsBuilder's append( ) method accepts all primitives, objects, and arrays, and one advantage of EqualsBuilder is the ability to compare two arrays by simply passing them to append( ). When this happens, EqualsBuilder compares every element of an array:

```
int[] array1 = new int[] { 1, 3, 4, 2, 5, 3, 4, 5, 3, 4 };
int[] array2 = new int[] { 1, 3, 4, 2, 5, 3, 4, 5, 3, 4 };
int[] array3 = new int[] { 3, 3, 3, 3, 3, 3, 3, 3, 3, 3 };

EqualsBuilder builder = new EqualsBuilder( );
builder.append( array1, array2 );
boolean firstTwoEqual = builder.isEquals( );
System.out.println( "Is array1 equal to array2? " + firstTwoEqual );

EqualsBuilder builder = new EqualsBuilder( );
builder.append( array2, array3 );
boolean lastTwoEqual = builder.isEquals( );
System.out.println( "Is array2 equal to array3? " + lastTwoEqual );
```

The EqualsBuilder compares the contents of two arrays, checking to see that the corresponding element is equal. The following output is produced:

```
Is array1 equal to array2? true
Is array2 equal to array3? false
```

If two classes are equal only if every field is equal, the EqualsBuilder can compare two objects using reflection as in the following code:

```
public boolean equals(Object o) {
    return EqualsBuilder.reflectionEquals(this, o);
}
```

Be careful when using reflection to automate hashCode( ) and equals( ), you may get more than you bargained for. In Example 1-2, a candidate is uniquely identified by first and last name; if this bean were mapped to a table in a relational database, firstName and lastName would be a composite key identifying each unique row. A HashMap or HashSet is similar to a database table in that the identifier is defined by the fields used by hashCode( ) and equals( ); putting an equal object with the same hash code into a HashMap replaces the previous entry. A poorly implemented hashCode( ) or equals( ) can have unintended consequences when storing objects in such a data structure. In other words, equals( ) and hashCode( ) should be based off of the properties that uniquely identify a class. This being the case, the equals( ) function should return true if two PoliticalCandidate objects have identical first and last names, and the hash code for two equal objects should be identical. The hashCode( ) and equals( ) in Example 1-2 are written to only take into account the firstName and lastName properties.

1.7   Automating compareTo( )

Problem

You need a quick way to implement compareTo( ) methods.

Solution

Commons Lang CompareToBuilder provides a builder for compareTo( ) methods. CompareToBuilder can perform a comparison via reflection, or a comparison can be customized by passing parameters to an instance of CompareToBuilder. The following example demonstrates the use of the reflection builder to implement a compareTo( ) method. This implementation compares all nonstatic and nontransient member variables in both classes.

```
import org.apache.commons.lang.builder.CompareToBuilder;

// Build a compareTo function from reflection
public int compareTo(Object o) {
    return CompareToBuilder.reflectionCompare(this, obj);
}
```

Discussion

CompareToBuilder.reflectionCompare( ) takes two objects and compares the nonstatic, nontransient member variables of these objects. In Example 1-2, the comparison involves the name properties of two PoliticalCandidate objects from Example 1-3, which are considered equal if both firstName and lastName are equal. reflectionCompare( ) ignores static fields and transients; therefore, in Example 1-3, averageAge and fullName do not contribute to the automated comparison.

Example 1-3. Implementing compareTo() using a reflection builder

```
public class PoliticalCandidate {

    // Static variable
    private static String averageAge;

    // Member variables
    private String firstName;
    private String lastName;
    private transient String fullName;

    // Constructors

    // get/set methods

    // Build a compareTo function from reflection
    public int compareTo(Object o) {
        return CompareToBuilder.reflectionCompare(this, obj);
    }
}
```

In addition to a comparison by reflection, the CompareToBuilder can be configured to compare two objects by a set of variables in a particular order. The order of comparisons plays a key role when a comparison involves multiple member variables; this order is not specified when using the reflectionCompare() method. Assume that the default sorting behavior for PoliticalCandidate objects should be lastName and then firstName; if two objects have the same lastName, then sort by the firstName. The following example demonstrates a customization of the compareTo() method.

Calling append() specifies what variables will be compared and in what order they will be compared. The order of the calls to append() are backward—similar to pushing an object onto the top of a stack. The last property "pushed" onto the CompareToBuilder is the first property to be compared. Objects are compared by last name, and first name is used as a "tiebreaker." Example 1-4 will compare two PoliticalCandidate objects by lastName, falling back to firstName only if the lastName values were equal.

Example 1-4. Customizing a compareTo() method with CompareToBuilder

```
// A compare to that mimics the behavior of equals()
public int compareTo(Object o) {
    int compare = -1; // By default return less-than
    if( o != null &&
        PoliticalCandidate.class.isAssignableFrom( o.getClass() ) ) {
            PoliticalCandidate pc = (PoliticalCandidate) o;
            compare = (new CompareToBuilder()
                        .append(firstName, pc.firstName)
                        .append(lastName, pc.lastName)).toComparison();
    }
    return compare;
}
```

Remember to keep the behavior of equals( ) and compareTo( ) consistent to avoid problems when sorting collections. Automating the compareTo( ) method via reflection may not compare objects in a way that is consistent with equals( ).

See Also

compareTo( ) methods provide the natural sorting order for a set of objects, and they are frequently used when sorting a collection of JavaBeans™. If you are trying to sort a collection of beans, you are better off using the BeanComparator, which is described in Recipe 3.10.

Instead of capturing comparison logic in a compareTo( ) method, consider using a Comparator object. The Jakarta Commons Collections project contains a number of supplements to the Comparator interface, such as utilities to reverse and chain comparators. Comparator utilities are discussed in Chapter 4.

1.8 Printing an Array

Problem

You need to print the contents of an array.

Solution

Use ArrayUtils.toString( ) to print the contents of an array. This method takes any array as an argument and prints out the contents delimited by commas and surrounded by brackets:

```
int[] intArray = new int[] { 2, 3, 4, 5, 6 };

int[] multiDimension = new int[][] { { 1, 2, 3 }, { 2, 3 }, {5, 6, 7} };

System.out.println( "intArray: " + ArrayUtils.toString( intArray ) );
System.out.println( "multiDimension: " + ArrayUtils.toString( multiDimension ) );
```

This example takes two arrays and prints them out using ArrayUtils.toString( ):

```
intArray: {2,3,4,5,6}
multiDimension: {{1,2,3},{2,3},{5,6,7}}
```

Discussion

This simple utility can be used to print the contents of an Object[], substituting an object for a null element:

```
String[] strings = new String[] { "Blue", "Green", null, "Yellow" };

System.out.println( "Strings: " + ArrayUtils.toString( strings, "Unknown" ) );
```

This example prints the strings array, and when `ArrayUtils` encounters a null element, it will print out "Unknown":

```
Strings: {Blue,Green,Unknown,Yellow}
```

This utility comes in handy when you need to print the contents of a `Collection` for debugging purposes. If you need to print out the contents of a `Collection`, convert it to an array, and pass that array to `ArrayUtils.toString()`:

```
List list = new ArrayList();
list.add( "Foo" );
list.add( "Blah" );

System.out.println( ArrayUtils.toString( list.toArray() ) );
```

1.9   Cloning and Reversing Arrays

Problem

You need to reverse and clone the contents of an array.

Solution

Use `ArrayUtils.clone()` and `ArrayUtils.reverse()` methods from Commons Lang. Example 1-5 demonstrates the reversal and cloning of a primitive array full of `long` primitives.

Example 1-5. Cloning and reversing a primitive array with ArrayUtils

```
import org.apache.commons.lang.ArrayUtils;

long[] array = { 1, 3, 2, 3, 5, 6 };
long[] reversed = ArrayUtils.clone( array );
ArrayUtils.reverse( reversed );

System.out.println( "Original: " + ArrayUtils.toString( array ) );
System.out.println( "Reversed: " + ArrayUtils.toString( reversed ) );
```

The array is cloned and reversed, and the contents of the original and the reversed array are displayed as output using `ArrayUtils.toString()`:

```
Original: { 1, 3, 2, 3, 5, 6 }
Reversed: { 6, 5, 3, 2, 3, 1 }
```

Discussion

In Example 1-5, `clone()` returns a reference to a new array, and `reverse()` operates on the array reference supplied as a parameter. It is important to realize that while `clone()` leaves the original array alone, `reverse()` operates directly on the supplied array. In addition to supporting all primitive arrays, `ArrayUtils.clone()` and

ArrayUtils.reverse( ) work with object arrays. If array had been an array of Long objects, the code would bear a striking resemblance to the previous example.

The only difference between Examples 1-6 and 1-5 is the type of array being cloned and reversed. Again, ArrayUtils.toString( ) is used to print out the contents of both the original and the reverse array:

```
Original: { 3, 56, 233 }
Reversed: { 233, 56, 3 }
```

Example 1-6. Cloning and reversing an Object[] with ArrayUtils

```
Long[] array = new Long[] { new Long(3), new Long(56), new Long(233) };
Long[] reversed = ArrayUtils.clone( array );
ArrayUtils.reverse( reversed );

System.out.println( "Original: " + ArrayUtils.toString( array ) );
System.out.println( "Reversed: " + ArrayUtils.toString( reversed ) );
```

Without the aid of ArrayUtils.clone( ) and ArrayUtils.reverse( ), this task would have involved writing a loop to populate a reversed array. The following code completes the same task, but, in order to reverse an array, this example assigns the values from the original array in reverse; elements are inserted starting at reversed[reversed.length - 1] and ending at reversed[0]:

```
// readTemps returns a 1000 member double[]
double[] temperature = readTemps( );

double[] reversed = new double[temperature.length];
for( int i = 0; i < temperature.length; i++ ) {
    reversed[reversed.length - (i+1)] = temperature[i];
}
```

Another option is the use of the Collections.reverse( ) method. J2SE contains a Collections object with a static reverse( ) method, but this only operates on a List object. If you had an array of double primitives, and you wanted to take advantage of the Collections class, you would need to convert your double array to a list. Without Java 1.5's autoboxing feature, a double[] will need to be translated into a Double[] before elements can be used to populate a list:

```
double[] temps = readTemps( );

List tempList = new ArrayList( );
for( int i = 0; i < temps.length; i++ ) {
    tempList.add( new Double[temps[i]] );
}

Collections.reverse( tempList );

double[] reversed = new double( tempList.size( ) );
Iterator i = tempList.iterator( );
int index = 0;
while( i.hasNext( ) ) {
```

```
    reversed[index] = ((Double) i.next()).doubleValue();
    index++;
}
```

That nasty translation between a double array and a list of Double objects compli-cates your code. The next recipe will touch upon an easier method for performing this translation.

Is ArrayUtils.clone() really necessary? All arrays have a clone() method, and all Java arrays implement Cloneable and Serializable, but I would be surprised if many Java developers have read the relevant section of the Java Language Specification (JLS), which discusses Array Members (section 10.7). All arrays can be cloned by calling the clone() method:

```
long[] temps = readTemps();
long[] cloned = (long[]) temps.clone();
```

ArrayUtils.clone() doesn't provide you with any performance benefits, it doesn't necessarily improve your code, and one could debate the assertion that it makes for more readable code. But, mainly, it exists as a safe way to handle null array refer-ences. If you attempt to clone a null reference, this utility will return a null instead of throwing a runtime exception.

1.10   Transforming Between Object Arrays and Primitive Arrays

Problem

You need a way to convert an object array to a primitive array.

Solution

Use ArrayUtils.toObject() and ArrayUtils.toPrimitive() to translate between primitive arrays and object arrays. The following example demonstrates the transla-tion from a primitive array to an object array and vice versa:

```
import org.apache.commons.lang.ArrayUtils;

long[] primitiveArray = new long[] { 12, 100, 2929, 3323 };
Long[] objectArray = ArrayUtils.toObject( primitiveArray );

Double[] doubleObjects = new Double[] { new Double( 3.22, 5.222, 3.221 ) };
double[] doublePrimitives = ArrayUtils.toPrimitive( doubleObject );
```

The result from both translations is an array of equal length and equal contents. The first translation takes a long[] and translates the array to a Long[], and the second translation takes a Double[] and turns it into a double[].

Discussion

Assume that the following example uses an external library that expects a list of Double objects. The existing system uses an array of double primitives, and you need to "step up" from a primitive array to an object array in order to pass a parameter to the complexCalculation( ) method:

```
// Assume that temps is a 4000 element double[]
double[] temps = readTemps( );

// Turn the double[] into an array of Double objects
Double[] objectArray = ArrayUtils.toObject( temps );

List inputList = Arrays.asList( objectArray );

// Assume that some process returns results as a List of Double
// objects
List outputList = externalLib.complexCalculation( inputList );

// Transform this List of doubles to an array of double primitives
Double[] resultObjArray =
    (Double[]) outputList.toArray( new Double[0] );

double[] result =
    ArrayUtils.toPrimitive( resultObjArray, Double.NaN );
```

The primitive array, temps, is transformed to an object array using ArrayUtils. toObject( ), and the results of our calculation are translated from a list to an array of primitives using ArrayUtils.toPrimitive( ). While an object array can contain a null element, a primitive array cannot; the second argument to ArrayUtils.toPrimitive( ) specifies a double value to be used if there is a null in the object array. In this example, null values in the object array are stored as Double.NaN in our primitive array. The second argument to ArrayUtils.toPrimitive( ) is optional; if it is not present and a null value is present in the object array, a NullPointerException is thrown.

ArrayUtils offers various static methods to transform between primitive and object arrays. Tables 1-2 and 1-3 summarize both the toObject( ) and toPrimitive( ) methods.

Table 1-2. The various flavors of ArrayUtils.toObject( )

Return type	Method signature
Boolean[]	ArrayUtils.toObject(boolean[] array)
Byte[]	ArrayUtils.toObject(byte[] array)
Double[]	ArrayUtils.toObject(double[] array)
Float[]	ArrayUtils.toObject(float[] array)
Integer[]	ArrayUtils.toObject(int[] array)
Short[]	ArrayUtils.toObject(short[] array)
Long[]	ArrayUtils.toObject(long[] array)

Table 1-3. The various flavors of ArrayUtils.toPrimitive()

Return type	Method signature
Boolean[]	ArrayUtils.toPrimitive(boolean[] array)
Byte[]	ArrayUtils.toPrimitive(byte[] array)
Double[]	ArrayUtils.toPrimitive(double[] array)
Float[]	ArrayUtils.toPrimitive(float[] array)
Integer[]	ArrayUtils.toPrimitive(integer[] array)
Short[]	ArrayUtils.toPrimitive(short[] array)
Long[]	ArrayUtils.toPrimitive(long[] array)

See Also

Java 1.5 has added a feature called autoboxing, which provides for automatic conversions between primitives and objects. For more information about autoboxing, see *http://www.jcp.org/aboutJava/communityprocess/jsr/tiger/autoboxing.html*.

1.11   Finding Items in an Array

Problem

You need to test an array to see if it contains an element. If the array contains the element, you need the index of the matching element.

Solution

Use ArrayUtils.contains( ) to see if an array contains a specified element, and use ArrayUtils.indexOf( ) or ArrayUtils.lastIndexOf( ) to find the position of a matching element. The following example demonstrates the use of these three methods:

```
import org.apache.commons.lang.ArrayUtils;

String[] stringArray = { "Red", "Orange", "Blue", "Brown", "Red" };

boolean containsBlue = ArrayUtils.contains( stringArray, "Blue" );
int indexOfRed = ArrayUtils.indexOf( stringArray, "Red");
int lastIndexOfRed = ArrayUtils.lastIndexOf( string, "Red" );

System.out.println( "Array contains 'Blue'? " + containsBlue );
System.out.println( "Index of 'Red'? " + indexOfRed );
System.out.println( "Last Index of 'Red'? " + lastIndexOfRed );
```

This example locates strings in a string array and produces the following output:

```
Array contains 'Blue'? true
Index of 'Red'? 0
Last Index of 'Red'? 4
```

Discussion

All three methods work with an object array or any primitive array; in fact, almost every method defined in ArrayUtils can be applied to every possible array type—boolean[], byte[], char[], double[], float[], long[], short[], and Object[]. When using a primitive array, ArrayUtils compares the value in question to each element of an array until a match is found. When using an object array, ArrayUtils calls the equals( ) method to check for a matching array element.

ArrayUtils.indexOf( ) and ArrayUtils.lastIndexOf( ) take an optional third parameter that controls where an element search begins. In the next example, you are searching an array of double primitives for the value –9999. Example 1-7 demonstrates how to establish that the value is contained within an array and how to locate the index for each matching element.

Example 1-7. Searching an array using ArrayUtils.contains() and ArrayUtils.indexOf()

```
// temps is a 1000 element long[]
long[] temps = readTemps( );

// Check to see if the array contains -9999
boolean hasErrorFlag = ArrayUtils.contains( temperature, -9999 );

// Print out the index of every errored reading
int start = 0;
while( hasErrorFlag &&
        (ArrayUtils.indexOf(temperature, -9999, start) != -1) ) {
    int errorIdx = ArrayUtils.indexOf(temperature, -9999, start);
    System.out.println( "Error reading at index: " + errorIdx );
    start = errorIdx + 1;
}
```

You could easily implement this method yourself; ArrayUtils.contains( ) and ArrayUtils.indexOf( ) are simply methods that iterate through every element of an array and test for equality. The simple savings you gain from ArrayUtils is one less for loop you have to test and maintain:

```
    long testValue = -9999;
    boolean hasErrors = false;

    for( int i = 0; i < temps.length; i++ ) {
        if( temps[i] == testValue ) {
            hasErrors = true;
        }
    }
```

The benefits are small, but maintaining your own custom utility classes is a pain—it is just another thing to test and maintain. ArrayUtils isn't going to change your application's architecture, but it will ultimately reduce the amount of trivial code you have to write, and you will not have to expend energy maintaining or testing trivial code.

See Also

Chapter 4 contains a number of recipes dealing with Predicate objects and filtering collections. Instead of using the three methods defined in this recipe, you can put objects into a collection and count or select the elements that match an EqualPredicate. See Chapter 4 for more information about querying collections with predicates.

1.12 Creating a Map from a Multidimensional Array

Problem

You need to create a Map from a multidimensional array.

Solution

Use ArrayUtils.toMap() to create a Map from a two-dimensional array (Object[][]). Example 1-8 demonstrates the creation of such a Map. Example 1-8 takes an Object[][] representing atomic symbols and atomic weights and turns it into a Map retrieving the atomic weight for hydrogen.

Example 1-8. Creating a Map from an Object[][]

```
import org.apache.commons.lang.ArrayUtils;

Object[] weightArray =
    new Object[][] { {"H" , new Double( 1.007)},
                     {"He", new Double( 4.002)},
                     {"Li", new Double( 6.941)},
                     {"Be", new Double( 9.012)},
                     {"B" , new Double(10.811)},
                     {"C" , new Double(12.010)},
                     {"N" , new Double(14.007)},
                     {"O" , new Double(15.999)},
                     {"F" , new Double(18.998)},
                     {"Ne", new Double(20.180)} };

// Create a Map mapping colors.
Map weights = ArrayUtils.toMap( weightArray );

Double hydrogenWeight = map.get( "H" );
```

Discussion

Instead of calling `weights.put( )` for each entry in the `Map`, an `Object[][]` is created and then passed to `ArrayUtils.toMap( )`. The `toMap( )` method then extracts the first item in each array as the key and the second item as the value. This is a simple way to quickly create a `Map` in a piece of code; the alternative to using `ArrayUtils.toMap( )` is to simply create a `Map` and repeatedly call the `put( )` method.

See Also

In the previous example, `Double` objects are added to a `Map`, and values are retrieved from the `Map` using `get( )`. Commons Collections contains utility methods for retrieving `Double` objects as `double` primitives; `MapUtils.getDouble( )` retrieves an object from a `Map`, casts it to a `Number`, and calls `doubleValue( )` using the default value supplied if there is no corresponding key in the `Map`. See Recipe 5.21 for more information about `MapUtils.getDouble( )`.

1.13   Formatting Dates

Problem

You need to format a date, and `SimpleDateFormat` is not thread-safe. You are also looking for standard International Organization of Standards (ISO) date formats.

Solution

Use `FastDateFormat`, a thread-safe formatter for Java `Date` objects, and use public static instances of `FastDateFormat` on `DateFormatUtils`, which correspond to ISO date and time formatting standards defined in ISO 8601. The following example outputs the international standard for representing a date and time in a given time zone:

```
Date now = new Date( );
String isoDT = DateFormatUtils.ISO_DATETIME_TIME_ZONE_FORMAT.format( now );

System.out.println( "It is currently: " + isoDT );
```

This produces the following output displaying the current time with time-zone information:

```
It is currently: 2004-03-26T16:20:00-07:00
```

If you need to use a custom date format, use `FastDateFormat` as a substitute for `SimpleDateFormat`:

```
// create a formatter that simply prints the year and month
FastDateFormat formatter =
    new FastDateFormat( "yyyy-mm",
                        TimeZone.getDefault( ),
                        Locale.getDefault( ) );
```

```
String output = formatter.format( new Date() );
// output equals "2003-10"
```

Discussion

The problem for this recipe is two-fold; your multithreaded application needs to print out standard date/time formats. Printing a standard format is a problem easily solved by static instances of FastDateFormat on DateFormatUtils. Ideally, every program that needs to deal with dates knows how to recognize an ISO 8601 date when parsing input. The world is getting smaller by the day; use international standards when presenting dates, times, measures, and country codes.

SimpleDateFormat is incapable of producing an ISO-8601-compliant time zone that matches the pattern: +11:30. Sun's SimpleDateFormat class can generate time zones without the colon separator, but these are incompatible with systems that need to be able to parse a standard format. FastDateFormat has achieved compliance with the ISO 8601 standard by adding a "ZZ" date format symbol, which is translated into the appropriate time-zone representation. In addition to the format demonstrated in the previous example, the DateFormatUtils class maintains a number of variations on the full ISO 8601 date format; there is a format to show only the time, a format to show only the date, and others, as well as the standard format for displaying dates in Simple Mail Transfer Protocol (SMTP). (See Table 1-4.)

Table 1-4. Static date/time formats in DateFormatUtils

Name	Format
ISO_DATE_FORMAT	yyyy-MM-dd "2004-01-02"
ISO_DATE_TIME_ZONE_FORMAT	yyyy-MM-ddZZ "2004-01-02-07:00"
ISO_DATETIME_FORMAT	yyyy-MM-dd'T'HH:mm:ss "2004-01-02T23:22:12"
ISO_DATETIME_TIME_ZONE_FORMAT	yyyy-MM-dd'T'HH:mm:ssZZ "2004-01-02T21:13:45-07:00"
ISO_TIME_FORMAT	'T'HH:mm:ss "T04:23:22"
ISO_TIME_NO_T_FORMAT	HH:mm:ss "05:12:34"
ISO_TIME_NO_T_TIME_ZONE_FORMAT	HH:mm:ssZZ "12:32:22-07:00"
ISO_TIME_TIME_ZONE_FORMAT	'T'HH:mm:ssZZ "T18:23:22-07:00"
SMTP_DATETIME_FORMAT	EEE, dd MMM yyyy HH:mm:ss Z "Wed, 01 Feb 2004 20:03:01 CST"

Why would you want to use `FastDateFormat` in the same way `SimpleDateFormat` is used? Isn't `SimpleDateFormat` enough? The simple answer is no; `SimpleDateFormat` is *not* thread-safe and `FastDateFormat` is. In fact, you should be aware that none of the Sun formatting classes are thread-safe. If multiple threads are using any Java formatting object there is a possibility of deadlock, `RuntimeException`, or inconsistent behavior. If your systems use a shared instance `SimpleDateFormat` across multiple threads, you should migrate to `FastDateFormat` immediately.

See Also

Java date and time classes have a number of issues—concurrency issues with date formatting being "only the tip of the iceberg." An active member of the Jakarta Commons Community, Stephen Colebourne, has taken time to create a clean room reimplementation of a date and time API. For more information about Joda, take a look at the Joda project page (*http://www.joda.org/*).

For more information about the ISO date and time standards, see *http://www.cl.cam. ac.uk/~mgk25/iso-time.html*.

For more information about nonthread-safe implementations of `SimpleDateFormat`, see Sun's Bug Database, and look for Bug #4264153. Sun specifically states that all of the format classes `Format`, `MessageFormat`, `NumberFormat`, `DecimalFormat`, `ChoiceFormat`, `DateFormat`, and `SimpleDateFormat` are not thread-safe. It is unclear if Sun has addressed this issue in Java 1.4, but if you are writing critical multithreaded applications, you should avoid Sun's formatting classes or synchronize access to them.

1.14   Rounding Date Objects

Problem

You need to round a date to the nearest second, minute, hour, day, month, or year.

Solution

Use `DateUtils` to round `Date` objects to the nearest `Calendar` field. `DateUtils.round()` can round to almost every `Calendar` field, including `Calendar.SECOND`, `Calendar.MINUTE`, `Calendar.HOUR`, `Calendar.DAY_OF_MONTH`, `Calendar.MONTH`, and `Calendar.YEAR`. The following example demonstrates the use of `DateUtils.round()`:

```
import org.apache.commons.lang.time.FastDateFormat;
import org.apache.commons.lang.time.DateFormatUtils;
import org.apache.commons.lang.time.DateUtils;

FastDateFormat dtFormat = DateFormatUtils.ISO_DATETIME_FORMAT;

Date now = new Date( );
Date nearestHour = DateUtils.round( now, Calendar.HOUR );
Date nearestDay = DateUtils.round( now, Calendar.DAY_OF_MONTH );
Date nearestYear = DateUtils.round( now, Calendar.YEAR );
```

```
System.out.println( "Now: " + dtFormat.format( now ) );
System.out.println( "Nearest Hour: " + dtFormat.format( nearestHour ) );
System.out.println( "Nearest Day: " + dtFormat.format( nearestDay ) );
System.out.println( "Nearest Year: " + dtFormat.format( nearestYear ) );
```

This example creates an object representing the current time and rounds this date to the nearest hour, day, and year. Assuming that the current date is March 28, 2004, and the current time is 1:48 P.M., this program creates the following output using the FastDateFormat class from the previous recipe:

```
Now: 2004-03-28T13:48:12
Nearest Hour: 2004-03-28T14:00:00
Nearest Day: 2004-03-29T00:00:00
Nearest Year: 2004-01-01T00:00:00
```

Discussion

If you are creating a system to record the time of an event, and you are not certain exactly when that event happened, it is appropriate to round that date and time to an approximate value. Are you certain that you woke up at 9:02 A.M., 23 seconds, and 879 milliseconds? Or, is it more likely that you remember that you woke up around 9 A.M.? It would be appropriate to round this time to the Calendar.MINUTE or Calendar.HOUR field at the very least—recording a general time, such as "around 9 A.M." In the following example, DateUtils.round( ) calculates an approximate time:

```
// Rounding to the nearest hour
Date wokeUp = new Date( );
Date wokeUpAround = DateUtils.round( now, Calendar.HOUR );
```

If your wokeUp Date object is 1:31 P.M., then wokeUpAround will be equal to 2:00 P.M. But, if you woke up at 1:15 P.M., your wokeUpAround object would then be rounded down to 1:00 P.M. When you round or truncate to a field, all of the date fields less significant than the specified field are set to zero. In this example, rounding to an hour causes the minutes, seconds, and milliseconds to be set to zero. Rounding a Date to a Calendar.YEAR sets the day of the year to one and the time to the first instance of the nearest year:

```
Date now = new Date( )
Date nearestYear = DateUtils.round( now, Calendar.YEAR );
```

This previous code rounds to the nearest year, and if now is 15 May 2004, the resulting Date will correspond to the first instance of 2004. Alternatively, if now is 15 July 2004, the resulting Date will be the first instance of 2005.

DateUtils.round( ) works with the following field values, listed in order of significance:

- Calendar.MILLISECOND
- Calendar.SECOND
- Calendar.MINUTE

- Calendar.HOUR_OF_DAY and Calendar.HOUR
- Calendar.DATE, Calendar.DAY_OF_MONTH, and Calendar.AM_PM
- Calendar.MONTH
- DateUtils.SEMI_MONTH
- Calendar.YEAR
- Calendar.ERA

DateUtils introduces a DateUtils.SEMI_MONTH field, which will cause dates to be rounded to the middle or beginning of a month. In DateUtils, the middle of the month is defined as the 15th day of the month with the second half of the month starting at midnight on the 16th day of the month:

```
Calendar cal = Calendar.getInstance();
cal.set( 2004, Calendar.MARCH, 5, 10, 2, 2 );

System.out.println( DateUtils.round( cal.getTime() , DateUtils.SEMI_MONTH ) );
```

This code will print out *Mon Mar 01 00:00:00 CST 2004* as the 5th of March and is closer to the beginning of the month than it is to the middle of the month. If the Calendar object was March, 14th, 2004, and it had been rounded to a DateUtils.SEMI_MONTH, the rounded date would have been set to midnight on March 16th. One would think that the middle of March is the 15th? Isn't that date the famous Ides of March—the date on which Brutus betrayed Caesar? According to DateUtils, the first half of the month ends at 11:59 P.M. on the 15th of the month; the DateUtils.round() method returns the first instant of the beginning of the second half of March: *March 16 12:00:00.000 A.M.*

See Also

The more you work with Java's Date and Calendar object, the more you will curse the J2SE. If your frustration is boiling over, take a look at Joda. Joda contains an entire package devoted to date, time, and duration formatting, and it is not based on the Date or Calendar classes. For more information about Joda, take a look at the Joda project page at: *http://www.joda.org/*.

1.15 Truncating Date Objects

Problem

You need to truncate a date to a calendar field.

Solution

Use DateUtils.truncate() to throw out all fields less significant than the specified field. When a Date is truncated to the Calendar.MONTH field, DateUtils.truncate()

will return a Date object set to the first instance of the month. The day, hour, minute, second, and millisecond field will each contain the minimum possible value for that field. Example 1-9 truncates a date at the month field and the hour field.

Example 1-9. Truncating a Date object at Calendar.MONTH

```
import org.apache.commons.lang.time.DateUtils;
import org.apache.commons.lang.time.FastDateFormat;
import org.apache.commons.lang.time.DateFormatUtils;

FastDateFormat dtFormat = DateFormatUtils.ISO_DATETIME_FORMAT;

Date now = new Date( );
Date truncatedMonth = DateUtils.truncate( now, Calendar.MONTH );
Date truncatedHour = DateUtils.truncate( now, Calendar.HOUR );

System.out.println( "Now: " + dtFormat.format( now ) );
System.out.println( "Truncated Month: "
                    + dtFormat.format( truncatedMonth ) );
System.out.println( "Truncated Hour: "
                    + dtFormat.format( truncatedHour ) );
```

Assuming that the current date is March 28, 2004, and the current time is 1:48 P.M., this example produces the following output:

```
Now: 2004-03-28T13:48:12
Truncated Month: 2004-03-01T00:00:00
Truncated Hour: 2004-03-28T13:00:00
```

Discussion

If you want to associate every event that happened between 2 P.M. and 3 P.M. with the 2 P.M. hour, or every event that happened in a particular year with the first instant of that year, you need to truncate a Date at a specified Calendar field. When a Date is truncated, it is rounded down; DateUtils.truncate( ) is the equivalent of Math.floor( ) for the Date class. If it is 4:02 P.M. on October 31, 1975, a Date object truncated at the Calendar.HOUR field will point to 4:00 P.M., and a Date truncated at the Calendar.YEAR field will point to the first millisecond of the first minute, of the first hour, of the first day of year 2005: *January 01 2005: 12:00:00.000 A.M.*

See Also

DateUtils.truncate( ) can also be used to truncate a date to the nearest DateUtils.SEMI_MONTH. Recipe 1.14 discusses DateUtils.SEMI_MONTH in more detail.

1.16   Creating an Enum

Problem

You need an Enum, but you are not using the new Java 1.5 release.

Solution

If you are stuck with Java 1.4 or lower, you can use Commons Lang Enum, ValuedEnum, and EnumUtils to create an enum "type," which approximates the new language feature. Example 1-10 extends Enum, providing three flavors: Flavor. CHOCOLATE, Flavor.VANILLA, and Flavor.STRAWBERRY.

Example 1-10. Defining a Flavor enumeration by extending Enum

```
import java.util.*;
import org.apache.commons.lang.enum.Enum;

public final class Flavor extends Enum {
    public static Flavor CHOCOLATE = new Flavor( "Chocolate" );
    public static Flavor VANILLA = new Flavor( "Vanilla" );
    public static Flavor STRAWBERRY = new Flavor( "Strawberry" );

    private Flavor(String name, int value) { super( name, value ); }

    public static Flavor getEnum(String flavor) {
        return (Flavor) getEnum(Flavor.class, flavor);
    }

    public static Map getEnumMap( ) {
        return getEnumMap(Flavor.class);
    }

    public static List getEnumList( ) {
        return getEnumList(Flavor.class);
    }

    public static Iterator iterator( ) {
        return iterator(Flavor.class);
    }
}
```

The key to an Enum is the private constructor; this guarantees that there are only three instances of Flavor in any virtual machine. This extension of Enum provides a number of useful utilities to get a List or Map of available Flavor instances:

```
// Using Flavor to create an ice cream cone
IceCreamCone cone = new IceCreamCone( );
cone.setScoops( 5 );
cone.setFlavor( Flavor.VANILLA );
cone.addTopping( "sprinkles" );
```

```
    List flavors = Flavor.getEnumList();
    System.out.println( ArrayUtils.toString( flavors.toString() ) );
    // prints "{ Chocolate, Vanilla, Strawberry }"
```

Discussion

Assume that you are writing a system to classify choral singers by voice type: soprano, alto, tenor, and bass. Your database has a table dbo.lu_VoicePart, which contains a part name and a numeric part code. This voice part is a coded type; it needs both a name and a code, and a straightforward design is achieved by extending ValuedEnum. ValuedEnum is an Enum that keeps track of a numeric code for each instance of the enumeration. PartEnum extends ValuedEnum to store static instances of the four possible voice parts: soprano, alto, tenor, and bass. (See Example 1-11.)

Example 1-11. Extending ValuedEnum to create an enum

```
import java.util.*;
import org.apache.commons.lang.enum.ValuedEnum;

public final class PartEnum extends ValuedEnum {
    public static int  SOPRANO_VAL = 1;
    public static int  ALTO_VAL = 2;
    public static int  TENOR_VAL = 3;
    public static int  BASS_VAL = 4;

    public static PartEnum SOPRANO = new PartsEnum( "Soprano", SOPRANO_VAL );
    public static PartEnum ALTO = new PartsEnum( "Alto", ALTO_VAL );
    public static PartEnum TENOR = new PartsEnum( "Tenor", TENOR_VAL );
    public static PartEnum BASS = new PartsEnum( "Bass", BASS_VAL );

    private PartsEnum(String name, int value) { super( name, value ); }

    public static PartEnum getEnum(String part) {
        return (PartEnum) getEnum(PartEnum.class, part);
    }

    public static PartEnum getEnum(int part) {
        return (PartEnum) getEnum(PartEnum.class, part);
    }

    public static Map getEnumMap() {
        return getEnumMap(PartEnum.class);
    }

    public static List getEnumList() {
        return getEnumList(PartEnum.class);
    }

    public static Iterator iterator() {
        return iterator(PartEnum.class);
    }
}
```

This class extends ValuedEnum and has a private constructor. This guarantees that the only instances of this enumeration will be defined in PartEnum; four instances of PartEnum are created as public static final constants, and a name is assigned to every part. (See Example 1-12.)

Example 1-12. Vocalist bean with a PartEnum

```java
public class Vocalist {
    private String name;
    private PartEnum part;

    public String getName() { return name; }
    public void setName(String name) { this.name = name; }

    public PartEnum getPart() { return part; }
    public void setPart(PartEnum part) { this.part = part; }
}
```

Checking for every voice part involves a call to PartEnum.iterator( ), which obviates the need for an if/else if control statement to catch every single voice part:

```java
Iterator parts = PartEnum.iterator();
while( parts.hasNext() ) {
  PartEnum part = (PartEnum) parts.next();
  if( part.equals( vocalist.getPart() ) ) {
    System.out.println( "Vocalist is a " + part.getValue() );
  }
}
```

This example did not include any reference to a specific voice part, but, if your code needs to reference a specific voice type, it can use the static constants in PartEnum— PartEnum.SOPRANO, PartEnum.ALTO, PartEnum.TENOR, and PartEnum.BASS. And, lastly, it is impossible to create a Vocalist object with an invalid voice part, as the part property must be one of the four static instances of PartEnum defined in a PartEnum or null.

Using Enum types becomes especially important if an object has multiple classifications. If you were creating an object to track a person, you could easily end up with two overlapping classifications. In Example 1-13, both jobStatus and gender can be UNKNOWN, and the valid options for both jobStatus and gender are defined as public static int variables.

Example 1-13. Using public static final constants for category information

```java
public class Person {
    public static final int STUDENT = -1;
    public static final int EMPLOYED = 0;
    public static final int UNEMPLOYED = 1;
    public static final int RETIRED = 2;
    public static final int UNKNOWN = 3;
    public static final int MALE = 0;
    public static final int FEMALE = 1;
```

```
    private int jobStatus;
    private int gender;

    public int getJobStatus() { return jobStatus; }
    public void setJobStatus(int jobStatus) { this.jobStatus = jobStatus; }

    public int getGender() { return gender; }
    public void setGender(int gender) { this.gender = gender; }
}
```

This class defines two properties—jobStatus and gender—and both correspond to codes stored in the database. This system needs to know; that MALE, FEMALE, and UNKNOWN are the valid values for the gender property; and STUDENT, EMPLOYED, UNEMPLOYED, UNKNOWN, and RETIRED all correspond to the jobStatus property. This class does not define which constants are related to which property. Is UNKNOWN a gender or a jobStatus? Some systems rename these static variables to reflect which properties they correspond to—GENDER_MALE, GENDER_FEMALE, and GENDER_UNKNOWN would clearly correspond to the gender property; and JOB_STUDENT, JOB_EMPLOYED, JOB_UNEMPLOYED, JOB_UNKNOWN, and JOB_RETIRED would correspond to the jobStatus property. This solution only draws a conceptual boundary in the mind of the programmer; no logical separation is achieved, and there is still no way to guarantee that a bean property will have a valid value. (See Example 1-14.)

Example 1-14. Simplifying with ValueEnum

```
public class Person {
    private JobStatusEnum jobStatus;
    private GenderEnum gender;

    public JobStatusEnum getJobStatus() { return jobStatus; }
    public void setJobStatus(JobStatusEnum jobStatus) {
        this.jobStatus = jobStatus;
    }

    public GenderEnum getGender() { return gender; }
    public void setGender(GenderEnum gender) { this.gender = gender; }
}
```

The solution to this problem can be solved by extending ValuedEnum and getting rid of the confusing mish-mash of public static constants. If you find yourself frequently creating static variables to reflect categories or types, enums are the solution. And, if you haven't upgraded to Java 1.5, use Commons Lang Enum and ValuedEnum.

See Also

As mentioned previously, Java 1.5 (or Tiger) has a new language feature: enums. If you are using Java 1.5, see the "Java 1.5 in a Nutshell" article from Sun Microsystems at *http://java.sun.com/developer/technicalArticles/releases/j2se15/*.

1.17 Generating Unique Numeric Identifiers

Problem

You need to generate numeric and alphanumeric identifiers.

Solution

Use IdentifierUtils to create an IdentifierFactory with both numeric and alphanumeric identifiers. Example 1-15 demonstrates the use of a LongIdentifierFactory to create unique numeric identifiers.

Example 1-15. Using a LongIdentifierFactory to create unique numeric identifiers

```
import org.apache.commons.lang.util.IdentifierUtils;
import org.apache.commons.lang.util.LongIdentifierFactory;

LongIdentifierFactory idFactory = factory.longGenerator(false, 0);

System.out.print( "Identifiers: " );
for( int i = 0; i < 10; i++ ) {
    System.out.println( idFactory.nextLongIdentifier() + " " );
}
```

This code will create 10 unique numeric identifiers and print them out on one line, producing the following output:

```
Identifiers: 0 1 2 3 4 5 6 7 8 9
```

Discussion

If you need a unique alphanumeric identifier, create a StringIdentifierFactory. This factory is created by calling the stringAlphanumericIdentifierFactory( ) method, passing true if you want the factory to wrap when it reaches a maximum value. The second parameter to this method specifies the length of the alphanumeric identifier; in this case, a length of four is specified. (See Example 1-16.)

Example 1-16. Using an IdentifierGenerator to create unique alphanumeric identifiers

```
import org.apache.commons.lang.util.IdentifierUtils;
import org.apache.commons.lang.util.StringIdentifierFactory;

StringIdentifierFactory idFactory =
    IdentifierUtils.stringAlphanumericIdentifierFactory(true, 4);

System.out.print( "Identifiers: " );
for( int i = 0; i < 10; i++ ) {
    System.out.println( idFactory.nextStringIdentifier() + " " );
}
```

This factory will create strings with four characters, which contain a base-36 representation of an integer that is incremented every time `nextStringIdentifier()` is called. The progression of alphanumeric identifiers follows this pattern:

0000, 0001, 0002, ... 000a, 000b, 000c, ... 000z, 0010, 0011, 0012, ... 001a, etc.

Once the identifier reaches the maximum value of "1111," it will wrap around to the start of the sequence. A factory that was not configured to wrap will throw an `IllegalStateException` when the maximum ID value has been reached.

If you do not feel like instantiating your own instance of a generator, `IdentifierUtils` contains static methods to access three static identifier factories: `LONG_IDENTIFIER_FACTORY`, `STRING_NUMERIC_IDENTIFIER_FACTORY`, and `STRING_ALPHANUMERIC_IDENTIFIER_FACTORY`. (See Example 1-17.)

Example 1-17. Static generators on IdentifierUtils

```
import org.apache.commons.lang.util.IdentifierUtils;

// Returns a Long identifier.
Long longId = IdentifierUtils.nextLongIdentifier();

// Returns a String numeric id.
String idNumber = IdentifierUtils.nextStringNumericIdentifier();

// Returns a String alphanumeric id.
String idAlpha = IdentifierUtils.nextStringAlphanumericIdentifier();
```

The `nextStringNumericIdentifier()` method returns a string that contains a number: "1," "2," "3," and so on. This static `STRING_ALPHANUMERIC_IDENTIFIER_FACTORY` is a wrapping alphanumeric generator that creates strings of length 15.

 This recipe demonstrates the use of the identifier generation utilities available in Commons Lang. Ongoing development of `IdentifierUtils` and `IdentifierFactory` has moved to the Commons Id project in the Jakarta Commons Sandbox.

See Also

The examples in this recipe provide a simple mechanism to create unique identifiers within a single JVM; the problem of generating truly unique identifiers across multiple systems is a job for the Universal Unique Identifier (UUID). The nascent Commons Id project contains a few utilities for working with UUID values, but, at the time of writing, these utilities are not yet ready for a final release. If you would like to either generate or use a UUID in a Java program, you are encouraged to follow the development of Commons Id UUID utilities at *http://jakarta.apache.org/commons/sandbox/id*.

The J2SE contains a class that can create a unique identifier across every JVM: a Virtual Machine Identifier (VMID). For more information about this class, which is associated with remote method invocation (RMI), see the Javadoc at *http://java.sun.com/j2se/1.4.2/docs/api/java/rmi/dgc/VMID.html*.

1.18   Validation of Method Parameters

Problem

You need to validate parameters passed to a method. You would prefer one line of code to test that a method parameter is valid.

Solution

Use Validate to check method parameters. Validate can check for empty or null parameters, as well as evaluate any logical conditions. Example 1-18 demonstrates the use of Validate to perform a few simple validations.

Example 1-18. Using Validate to perform simple validations

```
import org.apache.commons.lang.Validate;

public doSomething( int param1, Object[] param2, Collection param3 ) {

    Validate.isTrue( param1 > 0, "param must be greater than zero" );
    Validate.notEmpty( param2, "param2 must not be empty" );
    Validate.notEmpty( param3, "param3 must not be empty" );
    Validate.noNullElements( param3, "param3 cannot contain null elements" );

    // do something complex and interesting
}
```

Discussion

Write finicky methods. Don't just work with any input, have some standards. Don't hang around with garbage or nulls—clean up your act, and use Validate. Methods in Validate throw an IllegalArgumentException if invalid parameters are encountered. Validate.notEmpty( ) will throw an exception if the parameter is null or empty, and Validate.isTrue( ) takes a logical expression that must evaluate to true. Table 1-5 lists a number of static methods of Validate.

Table 1-5. Available static methods on Validate

Validate method	Description
isTrue(boolean expr)	Fails if expression evaluates to false
isTrue(boolean expr, String msg)	Same as above; constructs exception with a message
noNullElements(Collection col)	Fails if collection contains a null

Table 1-5. Available static methods on Validate (continued)

Validate method	Description
noNullElements(Object[] array)	Fails if array contains a null
notEmpty(Collection col)	Fails if collection is empty
notEmpty(Map map)	Fails if map is empty
notEmpty(Object[] array)	Fails if array is empty
notNull(Object obj)	Fails if object is null

Well-written code tests input and parameters. Is the number within a given range? Has the user supplied an index that is out of bounds for this array? Unless you want your applications to break down and throw exceptions, make sure that you are not trying to access the 15th element of a 10-element array; your code should be skeptical of parameters and refuse to run if it doesn't get its way. In fragile systems, parameter validation is not a top priority; errors are dealt with as different application layers throw a potpourri of exceptions. Other, more unstable, systems will pass a null all the way down the call stack until the lowest level blows up and spits back a NullPointerException—with a long-winded stack trace. Don't play around with null—avoid it, test your system exhaustively, and throw an IllegalArgumentException.

Consider the following method, which takes a latitude, longitude, and mode parameter. Both the latitude and longitude must fall within a valid range, and this method should throw an IllegalArgumentException if it encounters an unrealistic latitude, an unrealistic longitude, or an empty mode parameter. The Validate utility used in conjunction with a DoubleRange object can reduce the amount of code dedicated to range checking and method parameter validation. To test the validity of the coordinates, two constant DoubleRange objects are created outside of the method. DoubleRange.includesDouble(double d) returns true if the number falls within the defined range—if x <= rangeMax && x >= rangeMin. (See Example 1-19.)

Example 1-19. Using the Validator and the DoubleRange to validate method parameters

```
public static final DoubleRange LAT_RANGE = new DoubleRange(  -90.0,   90.0 );
public static final DoubleRange LON_RANGE = new DoubleRange( -180.0, 180.0 );

public double elevation( double latitude,
                         double longitude,
                         String mode ) {
    Validate.notEmpty( mode, "Mode cannot be empty or null" );
    Validate.isTrue( LAT_RANGE.includesDouble( latitude ),
                "Lat not in range " + latRange, latitude );
    Validate.isTrue( LON_RANGE.includesDouble( longitude ),
                "Lon not in range " + lonRange, longitude );
```

Example 1-19. Using the Validator and the DoubleRange to validate method parameters (continued)

```
    double elevation = 0.0;
    // code to implement the elevation method
    return elevation;
}
```

It takes a fair amount of institutional discipline to make sure that a code base has a sufficient amount of validation, and it is surprising how often systems scale to thousands of lines without it. Systems without good internal validation and sanity checks are characterized by frequent occurrences of `NullPointerException` and `RuntimeException`. Throwing `RuntimeException` in the form of `IllegalArgumentException` might seem like an odd recipe for increasing overall stability. But, if you actively throw exceptions and test exhaustively, it will be less toil and trouble to identify and fix defects—your application will fail sooner, and you will have short stack traces and well-defined problems. Performing rigorous parameter validation alone will not create a stable system, but it is part of a larger equation, which involves unit testing and validation.

In addition to parameter validation, you should be writing unit tests that test this validation. If you write good unit tests using JUnit and then measure your test coverage with a tool like Clover or JCoverage, you can save yourself an amazing amount of grief fixing unanticipated defects. Your unit tests should be covering close to 100% of your code, and they should throw curveballs. Don't just test the expected situation—if your method takes a double, see what it does with `Double.POSITIVE_INFINITY`; and if your method takes an array, pass it a `null`. Test the unexpected; if you find that your method melts down with a `null`, check the parameter with `Validate`. 100% test coverage is not an unrealistic ideal; it will drive your validation code. More test coverage always leads to a higher level of system quality.

See Also

Chapter 8 discusses `DoubleRange` and other utilities for capturing a range of numbers.

Chapters 4 to 7 of the *Java Extreme Programming Cookbook* by Eric Burke and Brian Coyner (O'Reilly) are great introductions to unit testing tools and concepts. Read this book for an introduction to JUnit, HttpUnit, mock objects, and the idea of unit testing. Think of `Validate` as a runtime test for a method; the methods on `Validate` are analogous to the `assert( )` methods in JUnit's `TestCase` class.

If you are interested in measuring code coverage of unit tests, take some time to look at Clover from Cortex eBusiness. Cortex eBusiness offers a free license to Open Source projects, but if you are using the product in a commercial environment, it is around $250. More information about Clover is available at *http://www.thecortex.net/clover/*. Other than Clover, there is another tool named JCoverage, which can also be used to measure test coverage. More information about JCoverage is available at *http://www.jcoverage.com/*. For more information about JUnit, go to *http://www.junit.org/*.

1.19 Measuring Time

Problem

You need to determine how much time has elapsed during the execution of a block of code.

Solution

Use StopWatch to measure the time it takes to execute a section of code. Example 1-20 demonstrates the use of this class to measure the time it takes to perform simple arithmetic operations.

Example 1-20. Using StopWatch to measure time

```
import org.apache.commons.lang.time.StopWatch;

StopWatch clock = new StopWatch();

System.out.println("Time to Math.sin(0.34) ten million times?" );
clock.start();
for( int i = 0; i < 100000000; i++ ) {
    Math.sin( 0.34 );
}
clock.stop();
System.out.println( "It takes " + clock.getTime() + " milliseconds" );

clock.reset();
System.out.println( "How long to multiply 2 doubles one billion times?" );

clock.start();
for( int i = 0; i < 1000000000; i++) {
    double result = 3423.2234 * 23e-4;
}
clock.stop();
System.out.println( "It takes " + clock.getTime() + " milliseconds." );
```

This example measures execution time with StopWatch and produces the following output:

```
Time to Math.sin(0.34) ten million times?
It takes 6865 milliseconds

How long to multiply 2 doubles one billion times?
It takes 1992 milliseconds.
```

Discussion

StopWatch performs the same functions as a physical stop watch; you can start, stop, pause, resume, reset, and split the clock. The name of this utility conveys unmistakable meaning: starting, stopping, pausing, and resuming a clock are methods that need no explanation, and resetting an instance of StopWatch simply resets the elapsed time to zero. When a StopWatch is "split" the clock continues to tick, but every call to StopWatch.getTime( ) will return the time at which split( ) was invoked. This is analogous to the "lap" button on a real stop watch; the StopWatch.split( ) causes StopWatch.getTime( ) to return "lap time." When a runner completes a lap, you can "freeze" the lap time while the clock continues to count seconds. Once you split a StopWatch, you will need to invoke the StopWatch.unsplit( ) method to measure the total time elapsed since the clock was started.

Example 1-21 demonstrates the split( ) method on StopWatch. The clock continues to tick for three seconds, and after one second the StopWatch is split. Calling getTime( ) between the split and unsplit times will return one second. After three seconds, the unsplit( ) method is invoked, and calling getTime( ) returns three seconds. Figure 1-1 shows a timeline for this example.

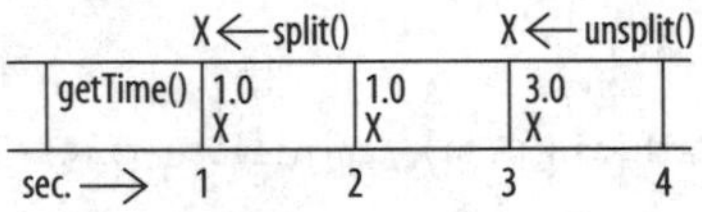

Figure 1-1. Timeline of StopWatch.split() and unsplit()

Example 1-21. Using the StopWatch.split() and StopWatch.unsplit() methods

```
import org.apache.commons.lang.time.StopWatch;

System.out.println( "Testing the split() method." );

clock.reset();
clock.start();
try { Thread.sleep(1000); } catch( Exception e ) {}

clock.split();
System.out.println( "Split Time after 1 sec: " + clock.getTime() );

try { Thread.sleep(1000); } catch( Exception e ) {}
System.out.println( "Split Time after 2 sec: " + clock.getTime() );

clock.unsplit();
try { Thread.sleep(1000); } catch( Exception e ) {}
System.out.println( "Time after 3 sec: " + clock.getTime() );
```

This example produces the following output, which shows that a split at one second resulted in 1001 being returned by the StopWatch after two seconds:

```
Split Time after 1 sec: 1001
Split Time after 2 sec: 1001
Time after 3 sec: 3004
```

The same requirements are easily fulfilled without the use of the StopWatch class. A program can measure time by calling System.currentTimeMillis() and subtracting the time after a section of code from a time measured before that same section of code; this yields the number of milliseconds elapsed. But the real benefit of using this little Commons Lang utility is to the readability and maintainability of a system. Writing good code is similar to writing a well-written essay, and StopWatch is a clear and concise noun that conveys direct meaning; it is a tangible analogy to a familiar object. In the previous example, the execution time of a block of code was obtained without adding clutter. Statements like clock.start() and clock.stop() are more apparent than long time1 = System.currentTimeMillis() and long time2 = System.currentTimeMillis(). And, for the same reasons, clock.getTime() conveys a stronger message than long timeElapsed = time2 - time1.

CHAPTER 2
Manipulating Text

2.0   Introduction

Parsing text fell out of fashion when Extensible Markup Language (XML) came to town. Java's text manipulation capabilities have only recently received some badly overdue attention, with the addition of regular expressions and numerous improvements in Java 1.5. Despite the improvements, using Java to manipulate plain text can inspire frustration. Hand a developer a fixed-length text file format to parse, and you will hear the groans—"Why can't we use something 'modern' like XML? I don't want to parse text." And while parsing and manipulating text may not build you a sexy resume, there is still a need to work with text in any program. For every snazzy XML file format, there is a widely accepted text file format with fixed-length fields; and for every XML web service, a vendor sends a proprietary feed that must be parsed character by character. Text manipulation is a must, but the Java 2 Standard Edition (J2SE) leaves developers wanting for more convenient ways to slice, dice, chomp, and manipulate text. This chapter introduces some simple utilities, which fill a few of Java's many gaps.

The recipes in this chapter deal with a collection of static methods on two classes in Jakarta Commons Lang—StringUtils and WordUtils. Some of the methods on StringUtils have been made obsolete by changes introduced in Java 1.4 and Java 1.5, but, regardless, there are times when you will want to split a string without regular expressions. Using StringUtils.chomp() achieves more readable logic than writing the equivalent logic using the String.indexOf() and String.substring() methods. These recipes will not change the basic architecture of a system with new, ground-breaking technology, but they are valuable "shortcuts" whose benefits will add up over time. Simple solutions to common tasks will save minutes of coding and hours of maintenance in the long run. Over time, many grow so accustomed to the efficiencies gained with Commons Lang, they consider it an indispensable supplement to the Java language.

Read the recipes in this chapter, and take some time to read the Javadoc for StringUtils and WordUtils. These utility classes provide some common string operations missing in Java, and they are simple and well-documented. These utilities are so simple that, throughout this chapter, you will notice recipes without a Discussion or See Also section—it's just not needed! These simple recipes have relevance to all skill levels; even if you are an experienced developer, you may be surprised at what Commons Lang string manipulation has to offer.

2.1   Setting Up StringUtils and WordUtils

Problem

You want the ability to use StringUtils and WordUtils to manipulate text.

Solution

To download the latest version of Commons Lang, refer to the steps outlined in Recipe 1.1.

Discussion

This chapter focuses on a very small subset of the Commons Lang project—StringUtils and WordUtils. To use either StringUtils or WordUtils in a Java class, add the following lines to your import statements:

```
import org.apache.commons.lang.StringUtils;
import org.apache.commons.lang.WordUtils;
```

Recipes that use StringUtils and WordUtils in this chapter will omit these import statements in code fragments. When StringUtils or WordUtils appears in an example, assume that it has already been imported.

See Also

If you have questions about these utilities, join the Jakarta Commons User mailing list; see Recipe 1.2. To download the source for Commons Lang, see Recipe 1.3.

2.2   Checking for an Empty String

Problem

You need to test for an empty or null string.

Solution

Use StringUtils.isBlank(). This method will return true if it is supplied with an empty, zero length, or whitespace-only string. This method gracefully handles a null input by returning true. The following example demonstrates isBlank( ) with four strings:

```
String test = "";
String test2 = "\n\n\t";
String test3 = null;
String test4 = "Test";

System.out.println( "test blank? " + StringUtils.isBlank( test ) );
System.out.println( "test2 blank? " + StringUtils.isBlank( test2 ) );
System.out.println( "test3 blank? " + StringUtils.isBlank( test3 ) );
System.out.println( "test4 blank? " + StringUtils.isBlank( test4 ) );
```

All four strings are tested, and the following output is produced:

```
test blank? true
test2 blank? true
test3 blank? true
test4 blank? false
```

Discussion

Checking for nonblank strings is just as easy; StringUtils.isNotBlank( ) will return the compliment of isBlank( ). If a string is empty, contains only whitespace, or is null, the StringUtils.isNotBlank( ) method will return false. This method comes in handy when a process expects a certain string to have content, and it gracefully handles a null input by returning false:

```
String test = "\t\t";
String test2 = "Test";

System.out.println( "test is not blank? " + StringUtils.isNotBlank( test ) );
System.out.println( "test2 is not blank? " + StringUtils.isNotBlank( test2 ) );
```

This produces the following output, which shows that a string containing only whitespace is considered blank:

```
test is not blank? false
test2 is not blank? true
```

Another method to test for an empty string is to "trim" a string to null if it contains only whitespace, and then test to see if the trimmed result is null. Use StringUtils. trimToNull( ) to transform empty strings to null. This method handles a null parameter value by returning null.

```
String test1 = "\t";
String test2 = "Test";
String test3 = null;

System.out.println( "test1 trimToNull: " + StringUtils.trimToNull( test1 ) );
System.out.println( "test2 trimToNull: " + StringUtils.trimToNull( test2 ) );
System.out.println( "test3 trimToNull: " + StringUtils.trimToNull( test3 ) );
```

This produces the following output, which shows that a string containing only whitespace is trimmed to null:

```
test1 trimToNull: null
test2 trimToNull: Test
test3 trimToNull: null
```

These three methods are laughably simple, but they will serve to reduce the amount of complexity in a system that needs to test strings. Use the methods from this recipe to avoid writing code to test for a null, and check the length of a string:

```
if( variable != null &&
    variable.length() > 0 &&
    !variable.trim().equals("") ) {
        // Do something
}
```

The code above can be rewritten with one call to StringUtils.isNotBlank():

```
if( StringUtils.isNotBlank( variable ) ) {
    // Do something
}
```

It is good practice to avoid using null whenever possible; code that uses null to signify emptiness or an error condition is harder to maintain and more likely to throw a nasty NullPointerException. Worse yet are methods that return a null whenever a problem occurs or an exception is thrown. While trimToNull() can accomplish the goal, it does increase the occurrence of nulls in code; use isBlank() and isNotBlank() to excise dangerous nulls from your code.

2.3   Abbreviating Strings

Problem

You want to abbreviate a string.

Solution

Use StringUtils.abbreviate(). Supply the string to abbreviate, and the maximum allowed length for the abbreviation. The following example will abbreviate the supplied text messages to 10 characters:

```
String test = "This is a test of the abbreviation."
String test2 = "Test"

System.out.println( StringUtils.abbreviate( test, 10 ) );
System.out.println( StringUtils.abbreviate( test2, 10 ) );
```

Here is the output of two string abbreviations:

```
This is...
Test
```

Discussion

`StringUtils.abbreviate( )` takes a string and abbreviates it, if necessary. When abbreviating to 20 characters, if the text is less than 20 characters, the method simply returns the original text. If the text is greater than 20 characters, the method displays 17 characters followed by three ellipses. Abbreviating a piece of text to 20 characters guarantees that the text will occupy 20 characters or less:

```
String message = "Who do you think you are?";
String abbrev = StringUtils.abbreviate( message, 20 );
String message2 = "Testing";
String abbrev2 = StringUtils.abbreviate( message, 40 );
System.out.println( "Subject: " + message );
System.out.println( "Subject2: " + messages2);
```

This simple example abbreviates the first message variable, `message`, to "Who do you think...?" The second message variable, `message2`, is not affected by the abbreviation because it is less than 40 characters long; `abbrev2` will equal the contents of `message2`.

`StringUtils.abbreviate( )` can also abbreviate text at an offset within a string. If you are writing an application that searches for a given word and prints that word out in context, you can use the `StringUtils.abbreviate( )` method to print the context in which a word appears:

```
String message = "There was a palpable sense that the rest of the world " +
                 "might, one day, cease to exist. In the midst of the " +
                 "confusion - the absence of firm ground - something would " +
                 "fail to recover. The whole city is still, in a way, " +
                 "holding it's breath, hoping the the worst has come and " +
                 "gone.";
int index = message.indexOf( "ground" );
int offset = index - 20;
int width = 20 + message.length();

String context = StringUtils.abbreviate(message, offset, width);
System.out.println( "The word 'ground' in context: " + context );
```

The output of this example is:

```
The word 'ground' in context: ... absence of firm ground, something would...
```

This code attempts to locate "ground." Once the index of the word has been located, an offset abbreviation is used to show the context of the word. The `offset` parameter tells `StringUtils.abbreviate( )` to start at a specific index in the string. Once the index of "ground" has been found, an offset and a width are computed to print 20 characters before and after the word "ground."

If an offset is less than four, output will start from the beginning of a string. If the offset is greater than four, the first three characters will be ellipses.

If a width less than four is specified, abbreviate( ) will throw an IllegalArgumentException. A width less than four does not give the abbreviate( ) method enough room to print ellipses and content.

2.4 Splitting a String

Problem

You want to split a string on a number of different character delimiters.

Solution

Use StringUtils.split( ), and supply a series of characters to split upon. The following example demonstrates splitting strings of a comma and a space:

```
import org.apache.commons.lang.ArrayUtils;

String input = "Frantically oblong";
String input2 = "Pharmacy, basketball,funky";

String[] array1 = StringUtils.split( input, " ,", 2 );
String[] array2 = StringUtils.split( input2, " ,", 2 );

System.out.println( ArrayUtils.toString( array1 ) );
System.out.println( ArrayUtils.toString( array2 ) );
```

This produces the output:

```
{ "Frantically", "oblong" }
{ "Pharmacy", "basketball" }
```

Discussion

The StringUtils.split( ) function does not return empty strings for adjacent delimiters. A number of different delimiters can be specified by passing in a string with a space and a comma. This last example limited the number of tokens returned by split with a third parameter to StringUtils.split( ). The input2 variable contains three possible tokens, but the split function only returns an array of two elements.

The most recent version of J2SE 1.4 has a String.split( ) method, but the lack of split( ) in previous versions was an annoyance. To split a string in the old days, one had to instantiate a StringTokenizer, and iterate through an Enumeration to get the components of a delimited string. Anyone who has programmed in Perl and then had to use the StringTokenizer class will tell you that programming without split( ) is time consuming and frustrating. If you are stuck with an older Java Development Kit (JDK), StringUtils adds a split function that returns an Object array. Keep this in mind when you question the need for StringUtils.split( ); there are still applications and platforms that do not have a stable 1.4 virtual machine.

The J2SE 1.4 String class has a split( ) method, but it takes a regular expression. Regular expressions are exceedingly powerful tools, but, for some tasks, regular expressions are needlessly complex. One regular expression to match either a space character or a comma character is [' '','']. I'm sure there are a thousand other ways to match a space or a comma in a regular expression, but, in this example, you simply want to split a string on one of two characters:

```
String test = "One, Two Three, Four Five";
String[] tokens = test.split( "[' '','']" );

System.out.println( ArrayUtils.toString( tokens );
```

This example prints out the tokens array:

```
{ "One", "", "Two", "Three", "", "Four", "Five" }
```

The array the previous example returns has blanks; the String.split( ) method returns empty strings for adjacent delimiters. This example also uses a rather ugly regular expression involving brackets and single quotes. Don't get me wrong, regular expressions are a welcome addition in Java 1.4, but the same requirements can be satisfied using StringUtils.split(" .")—a simpler way to split a piece of text.

See Also

Note the use of ArrayUtils.toString( ) in the solution section. See Chapter 1 for more information about ArrayUtils in Commons Lang.

2.5   Finding Nested Strings

Problem

You want to locate strings nested within other strings.

Solution

Use StringUtils.substringBetween( ). This method will return a string surrounded by two strings, which are supplied as parameters. The following example demonstrates the use of this method to extract content from HTML:

```
String htmlContent = "<html>\n" +
                "  <head>\n" +
                "    <title>Test Page</title>\n" +
                "  </head>\n" +
                "  <body>\n" +
                "    <p>This is a TEST!</p>\n" +
                "  </body>\n" +
                "</html>";
```

```
// Extract the title from this XHTML content
String title = StringUtils.substringBetween(htmlContent, "<title>", "</title>");

System.out.println( "Title: " + title );
```

This code extracts the title from this HTML document and prints the following:

```
Title: Test Page
```

Discussion

In the Solution section, the substringBetween( ) method returns the first string between the open and close strings—the title of an HTML document. The previous example only contained one nested element, but what happens when a string contains multiple elements nested in the same two strings? In the following example, three variables are extracted from a string using substringBetween( ):

```
String variables = "{45}, {35}, {120}" ;
List numbers = new ArrayList( );

String variablesTemp = variables;
while( StringUtils.substringBetween( variablesTemp, "{", "}" ) != null ) {
    String numberStr = StringUtils.substringBetween( variables, "{", "}" );
    Double number = new Double( numberStr );
    numbers.add( number );
    variablesTemp = variablesTemp.substring( variablesTemp.indexOf(",") );
}

double sum = StatUtil.sum( ArrayUtils.toPrimitive( numbers.toArray( ) ) );
System.out.println( "Variables: " + variables + ", Sum: " + sum );
```

The output of this example is:

```
Variable: {45}, {35}, {120}, Sum: 200
```

After each number is extracted from the curly braces, the system finds the index of the next comma and reduces the size of the string to search for the next call to StringUtils.

StringUtils.substringBetween( ) can also find text that is delimited by the same character:

```
String message = "|TESTING| BOUNDARYExampleBOUNDARY";
String first = StringUtils.substringBetween( message, "|");
String second = StringUtils.substringBetween( message, "BOUNDARY");
```

The first string would return "TESTING" as it is between the | characters, and the second string would contain "Example."

2.6   Stripping and Trimming a String

Problem

You need to strip or trim a string of extraneous whitespace, control characters, or other specified characters.

Solution

`StringUtils.trim( )` takes a string and removes every whitespace and control character from the beginning and the end:

```
String test1 = " \a\r Testing 1 2 3 ";
String test2 = " \r\n ";

String trimTest1 = StringUtils.trim( test1 );
String trimTest2 = StringUtils.trimToNull( test2 );

System.out.println( trimTest1 );
System.our.println( trimTest2 );
```

This code produces the following result. The `test1` variable is trimmed of leading and trailing whitespace, and the `test2` variable is trimmed to `null`:

```
Testing 1 2 3
null
```

Discussion

A *control character* is defined as all characters below 32 on the ASCII table—everything from 0 (NUL) to 31 (unit separator). `StringUtils.trim( )` delegates to the `trim( )` function on `String` and gracefully handles null. When you pass a `null` to `StringUtils.trim( )`, it returns a `null`.

Stripping a string

If a string contains leading and trailing characters to be removed, you can remove them with `StringUtils.strip( )`. The `strip( )` method differs from `trim( )` in that you can specify a set of characters to strip from the beginning and end of a string. In this example, dashes and asterisks are stripped from the start and end of a string:

```
String original = "-------***---SHAZAM!---***-------";
String stripped = StringUtils.strip( original, "-*" );

System.out.println( "Stripped: " + stripped )
```

This produces the following output:

```
Stripped: SHAZAM!
```

Trimming to null

Use `trimToNull( )` to test if a given parameter is present. Take the following servlet code as an example:

```
public void doGet(HttpServletRequest request, HttpServletResponse response)
    throws IOException, ServletException {

    String companyName =
        StringUtils.trimToNull( request.getParameter("companyName") );
    if( companyName != null ) {
        response.getWriter().write( "You supplied a company name!" );
    }
}
```

Using `StringUtils` reduces code complexity incrementally—four or five lines of code at a time. Testing for the absence or emptiness of a string usually entails checking to see if a string is empty or of zero length, and because a string could be `null`, you always need to check for `null` to avoid throwing a `NullPointerException`. In this last example, empty has the same meaning as `null`—the `StringUtils.trimToNull( )` method takes a string as a parameter, and if it is `null` or empty, the method returns a `null`.

2.7 Chomping a String

Problem

You need to remove a trailing newline or carriage return from a string.

Solution

Use `StringUtils.chomp( )` to remove the last line termination sequence from a string:

```
String input = "Hello\n";
String chomped = StringUtils.chomp( input );
// chomped equals "Hello"

String input2 = "Another test\r\n";
String chomped2 = StringUtils.chomp( input2 );
// chomped2 equals "Another test";
```

2.8 Creating an Emphasized Header

Problem

You would like to print an attention-grabbing header.

Solution

Combine the powers of StringUtils.repeat( ), StringUtils.center( ), and StringUtils.join( ) to create a textual header. The following example demonstrates the use of these three methods to create a header:

```java
public String createHeader( String title ) {
    int width = 30;
    // Construct heading using StringUtils: repeat(), center(), and join()
    String stars = StringUtils.repeat( "*", width);
    String centered = StringUtils.center( title, width, "*" );
    String heading =
        StringUtils.join(new Object[]{stars, centered, stars}, "\n");
    return heading;
}
```

Here's the output of createHeader("TEST"):

```
******************************
*********** TEST ************
******************************
```

Discussion

In the example, StringUtils.repeat( ) creates the top and bottom rows with StringUtils.repeat("*", 30), creating a string with 30 consecutive * characters. Calling StringUtils.center(title, width, "*") creates a middle line with the header title centered and surrounded by * characters. StringUtils.join( ) joins the lines together with the newline characters, and out pops a header.

2.9   Reversing a String

Problem

You need to reverse a string.

Solution

Use StringUtils.reverse( ). Supply a string parameter to this method, and it will return a reversed copy. The following example reverses two strings:

```java
String original = "In time, I grew tired of his babbling nonsense.";
String reverse = StringUtils.reverse( original );
String originalGenes = "AACGTCCCTTGGTTTCCCAAAGTTTCCCTTTGAAATATATGCCCGCG";
String reverseGenes = StringUtils.reverse( originalGenes );

System.out.println( "Original: " + original );
System.out.println( "Reverse: " + reverse );
System.out.println( "\n\nOriginal: " + originalGenes );
System.out.println( "Reverse: " + reverseGenes );
```

The output contains a reversed string along with an original string:

```
Original: In time, I grew tired of his babbling nonsense.
Reverse: .esnesnon gnilbbab sih fo derit werg I ,emit nI

Original: AACGTCCCTTGGTTTCCCAAAGTTTCCCTTTGAAATATATGCCCGCG
Reverse: GCGCCCGTATATAAAGTTTCCCTTTGAAACCCTTTGGTTCCCTGCAA
```

Discussion

Reversing a String is easy, but how would you rearrange the words in a sentence? StringUtils.reverseDelimited( ) can reverse a string of tokens delimited by a character, and a sentence is nothing more than a series of tokens separated by whitespace and punctuation. To reverse a simple sentence, chop off the final punctuation mark, and then reverse the order of words delimited by spaces. The following example reverses an unrealistically simple English sentence:

```
public Sentence reverseSentence(String sentence) {
    String reversed = StringUtils.chomp( sentence, "." );
    reversed = StringUtils.reverseDelimited( reversed, ' ' );
    reversed = reversed + ".";
    return reversed;
}

....

String sentence = "I am Susan.";
String reversed = reverseSentence( sentence ) );
System.out.println( sentence );
System.out.println( reversed );
```

The sentence is reversed and printed alongside the original:

```
I am Susan.
Susan am I.
```

Here, the order of the characters within each delimited token is preserved. Notice that this example includes StringUtils.chomp( ) with two parameters, the last specifying the character to chomp from the string. Instead of chomping a newline, in this example, the period is chomped off of the sentence before performing the delimited reversal.

2.10 Wrapping Words

Problem

You want to wrap lines of text using different line widths and various line termination sequences.

Solution

Use WordUtils to wrap words. Supply the number of columns and a line termination string, and WordUtils will wrap text. The following example wraps a small string to 20 columns:

```
// Define original String
String message = "One Two Three Four Five";

// Wrap the text.
String wrappedString =
    WordUtils.wrapText( message, 20, "\n", false );

System.out.println( "Wrapped Message:\n\n" + wrappedString );
```

This produces the following output:

```
Wrapped Message:

One Two Three Four
Five
```

Discussion

When WordUtils wraps a string, it takes a user-supplied line termination sequence like \n or \r\n and inserts this line termination sequence after a specified number of characters, without splitting a word. In the next example, if the user is using a hand-held device, the number of columns in the display is 40, and a new line is represented by the sequence \r\n. On a workstation, the number of available columns is 80, and a new line is a single \n character. The platform is available as the System property application.platform:

```
String message = "Four score and seven years ago, our fathers " +
                 "brought forth upon this continent a new nation: " +
                 "conceived in liberty, and dedicated to the proposition " +
                 "that all men are created equal. ";

// Define variables to hold two parameters to word wrapping
int cols;
String lineSeparator = "";

// Retrieve the platform property from System
String platform = System.getProperty("application.platform");
if( platform.equals( "Handheld" ) ) {
    cols = 40;
    lineSeparator = "\r\n";
} else if( platform.equals( "Workstation" ) ) {
    cols = 80;
    lineSeparator = "\n";
}

// Wrap the text.
String wrappedString =
    WordUtils.wrapText( message, cols, lineSeparator, true );
```

Depending on the platform, the `wrappedString` variable now holds the initial paragraph of the Gettysburg Address wrapped to fit either a 40-column handheld device or an application running on a workstation with an 80-column display.

To wrap text for presentation on the Web, use the line termination sequence `<br/>` to add an HMTL line break. The following example wraps text with `<br/>`, and introduces an option to prevent `WordUtils` from wrapping larger words:

```
String message = "Four score and seven years ago, our fathers " +
                "brought forth upon this continent a new nation: conceived " +
                "in liberty, and dedicated to the proposition that all men " +
                "are created equal. http://www.oreilly.com/Gettysburg ";

// Wrap the text.
String wrappedString = WordUtils.wrap( message, 40, "<br/>", false );
```

In this example, the Gettysburg Address is formatted to fit into 40 columns in an HTML document. The final parameter to the `WordUtils.wrap()` method tells the wrapping algorithm not to bother wrapping large words, such as the long URL at the end of the text. Wrapping a long word would prevent people from being able to copy this URL correctly.

2.11   Testing the Contents of a String

Problem

You need to make sure a string contains only numbers, letters, or a combination of both.

Solution

Use the various `StringUtils` methods to validate user input; `isNumeric()`, `isAlpha()`, `isAlphanumeric()`, and `isAlphaSpace()` verify that a string does not contain any undesired characters:

```
String state = "Virginia"

System.our.println( "Is state number? " +
                    StringUtils.isNumeric( state ) );
System.our.println( "Is state alpha? " +
                    StringUtils.isAlpha( state ) );
System.our.println( "Is state alphanumeric? " +
                    StringUtils.isAlphanumeric( state ) );
System.our.println( "Is state alphaspace? " +
                    StringUtils.isAlphaspace( state ) );
```

This code tests the string "Virginia" against four validation methods, producing the following output:

```
Is state a number? false
Is state alpha? true
```

```
Is state alphanumeric? true
Is state alphaspace? true
```

Discussion

`StringUtils.isNumeric( )` returns true if the string being tested contains only digits from 0 to 9. If you are asking a user to input a numerical value, such as year or age, you need to have a way to ensure that the input supplied is, in fact, a numeric value:

```
String test1 = "1976";
String test2 = "Mozart";

boolean t1val = StringUtils.isNumeric( test1 );
boolean t2val = StringUtils.isNumeric( test2 );

System.out.println( "Is " + test1 + " a number? " + t1val );
System.out.println( "Is " + test2 + " a number? " + t2val );
```

This code tests two strings and produces the following output:

```
Is 1976 a number? true
Is Mozart a number? false
```

You can use the following code to see if a string contains only letters or a combination of letters and numbers:

```
String test1 = "ORANGE";
String test2 = "ICE9";
String test3 = "ICE CREAM";
String test4 = "820B Judson Avenue";

boolean t1val = StringUtils.isAlpha( test1 ); // returns true
boolean t2val = StringUtils.isAlphanumeric( test2 ); // returns true
boolean t3val = StringUtils.isAlphaSpace( test3 ); // returns true
boolean t4val =
    StringUtils.isAlphanumericSpace( test4 ); // returns true
```

User supplied input can rarely be trusted. If you have asked the user to supply an age, a year, or a day of the week, you will need to then validate that input. Or, if you have asked the user to type in a name, you will want to make sure that the supplied name contains only letters and acceptable punctuation. An application with inadequate input validation will frequently fail, and produce unsightly stack traces caused by either `NumberFormatExceptions` or `NullPointerExceptions`. An application should be able to gracefully handle the most nonsensical input without missing a beat, and prompt the user for a valid input. Tools such as Jakarta Commons Validator provide a framework to validate the contents of a JavaBean, but at a much lower level, the `StringUtils` class in Commons Lang provides some useful utilities for examining the contents of a string.

Input forms frequently need to validate a user's name. In this case, it is important to remember that certain names have apostrophes and dashes. If you are validating a name, always make sure that you allow for names with punctuation. Here is an example that validates a name with a dash, an apostrophe, and a period:

```
String name1 = "Tim O'Reilly";
String name2 = "Mr. Mason-Dixon!";

String punctuation = ".-'";
String name1Temp = StringUtils.replaceChars( name1, punctuation, "");
String name2Temp = StringUtils.replaceChars( name1, punctuation, "");

boolean t1val = StringUtils.isAlpha( name1Temp ); // returns true
boolean t2val = StringUtils.isAlpha( name2Temp ); // returns false
```

"Tim O'Reilly" is a valid name, but you need to use the `StringUtils.replaceChars()` method to throw out punctuation before you can pass both of the names to the `StringUtils.isAlpha()` method. "Mr. Mason-Dixon!" is not a valid name, because an exclamation point is not on the list of valid name punctuation. As an Irishman, I encourage you to always check your name validation with names like "O'Toole" or "O'Brien," and, as the world continues to shrink, more exceptions to the rule, like "Al-Sa'ud," will become more prevalent; your system should not force someone to change their name. Speaking from personal experience, it is insulting when a web site or an application forces you to change your name, and it is a quick way to alienate your customers. I cannot begin to tell you how many web sites have shown me a nasty Open Database Connectivity (ODBC) error page or stack trace after I've told them my last name—it is frustrating.

2.12   Measuring the Frequency of a String

Problem

You need to find out how many times a certain word or piece of text occurs in a string.

Solution

`StringUtils.countMatches()` returns the frequency of a piece of text within another string:

```
File manuscriptFile = new File("manuscript.txt");
Reader reader = new FileReader( manuscriptFile );
StringWriter stringWriter = new StringWriter();
while( reader.ready() ) { writer.write( reader.read() ); }
String manuscript = stringWriter.toString();

// Convert string to lowercase
manuscript = StringUtils.lowerCase(manuscript);

// count the occurrences of "futility"
int numFutility = StringUtils.countMatches( manuscript, "futility" );
```

Converting the entire string to lowercase ensures that all occurrences of the word "futility" are counted, regardless of capitalization. This code executes and numFutility will contain the number of occurrences of the word "futility."

Discussion

If the *manuscript.txt* file is large, it makes more sense to search this file one line at a time, and sum the number of matches as each line is read. A more efficient implementation of the previous example would look like this:

```
File manuscriptFile = new File("manuscript.txt");
Reader reader = new FileReader( manuscriptFile );
LineNumberReader lineReader = new LineNumberReader( reader );
int numOccurences = 0;

while( lineReader.ready( ) ) {
    String line = StringUtils.lowerCase( lineReader.readLine( ) );
    numOccurences += StringUtils.countMatches( , "futility" );
}
```

Your random access memory will thank you for this implementation. Java programmers are often lulled into a sense of false security knowing that they do not have to worry about memory management. Poor design decisions and inefficient implementation often lead to slow running or hard-to-scale applications. Just because you don't have to allocate and deallocate memory does not mean that you should stop thinking about efficient memory use. If you are trying to search for the frequency of a word in a 20 megabyte file, please try not to read the entire file into memory before searching. Performing a linear search on a large string is an inappropriate way to search a large database of documents. When searching large amounts of text, it is more efficient to create an index of terms than to perform a linear search over a large string. A method for indexing and searching documents using Jakarta Lucene and Jakarta Commons Digester will be discussed in a later chapter.

See Also

Chapter 12 contains a number of recipes devoted to searching and filtering content. If you are creating a system that needs to search a large collection of documents, consider using Jakarta Lucene (*http://jakarta.apache.org/lucene*) to index your content.

2.13   Parsing Formatted Strings

Problem

You need to parse a string containing control characters and the delimiters (, [,),], and ,.

Solution

Use variations of substring( ) from StringUtils. This next example parses a string that contains five numbers delimited by parentheses, brackets, and a pipe symbol (*N0 * (N1,N2) [N3,N4] | N5*):

```
String formatted = " 25 * (30,40) [50,60] | 30"

PrintWriter out = System.out;
out.print("N0: " + StringUtils.substringBeforeLast( formatted, "*" ) );
out.print(", N1: " + StringUtils.substringBetween( formatted, "(", "," ) );
out.print(", N2: " + StringUtils.substringBetween( formatted, ",", ")" ) );
out.print(", N3: " + StringUtils.substringBetween( formatted, "[", "," ) );
out.print(", N4: " + StringUtils.substringBetween( formatted, ",", "]" ) );
out.print(", N5: " + StringUtils.substringAfterLast( formatted, "|" ) );
```

This parses the formatted text and prints the following output:

```
N0: 25, N1: 30, N2: 40, N3: 50, N4: 60, N5: 30
```

Discussion

The following public static methods come in handy when trying to extract information from a formatted string:

StringUtils.substringBetween( )
> Captures content between two strings

StringUtils.substringAfter( )
> Captures content that occurs after the specified string

StringUtils.substringBefore( )
> Captures content that occurs before a specified string

StringUtils.substringBeforeLast( )
> Captures content after the last occurrence of a specified string

StringUtils.substringAfterLast( )
> Captures content before the last occurrence of a specified string

To illustrate the use of these methods, here is an example of a feed of sports scores. Each record in the feed has a defined format, which resembles this feed description:

```
\(SOT)<sport>[<team1>,<team2>] (<score1>,<score2>)\(ETX)

Notes:
 \(SOT) is ASCII character 2 "Start of Text",
 \(ETX) is ASCII character 4 "End of Transmission".

Example:
 \(SOT)Baseball[BOS,SEA] (24,22)\(ETX)
 \(SOT)Basketball[CHI,NYC] (29,5)\(ETX)
```

The following example parses this feed using `StringUtils` methods `trim()`, `substringBetween()`, and `substringBefore()`. The `boxScore` variable holds a test string to parse, and, once parsed, this code prints out the game score:

```
// Create a formatted string to parse - get this from a feed
char SOT = '\u0002';
char ETX = '\u0004';
String boxScore = SOT + "Basketball[CHI,BOS](69,75)\r\n" + ETX;

// Get rid of the archaic control characters
boxScore = StringUtils.trim( boxScore );

// Parse the score into component parts
String sport = StringUtils.substringBefore( boxScore, "[" );
String team1 = StringUtils.substringBetween( boxScore, "[", "," );
String team2 = StringUtils.substringBetween( boxScore, ",", "]" );
String score1 = StringUtils.substringBetween( boxScore, "(", "," );
String score2 = StringUtils.substringBetween( boxScore, ",", ")" );

PrintWriter out = System.out
out.println( "**** " + sport + " Score" );
out.println( "\t" + team1 + "\t" + score1 );
out.println( "\t" + team2 + "\t" + score2 );
```

This code parses a score, and prints the following output:

```
**** Basketball
 CHI 69
 BOS 75
```

In the previous example, `StringUtils.trim()` rids the text of the SOT and ETX control characters. `StringUtils.substringBefore()` then reads the sport name—"Basketball"—and `substringBetween()` is used to retrieve the teams and scores.

At first glance, the value of these `substring()` variations is not obvious. The previous example parsed this simple formatted string using three static methods on `StringUtils`, but how difficult would it have been to implement this parsing without the aid of Commons Lang? The following example parses the same string using only methods available in the Java 1.4 J2SE:

```
// Find the sport name without using StringUtils
boxScore = boxScore.trim();

int firstBracket = boxScore.indexOf( "[" );
String sport = boxScore.substring( 0, firstBracket );

int firstComma = boxScore.indexOf( "," );
String team1 = boxScore.substring( firstBracket + 1, firstComma );

int secondBracket = boxScore.indexOf( "]" );
String team2 = boxScore.substring( firstComma + 1, secondBracket );

int firstParen = boxScore.indexOf( "(" );
int secondComma = boxScore.indexOf( ",", firstParen );
String score1 = boxScore.substring( firstParen + 1, secondComma );
```

```
int secondParen = boxScore.indexOf( ")" );
String score2 = boxScore.substring( secondComma + 1, secondParen );
```

This parses the string in a similar number of lines, but the code is less straight-forward and much more difficult to maintain. Instead of simply calling a substringBetween( ) method, the previous example calls String.indexOf( ) and performs arithmetic with an index while calling String.substring( ). Additionally, the substring( ) methods on StringUtils are null-safe; the Java 1.4 example could throw a NullPointerException if boxScore was null.

String.trim( ) has the same behavior as StringUtils.trim( ), stripping the string of all whitespace and ASCII control characters. StringUtils.trim( ) is simply a wrapper for the String.trim( ) method, but the StringUtils.trim( ) method can gracefully handle a null input. If a null value is passed to StringUtils.trim( ), a null value is returned.

2.14   Calculating String Difference

Problem

Your application needs to compare two strings and print out the difference.

Solution

Use StringUtils.difference( ), StringUtils.indexOfDifference( ), and StringUtils.getLevenshteinDistance( ). StringUtils.difference( ) prints out the difference between two strings, StringUtils.indexOfDifference( ) returns the index at which two strings begin to differ, and StringUtils.getLevenshteinDistance( ) returns the "edit distance" between two strings. The following example demonstrates all three of these methods:

```
int dist = StringUtils.getLevenshteinDistance( "Word", "World" );
String diff = StringUtils.difference( "Word", "World" );
int index = StringUtils.indexOfDifference( "Word", "World" );

System.out.println( "Edit Distance: " + dist );
System.out.println( "Difference: " + diff );
System.out.println( "Diff Index: " + index );
```

This code compares the strings "Word" and "World," producing the following output:

```
Edit Distance: 2
Difference: ld
Diff Index: 3
```

Discussion

StringUtils.difference( ) returns the difference between two strings, returning the portion of the second string, which starts to differ from the first. StringUtils.

indexOfDifference( ) returns the index at which the second string starts to diverge from the first. The difference between "ABC" and "ABE" is "E," and the index of the difference is 2. Here's a more complex example:

```
String a = "Strategy";
String b = "Strategic";

String difference = StringUtils.difference( a, b );
int differenceIndex = StringUtils.indexOfDifference( a, b );

System.out.println( "difference(Strategy, Strategic) = " +
                    difference );
System.out.println( "index(Strategy, Strategic) = " +
                    differenceIndex );

a = "The Secretary of the UN is Kofi Annan.";
b = "The Secretary of State is Colin Powell.";

difference = StringUtils.difference( a, b );
differenceIndex = StringUtils.indexOfDifference( a, b );

System.out.println( "difference(..., ...) = " +
                    difference );
System.out.println( "index(..., ...) = " +
                    differenceIndex );
```

This produces the following output, showing the differences between two strings:

```
difference(Strategy, Strategic) = ic
index(Strategy, Strategic) = 7
difference(...,...) = State is Colin Powell.
index(...,...) = 17
```

The Levenshtein distance is calculated as the number of insertions, deletions, and replacements it takes to get from one string to another. The distance between "Boat" and "Coat" is a one letter replacement, and the distance between "Remember" and "Alamo" is 8—five letter replacements and three deletions. Levenshtein distance is also known as the *edit distance*, which is the number of changes one needs to make to a string to get from string A to string B. The following example demonstrates the getLevenshteinDistance( ) method:

```
int distance1 =
    StringUtils.getLevenshteinDistance( "Boat", "Coat" );
int distance2 =
    StringUtils.getLevenshteinDistance( "Remember", "Alamo" );
int distance3 =
    StringUtils.getLevenshteinDistance( "Steve", "Stereo" );

System.out.println( "distance(Boat, Coat): " + distance1 );
System.out.println( "distance(Remember, Alamo): " + distance2 );
System.out.println( "distance(Steve, Stereo): " + distance3 );
```

This produces the following output, showing the Levenshtein (or edit) distance between various strings:

```
distance(Boat, Coat): 1
distance(Remember, Alamo): 8
distance(Steve, Stereo): 3
```

See Also

The Levenshtein distance has a number of different applications, including pattern recognition and correcting spelling mistakes. For more information about the Levenshtein distance, see *http://www.merriampark.com/ld.htm*, which explains the algorithm and provides links to implementations of this algorithm in 15 different languages.

2.15   Using Commons Codec

Problem

You want to use Commons Codec.

Solution

You must download the latest version of Jakarta Commons Codec, and place the Commons Codec JAR in your project's classpath. Follow the steps outlined in Recipe 1.1, downloading Commons Codec 1.2 instead of Commons Lang.

Discussion

The Commons Codec library is a small library, which includes encoders and decoders for common encoding algorithms, such as Hex, Base64; and phonetic encoders, such as Metaphone, DoubleMetaphone, and Soundex. This tiny component was created to provide a definitive implementation of Base64 and Hex, encouraging reuse and reducing the amount of code duplication between various Apache projects.

If you have a Maven project that needs to use Commons Codec, add a dependency on Commons Codec 1.2 with the following section in *project.xml*:

```xml
<dependencies>
  <dependency>
    <id>commons-codec</id>
    <version>1.2</version>
  </dependency>

  ....other dependencies...
</dependencies>
```

See Also

For information on obtaining the source code for Commons Codec, see Recipe 2.16. To learn more about Commons Codec, visit the Jakarta Commons Codec web site at *http://jakarta.apache.org/commons/codec/*.

2.16   Getting the Commons Codec Source Code

Problem

You want the source code for the Commons Codec project.

Solution

Download the source from *http://jakarta.apache.org/site/sourceindex.cgi*. Follow the same procedure as outlined in Recipe 1.1. Download a file named *commons-codec-1.2-src.zip* (or *commons-lang-1.2-src.tar.gz*), and once you unzip this file, you will have the source to Commons Codec in *./commons-codec-1.2-src/src*.

See Also

Most Commons components follow a similar convention for the layout of binary and source distributions. For more information about the contents layout of the Codec source distribution, see Recipe 1.3.

For information on obtaining the binary distribution for Commons Codec, see Recipe 2.15.

2.17   Calculating Soundex

Problem

You need the Soundex code of a word or a name.

Solution

Use Jakarta Commons Codec's Soundex. Supply a surname or a word, and Soundex will produce a phonetic encoding:

```
// Required import declaration
import org.apache.commons.codec.language.Soundex;

// Code body
Soundex soundex = new Soundex( );
String obrienSoundex = soundex.soundex( "O'Brien" );
String obrianSoundex = soundex.soundex( "O'Brian" );
String obryanSoundex = soundex.soundex( "O'Bryan" );
```

```
System.out.println( "O'Brien soundex: " + obrienSoundex );
System.out.println( "O'Brian soundex: " + obrianSoundex );
System.out.println( "O'Bryan soundex: " + obryanSoundex );
```

This will produce the following output for three similar surnames:

```
O'Brien soundex: 0165
O'Brian soundex: 0165
O'Bryan soundex: 0165
```

Discussion

Soundex.soundex( ) takes a string, preserves the first letter as a letter code, and proceeds to calculate a code based on consonants contained in a string. So, names such as "O'Bryan," "O'Brien," and "O'Brian," all being common variants of the Irish surname, are given the same encoding: "O165." The 1 corresponds to the B, the 6 corresponds to the R, and the 5 corresponds to the N; vowels are discarded from a string before the Soundex code is generated.

The Soundex algorithm can be used in a number of situations, but Soundex is usually associated with surnames, as the United States historical census records are indexed using Soundex. In addition to the role Soundex plays in the census, Soundex is also used in the health care industry to index medical records and report statistics to the government. A system to access individual records should allow a user to search for a person by the Soundex code of a surname. If a user types in the name "Boswell" to search for a patient in a hospital, the search result should include patients named "Buswell" and "Baswol;" you can use Soundex to provide this capability if an application needs to locate individuals by the sound of a surname.

The Soundex of a word or name can also be used as a primitive method to find out if two small words rhyme. Commons Codec contains other phonetic encodings, such as RefinedSoundex, Metaphone, and DoubleMetaphone. All of these alternatives solve similar problems—capturing the *phonemes* or sounds contained in a word.

See Also

For more information on the Soundex encoding, take a look at the Dictionary of Algorithms and Data Structures at the National Institute of Standards and Technology (NIST), *http://www.nist.gov/dads/HTML/soundex.html*. There you will find links to a C implementation of the Soundex algorithm.

For more information about alternatives to Soundex encoding, read "The Double Metaphone Search Algorithm" by Lawrence Philips (*http://www.cuj.com/documents/ s=8038/cuj0006philips/*). Or take a look at one of Lawrence Philips's original Metaphone algorithm implementations at *http://aspell.sourceforge.net/metaphone/*. Both the Metaphone and Double Metaphone algorithms capture the sound of an English word; implementations of these algorithms are available in Commons Codec as Metaphone and DoubleMetaphone.

CHAPTER 3
JavaBeans

3.0   Introduction

Beans are everywhere, popping up in web-application frameworks, enterprise applications, Swing Graphical User Interface (GUIs), templating engines, and object-relational mapping (ORM) tools. Most systems have some sort of object model; for example, an electronic commerce application would have an object model involving an `Invoice`, which relates to a `Customer`; or a sports news web site would have related `Athlete`, `Sport`, and `Team` objects. Frequently, objects in these object models are beans—simple objects with properties, encapsulating access to these properties via public getter and setter methods.

In 1997, Sun Microsystems published Version 1.01 of the JavaBeans™ specification. Initially, Sun offered beans as visual components for graphical user interfaces; JavaBeans were to be the equivalent of Microsoft's ActiveX controls—a framework and set of interfaces for creating reusable and pluggable GUI components. Used as components, which exposed states through a series of accessor and mutator (`getX( )` and `setX( )`) methods, a developer would develop a GUI Java application by creating a visual layout using an IDE like Visual Cafe or JBuilder. If you've ever developed with Microsoft tools, you'll know exactly what this means—Java was going to unseat Visual Basic, and GUI development was going to be easier than easy. According to the JavaBeans Specification Version 1.01 from 1997:

> A Java Bean is a reusable software component that can be manipulated visually in a builder tool.

Don't be misled; 1997 was ages ago, and the concept of the bean has evolved. In the last seven years, Java has become a dominant technology for server-side applications; impressive Swing applications do exist, but Java has not been an attractive platform for desktop application development due to reasons technical, economic, and judicial.

Don't be confused by the 1997 JavaBeans specification, either; it is still relevant, but, when used in the context of this book, the term *bean* is any object with a no-argument constructor, which encapsulates access to private member variables via getter and setter methods. Example 3-1 defines a bean, SimpleBean, which contains two bean properties—name1 and name2.

Example 3-1. Sample bean

```
package org.test.bean;

public class SimpleBean {
    private String name1;
    private String name2;

    public SimpleBean() {}

    public String getName1() { return name1; }
    public void setName1(String name1) { this.name1 = name1; }

    public String getName2() { return name2; }
    public void setName2(String name2) { this.name2 = name2; }
}
```

The presence of the public methods getName1( ) and getName2( ) make the bean properties name1 and name2 readable, and the public methods setName1( ) and setName2( ) make these properties writable. A bean should also have a public no-argument constructor; other constructors are not prohibited, but, since many tools need to dynamically create and populate beans, a no-argument constructor is required.

The original JavaBeans specification is available at *http://java.sun.com/products/ javabeans/docs/spec.html*. The JavaBeans specification still exists and features have been added to the Java 1.4 release to support reading and writing JavaBeans to Extensible Markup Language (XML) documents. More information about more modern additions to the JavaBeans specification can be found at *http://java.sun.com/ j2se/1.4.2/docs/guide/beans/changes14.html*.

3.1   Representing Beans Graphically

Problem

You need to draw a diagram of a simple bean that shows the relationships between different objects.

Solution

Use a simplified variant of a Unified Modeling Language (UML) class diagram that contains only class names, attribute names, and attribute types. Figure 3-1 describes two related beans—Person and Job.

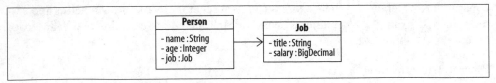

Figure 3-1. *Structure of Person and Job beans*

Discussion

Many of the recipes in this book deal with an object model consisting of JavaBeans, and, to save paper, I've devised this simple shorthand for describing a collection of related beans. Every time you see a diagram like Figure 3-1, mentally translate it to a set of classes, one for each box; each class attribute in that box is a private member variable, with a getter method and a setter method. The beans represented by these diagrams are simply objects with attributes, and the only operations on a bean are getter and setter methods and no-argument constructors. To help you get used to translating these diagrams into code, the Person and Job classes are defined in Examples 3-2 and 3-3.

Example 3-2. The Person bean

```
public class Person {
    private String name;
    private Integer age;
    private Job job;

    public String getName() { return name; }
    public void setName(String name) { this.name = name; }

    public Integer getAge() { return age; }
    public void setAge(Integer age) { this.age = age; }

    public Job getJob() { return job; }
    public void setJob(Job job) { this.job = job; }
}
```

Example 3-3. The Job bean

```
public class Job {
    private String title;
    private BigDecimal salary;

    public String getTitle() { return title; }
    public void setTitle(String title) { this.title = title; }

    public BigDecimal getSalary() { return salary; }
    public void setSalary(BigDecimal salary) { this.salary = salary; }
}
```

When an object contains an attribute of type List, it is helpful to know the type of object that List contains. To convey the type of object contained in a List, every list attribute will be followed by the type it is intended to contain surrounded by brackets: *List<Integer>*. Similarly, if an object contains a Map, the type of the key and value will be separated by a comma and surrounded by brackets: *Map<String,Integer>*. If the Person object had contained a list of Job objects instead of a single Job object, the attribute type would be written *List<Job>*, as in Figure 3-2.

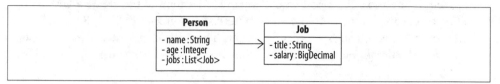

Figure 3-2. Representing a list of Job objects

 The angle bracket syntax is actually the standard means of representing these objects in the newest version of Java, JDK 1.5. For more on JDK 1.5, check out *Java 1.5 Tiger: A Developer's Notebook*, by David Flanagan and Brett McLaughlin(O'Reilly).

See Also

Don't confuse UML with object-oriented design, as this is a mistake all too often made; UML captures the form and function of a system, but it is no substitute for a good design. All the drawings in the world won't make a bad design good, and spending a day drawing a big UML diagram is simply a creative form of procrastination. That said, if you insist on drawing UML diagrams, check out some of the following tools:

ArgoUML
> ArgoUML is a UML editor from Tigris.org, an open source community hosted by CollabNet (*http://www.collabnet.com*). ArgoUML supports reverse engineering and code generation to Java, C++, C#, and PHP. For more information about ArgoUML, see the project page at *http://argouml.tigris.org/*. To launch ArgoUML via Java Web Start, click on *http://argouml.tigris.org/files/documents/4/383/ArgoUML-stable.jnlp*.

Poseidon for UML
> Gentleware AG has taken ArgoUML and extended it, providing additional features, such as language export options and improved usability. A community edition is free to download and use. For more information about this product, see the Gentleware AG site at *http://www.gentleware.com*. If you have Java Web Start installed, you can launch the community edition of Poseidon through a browser by clicking on *http://www.gentleware.com/products/webstart.php4*.

SmartDraw

SmartDraw, from SmartDraw.com, offers a very usable general purpose tool for creating diagrams. This tool stands out from the rest because it is simple, and, unlike other tools, it is solely concerned with the creation of diagrams; it makes no attempt to get involved with your application, and it has an attractive price of around $129. Details are at *http://www.smartdraw.com*.

Other Tools

It seem that almost every software company has attempted to create a UML modeling tool, some of the well-known commercial products are IBM's Rational Rose, Microsoft's Visio, and Borland's Together. The URL *http://www.objectsbydesign. com/tools/umltools_byCompany.html* contains an exhaustive list of other UML tools.

3.2   Obtaining Commons BeanUtils

Problem

You want to use Jakarta Commons BeanUtils to manipulate and access simple, indexed, and nested bean properties.

Solution

You must download the latest version of Commons BeanUtils, and place the Commons BeanUtils JAR in your project's classpath. Following the steps outlined in Recipe 1.1, download Commons BeanUtils 1.7 instead of Commons Lang.

Commons BeanUtils depends on Commons Logging 1.0.3 and Commons Collections 3.0; both of these can be downloaded from the same location as Commons BeanUtils.

Discussion

Commons BeanUtils is a collection of utilities that makes working with beans and bean properties much easier. This project contains utilities that allow one to retrieve a bean property by name, sort beans by a property, translate beans to maps, and more. BeanUtils is simple and straightforward, and, as such, you will find that it is one of the most widely used and distributed libraries in open source Java. Along with Commons Lang and Commons Collections, Commons BeanUtils is part of the core of Jakarta Commons. Unless specified otherwise, every utility mentioned in this chapter is from Commons BeanUtils.

If you have a Maven project that needs to use Commons BeanUtils, add a dependency on Commons BeanUtils 1.7 with the following section in *project.xml*:

```
<dependencies>
  <dependency>
```

```
    <id>commons-beanutils</id>
    <version>1.7</version>
  </dependency>

  ....other dependencies...
</dependencies>
```

The rest of this chapter focuses on Commons BeanUtils.

In the Beginning...

BeanUtils was originally a part of Jakarta Struts, a widely used Model-View-Controller (MVC) framework for web applications, which originated in the Jakarta project. The Struts framework hinges upon *form beans*, which are used to present and communicate user input to and from a Struts action. The Struts `ActionServlet` and the bean Java-Server Pages (JSP) tag libraries use the `BeanUtils`, `PropertyUtils`, and `ConvertUtils` classes to populate and manipulate beans. Refactoring BeanUtils from Struts has created new possibilities of reuse throughout the Jakarta project and the larger open source Java community.

See Also

For more information about downloading Commons Logging 1.0.3, see Recipe 7.9. For more information about downloading Commons Collections, see Recipe 4.1. For information on obtaining the source code for Commons BeanUtils, see Recipe 3.3.

To learn more about Commons BeanUtils, visit the Commons BeanUtils web site: *http://jakarta.apache.org/commons/beanutils/*.

If you have questions about how to use Commons BeanUtils, you can join the *commons-user@jakarta.apache.org* mailing list. Refer to Recipe 1.2 for instructions on joining the Commons-user mailing list.

3.3   Getting the Commons BeanUtils Source Code

Problem

You need the source code for the Commons BeanUtils project.

Solution

Download the source from *http://jakarta.apache.org/site/sourceindex.cgi*, following the same procedure as outlined in Recipe 1.1. Download a file named *commons-beanutils-1.7-src.zip* (or *commons-beanutils-1.7-src.tar.gz*); once you unzip this archive, you will have the source to Commons BeanUtils in *./commons-beanutils-1.7-src/src*.

See Also

Most Commons components follow a similar convention for the layout of binary and source distributions. For more information about the layout of the BeanUtils source distribution, see Recipe 1.3.

For information on obtaining the binary distribution for Commons BeanUtils, see Recipe 3.2.

3.4   Accessing Simple Bean Properties

Problem

You need to access a simple bean property by name.

Solution

Use `PropertyUtils.getSimpleProperty()` to access a bean property by name; this method takes the name of a property and returns the value of that property. The following example uses this method to retrieve the `name` property from a `Person` bean:

```
import org.apache.commons.beanutils.PropertyUtils;

Person person = new Person();
person.setName( "Alex" );

String name = (String) PropertyUtils.getSimpleProperty( person, "name" );
System.out.println( name );
```

`PropertyUtils.getSimpleProperty()` invokes the public method `getName()` on an instance of `Person`, returning the value of the `name` property. The previous example executes and prints out the name "Alex."

Discussion

A simple bean property is a private member variable that can be accessed with a getter method. If a property can be read via a getter method, that getter method is said to be the *read method* for the named property. If the property can be modified with a setter method, that setter method is said to be the *write method* for the named property. The `Person` bean in Example 3-4 defines two simple bean properties, `name` and `favoriteColor`.

Example 3-4. A Person bean with two simple properties

```
package com.discursive.jccook.bean;

public class Person {
    private String name;
    private String favoriteColor;

    public Person() {}

    public String getName() { return name; }
    public void setName(String name) {
        this.name = name;
    }

    public String getFavoriteColor() { return favoriteColor; }
    public void setFavoriteColor(String favoriteColor) {
        this.favoriteColor = favoriteColor;
    }
}
```

The class defined in Example 3-4 is used in the following sample code, which creates a Person object, sets the name and favoriteColor properties, and demonstrates the use of Property.getSimpleProperty( ) to retrieve both properties by name:

```
import org.apache.commons.beanutils.PropertyUtils;

// Create a person
Person person = new Person();
person.setName( "Alex Wolfe" );
person.setFavoriteColor( "Green" );

try {
    String name = (String) PropertyUtils.getSimpleProperty( person, "name" );
    String favoriteColor =
        (String) PropertyUtils.getSimpleProperty( person, "favoriteColor" );
    System.out.println( "The Person: " + name + " likes " + favoriteColor );
} catch (IllegalAccessException e) {
    System.out.println( "You are not allowed to access a property!" );
} catch (InvocationTargetException e) {
    System.out.println( "There was a problem invoking the method." );
} catch (NoSuchMethodException e) {
    System.out.println( "There is no method to get a property." );
}
```

Take note of the extensive exception handling required to retrieve two bean properties; three separate exceptions can be thrown by getSimpleProperty( ). The first, IllegalAccessException, is thrown if the getter method is not accessible (not public). InvocationTargetException is thrown if the getter method throws an exception, and NoSuchMethodException is thrown if you specify a bean property that does not exist on an object; for example, attempting to retrieve the numberOfDoors property from the person object above would throw a NoSuchMethodException because there is no getNumberOfDoors( ) method.

To simplify the examples in this chapter, most examples will omit the try/catch or catch the general Exception—to do otherwise would be a needless waste of paper. As a general programming practice, catching the general Exception should be avoided; well-written code usually catches individual, specific exceptions. But, in this case, catching the general Exception may save you a great deal of hassle.

Using PropertyUtils.getSimpleProperty( ) when you could simply call a get method might seem like an unwieldy solution to a very simple problem, but the alternative— calling a getter method—locks you into a specific bean property at compile time. This may be unacceptable if you are designing something generic like a templating system or an expression language interpreter; you may need to access an arbitrary property of an arbitrary object known only at runtime. The ability to retrieve the value of a bean property by name lies at the heart of a number of important tools, such as Struts, Jakarta Velocity, Jakarta Commons JEXL, and utilities from Jakarta Commons Collections. Accessing bean properties by name is an appropriate solution for a system that needs a high level of flexibility.

See Also

The next three recipes focus on accessing different types of bean properties: nested, indexed, and mapped. Simple properties may also be retrieved with PropertyUtils. getProperty( ); this method is described in Recipe 3.8.

This recipe mentions Struts, a web application MVC framework. For more information about the Struts project, see *http://jakarta.apache.org/struts*. Jakarta Velocity and Jakarta Commons JEXL are discussed in Chapter 9, and Commons Collections is discussed in Chapter 5.

3.5   Accessing Nested Bean Properties

Problem

You need to access a nested bean property.

Solution

Use PropertyUtils.getNestedProperty( ) to retrieve a nested bean property. Use a period as a delimiter to identify nested bean properties; *one.two.three.four* refers to a property nested three levels deep—the four property of the three property of the two property of the one property. The following example accesses a nested bean property on a Person bean, *author.name*:

```
import org.apache.commons.beanutils.PropertyUtils;

Book book = new Book( );
book.setName( "Emerson's Essays" );
```

```
Person author = new Person( );
author.setName( "Ralph Waldo Emerson" );
book.setAuthor( author );

String authorName = (String) PropertyUtils.getNestedProperty(book, "author.name");
System.out.println( "authorName" );This example retrieves the name property of the
author property on the Book object, printing "Ralph Waldo Emerson".
```

Discussion

The author property of Book is a Person bean with a name property; calling
getNestedProperty( ) with *author.name* retrieves the simple property author from
Book and the property name, which is nested in the author property. Figure 3-3 shows
the Book and Person beans that were used in the previous example.

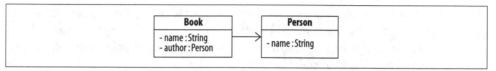

Figure 3-3. Structure of two simple beans: Book and Person

The following example demonstrates a combination of getSimpleProperty( ) and
getNestedProperty( ), retrieving a book name and an author name:

```
General Exception is caught.

import org.apache.commons.beanutils.PropertyUtils;

// Create an author
Person author = new Person( );
author.setName( "Chaucer" );

Book book = new Book( );
book.setName( "The Canterbury Tales" );
book.setAuthor( author );

try {
    String bookName = (String) PropertyUtils.getSimpleProperty( book, "name" );
    String authorName =
        (String) PropertyUtils.getNestedProperty( book, "author.name" );

    System.out.println( "The book is " + bookName );
    System.out.println( "The author is " + authorName );

} catch (Exception e) {
    System.out.println( "There was a problem getting a bean property." );
    e.printStackTrace( );
}
```

To reduce the size of the example code, only the general Exception is caught.

When using getNestedProperty( ), there is no limit to the number of nesting levels for a property; demonstrating the retrieval of a deeply nested property, the following example retrieves the name property from the state property of the address property of a Person object:

```
String propertyName = "address.state.name";

String stateName =
    (String) PropertyUtils.getNestedProperty( person,  propertyName );
```

This example assumes that the Person class has a getAddress( ) method that returns an Address object with a getState( ) method and returns a State object with a getName( ) method. The emphasized code in the previous example is the equivalent of the following three lines of code:

```
Address address = person.getAddress( );
State state = address.getState( );
String stateName = state.getName( );
```

3.6   Accessing Indexed Bean Properties

Problem

You need to access the nth element of a bean property, which is an array or a List.

Solution

Use PropertyUtils.getIndexed( ) to retrieve an element at a specific index of an array or a List property. Assuming that the chapters property of the Book object is an instance of List, the following demonstrates the use of getIndexedProperty( ) to access the first element of the list of chapters.

```
import org.apache.commons.beanutils.PropertyUtils;

// Create a new Book
Book book = new Book( );

// Create a list of Chapters
Chapter chapter1 = new Chapter( );
Chapter chapter2 = new Chapter( );
book.getChapters( ).add( chapter1 );
book.getChapters( ).add( chapter2 );

// Retrieve the first Chapter via a property name and an index.
Chapter chapter =
    (Chapter) PropertyUtils.getIndexedProperty(book, "chapters[0]");
```

Discussion

There are two ways of accessing an indexed property via `PropertyUtils`: the index can be specified in the name, or it can be specified as a third parameter. The following code uses both versions of `getIndexedProperty()` to retrieve the first chapter from the list of chapters:

```
import org.apache.commons.beanutils.PropertyUtils;

Book book = new Book();

Chapter chapter1 = new Chapter();
Chapter chapter2 = new Chapter();
List chapters = new ArrayList();
chapters.add( chapter1 );
chapters.add( chapter2 );

book.setChapters( chapters );

// You can retrieve the first chapters like this...
Chapter chapterOne =
    (Chapter) PropertyUtils.getIndexedProperty( book, "chapters[0]" );

// Or... you can retrieve the first chapter like this...
chapterOne =
    (Chapter) PropertyUtils.getIndexedProperty( book, "chapters", 0 );
```

In the previous example, the first version of `getIndexedProperty()` accepts a string specifying an indexed bean property—`chapters[0]`. If this string is not well-formed, `PropertyUtils` will throw an `IllegalArgumentException`; `chapters[zero]` and `chapters['zero']` will cause an exception because neither index is an integer value, and `chapters]0[` will cause an exception because the brackets are transposed. The second call to `getIndexedProperty()` is preferred because there is less risk that a parsing error will throw an `IllegalArgumentException`.

3.7 Accessing Mapped Bean Properties

Problem

You need to retrieve values from a bean property of type `Map`.

Solution

Use `PropertyUtils.getMappedProperty()` to obtain values from a map property. The code here retrieves the value corresponding to the key "Dining Room" from the room map property of the Apartment bean:

```
import org.apache.commons.beanutils.PropertyUtils;

Room dining = new Room();
dining.setArea( 20 );
```

```
dining.setCarpeted( true );
dining.setFurnished( true );

Map rooms = new HashMap( );
rooms.put( "Dining Room", dining );

Apartment apartment = new Apartment( );
apartment.setRooms( rooms );

// Retrieve the Dining Room object
Room room =
    PropertyUtils.getMappedProperty( apartment, "rooms(Dining Room)" );
```

Discussion

The code shown in the Solution section retrieves the value from the rooms map corresponding to the key "Dining Room"—rooms(Dining Room). The call to getMappedProperty( ) is the equivalent of calling apartment.getRooms( ).get("Dining Room"). Figure 3-4 illustrates the structure and relationship of these two beans used, Apartment and Room.

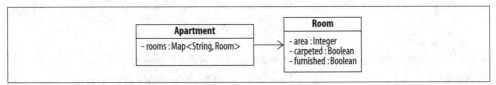

Figure 3-4. Diagram of the Apartment and Room beans

getMappedProperty( ) works only if the specified Map has String keys. getMappedProperty( ) takes the string between (and) and retrieves the value corresponding to this string.

There is another version of PropertyUtils.getMappedProperty( ) that takes a third argument, allowing you to specify the map property in the second argument and the key in the third argument. The code here uses two different versions of getMappedProperty( ) to retrieve the same value from the rooms map property:

```
import java.util.Map;
import java.util.HashMap;
import org.apache.commons.beanutils.PropertyUtils;

Room dining = new Room( );
dining.setArea( 20 );
dining.setCarpeted( true );
dining.setFurnished( true );

Map rooms = new HashMap( );
rooms.put( "Dining Room", dining );

Apartment apartment = new Apartment( );
apartment.setRooms( rooms );
```

```
// Retrieve the livingRoom key
Room room =
    (Room) PropertyUtils.getMappedProperty( apartment, "rooms(Dining Room)" );

// Or.. retrieve the livingRoom key with 3 parameters - equivalent to previous
room =
    (Room) PropertyUtils.getMappedProperty( apartment, "rooms", "Dining Room" );
```

What was true for getIndexedProperty( ) is also true for getMappedProperty( ). In the previous example, the first call to getMappedProperty( ) specifies a key with a string—rooms(Dining Room). If getMappedProperty( ) is unable to parse this string, an IllegalArgumentException will be thrown; rooms[DiningRoom) and rooms((DiningRoom) will both throw IllegalArgumentException because the property string is not well-formed. The second call to getMappedProperty( ) reduces the risk of a property string parsing error because the key is specified in a third parameter.

3.8   Accessing a Simple, Nested, Indexed, and Mapped Bean Property

Problem

You need to access a nested, indexed, and mapped bean property by name.

Solution

Use PropertyUtils.getProperty( ) to access any bean property. This single utility can be used to access any bean property be it simple, nested, indexed, mapped, or any combination thereof. The following example accesses a simple property, population, of a nested mapped property, cities, on an indexed property, regions:

```
import java.util.*;
import org.apache.commons.beanutils.PropertyUtils;

// Create a series of nested beans
City richmond = new City();
richmond.setName( "Richmond" );
richmond.setPopulation( new Long(500000) );

Map cities = new HashMap();
cities.put( "richmond", richmond );

Region midAtlantic = new Region();
midAtlantic.setName( "Mid-Atlantic" );
midAtlantic.setCities( cities );

List regions = new ArrayList();
regions.add( midAtlantic );
```

```
Country country = new Country( );
country.setName( "United States" );
country.setRegions( regions );

// Retrieve the population of Richmond
Long population =
    (Long) PropertyUtils.getProperty( country,
                "regions[0].cities(richmond).population" );
```

Most of this code sets up a complex nested object hierarchy to be queried by
PropertyUtils.getProperty( ). Retrieving the regions[0].cities(richmond).population
property is the equivalent of traversing down a tree of objects and retrieving the bot-
tom-most element—population.

Discussion

The emphasized code retrieves the population of the City object richmond; it is equivalent to the following code excerpt:

```
Region region = (Region) country.getRegions( ).get(0);
City city = (City) region.getCities( ).get("Richmond");
Long population = city.getPopulation( );
```

Figure 3-5 displays the structure of these three beans: Country, Region, and City.

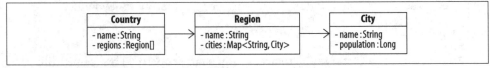

Figure 3-5. The Country, Region, and City beans

When accessing a bean property, you can use PropertyUtils.getProperty( ) in lieu of
the methods introduced in the previous four recipes. The getProperty( ) method parses
the supplied property name, splitting the name as the period character. Once this property has been split, this utility parses each token and passes the string to the appropriate method—getSimpleProperty( ), getNestedProperty( ), getIndexedProperty( ), or
getMappedProperty( ).

See Also

Bean properties may also be retrieved using a simple expression language, such as
Expression Language (EL) or Java Expression Language (JEXL). For more information about retrieving bean properties using an expression language, see Recipe 12.1.

Bean properties may also be retrieved using an XPath expression. For more information, see Recipe 12.1.

3.9   Determining the Type of a Bean Property

Problem

You need to determine the type of a bean property.

Solution

Use `PropertyUtils.getPropertyType()` to determine the type of a bean property. This utility will return a `Class` object that represents the return type of the property's getter method. The following example uses this method to obtain the return type for the author property on the Book bean:

```
import org.apache.commons.beanutils.PropertyUtils

Book book = new Book();

Class type = PropertyUtils.getPropertyType( book, "author" );

System.out.println( "book.author type: " + type.getName() );
```

This example retrieves and displays the type of the `author` property on Book, which happens to be a `Person` object. The type of the property is returned and printed to the console:

```
book.author type: org.test.Person
```

Discussion

`PropertyUtils.getPropertyType()` also works for a complex bean property. Passing a nested, indexed, or mapped bean property to this utility will return the type of the last property specified. The following code retrieves the type of a nested, indexed property—chapters[0].name:

```
import org.apache.commons.beanutils.PropertyUtils;

Chapter chapter = new Chapter();
chapter.setName( "Chapter 3 BeanUtils" );
chapter.setLength( new Integer(40) );

list chapters = new ArrayList();
chapters.add( chapter );

Book book = new Book();
book.setName( "Jakarta Commons Cookbook" );
book.setAuthor( "Dude" );
book.setChapters( chapters );

String property = "chapters[0].name";
Class propertyType = PropertyUtils.getPropertyType(book, property);

System.out.println( property + " type: " + propertyType.getName() );
```

This code retrieves the type of the name property from an instance of the Chapter retrieved as an indexed property, and it prints the following output:

```
chapters[0].name type: java.lang.String
```

PropertyUtils contains another method to retrieve a PropertyDescriptor– PropertyUtils.getPropertyDescriptor( ). This method takes a reference to any bean property, simple or complex, and returns an object describing the type of a property and providing access to the read and write methods of a property. The following code excerpt obtains the PropertyDescriptor of a nested, indexed property— chapters[0].name:

```
String property = "chapters[0].name";

PropertyDescriptor descriptor =
    PropertyUtils.getPropertyDescriptor(book, property);

Class propertyType = descriptor.getPropertyType( );
Method writeMethod = descriptor.getWriteMethod( );
Method readMethod = descriptor.getReadMethod( );
```

3.10 Comparing Beans

Problem

You need to sort or compare beans by a bean property.

Solution

Use BeanComparator to compare two beans using a bean property, which can be simple, nested, indexed, or mapped. BeanComparator obtains the value of the same bean property from two objects and, by default, compares the properties with a ComparableComparator. The following example sorts a list of Country objects using a BeanComparator and the default ComparableComparator:

```
import java.util.*;
import org.apache.commons.beanutils.BeanComparator;

Country country1 = new Country( );
country1.setName( "India" );

Country country2 = new Country( );
country2.setName( "Pakistan" );

Country country3 = new Country( );
country3.setName( "Afghanistan" );

// Create a List of Country objects
Country[] countryArray = new Country[] { country1, country2, country3 };
List countryList = Arrays.asList( countryArray );
```

```
// Sort countries by name
Comparator nameCompare = new BeanComparator( "name" );
Collections.sort( countryList, nameCompare );

System.out.println( "Sorted Countries:" );
Iterator countryIterator = countryList.iterator();
while( countryIterator.hasNext() ) {
    Country country = (Country) countryIterator.next();
    System.out.println( "\tCountry: " + country.getName() );
}
```

This code creates three Country objects with different names, places the Country objects into a list, and sorts this list with a BeanComparator configured to compare by the bean property name. This code executes and prints the sorted list of countries:

```
Sorted Countries:
    Country: Afghanistan
    Country: India
    Country: Pakistan
```

Discussion

The previous example demonstrated the default behavior of BeanComparator; when a BeanComparator is constructed with only one parameter, it uses a ComparableComparator to compare the values of the properties it retrieves. You can also construct a BeanComparator with an instance of Comparator; in this case, BeanComparator decorates another Comparator, retrieving the values of a property and passing these values on to an instance of Comparator. The following example demonstrates the use of BeanComparator with a custom Comparator implementation. This example involves two objects shown in Figure 3-6: ElectricVehicle and Engine.

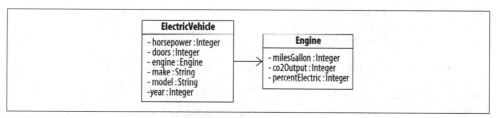

Figure 3-6. Objects involved in a sorting example

An application needs to sort ElectricVehicle objects by efficiency, and, in this contrived example, efficiency is defined as the number of miles per gallon times the percentage of electric operation; an 80% electric hybrid vehicle is more efficient than a 25% electric hybrid vehicle with the same mileage because of reduced emissions. The code fragments shown in Example 3-5 sort a collection of beans by wrapping a custom Comparator with a BeanComparator.

Example 3-5. Decorating a Comparator with a BeanComparator

```java
import java.util.*;
import org.apache.commons.beanutils.BeanComparator;

// Create Engines
Engine engine1 = new Engine( );
engine1.setMilesGallon( new Integer(60) );
engine1.setPercentElectric( new Integer(50) );

Engine engine2 = new Engine( );
engine2.setMilesGallon( new Integer(90) );
engine2.setPercentElectric( new Integer(50) );

Engine engine3 = new Engine( );
engine3.setMilesGallon( new Integer(65) );
engine3.setPercentElectric( new Integer(45) );

// Create Vehicles
ElectricVehicle vehicle1 = new ElectricVehicle( );
vehicle1.setMake( "Toy Yoda" );
vehicle1.setModel( "Electro" );
vehicle1.setYear( 2005 );
vehicle1.setEngine( engine1 );

ElectricVehicle vehicle2 = new ElectricVehicle( );
vehicle2.setMake( "Fjord" );
vehicle2.setModel( "Photon" );
vehicle2.setYear( 2004 );
vehicle2.setEngine( engine2 );

ElectricVehicle vehicle3 = new ElectricVehicle( );
vehicle3.setMake( "Ford" );
vehicle3.setModel( "Electric Pinto" );
vehicle3.setYear( 2005 );
vehicle3.setEngine( engine3 );

// Create List of Vehicles
List vehicles = new ArrayList( );
vehicle.add( vehicle1 );
vehicle.add( vehicle2 );
vehicle.add( vehicle3 );

// Define Engine Comparison Logic in an Anonymous inner class
// which implements the Comparator interface
Comparator engineCompare = new Comparator( ) {
    public int compare(Object o1, Object o2) {
        Engine engine1 = (Engine) o1;
        Engine engine2 = (Engine) o2;

        int engine1Temp = engine1.getMilesGallon( ).intValue( ) *
                    engine1.getPercentElectric( ).intValue( );
        int engine2Temp = engine2.getMilesGallon( ).intValue( ) *
                    engine2.getPercentElectric( ).intValue( );
```

Example 3-5. Decorating a Comparator with a BeanComparator (continued)

```
        Integer engine1Factor = new Integer( engine1Temp );
        Integer engine2Factor = new Integer( engine2Temp );

        return engine1Factor.compareTo( engine2Factor );
    }
}


Comparator vehicleCompare = new BeanComparator( "engine", engineCompare );
Collections.sort( vehicles, vehicleCompare );

// Print Sorted Results
System.out.println( "Vehicles Sorted by Efficiency:" );
Iterator vehicleIter = vehicles.iterator();
while( vehicleIter.hasNext() ) {
    ElectricVehicle vehicle = (ElectricVehicle) vehicleIter.next();
    System.out.println( "\tVehicle: " + vehicle.getModel() + ", " +
        vehicle.getEngine().getMilesGallon() + " MPG, " +
        vehicle.getEngine().getPercentElectric() + "% Electric" );
}
```

engineCompare contains the logic used to sort vehicles by efficiency, and
BeanComparator supplies the engine properties to this Comparator implementation.
This previous example creates three vehicles and sorts the vehicles in order of effi-
ciency, the following results are printed:

```
    Vehicles Sorted by Efficiency:
        Vehicle: Photon, 90 MPG, 50% Electric
        Vehicle: Electro, 60 MPG, 50% Electric
        Vehicle: Electric Pinto, 65 MPG, 45% Electric
```

See Also

Chapter 4 provides examples of various Comparator implementations, which can be
used to decorate other comparators. One Comparator in particular is important if you
plan to sort beans on a bean property, which could be null. If a bean property could
be null, make sure to pass a NullComparator to BeanComparator; otherwise,
ComparableComparator will throw a NullPointerException if a property value is null.
Recipe 4.5 discusses techniques for decorating a Comparator with NullComparator.

Recipe 3.15 discusses a BeanPredicate object that can be used to validate beans. The
BeanPredicate is similar to the BeanComparator as it decorates another instance of
Predicate, providing access to a bean property.

3.11   Copying Bean Properties

Problem

You have two instances of a bean, and you need to copy the properties of one bean to another instance of the same class.

Solution

Use `PropertyUtils.copyProperties()` to copy the properties from one bean to another. The first parameter is the destination bean, and the second parameter is the bean to copy properties from:

```
import org.apache.commons.beanutils.PropertyUtils;

Book book = new Book( );
book.setName( "Prelude to Foundation" );
book.setAuthorName( "Asimov" );

Book destinationBook = new Book( );

PropertyUtils.copyProperties( destinationBook, book );
```

After executing this code, `destinationBook.getName( )` should return "Prelude to Foundation," and `destinationBook.getAuthorName( )` should return "Asimov"; the name and `authorName` properties of book were both copied to `destinationBook`.

Discussion

`PropertyUtils.copyProperties( )` retrieves the values of all properties from a source instance of a bean, assigning the retrieved values to a matching property on a destination instance. If the `Book` bean in the previous example had an `author` property of type `Author`, `copyProperties( )` would have assigned the same reference object to the `destinationBook`. In other words, `copyProperties( )` does *not* clone the values of the bean properties. The following example demonstrates this explicitly:

```
Author author = new Author( );
author.setName( "Zinsser" );

Book book = new Book( );
book.setName( "On Writing Well" );
book.setAuthor( author );

Book destinationBook = new Book( );

PropertyUtils.copyProperties( destinationBook, book );

// At this point book and destinationBook have the same author object
if( book.getAuthor( ) == destinationBook.getAuthor( ) ) {
    system.out.println( "Author objects identical" );
}
```

The author properties of these two objects are now identical references to the same instance of the Author class. copyProperties() does not clone the values of bean properties.

copyProperties() can also copy the contents of a Map to a bean if the keys of a Map correspond to names of simple bean properties on the destination bean:

```
Map mapProps = new HashMap();
mapProps.put( "name", "The Art of Computer Programming" );
mapProps.put( "author", "Knuth" );

Book destinationBook = new Book();

PropertyUtils.copyProperties( destinationBook, mapProps );
```

See Also

If you need to clone a bean, take a look at Recipe 3.12

3.12   Cloning a Bean

Problem

You need to clone a bean.

Solution

Use BeanUtils.cloneBean(). This method creates a new instance of a bean with the default constructor, and it copies every property to the new bean instance. The following instance creates a cloned instance of a Book object:

```
import org.apache.commons.beanutils.BeanUtils;

Book book1 = new Book();
book1.setName( "Count of Monte Cristo" );

Book book2 = (Book) BeanUtils.cloneBean( book1 );
```

Discussion

cloneBean() instantiates a new instance of the bean to be cloned and calls BeanUtils. copyProperties() to transfer all readable bean properties to the newly instantiated bean. The following code demonstrates the steps that cloneBean() is taking to clone an instance of a bean:

```
Book book1 = new Book();
book1.setName( "Practical C Programming" );

Book book2 = book1.getClass().newInstance();
PropertyUtils.copyProperties( book2, book1 );
```

3.13   Setting a Bean Property

Problem

You need to set a simple, indexed, nested, or mapped bean property by name.

Solution

Use PropertyUtils.setProperty( ) to set any bean property: simple, nested, indexed, or mapped. Pass the bean object to be modified, the name of the property, and the value to setProperty( ); this method will call the appropriate setter method on the supplied object. The following example demonstrates the use of this method to set two properties on a Book bean:

```
import org.apache.commons.beanutils.PropertyUtils;

Person person1 = new Person( );
person1.setName( "Blah" );

Book book1 = new Book( );
book1.setName( "Blah" );
book1.setAuthor( "Blah" );

PropertyUtils.setProperty( book1, "name", "Some Apache Book" );
PropertyUtils.setProperty( book1, "author", new Person( ) );
PropertyUtils.setProperty( book1, "author.name", "Ken Coar" );
```

This code created an instance of the Book bean and the Person bean, and PropertyUtils.setProperty( ) set both a simple and a nested bean property.

Discussion

In addition to simple and nested bean properties, this utility can populate indexed and mapped properties. The following example demonstrates the setting of mapped and indexed bean properties on a Book object:

```
Book book1 = new Book( );
book1.getChapters( ).add( new Chapter( ) );
book1.getChapters( ).add( new Chapter( ) );

PropertyUtils.setProperty( book1, "name", "Apache: The Definitive Guide" );
PropertyUtils.setProperty( book1, "author", new Person( ) );
PropertyUtils.setProperty( book1, "author.name", "Laurie" );
PropertyUtils.setProperty( book1, "chapters[0].name", "Introduction" );

Apartment apartment = new Apartment( );
apartment.getRooms( ).put( "livingRoom", new Room( ) );

PropertyUtils.setProperty( apartment, "rooms(livingRoom).length",
                new Integer(12) );
```

Assume that the Book bean is associated with a series of Chapter objects each of which have a name property. The Book bean has a chapters property, which is a list. The name of the first chapter is set by referencing the chapters[0].name property.

3.14   Testing Property Access

Problem

You need to test a bean property to see if it can be read from or written to.

Solution

Use PropertyUtils.isReadable() and PropertyUtils.isWritable() to see if a bean property is readable or writable. The following code tests the name property of the Book bean to see if it is readable and writable:

```
import org.apache.commons.beanutils.PropertyUtils;

// Create a Book demonstrating the getter and setter for "name"
Book book1 = new Book();
book1.setName( "Blah" );
String name = book1.getName( );

// Can we read and write "name"
boolean nameReadable = PropertyUtils.isReadable( book, "name" );
boolean nameWritable = PropertyUtils.isWritable( book, "name" );

System.out.println( "Is name readable? " + nameReadable );
System.out.println( "Is name writable? " + nameWritable );
```

The name property is both readable and writable, so the nameReadable and nameWritable variables will both be true. The output of this example is as follows:

```
Is name readable? true
Is name writable? true
```

Discussion

In addition to working with simple properties, isReadable() and isWritable() also work on nested, indexed, and mapped properties. The following example demonstrates the use of these methods to check access to the indexed, quadruple-nested, mapped bean property length:

```
Book book1 = new Book();
book1.getChapters().add( new Chapter() );

boolean isReadable =
    PropertyUtils.isReadable( book,
        "chapters[0].author.apartment.rooms(livingRoom).length");
```

```
boolean isWritable =
    PropertyUtils.isWritable( book,
        "chapters[0].author.apartment.rooms(livingRoom).length");
```

`PropertyUtils.isReadable( )` returns true if a specified bean property can be obtained via a public getter method, and `PropertyUtils.isWritable( )` returns true if a specified bean property corresponds to a public setter method. This is an overly complex example, but it demonstrates the versatility of `PropertyUtils.isReadable( )` and of `PropertyUtils.isWritable( )`.

3.15 Validating Beans with Predicates

Problem

You need to test the state of a bean, testing for the presence or absence of simple and nested bean properties.

Solution

Use a `BeanPredicate` from Commons BeanUtils. A `BeanPredicate` is an implementation of the `Predicate` interface defined in Commons Collections. As described in Chapter 4, a `Predicate`'s `evaluate( )` method takes an object and returns a boolean; `BeanPredicate` decorates another `Predicate`, allowing that `Predicate` to evaluate a bean property: simple, nested, indexed, or mapped. The following code demonstrates the use of `BeanPredicate` to validate the condition of a bean:

```
import org.apache.commons.beanutils.*;
import org.apache.commons.collections.*;

// A Predicate that returns true if the "name" property is not null
Predicate teamNotNull = new BeanPredicate( "name", new NotNullPredicate() );

// A Predicate that returns true if the "coach.firstName" property
// is "Tom"
Predicate coachFirstName = new BeanPredicate( "coach.firstName",
                                              new EqualsPredicate("Tom") );

// Tie two Predicates together into an AndPredicate
Predicate validateTeam = new AllPredicate( predicateArray );

// Create Team Objects
Team fish = new Team( "Swordfish", new Coach( "Tom", "O'Connell") );
Team hens = new Team( "Hens", new Coach( "Bob", "McGarry") );

boolean fishValid = validateTeam.evaluate( fish );
boolean henValid = validateTeam.evaluate( hens );

System.out.println( "Is Swordfish team valid? " + fishValid );
System.out.println( "Is Hens team valid? " + hensValid );
```

Assume that the two Team objects contain two properties: name and coach. The coach property on Team is a Coach object with two properties: firstName and lastName. The first BeanPredicate, teamNotNull, uses a NotNullPredicate to test the simple property name. The second BeanPredicate uses an EqualPredicate to test the nested property coach.firstName. In the previous example, a Team object is only valid if it has a name, and the first name of the coach is "Tom." Two teams are created and the following output is printed:

```
Is Swordfish team valid? true
Is Hens team valid? false
```

Discussion

A BeanPredicate obtains the value of the specified bean property using PropertyUtils and passes the resulting property value to the Predicate it was constructed with; BeanPredicate decorates another Predicate. The following example demonstrates the use of BeanPredicate, wrapping an EqualPredicate, InstanceofPredicate, and a composite AnyPredicate:

```
import org.apache.commons.collections.Predicate;
import org.apache.commons.beanutils.BeanPredicate;
import org.apache.commons.collections.functors.AnyPredicate;
import org.apache.commons.collections.functors.EqualPredicate;
import org.apache.commons.collections.functors.InstanceofPredicate;
import org.apache.commons.collections.functors.OrPredicate;

// A predicate to validate the value of the age property
Predicate example1 = new BeanPredicate( "age",
    new EqualPredicate( new Integer( 10 ) );

// A predicate to validate the type of the title property
Predicate example2 = new BeanPredicate( "book[4].title",
    new InstanceofPredicate( String.class ) );

// A composite predicate definition
Predicate equalA = new EqualsPredicate("A");
Predicate equalB = new EqualsPredicate("B");
Predicate equalC = new EqualsPredicate("C");
Predicate eitherABC =
    new AnyPredicate( new Predicate[] { equalA, equalB, equalC } );

// A predicate to validate the type of the title property
Predicate example3 = new BeanPredicate( "mode", eitherABC );
```

Predicate example1 tests the age property of a bean, passing the property value to an EqualPredicate, which returns true if age is 10. Predicate example2 tests the property title from the fifth element in the book property; if the book's title property value is of type String, example2 returns true. Predicate example3 tests the value of the mode property of a bean, it evaluates to true if mode equals "A," "B," or "C." These three examples demonstrate that a BeanPredicate is a simple decorator, which allows one to apply any Predicate to a bean property.

See Also

Chapter 4 contains more recipes focused on using `Predicate` implementations to perform complex validation and to create intelligent, self-validating collections. This recipe introduces two simple predicates; `EqualPredicate` and `NotNullPredicate` are discussed in Recipe 4.7. For more information about using predicates, see Chapter 4 and the Commons Collections project site at *http://jakarta.apache.org/commons/collections*.

3.16   Creating a Map of Bean Properties

Problem

You need to create a `Map` that contains every property in a bean.

Solution

Use `PropertyUtils.describe( )` to generate a `Map` containing all of the readable bean properties from a bean instance. Supply an instance of a bean and this method will return a `Map` containing all readable bean properties. The code shown here demonstrates the use of `PropertyUtils.describe( )` to describe a `Person` bean:

```
import java.util.*;
import org.apache.commons.beanutils.PropertyUtils;

// Create a Person and a Book bean instance
Person person = new Person( );
person.setName( "Some Dude" );

Book book = new Book( );
book.setName( "Some Silly Computer Book" );
book.setAuthor( person );

// Describe both beans with a Map
Map bookMap = PropertyUtils.describe( book );
Map authorMap = PropertyUtils.describe( bookMap.get("book") );

System.out.println( "Book Name: " + bookMap.get( "name" ) );
System.out.println( "Author Name: " + authorMap.get( "name" ) );
```

Discussion

The previous example involves a `Book` bean with a `name` and `author` property; the author property is a `Person` bean with one property: `name`. The two maps, `bookMap` and `authorMap`, contain keys for every defined bean property, and two of those properties are printed out:

```
Book Name: Some Silly Computer Book
Author Name: Some Dude
```

The map returned from `PropertyUtils.describe( )` is a `HashMap` that contains every property from the bean to be described. Internally, `PropertyUtils.describe( )` uses `PropertyUtils.getPropertyDescriptors( )` to obtain the list of properties to put into this map.

See Also

Recipe 3.17 demonstrates the use of the `BeanMap` to wrap a bean and expose a bean's properties via the `Map` interface.

3.17 Wrapping a Bean with a Map

Problem

You need to expose a bean's properties as a `Map`, and operate on the bean properties as if they were entries in a `Map`.

Solution

Wrap any bean in a `BeanMap`. This `Map` implementation uses introspection to provide access to bean properties as if they were key/value pairs in a map. This code wraps a Person bean with `BeanMap`, iterating through every key and accessing bean properties with `get( )`:

```java
import java.util.*;
import org.apache.commons.collections.BeanMap;

Person person = new Person( );
person.setName( "Jim" );
person.setAge( new Integer( 28 ) );
person.setOccupation( "Developer" );

Map beanMap = new BeanMap( person );

Set keys = beanMap.keySet( );
Iterator keyIterator = keys.iterator( );
while( keyIterator.hasNext( ) ) {
   String propertyName = (String) keyIterator.next( );

   System.out.println( "Property: " + propertyName +
                    ", Value: " + beanMap.get( propertyName ) +
                    ", Type: " + beanMap.getType( propertyName ).toString( ) );
}
```

The `Person` bean has the following properties: age, name, and occupation; an instance of this bean is created and passed to the constructor of `BeanMap`. The following output is created by iterating over the key set of beanMap:

```
Property: Age, Value: 28, Type: java.lang.String
Property: Name, Value: Jim, Type: java.lang.Integer
Property: Occupation, Value: Developer, Type: java.lang.String
```

Discussion

The previous example demonstrates the use of PropertyUtils.describe( ) to create a Map containing bean properties. BeanMap not only exposes bean properties with a Map interface, it wraps a bean instance, allowing you to alter the contents of the underlying bean via put( ). In addition to implementing the Map interface, BeanMap provides a number of additional methods for obtaining Method objects and the types of bean properties. Table 3-1 describes a few of these methods.

Table 3-1. Methods provided by BeanMap

Method	Description
clear( )	Constructs a new instance of a bean using the no-argument constructor of the class that corresponds to getBean( ).getClass( )
clone( )	If possible, creates another instance of BeanMap, wrapping a copy of the wrapped bean
getBean( )	Returns the bean wrapped by this BeanMap
setBean(Object bean)	Causes an instance of BeanMap to wrap the supplied bean
getType(String name)	Retrieves the type of the specified bean property
getReadMethod(String name)	Retrieves a Method object for the read method (or getter) of the specified property
getWriteMethod(String name)	Retrieves a Method object for the write method (or setter) of the specified property

Example 3-6 demonstrates the use of the methods listed above to manipulate and alter properties of a Person bean. Remember, when you alter a BeanMap, you are modifying the underlying bean.

Example 3-6. BeanMap methods getBean(), setBean(), getType(), getReadMethod(), and getWriteMethod()

```
package com.discursive.jccook.collections;

import java.lang.reflect.Method;

import org.apache.commons.collections.BeanMap;

public class BeanMapExample {
    public static void main(String[] args) throws Exception {
        BeanMapExample example = new BeanMapExample( );
        example.start( );
    }

    public void start( ) throws Exception {

        // Create a Person bean
        Person person = new Person( );
        person.setName( "Todd" );
```

Example 3-6. BeanMap methods getBean(), setBean(), getType(), getReadMethod(), and getWriteMethod() (continued)

```
        person.setAge( new Integer( 45 ) );
        person.setOccupation( "Record Collector" );

        // Wrap person with a Map
        BeanMap map = new BeanMap( person );

        // Set the age to 24 using a Method from this map
        Method method = map.getWriteMethod( "age" );
        method.invoke( person, new Integer(24) );

        // Set the name to "John" using map.put
        map.put( "name", "John" );

        // Create a Person bean
        Person person2 = new Person( );
        person2.setName( "Cindy" );
        person2.setAge( new Integer( 39 ) );
        person2.setOccupation( "Transcriptionist" );

        // Make the BeanMap operate on another bean
        map.setBean( person2 );

        // Get the type of the Age property
        Class type = map.getType( "age" );
    }
}
```

See Also

BeanMap provides a convenient shortcut for accessing and manipulating beans, providing the same abilities that are provided by PropertyUtils. For more information about accessing and manipulating bean properties with PropertyUtils, see Recipes 3.8 and 3.13.

3.18   Creating a Dynamic Bean

Problem

You need to be able to create a bean dynamically at runtime.

Solution

Use a DynaBean. You can create a DynaBean with an arbitrary set of properties at runtime, and the resulting DynaBean object will function properly with all Commons BeanUtils utilities, such as PropertyUtils. The following example demonstrates the use of a BasicDynaBean to model a politician:

```
import java.util.*;
import org.apache.commons.beanutils.*;
```

```
DynaProperty[] beanProperties = new DynaProperty[]{
    new DynaProperty("name", String.class),
    new DynaProperty("party", Party.class),
    new DynaProperty("votes", Long.class)
};

BasicDynaClass politicianClass =
    new BasicDynaClass("politician", BasicDynaBean.class, props);

DynaBean politician = politicianClass.newInstance();

// Set the properties via DynaBean
politician.set( "name", "Tony Blair" );
politician.set( "party", Party.LABOUR );
politician.set( "votes", new Long( 50000000 ) );

// Set the properties with PropertyUtils
PropertyUtils.setProperty( politician, "name", "John Major" );
PropertyUtils.setProperty( politician, "party", Party.TORY );
PropertyUtils.setProperty( politician, "votes", new Long( 50000000 ) );
```

In this code, the properties of the politician bean are set using two different methods. The first method is to manipulate properties via the DynaBean interface, and the second method involves using PropertyUtils.setProperty( ). Both regions of code accomplish the same goal, and PropertyUtils was included to emphasize the fact that most utilities in BeanUtils will understand how to work with DynaBean implementations.

Discussion

DynaBean objects come in handy when your system uses beans to represent a data model. Since a bean is just a collection of properties, you can avoid having to maintain a bean class by automatically generating a bean from a description of the objects and properties; for example, a complex data model could be described in an XML document, and a utility would parse such a document and create a number of DynaClass objects at runtime.

A DynaBean contains the methods listed in Table 3-2. There are methods to get and set indexed and mapped properties, and two operations—remove( ) and contains( )—allow you to manipulate the contents of a Map property.

Table 3-2. Methods available on a DynaBean

Method	Description
get(String name)	Retrieves a simple bean property
get(String name, int i)	Retrieves an indexed been property
get(String name, String key)	Retrieves a mapped bean property
set(String name, Object value)	Sets a simple bean property
set(String name, int i, Object value)	Sets an indexed bean property

Table 3-2. *Methods available on a DynaBean (continued)*

Method	Description
set(String name, String key, Object value)	Sets a mapped bean property
remove(String name, String key)	Removes a key from a mapped bean property
contains(String name, String key)	Tests a map property for the presence of a key

See Also

Chapter 6 combines the power of Commons Digester and Commons BeanUtils to create a utility that reads in bean definitions from an XML document. A data model is described using an XML document, and it is realized into a set of DynaClass objects.

Chapter 12 discusses the power of Commons BeanUtils as it relates to working with a database. A ResultSetDynaClass enables you to wrap a JDBC ResultSet.

3.19   Getting and Setting Properties as Strings

Problem

You need to persist a bean to a text file, or populate a bean's properties from a String.

Solution

Use BeanUtils to get and set bean properties with strings. This utility contains many of the same functions as PropertyUtils with one major exception; instead of returning the Object value of the property, BeanUtils returns and expects a string representation of a value. The following code uses BeanUtils to populate a bean that is dependent on user input:

```
import java.util.*;
import org.apache.commons.beanutils.*;

Person person = new Person( );
person.setAge( new Integer( 45 ) );
person.setName( "Donald" );
person.setOccupation( "Salesman" );

// Get the Age as a String
String ageString = BeanUtils.getProperty( person, "age" );

// Set the Age from a String
BeanUtils.setProperty( person, "age", "50" );
```

Discussion

BeanUtils come in handy when a bean is populated from a user-supplied input like standard input or the parameters of an HTTP request. In fact, BeanUtils started as the mechanism used to populate a Struts ActionForm from the contents of an HTTP request. When the Struts ActionServlet receives a request that is mapped to an Action, the ActionServlet calls a method in RequestUtils, which examines the request and sets any properties on the relevant ActionForm. Because the inner workings of Struts are outside the scope of this book, Example 3-7 takes a String input from System.in and sets the age property of Person.

Example 3-7. Using BeanUtils to populate a bean from user input

```
import java.io.*;

public class ReadAge {
    public static void main (String[] args) throw Exception {
        //  Prompt for an Age
        System.out.print("Enter Age: ");

        //  open up standard input
        BufferedReader br =
            new BufferedReader(new InputStreamReader(System.in));

        String ageString = null;
        ageString = br.readLine( );

        // Set the Integer property with a String
        Person person = new Person( );
        BeanUtils.setProperty( person, "age", ageString );
    }
}
```

When BeanUtils sets the age property, it uses a set of registered Converter instances that are available to translate between a String and an Object. Behind the scenes, BeanUtils used the IntegerConverter class to convert the user-supplied String to an Integer object. For a full list of converters, read the documentation for the org.apache.commons.beanutils.converters package.

See Also

The BeanUtils Javadoc is available at *http://jakarta.apache.org/commons/beanutils/api/index.html*.

## CHAPTER 4

Functors

4.0 Introduction

The American Heritage Dictionary defines a *functor* as "one that performs an operation or a function," and, in the context of programming, a functor is an object that encapsulates "functional logic"—a functional object. So with a definition as abstract as "something that does stuff," you won't find a lot of satisfying, concise explanations of what a functor can do; in the abstract, anything that performs an operation or function could be considered a functor, and the process of drawing divisions between what should and should not be implemented with functors becomes a matter of personal preference. I'm not going to attempt to give a well-polished, textbook definition of a functor; this chapter simply demonstrates the set of basic functors from Commons Collections. Functors are less of an impressive new technology and are more of an approach to programming. Even if you are unfamiliar with the term, you've likely used functors without realizing it; two functors in common usage are Comparator and Iterator.

Both Comparator and Iterator serve to isolate an algorithm; Comparator encapsulates logic to compare two objects, and Iterator encapsulates logic used to iterate over a collection of objects. Functors often lead to more code reuse and a cleaner design because functional logic can be abstracted and extracted out of logic dealing with a specific data structure. For example, to compare two Person beans, you could make the Person class implement Comparable and provide a compareTo( ) method in the Person class, or you could write a PersonComparator, separating the comparison logic from the Person class. It is this separation of functional logic and the ability to combine functors together that make functors an interesting solution to a number of problems, from the creation of a Closure pipeline to a series of Predicate objects used to model a digital logic circuit.

Jakarta Commons Collections 3.0 introduces a set of functor interfaces in the org. apache.commons.collections package: Predicate, Transformer, Factory, and Closure objects. Predicate objects evaluate criteria or conditions, returning a boolean result.

Transformer objects create a new object based on an input object, Closure objects act on an input object, and Factory objects create objects. The powerful part of functors isn't that Commons Collections has introduced a few new interfaces—the power is only evident once you realize how they can be used in concert with other Jakarta Commons utilities such as Commons BeanUtils and Commons Collections. Chapter 5 makes heavy use of the functors introduced in this chapter, and Chapter 3 discusses a BeanComparator and a BeanPredicate.

This chapter focuses on the functors introduced in Commons Collections 3.0 and also deals with improvements to the Comparator interface. Commons Collections introduces some improvements to the Iterator interface, but, since people usually use Iterator objects with Collections, recipes involving Iterator objects are in the next chapter, which covers Java Collections. Functors, part of Commons Collections, are somewhat misplaced, and, even as this chapter is written, a Commons Functor project is being finalized in the Jakarta Commons Sandbox. By the time you read this chapter, the Commons Functor project may have been released. This book assumes that you are using the functors available in the 3.0 release of Commons Collections. The Commons Functor release contains a number of changes and improvements to the set of functors introduced in Commons Collections 3.0, and, when possible, the See Also sections in each recipe discuss the relevant class or interface in the fast-developing Commons Functor project.

4.1   Obtaining Commons Collections

Problem

You need to use Jakarta Commons Collections because your system could benefit from the various functor interfaces and implementations provided by this component.

Solution

You must download the latest version of Commons Collections and place the Commons Collections JAR in your project's classpath. Following the steps outlined in Recipe 1.1, download Commons Collections 3.0 instead of Commons Lang.

Discussion

Commons Collections was introduced as a series of utilities that augment the Java Collections API. Commons Collections contains functors such as Predicate and Closure, utilities for filtering and selecting elements in a collection, and some new collections: Bag and Buffer. Commons Collections is as widely used as Commons BeanUtils and Commons Lang, and with these two projects, it forms the core of the Jakarta Commons components.

If you have a Maven project that needs to use Commons Collections, add a dependency on Commons Collections 3.0 with the following section in *project.xml*:

```
<dependencies>
  <dependency>
    <id>commons-collections</id>
    <version>3.0</version>
  </dependency>

  ....other dependencies...
</dependencies>
```

See Also

For more information about the Commons Collections project, see the project page at *http://jakarta.apache.org/commons/collections*. If you have questions about using Commons Collections, feel free to join the *commons-user@jakarta.apache.org* mailing list. Instructions for joining the user mailing list can be found in Recipe 1.2. For information on obtaining the source code for Commons Collections, see Recipe 4.2.

4.2   Getting the Commons Collections Source Code

Problem

You need the source code for the Commons Collections project.

Solution

Download the source from *http://jakarta.apache.org/site/sourceindex.cgi*. Following the same procedure outlined in Recipe 1.3, download a file named *commons-collections-3.0-src.zip* (or *commons-collections-3.0-src.tar.gz*); once you unzip this archive, you will have the source to Commons Collections in *./commons-collections-3.0-src/src*.

See Also

Most Commons components follow a similar convention for the layout of binary and source distributions. For more information about the layout of the Collections source distribution, see Recipe 1.3. For information on obtaining the binary distribution for Commons Collections, see Recipe 4.1.

4.3   Reversing a Comparator

Problem

You need to reverse the effects of a Comparator. You need to return less than when this Comparator returns greater than, and greater than when it returns less than.

Solution

Use ReverseComparator to reverse the effects of a Comparator. Supply an existing Comparator to the constructor of ReverseComparator, and it reverses the effects of that Comparator. The following example demonstrates the use of ReverseComparator to reverse the result of a custom MyComparator instance:

```
Comparator myComparator = new MyComparator( );

Comparator reverseComparator = new ReverseComparator( myComparator );

Book book1 = new Book( );
Book book2 = new Book( );

int comparison = myComparator.compare( book1, book2 );
int reversedComparison = reverseComparator( book1, book2);
```

The value of reversedComparison is simply the negative of comparison; if MyComparator decides that book1 is less than book2, the ReverseComparator returns the opposite result—greater than. ReverseComparator simply wraps the original Comparator and multiplies the result by negative one.

Discussion

Example 4-1 is an implementation of a Comparator that is reversed using the ReverseComparator. This BookComparator compares two Book objects by the name and author bean properties. Sorting a list of books using this Comparator results in a list sorted alphabetically by book name and author name; if two books have the same name, they are sorted by author name.

Example 4-1. A Comparator that compares Book objects by name and author

```
package com.discursive.jccook.collections.compare;

import java.util.*;
import org.apache.commons.lang.StringUtils;
import org.apache.commons.collections.comparators.ReverseComparator;

public class BookComparator implements Comparator {

    public int compare(Object o1, Object o2) {
      int comparison = -1;
```

```
        if( o1 instanceof Book && o2 instanceof Book ) {
            Book b1 = (Book) o1;
            Book b2 = (Book) o2;

        String b1Name = b1.getName( );
        String b2Name = b2.getName( );

        String b1Author = b1.getAuthor( );
        String b2Author = b2.getAuthor( );

          if( StringUtils.isNotEmpty( b1Name ) &&
              StringUtils.isNotEmpty( b2Name ) ) {
              comparison = b1Name.compareTo( b2Name );
          }

          if( comparison == 0 &&
              StringUtils.isNotEmpty( b1Author ) &&
              StringUtils.isNotEmpty( b2Author ) ) {
              comparison = b1Author.compareTo( b2Author );
          }
        }
        return comparison;
    }
}
```

Example 4-2 sorts an array of Book objects in reverse order.

Example 4-2. Using ReverseComparator to sort Book objects

```
package com.discursive.jccook.collections.compare;

import java.util.*;
import org.apache.commons.collections.comparators.ReverseComparator;

public class ReverseExample {

    public static void main(String[] args) throws Exception {
        ReverseExample example = new ReverseExample( );
        example.start( );
    }

    public void start( ) throws Exception {

        // Create a Reversed BookComparator
        Comparator bookCompare = new BookComparator( );
        Comparator reverseComparator = new ReverseComparator( bookComparator );

        // Create a List of Book objects
        List books = new ArrayList( );

        Book book1 = new Book( );
        book1.setName( "TitleA" );
```

Example 4-2. Using ReverseComparator to sort Book objects (continued)

```
        book1.setAuthor( "John" );
        books.add( book1 );

        Book book2 = new Book( );
        book2.setName( "TitleB" );
        book2.setAuthor( "Donald" );
        books.add( book2 )

        Book book3 = new Book( );
        book3.setName( "TitleA" );
        book3.setAuthor( "Doug" );
        books.add( book3 );

        // Sort the List of Book objects with the Reversed BookComparator
        Collections.sort( books, reverseComparator );

    }
}
```

After `Collections.sort( )`, the books array is sorted in reverse alphabetical order by book name and author name: "TitleB by Donald" followed by "TitleA by John" followed by "TitleA by Doug."

See Also

If you were using a simple `Comparator` to sort an array, you could sort and reverse the resulting array with `Arrays.reverse( )`, or you could reverse a `List` with `Collections.reverse( )`. Wrapping a `Comparator` in `ReverseComparator` may help you avoid the call to `reverse( )`, but the benefit is miniscule. `ReverseComparator` makes more sense when used in the context of a `ChainedComparator`; see Recipe 4.4 for more information about the `ChainedComparator`.

Note that use of `StringUtils.isNotEmpty( )` is used in `BookComparator` to check if either of the bean properties are null or blank. This utility, is from `StringUtils`, and it is introduced in Recipe 2.2.

4.4   Chaining Comparators

Problem

You need to sort a collection of objects by more than one property.

Solution

Use `ComparatorChain` to create a series of `Comparator` objects that appear as a single `Comparator`. A `ComparatorChain` compares two objects with each `Comparator` in the chain until a `Comparator` returns a nonzero value. If a `Comparator` returns equality (zero), the ComparatorChain then moves to the next Comparator to obtain another comparison. The following example demonstrates the use of chained BeanComparators; if two Person objects have the same lastName, the chain created in this example tries to compare the objects by firstName:

```
Person person1 = new Person( );
person1.setLastName( "Payne" );
person1.setFirstName( "James" );
person1.setAge( 21 );

Person person2 = new Person( );
person2.setLastName( "Payne" );
person2.setFirstName( "James" );
person2.setAge( 85 );

Person person3 = new Person( );
person3.setLastName( "Payne" );
person3.setFirstName( "Susan" );
person3.setAge( 29 );

Person[] persons = new Person[] { person1, person2, person3 };

ComparatorChain comparatorChain = new ComparatorChain( );
comparatorChain.addComparator( new BeanComparator( "lastName" ) );
comparatorChain.addComparator( new BeanComparator( "firstName" ) );
comparatorChain.addComparator( new BeanComparator( "age" ), true );

Arrays.sort( persons, comparatorChain );
```

This example sorts an array of Person objects: by lastName ascending, firstName ascending, and age descending. The sorted persons array will be in the following order: the older James Payne, the younger James Payne, followed by Susan Payne. The ChainedComparator successfully sorts two objects with the same first and last names—falling back to the age to provide the correct sort order.

Discussion

A ComparatorChain evaluates every Comparator in the chain as needed. If the current Comparator returns a zero, the next Comparator is invoked until there are no more Comparator objects left in the chain. If the final Comparator returns a zero value, the ComparatorChain returns a zero. The ComparatorChain implements the Comparator interface and is an aggregate of other Comparator objects; it can be used wherever a Comparator is used, including array sorting and as a Comparator for a tree-based Collection implementation.

The ReverseComparator (introduced in Recipe 4.3) makes more sense in light of the ComparatorChain. If you need to sort a collection of objects for display, you might want to reverse a particular Comparator in a ComparatorChain. In the previous example, there are two people named "James Payne": one is 21 and the other is 85. Your application respects age and you want to put the older James Payne in front of the younger James Payne in the sorted list. Sorting by lastName ascending, firstName ascending, and age descending calls for the last Comparator in the chain to be reversed; the following code calls addComparator( ) with a second parameter, true, causing the BeanComparator for age to be reversed with ReverseComparator:

```
comparatorChain.addComparator( new BeanComparator( "age" ), true );
```

The previous statement is equivalent to the following code:

```
comparaterChain.addComparator( new ReverseComparator(new BeanComparator("age") );
```

Using a ComparatorChain may remind you of the way a result set is sorted in a SQL SELECT statement. This recipe's Solution implements the following SQL statement in a ComparatorChain:

```
SELECT * FROM person ORDER BY lastName ASC, firstName ASC, age DESC;
```

Where to Sort?

In many organizations, there is a debate over where to sort data in an application: should sorting be done in the database or in an application server? The answer depends on a number of factors, but, now that you have seen how a ComparatorChain works, you can implement *any* complex sort in Java. The use of a ComparatorChain is especially relevant if you are writing a web application that presents a sortable table and you have decided to implement sorting logic in your presentation layer. If you are sorting beans, load your data into a collection and use a ComparatorChain made up of BeanComparators.

See Also

The BeanComparator was introduced in the previous chapter; for more information, see Recipe 3.10. The ReverseComparator was introduced in Recipe 4.3.

4.5   Comparing Nulls

Problem

You need to sort an object array that contains null elements, and you want to have control over whether the null values are at the beginning or end of a sorted array.

Solution

Wrap your Comparator in a NullComparator from Commons Collections. The NullComparator can sort null values higher or lower than non-null values, depending on options passed into the constructor. The following example shows a custom BookComparator wrapped with a NullComparator:

```
import org.apache.commons.collections.comparators.NullComparator;
import java.util.*;

Comparator bookComparator = new BookComparator( );
Comparator nullComparator = new NullComparator( BookComparator );

Book[] bookArray = new Book[] { new Book(), null, new Book() };

Arrays.sort( bookArray, nullComparator );
```

This example sorts an array of Book objects, placing null at the end of the sorted array; after the sort, bookArray contains two Book objects at index zero and index one and a null reference at index two.

 If a Comparator does not handle null values gracefully, wrap it in a NullComparator and avoid a NullPointerException.

Discussion

To configure NullComparator to sort null values as less than non-null values, pass false to the constructor of NullComparator; to sort null values as greater than non-null values, pass true. By default, null values are sorted higher:

```
// null is less than non-null
Comparator nullComparator = new NullComparator( bookComparator, false );

// null is greater than non-null (default)
Comparator nullComparator = new NullComparator( bookComparator, true );
```

While the NullComparator usually decorates another instance of Comparator, the NullComparator can also be used by itself to compare null and non-null objects, as in the following example:

```
Comparator nullHighComparator = new NullComparator( );
Comparator nullLowComparator = new NullComparator(false);

// Returns 1
nullHighComparator.compare( null, new Double(3.0) );

// Returns -1
nullLowComparator.compare( null, new Double(3.0) );

// Returns 0
nullLowComparator.compare( null, null );
```

See Also

Both ReverseComparator and NullComparator are objects that decorate an existing Comparator. Take note of the decorator pattern as it is a common pattern used throughout Commons Collections. For more information about the decorator design pattern, read *Design Patterns: Elements of Reusable Object-Oriented Software* (Addison Wesley).

4.6   Fixed-Order Comparison

Problem

You need to sort a collection of objects that have a preestablished order, such as the days of the week or the order of planets in the solar system.

Solution

Use FixedOrderComparator in Jakarta Commons Collections. When using FixedOrderComparator, you supply an array of objects in a sorted order and the Comparator returns comparison results based on the order of the objects in this array. The following example uses a fixed string array to compare different Olympic medals:

```
import java.util.*;
import org.apache.commons.beanutils.BeanComparator;
import org.apache.commons.collections.comparators.FixedOrderComparator;

String[] medalOrder = {"tin", "bronze", "silver", "gold", "platinum"};

Comparator medalComparator = new FixedOrderComparator( medalOrder );
Comparator athleteComparator = new BeanComparator( "medal", medalComparator );

Athlete athlete1 = new Athlete( );
Athlete athlete2 = new Athlete( );

int compare = medalComparator.compare( athlete1.getMedal(), athlete2.getMedal() );
```

In this code, a FixedOrderComparator compares two Athletes by the value of the medal property. The medal property can be "tin," "bronze," "silver," "gold," or "platinum," and a FixedOrderComparator uses the order of the medalOrder array to compare these values. The medalOrder array establishes a fixed relationship between the three medal types; "bronze" is less than "silver," which is less than "gold."

Discussion

Use FixedOrderComparator when sorting an array or a collection that contains values that are ordered in a pre-determined fashion: days of the week, planets in the solar system, colors in the spectrum, or hands dealt in a poker game. One way to sort an array containing the days of the week would be to assign a numerical value to each day—"Monday" is one, "Tuesday" is two, "Wednesday" is three, etc. Then you could sort the array with a Comparator that takes each day's name, sorting elements based on the numerical value corresponding to a day's name. An alternative is the use of FixedOrderComparator, letting the comparator order objects based on the order of an array of day names.

If a bean contains a property to be sorted according to a fixed-order array, you can use the BeanComparator in conjunction with FixedOrderComparator. The following example sorts cards by value and suit using a FixedOrderComparator and a BeanComparator; A PlayingCard object, defined in Example 4-3, is sorted according to the order of two arrays—one for the face value of the PlayingCard and one for the suit of the PlayingCard.

Example 4-3. A bean representing a playing card

```java
package org.discursive.jccook.collections.compare;

public class PlayingCard() {

    public static String JOKER_VALUE = null;
    public static String JOKER_SUIT = null;

    private String value;
    private String suit;

    public PlayingCard() {}
    public PlayingCard(String value, String suit) {
        this.value = value;
        this.suit = suit;
    }

    public String getValue() { return value; }
    public void setValue(String value) { this.value = value; }

    public String getSuit() { return suit; }
    public void setSuit(String suit) { this.suit = suit; }

    public String toString() {
        String cardString = "JOKER";
        if( value != null && suit != null ) {
            cardString = value + suit;
        }
        return cardString;
    }
}
```

Example 4-4 creates a ComparatorChain of BeanComparators, which compares the value and suit properties using a FixedOrderComparator. Each card's suit is compared first, and, if two cards have the same suit, they are compared by face value. Jokers do not have suits or a face value, and this example handles jokers with a null-valued suit and value property by wrapping each FixedOrderComparator with a NullComparator.

Example 4-4. Combining FixedOrderComparator with BeanComparator, NullComparator, and ComparatorChain

```
package com.discursive.jccook.collections.compare;

import java.util.ArrayList;
import java.util.Comparator;
import java.util.List;

import org.apache.commons.beanutils.BeanComparator;

import org.apache.commons.collections.comparators.NullComparator;
import org.apache.commons.collections.comparators.FixedOrderComparator;
import org.apache.commons.collections.comparators.ComparatorChain;

public class FixedOrderExample {

    // Suit order "Spades", "Clubs", "Diamonds", "Hearts"
    private String[] suitOrder = { "S", "C", "D", "H" };

    private String[] valueOrder = { "2", "3", "4", "5", "6", "7", "8",
                                    "9", "10", "J", "Q", "K", "A" };

    public static void main(String[] args) {
        FixedOrderExample example = new FixedOrderExample();
        example.start();
    }

    public void start() {

        List cards = new ArrayList();
        cards.add( PlayingCard( "J", "C" ) );
        cards.add( PlayingCard( "2", "H" ) );
        cards.add( PlayingCard( PlayingCard.JOKER_VALUE, PlayingCard.JOKER_SUIT));
        cards.add( PlayingCard( "2", "S" ) );
        cards.add( PlayingCard( "Q", "S" ) );
        cards.add( PlayingCard( "4", "C" ) );
        cards.add( PlayingCard( "J", "D" ) );

      System.out.println( "Before sorting: " + printCards( cards ) );

        // Create a null-safe suit order comparator that will compare the
        // suit property of two Java beans
        Comparator suitComparator = new FixedOrderComparator( suitOrder );
        suitComparator = new NullComparator( suitComparator );
        suitComparator = new BeanComparator( "suit", suitComparator );

        // Create a null-safe value order comparator that will compare the
        // value property of two Java beans
        Comparator valueComparator = new FixedOrderComparator( valueOrder );
```

Example 4-4. Combining FixedOrderComparator with BeanComparator, NullComparator, and ComparatorChain (continued)

```
        valueComparator = new NullComparator( valueComparator );
        valueComparator = new BeanComparator( "value", valueComparator );

        // Create a chain of comparators to sort a deck of cards
        Comparator cardComparator = new ComparatorChain( );
        cardComparator.addComparator( suitComparator );
        cardComparator.addComparator( valueComparator );

        Collections.sort( cards, cardComparator );

        System.out.println( "After sorting: " + printCards( cards ) );
    }

    private String printCards( List cards ) {
        StringBuffer resultBuffer = new StringBuffer( );
        Iterator cardIter = cards.iterator( );
        while( cardIter.hasNext( ) ) {
            PlayingCard card = (PlayingCard) cards.next( );
            resultBuffer.append( " " + card.toString( ) );
        }
        return resultBuffer.toString( );
    }
}
```

This example sorts the `PlayingCard` objects and produces the following output:

```
Before sorting: JC 2H JOKER 2S QS 4C JD
After sorting: 2S QS 4C JC JD 2H JOKER
```

The list is sorted such that all the cards of a similar suit are grouped together—spades are less than clubs, clubs are less than diamonds, and diamonds are less than hearts. A sorted collection of cards is grouped by suits, and, within each suit, cards are organized according to face value—2 is low and aces is high. The order used in the sorting is captured in two fixed-order arrays, `suitOrder` and `faceOrder`. If a shuffled deck were used in the example, it would end up as a perfectly sorted deck of cards.

Example 4-4 ties a number of simple `Comparators` together to perform a fairly complex sort. A `FixedOrderComparator` is wrapped in a `NullComparator`, which is then wrapped with a `BeanComparator`. These `BeanComparator` instances are then combined in a `ComparatorChain`. The use of `NullComparator` with a `BeanComparator` is recommended to avoid a `NullPointerException` from `BeanComparator`; `BeanComparator` is not designed to handle null-valued bean properties, and it throws an exception if you ask it to play nice with `null`s.

See Also

`BeanComparator` is discussed in Recipe 3.10. This helpful utility is indispensable if you are working with systems that need to sort JavaBeans.

For more information about the ComparatorChain object, see Recipe 4.4. For more information on the NullComparator, see Recipe 4.5.

4.7   Using Simple Predicates

Problem

You need to perform logic that is predicated on a certain condition being satisfied, and you want to encapsulate this condition in an object.

Solution

Use a Predicate to evaluate a criteria or a condition. A Predicate is an object that evaluates another object and returns true or false; predicates are used throughout the Commons Collections packages for filtering, selecting, and validating the contents of collections. This code demonstrates the use of simple predicates to test the type and contents of an object:

```
import org.apache.commons.collection.Predicate;
import org.apache.commons.collection.functors.*;

String name = "Tim";

Predicate nameJohn = new EqualPredicate( "John" );
Predicate nameTim = new EqualPredicate( "Tim" );

Predicate instanceString = new InstanceofPredicate( String.class );
Predicate instanceDouble = new InstanceofPredicate( Double.class );

// Testing all predicates for "Tim"
System.out.println( "Is Name John?: " + nameJohn.evaluate( name ) );
System.out.println( "Is Name Tim?: " + nameTim.evaluate( name ) );
System.out.println( "Is this a String?: " + instanceString.evaluate( name ) );
System.out.println( "Is this a Double?: " + instanceDouble.evaluate( name ) );
```

The previous example tests the name object against a few Predicate implementations producing the following console output:

```
Is Name John?: false
Is Name Tim?: true
Is this a String?: true
Is this a Double?: false
```

The string "Tim" is subjected to various Predicate tests. The first two EqualPredicate objects test the contents of the string, returning true if the object being evaluated is equal to the object passed into the EqualPredicate's constructor. The last two Predicate objects are InstanceofPredicate instances, which test the type of object being evaluated; if an InstanceofPredicate constructor is passed to the String class, it returns true if the object being evaluated is a java.lang.String type.

Discussion

The simple `Predicate` interface is central to a number of utilities introduced in this chapter. To implement `Predicate`, define an `evaluate( )` method that returns a boolean; a `Predicate` is a function object (or functor) that captures a criteria in an object that can be created and altered at runtime. Creating and evaluating a `Predicate` is just as valid as writing an `if` statement; for example, the code in the Solution of this recipe could have been implemented as a series of `if` statements:

```
String name = "Tim";

if( name.equals( "John" ) ) {
    System.out.println( "The name is John." );
}

if( name.equals( "Tim" ) ) {
    System.out.println( "The name is Tim." );
}

if( name instanceof String ) ) {
    System.out.println( "name is as String object" );
}

if( name instanceof Double ) ) {
    System.out.println( "name is as Double object" );
}
```

`Predicate` instances capture an `if` statement in an object, and if you are going to constantly change the behavior of your application, you might want to consider placing conditional expressions in `Predicate` instances. For example, if a system is designed to classify a storm as being a hurricane, you may want to capture all of your classification criteria in an XML file—parsing this file at runtime and creating a series of `Predicate` objects. A storm is a hurricane when the winds exceed a certain value, and the barometric pressure falls below a certain point. But, in a few years those criteria might change to involve a new, or more complex, set of measurements. If your decision logic is encapsulated in a `Predicate` object, it will be easier to upgrade the program to take new criteria into account; all of this logic will be encapsulated in an instance of `Predicate`.

Commons Collections provides a number of basic predicates for common situations, such as testing to see if an object equals another object (`EqualPredicate`), or that an object is of a certain type (`InstanceofPredicate`). Table 4-1 lists a number of simple `Predicate` implementations.

Table 4-1. Predicate implementations

Name	Description
EqualPredicate	Compares each object to an object passed via a constructor—returning true if the two are equal.
IdentityPredicate	Returns true if the object being evaluated is the same object reference as the object passed to its constructor. The IdentityPredicate uses the == operator to compare two object references.
NotPredicate	Wraps a Predicate and returns the opposite result.
InstanceOfPredicate	Returns true if the object being evaluated matches the type passed into its constructor.
NullPredicate NullIsTruePredicate	Returns true if the object being evaluated is null.
NotNullPredicate NullIsFalsePredicate	Returns true if the object being evaluated is not null.
TruePredicate	Always returns true.
FalsePredicate	Always returns false.
UniquePredicate	Returns true if it is the first time a particular object has been evaluated. The UniquePredicate maintains a HashSet of objects it has evaluated; if an object is already in that HashSet, this Predicate returns false. UniquePredicate can be used to select distinct objects from a collection.

The following example demonstrates simple Predicate objects with a test for equality, inequality, and equality by identity:

```
import org.apache.commons.collections.Predicate;
import org.apache.commons.collections.functors.*;
...

String testName = "Ben";

Predicate equals = new EqualPredicate( testName );
Predicate notEquals = new NotPredicate( equals );
Predicate identity = new IdentityPredicate( testName );

System.out.println( "Does name equal 'Ben'? " + equals.evaluate( "Ben" ) );
System.out.println( "Is object 'Ben'? " + identity.evaluate( testName ) );
System.out.println( "Does name equal 'Tim'? " + equals.evaluate( "Tim" ) );
System.out.println( "Does name not equal 'Tim'? " + notEquals.evaluate( "Tim" ) );
System.out.println( "Is object 'Tim'? " + identity.evaluate( "Tim" ) );
```

This code demonstrates the use of Predicate objects to determine if objects are equal or if two object references reference the same instance. When executed, the following is output to the console:

```
Does name equal 'Ben'? true
Is object 'Ben'? true
Does name equal 'Tim'? false
Does name not equal 'Tim'? true
Is object 'Tim'? false
```

The following code demonstrates simple predicates that test for the presence or absence of null or if an object being evaluated is of a certain type. The example also demonstrates the use of a UniquePredicate that returns true when it encounters an object for the first time:

```
import org.apache.commons.collections.Predicate;
import org.apache.commons.collections.functors.*;

String nullString = null;
Double testDouble = new Double(3.4);

Predicate isString = new InstanceofPredicate( String.class );
Predicate isLong = new InstanceofPredicate( Long.class );
Predicate isNumber = new InstanceofPredicate( Number.class );

Predicate isNotNull = NotNullPredicate.INSTANCE;
Predicate isNull = NullPredicate.INSTANCE;

Predicate unique = new UniquePredicate();

System.out.println("'nullString' not null?: " + isNotNull.evaluate(nullString));
System.out.println("'nullString' null?: " + isNull.evaluate(nullString));

System.out.println("'testDouble' a String?: " + isString.evaluate(testDouble));
System.out.println("'testDouble' a Long?: " + isLong.evaluate(testDouble));
System.out.println("'testDouble' a Number?: " + isNumber.evaluate(testDouble));

System.out.println("'A' Unique?: " + unique.evaluate("A"));
System.out.println("'C' Unique?: " + unique.evaluate("C"));
System.out.println("'A' Unique?: " + unique.evaluate("A"));
System.out.println("'B' Unique?: " + unique.evaluate("B"));
```

The sample evaluates objects against the InstanceofPredicate, the NullPredicate, the NotNullPredicate, and the UniquePredicate, and the following is output to the console:

```
'nullString' not null?: false
'nullString' null?: true

'testDouble' a String?: false
'testDouble' a Long?: false
'testDouble' a Number?: true

'A' Unique?: true
'C' Unique?: true
'A' Unique?: false
'B' Unique?: true
```

The UniquePredicate returns false the second time it encounters "A." The Double object testDouble is shown to be a Number object, and the nullString is evaluated as non-null.

See Also

This recipe mentions function pointers in C and C++. Function pointers are pointers to the address of a function, and they allow for some interesting logical acrobatics. For more information about function pointers in C and C++, see *http://www.function-pointer.org/*.

Predicate, Closure, and Transformer are all functor objects that are used throughout the Commons Collections component. You may be familiar with functors if you have used the Standard Template Library (STL) in C++. STL documentation contains rigorous definitions for function objects and predicates. For more information about functors in STL, see *http://www.sgi.com/tech/stl/functors.html*.

4.8   Writing a Custom Predicate

Problem

You need to evaluate an object to see if it meets criteria, and you want to capture these criteria in a custom Predicate.

Solution

Implement the Predicate interface and capture your logic in an evaluate( ) method. Example 4-5 is a simple Predicate implementation that always returns true; it is intended as a basic example of how to implement the Predicate interface.

Example 4-5. A simple Predicate implementation

```
import org.apache.commons.collections.Predicate;

public class SimplePredicate implements Predicate {
    public boolean evaluate(Object object) {
        // do something.
        boolean result = true;
        return result;
    }
}
```

Discussion

Predicates can be used in any number of situations, such as validating user input, filtering a Collection, or just as a replacement for complex conditional logic. A Predicate can be as simple or as complex as you need it to be; the only contract it must satisfy is the production of a boolean result from an evaluate( ) method.

To demonstrate the process of writing a fairly complex implementation of the Predicate interface, a contrived example is developed in Example 4-6. Your application evaluates the condition of the space shuttle and makes a determination for launch—go or no go. Some of the criteria include the temperature of the launch pad, the status of the crew, and the presence (or absence) of fuel. In the end, your boss is looking for thumbs up or thumbs down, and you decide to write a program that returns a boolean decision. This decision is implemented in the LaunchPredicate class.

Example 4-6. Implementing the Predicate interface

```
package com.discursive.jccook.collections.predicate;

import org.apache.commons.collections.Predicate;

public class LaunchPredicate implements Predicate {

    public LaunchPredicate() {}

    public boolean evaluate(Object object) {
        boolean launchGo = false;

        LaunchStats stats = (LaunchStats) object;

        boolean crewReady = stats.isCrewPresent() && stats.isCrewHealthy();
        boolean fueled = stats.isShuttleFueled() && stats.isFuelIgnitionReady();
        boolean withinLaunchWindow = stats.isLaunchWindowOpen();

        boolean properWeather =
          ( stats.temperature() > 35 ) &&
              ( !stats.isLightningDangerPresent() );

        // Check the crew, fuel, and launch time
        if( crewReady && fueled && withinLaunchWindow ) {
            launchGo = true;
        }

        // Override a GO decision if the weather is bad
        if( !properWeather ) {
            launchGo = false;
        }

        return launchGo;
    }
}
```

A shuttle launch is predicated on the presence and health of the crew, the state of the fuel, and the time of the launch event. A final weather check is performed to ensure that the temperature of the shuttle is not below 35 degrees Fahrenheit. If this critical temperature limit is not met, the Predicate overrides the previous decision to launch. Using a LaunchPredicate encapsulates your decision logic in one object, making it easier to upgrade, maintain, and test this decision process. Your unit tests can pass a mock object to this predicate, testing every possible permutation of possible inputs. The following example demonstrates the use of the LaunchPredicate:

```
LaunchPredicate launchDecision = new LaunchPredicate( );

LaunchStats stats = measureLaunchStatistics( );

if( launchDecision.evaluate( stats ) ) {
    System.out.println( "We are Go for Ignition." );
} else {
    System.out.println( "Abort mission." );
}
```

See Also

The real Space Shuttle Launch Team has the outrageously complex job of monitoring and controlling every aspect of launching a spacecraft, and I'm sure that NASA doesn't implement the Predicate interface from Jakarta Commons Collections. While it isn't related to the topic of open source Java programming, it is a fascinatingly complex piece of software that maintains a shuttle launch. It is written in something called high-order assembly language/shuttle (HAL/S). If you are interested in learning more about one of the most complex pieces of software, take a look at NASA's Space Shuttle Launch Team website at *http://science.ksc.nasa.gov/shuttle/countdown/launch-team.html*. (Besides, I'm sure you are amused that NASA controls spacecraft with an assembly language known as HAL.)

This recipe mentions the use of a mock object to test a Predicate. One of the attractions of using a Predicate to encapsulate any complex condition is the ability to write a test for this condition logic; *mock objects* are a method of unit testing that involves passing a mock implementation of an object to a class in a test. For more information about mock objects, see *http://www.mockobjects.com/*.

4.9   Creating Composite Predicates

Problem

You need to perform complex conditional logic using multiple Predicate objects, and you need to combine and expose multiple criteria as one Predicate.

Solution

To combine several Predicate instances, create a Predicate to capture each portion of a compound condition, and combine each condition with AndPredicate, OrPredicate, AllPredicate, OnePredicate, AnyPredicate, or NonePredicate. All of these predicate implementations are used to combine the results of multiple predicates—creating a compound predicate. The following code demonstrates the use of the AndPredicate, OrPredicate, AllPredicate, and OnePredicate:

```
import org.apache.commons.collections.Predicate;
import org.apache.commons.collections.functors.*;

// Create Base Predicates
Predicate isTim = new EqualsPredicate("Tim");
Predicate isDouble = new InstanceOfPredicate( Double.class );
Predicate isNotNull = NotNullPredicate.INSTANCE;

Predicate[] predicates = new Predicate[] { isTim, isDouble, isNotNull };

// Create 2 argument logical predicate composites
Predicate andPredicate = new AndPredicate( isTim, isNotNull );
Predicate orPredicate = new OrPredicate( isTim, isNotNull );

// Create n-argument logical predicate composites
Predicate allPredicate = new AllPredicate( predicates );
Predicate onePredicate = new OnePredicate( predicates );

System.out.println( "'Tim' and not null?: " + andPredicate.evalute( "Tim" ) );
System.out.println( "'Tim' or not null?: " + andPredicate.evalute(new Long(3)));

System.out.println( "'Tim', not null, and Double?: "
            + allPredicate.evaluate( "Impossible" ) );
System.out.println( "XOR ('Tim', not null, or Double?): "
            + allPredicate.evaluate( "Impossible" ) );
```

This example creates the following output:

```
'Tim' and not null?: true
'Tim' or not null?: true

'Tim', not null, and Double?: false
XOR('Tim', not null, or Double?): true
```

Discussion

An AndPredicate returns true if both predicates supplied to its constructor return true, and an OrPredicate returns true if at least one of the two predicates passed to its constructor returns true. An AllPredicate takes an array of predicates, only returning true if every predicate evaluates to true. The OnePredicate also takes an array of predicates, only returning true if exactly one predicate evaluates to true.

In the code sample, the use of the second to last predicate, AllPredicate, is impossible to satisfy; an object can never be a String and a Double at the same time. This example fails to demonstrate AnyPredicate and NonePredicate—both take an array of predicates. AnyPredicate returns true if any of the predicates evaluate to true, and NonePredicate returns true only if none of the predicates evaluate to true. The behavior of these objects is easily inferred from the names: And, Or, All, One, Any, or None.

Any logical expression can be modeled by connecting Predicate objects together—similar to the way that simple logic gates are connected to create complex digital logic. Logical inputs (1 and 0) are routed to logic gates (AND, OR, NOR, NAND, XOR, etc.), and the outputs of a logic circuit are a result of stages that perform the same function as the Predicate objects introduced in this recipe. In the next example, a logic circuit will be used to demonstrate a complex hierarchy of Predicate objects; a circuit diagram is drawn, and a series of predicates are developed to model this circuit. Figure 4-1 contains a logical expression that is implemented with digital logic and Predicate objects.

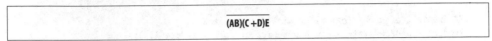

Figure 4-1. Logical expression to be modeled with Predicate

Assuming that every letter corresponds to a boolean variable, this expression corresponds to the circuit diagram in Figure 4-2. Each gate can be modeled as a composite Predicate, and from Figure 4-2 it is clear that this example will include two AndPredicates, an OrPredicate, and a NotPredicate. The "AND" gate is modeled with an AndPredicate, and an "OR" gate with an OrPredicate. The "NAND" gate is transformed into a three-input "AND" gate followed by an inverter that is modeled with an AllPredicate wrapped in a NotPredicate.

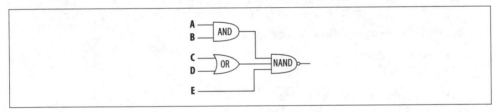

Figure 4-2. Circuit representing logical expression

The system has five inputs, which will be stored in a Map with five keys: A, B, C, D, and E. A simple InputPredicate is developed to handle the inputs to the system—a map of Boolean input objects is passed to the top-level Predicate. An InputPredicate is configured to evaluate the input Map and return the boolean value of one of the inputs; in other words, an InputPredicate selects a boolean value from a Map, always returning the value of that input from the Map it evaluates. (See Example 4-7.)

Example 4-7. InputPredicate: a predicate that selects an input from a Map

```
package com.discursive.jccook.collections.predicate;

import org.apache.commons.collections.Predicate;

public class InputPredicate implements Predicate {

    private String inputKey;
```

```java
    public BooleanPredicate(String inputKey) {
        this.inputKey = inputKey;
    }

    public boolean evaluate(Object object) {
        boolean satisfies = false;

        Map inputMap = (Map) object;
        Boolean input = (Boolean) inputMap.get( inputKey );
        if( input != null ) {
            satisfies = input.booleanValue();
        }

        return satisfies;
    }
}
```

The entire circuit is modeled by one top-level `Predicate` and a `Map` of `Boolean` input signals is passed down a hierarchy of predicates as needed. Unlike a real circuit, where inputs would cause gates to fire sequentially, the predicate hierarchy is evaluated from the final stage backward—the example evaluates the `Predicate` variable circuit. The input map is passed to the top-most `Predicate`, which, in turn, passes this same map to the `Predicate` that precedes it in the circuit. Example 4-8 ties everything together, and the logic to create our circuit-modeling predicate has been confined to the `createPredicate( )` method.

Example 4-8. Implementing a multilevel composite Predicate

```java
package com.discursive.jccook.collections.predicate;

import org.apache.commons.collections.Predicate;
import org.apache.commons.collections.functors.*;

public class CompoundPredicateExample {

    public static void main(String[] args) {
        CompoundPredicateExample example = new CompoundPredicateExample( );
        example.start( );
    }

    public void start( ) {

    Predicate circuit = createPredicate( );
      Object[] inputsArray =
          new Object[][] { {"A", Boolean.TRUE},
                           {"B", Boolean.FALSE},
                           {"C", Boolean.TRUE},
                           {"D", Boolean.FALSE},
                           {"E", Boolean.FALSE} };
      Map inputs = ArrayUtils.toMap( inputsArray );
      boolean result = circuit.evaluate( inputs );
```

Example 4-8. Implementing a multilevel composite Predicate (continued)

```
    System.out.println( "The circuit fired?: " + result );
}

public Predicate createPredicate() {
    Predicate aPredicate = new InputPredicate("A");
    Predicate bPredicate = new InputPredicate("B");
    Predicate cPredicate = new InputPredicate("C");
    Predicate dPredicate = new InputPredicate("D");
    Predicate ePredicate = new InputPredicate("E");

    Predicate expression1 = new AndPredicate( aPredicate, bPredicate );
    Predicate expression2 = new OrPredicate( cPredicate, dPredicate );

    Predicate[] secondLevel =
        new Predicate() { expression1, expression2, ePredicate };

    Predicate topLevel = new NotPredicate( secondLevel );
    return topLevel;
}
}
```

This code prints The circuit fired?: true. This complex example has demonstrated
the process of modeling composite, multistage logic with a hierarchy of predicates.
A Predicate is the most basic functor and when combined with other Predicate
instances, there is no limit to the level of complexity that can be achieved. Logic cir-
cuits were used in this example because a logic gate is a great analogy for a
Predicate. Think of a Predicate as a component—a gate in a logic circuit.

4.10 Transforming Objects

Problem

You need to perform a transformation, taking an object and creating a new object.

Solution

Implement the Transformer interface. A Transformer takes an object and returns a
new object instance. The following example demonstrates the joinArmy Transformer;
the transform( ) method takes a Recruit object instance and returns a Soldier object:

```
import org.apache.commons.collections.Transformer;

Transformer joinArmy = new Transformer() {
    public Object transform(Object input) {
        Recruit recruit = (Recruit) input;
        BootCamp.obstacleCourse( recruit );
        Soldier soldier = BootCamp.graduate( recruit );
    }
}
```

```
Recruit recruit1 = new Recruit("Pat T.");
System.out.println( "Status before transformation: " + recruit );

Soldier soldier1 = (Soldier) joinArmy.transform( recruit1 );
System.out.println( "Status after transformation: " + soldier );
```

A Recruit object is passed to the joinArmy.transform( ) method, and a Soldier object is returned. The state of the recruit and soldier instances are printed before and after the transformation:

```
Status before transformation: Pat T., Recruit
Status after transformation: Pat T., Soldier
```

Discussion

This object isolates and encapsulates a transition; a system that needs to translate between two domain models or two object types should encapsulate such a transition in a Transformer. Transformer may be something of a misnomer. When an object undergoes a transformation, it is common to think of an object being modified or acted upon, but this is contrary to the design of the Transformer interface. The Javadoc for Transformer expressly states, "The original object is left unchanged." Figure 4-3 illustrates the simple joinArmy Transformer.

Figure 4-3. Diagram of the joinArmy Transformer

See Also

Jakarta Commons Functor in the Commons Sandbox expands on the initial functors introduced in Commons Collections, introducing a UnaryFunction object that provides a simple interface equivalent to Transformer. For more information about UnaryFunction, see the Commons Functor page at *http://jakarta.apache.org/commons/ sandbox/functor*.

4.11   Creating a Chain of Transformations

Problem

You have a series of transformations and you need to chain them together, passing the output of one stage to the input of the next.

Solution

Create multiple implementations of Transformer, and chain them together with ChainedTransformer. A ChainedTransformer takes an array of Transformer objects, passing the output of each Transformer to the next Transformer in the chain. The following example demonstrates a ChainedTransformer with two Transformer stages. The first stage, multiply, multiplies a number by 100, and the second stage, increment, adds one to the result from the first stage:

```java
import org.apache.commons.collections.Transformer;
import org.apache.commons.collections.functors.ChainedTransformer;

Transformer multiply = new Transformer() {
    public Object transform(Object input) {
        Long number = (Long) input;
        return( new Long( number.longValue() * 100 ) );
    }
}

Transformer increment = new Transformer() {
    public Object transform(Object input) {
        Long number = (Long) input;
        return( new Long( number.longValue() + 1 ) );
    }
}

Transformer[] chainElements = new Transformer[] { multiply, increment };
Transformer chain = new ChainedTransformer( chainElements );

Long original = new Long( 34 );
Long result = chain.transform( original );

System.out.println( "Original: " + original );
System.out.println( "Result: " + result );
```

The Transformer chain takes the Long instance original and transforms it into a result:

```
Original: 34
Result: 3401
```

Discussion

Since a Transformer leaves the input parameter passed to transform() intact, this two-stage ChainedTransformer creates a new instance of Long for each stage in the ChainedTransformer. A Long is passed to the first stage, multiply, which transforms 34 to 3400. The result from the first stage, 3400, is then passed to the second stage, increment, which produces the final Long result, 3401. A real example would involve more complex implementations of Transformer, but this simple example demonstrates the mechanics of creating a simple pipeline of transformations, one leading to another. Figure 4-4 illustrates the simple structure of this two-staged ChainedTransformer.

Figure 4-4. A ChainedTransformer with two Transformers

See Also

Jakarta Commons Functor in the Commons Sandbox introduces a UnaryFunction interface that provides an interface equivalent to Transformer, and multiple UnaryFunction instances can be chained together using the CompositeUnaryFunction class. For more information about CompositeUnaryFunction, see the Commons Functor page at *http://jakarta.apache.org/commons/sandbox/functor*.

4.12   Applying Conditional Transformations

Problem

You need to perform a different transformation depending on a series of conditions or cases.

Solution

Use a SwitchTransformer to apply a Transformer that is dependent on a Predicate. A SwitchTransformer models a switch statement, and it takes three parameters: an array of Predicate instances, an array of Transformer instances, and a default Transformer. Example 4-9 uses a SwitchTransformer to apply a different Transformer implementation to odd and even numbers.

Example 4-9. Using a SwitchTransformer

```
Transformer oddTransform = new Transformer() {
    public Object transform(Object input) {
        Integer number = new Integer( input );
        return ( new Integer( number.intValue() * 2 );
    }
}

Transformer evenTransform - new Transformer() {
    public Object transform(Object input) {
        Integer number = new Integer( input );
        return ( new Integer( number.intValue() * 3 );
    }
}

Predicate isEven = new Predicate() {
    public boolean evaluate(Object input) {
        Integer number = (Integer) input;
        return( number.intValue() % 2 == 0 );
    }
}
```

Example 4-9. Using a SwitchTransformer (continued)

```
Predicate isOdd = new NotPredicate(isEven);

Predicate[] pArray = new Predicate[] { isOdd, isEven };
Transformer[] tArray = new Transformer[] { oddTransform, evenTransform };

Transform predicateTransform =
    new SwitchTransform( pArray, tArray, new NOPTransformer() );

Integer one = new Integer( 1 );
Integer two = new Integer( 2 );
Integer three = new Integer( 3 );
Integer four = new Integer( 4 );

System.out.println( "Transform of 1 = " + predicateTransform.transform( one ) );
System.out.println( "Transform of 2 = " + predicateTransform.transform( two ) );
System.out.println( "Transform of 3 = " + predicateTransform.transform( three ) );
System.out.println( "Transform of 4 = " + predicateTransform.transform( four ) );
```

If an object being transformed satisfies the isOdd Predicate, it is passed to the oddTransform Transformer. If an object being transformed satisfies the isEven Predicate, it is passed to the evenTransform Predicate. If the object satisfies neither Predicate, it is passed to an instance of NOPTransformer, which is a Transformer implementation that returns the object passed to transform( ):

```
Transform of 1 = 2
Transform of 2 = 6
Transform of 3 = 6
Transform of 4 = 12
```

Discussion

The array of Predicate instances and the array of Transformer instances passed to the constructor of SwitchTransformer must be of equal length. The SwitchTransformer evaluates each of the Predicate instances in the array. If a Predicate evaluates to true, the SwitchTransformer retrieves the Transformer that corresponds to the matching Predicate. If no Predicate evaluates to true, the SwitchTransformer passes the object being transformed to the third parameter—the default Transformer. In Example 4-9, the default Transformer was a NOPTransformer, which is a Transformer implementation that performs no transformation and returns the object passed to transform( ). Figure 4-5 illustrates the SwitchTransformer from the Solution; the two Predicate instances correspond to two Transformer instances.

See Also

Jakarta Commons Functor in the Commons Sandbox introduces a UnaryFunction interface that provides an interface equivalent to Transformer. A UnaryFunction can be predicated with a UnaryPredicate object via the ConditionalUnaryFunction class.

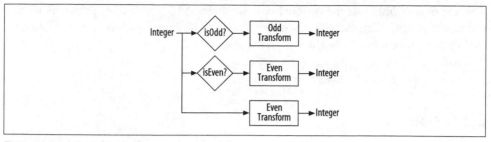

Figure 4-5. A SwitchTransform with two Predicate instances, two Transformer instances, and a default Transformer

For more information about `UnaryPredicate` and `ConditionalUnaryFunction`, see the Commons Functor page at *http://jakarta.apache.org/commons/sandbox/functor*.

4.13   Writing a Closure

Problem

You need a functor that operates on an object.

Solution

Use a `Closure` to encapsulate a block of code that acts on an object. In this example, a discount `Closure` operates on a `Product` object, reducing the price by 10 percent:

```
Closure discount = new Closure( ) {
    int count = 0;
    public int getCount( ) { return count; }

    public void execute(Object input) {
        count++;
        (Product) product = (Product) input;
        product.setPrice( product.getPrice( ) * 0.90 );
    }
}

Product shoes = new Product( );
shoes.setName( "Fancy Shoes" );
shoes.setPrice( 120.00 );
System.out.println( "Shoes before discount: " + shoes );

discount.execute( shoes );
System.out.println( "Shoes after discount: " + shoes );

discount.execute( shoes );
discount.execute( shoes );
System.out.println( "Shoes after " + discount.getcount( ) +
                    " discounts: " + shoes );
```

The example prints out the original cost of shoes ($120) and then proceeds to discount shoes and print out the discounted price. The Product object, shoes, is modified by the discount Closure three separate times:

```
Shoes before discount: Fancy Shoes for $120.00
Shoes after discount: Fancy Shoes for $108.00
Shoes after 3 discounts: Fancy Shoes for $87.48
```

Discussion

A Closure operates on the input object passed to the execute( ) method, while a Transformer does not alter the object passed to transform( ). Use Closure if your system needs to act on an object. Like the Transformer and Predicate interfaces, there are a number of Closure implementations that can be used to chain and combine Closure instances.

See Also

Jakarta Commons Functor in the Commons Sandbox expands on the initial functors introduced in Commons Collections, introducing a UnaryProcedure object that provides a simple interface equivalent to Closure. For more information about UnaryProcedure, see the Commons Functor page at *http://jakarta.apache.org/commons/sandbox/functor*.

4.14 Chaining Closures

Problem

An object needs to be acted on by a series of Closure instances.

Solution

Use ChainedClosure to create a chain of Closure instances that appears as a single Closure. A ChainedClosure takes an array of Closure objects and passes the same object sequentially to each Closure in the chain. This example sends an object through a ChainedClosure containing two stages that modify different properties on the object:

```
Closure fuel = new Closure() {
    public void execute(Object input) {
        Shuttle shuttle = (Shuttle) input;
        shuttle.setFuelPercent( 100.0 );
    }
}

Closure repairShielding = new Closure() {
    public void execute(Object input) {
```

```
        Shuttle shuttle = (Shuttle) input;
        shuttle.setShieldingReady( true );
    }
}

Closure[] cArray = new Closure[] { repairShielding, fuel };
Closure preLaunch = new ChainedClosure( cArray );

Shuttle endeavour = new Shuttle();
endeavour.setName( "Endeavour" );
System.out.println( "Shuttle before preLaunch: " + shuttle );

preLaunch.execute( endeavour );
System.out.println( "Shuttle after preLaunch: " + shuttle );
```

A Shuttle object is passed through a ChainedClosure, preLaunch, which consists of the stages fuel and repairShielding. These two Closure objects each modify the internal state of the Shuttle object, which is printed out both before and after the execution of the preLaunch Closure:

```
Shuttle before preLaunch: Shuttle Endeavour has no fuel and no shielding.
Shuttle before preLaunch: Shuttle Endeavour is fueled and is ready for reentry.
```

Discussion

This example should remind you of Recipe 4.11. When chaining Transformer objects, the result of each transformation is passed between stages—the results of stage one are passed to stage two, the results of stage two are passed to stage three, and so on. A ChainedClosure is different; the same object is passed to each Closure in sequence like a car moving through a factory assembly line.

See Also

Jakarta Commons Functor in the Commons Sandbox introduces a UnaryProcedure interface that is equivalent to Closure. Two or more UnaryProcedure instances can be chained together using the CompositeUnaryProcedure class. For more information about CompositeUnaryProcedure, see the Commons Functor page at *http://jakarta.apache.org/ commons/sandbox/functor*.

4.15 Modeling Conditional Statements with Closures

Problem

You need to model a conditional statement with functors.

Solution

Use an IfClosure, supplying a Predicate and two Closure objects. If the Predicate evaluates to true, the first Closure is executed; if the Predicate evaluates to false, the second Closure is executed. The following closure deals with a financial decision; a Predicate, isWinning, evaluates a Stock object. If the purchase price is less than the current price, the stock is a winner, causing the buy Closure to be executed. If the purchase price is higher than the current price, the stock is a loser and it is sold by passing it to the sell Closure:

```
Closure sell = new Closure() {
    public void execute(Object input) {
        Stock stock = (Stock) input;
        stock.sell( stock.getShares() );
        System.out.println( "\tSold all shares" );
    }
}

Closure buy = new Closure() {
    public void execute(Object input) {
        Stock stock = (Stock) input;
        int buyShares = stock.getShares() * 0.10;
        stock.buy( buyShares );
        System.out.println( "\tBought " + buyShares );
    }
}

Predicate isWinning = new Predicate() {
    public boolean evaluate(Object object) {
        Stock stock = (Stock) object;
        if( stock.getPurchasePrice() < stock.getCurrentPrice() ) {
            System.out.println( stock.getSymbol() + " is a winner";
            return true;
        } else {
            System.out.println( stock.getSymbol() + " is a loser";
            return false;
        }
    }
}

Closure stockAction = new IfClosure( isWinning, buy, sell );

Stock yahoo = new Stock("YHOO");
yahoo.setPurchasePrice( 10.0 );
yahoo.setCurrentPrice( 20.0 );
yahoo.setShares( 100 );

Stock tibco = new Stock("TIB");
tibco.setPurchasePrice( 50.0 );
tibco.setCurrentPrice( 30.0 );
tibco.setShares( 50 );
```

```
// Execute the IfClosure, take action on stocks based on performance
stockAction.execute( yahoo );
stockAction.execute( tibco );
```

The example evaluates two stocks, a winner and a loser. The following output is generated:

```
YHOO is a winner
    Bought 10 shares
TIB is a loser
    Sold All Shares
```

Discussion

Because an IfClosure is an implementation of a Closure, you can nest IfClosures within other IfClosures. The following code uses the Closure objects and the Predicate defined in the Solution, adding a third Closure, isUnchanged, to create a nested IfClosure–sellOrHold:

```
Predicate isUnchanged = new Predicate() {
    public boolean evaluate(Object object) {
        Stock stock = (Stock) object;
        if( stock.getPurchasePrice() == stock.getCurrentPrice() ) {
            System.out.println( stock.getSymbol() + " is unchanged";
            return true;
        }
        return false;
    }
}

Closure sellOrHold = new IfClosure( isUnchanged, new NOPClosure(), sell );
Closure stockAction = new IfClosure( isWinning, buy, sellOrHold );

Stock tibco = new Stock("TIB");
tibco.setPurchasePrice( 50.0 );
tibco.setCurrentPrice( 30.0 );
tibco.setShares( 50 );

Stock lucent = new Stock("LU");
tibco.setPurchasePrice( 30.0 );
tibco.setCurrentPrice( 30.0 );
tibco.setShares( 150 );

stockAction.execute( tibco );
stockAction.execute( lucent );
```

When stockAction is executed, and a Stock does not satisfy the isWinning Predicate, it is passed to the sellOrHold Closure, which is another IfClosure. The sellOrHold Closure then evaluates the Stock to see if it is a loser or unchanged. If the stock price is unchanged, it is passed to a NOPClosure, which performs no operation on the Stock object. If the stock price is less than the purchase price, the Stock is passed to the sell Closure.

4.16 Modeling Loops with Closures

Problem

You need to execute a Closure multiple times.

Solution

Use a WhileClosure, passing in a Predicate and a Closure. The WhileClosure will execute the Closure as long as a Predicate evaluates to true. The following example demonstrates a Closure named drive, which operates on a Car object and a Predicate named hasFuel, which evaluates the Car object. Each time a Car is passed to drive, a gallon of fuel is used, and hasFuel will evaluate to true if the amount of fuel in a car is greater than zero. The WhileClosure, useAllFuel, evaluates drive until hasFuel evaluates to false:

```
import org.apache.commons.collections.Closure;
import org.apache.commons.collections.Predicate;
import org.apache.commons.collections.functors.WhileClosure;

Closure drive = new Closure( ) {
    public void execute(Object input) {
        Car car = (Car) input;
        car.setFuel( car.getFuel( ) - 1 );
    }
}

Predicate hasFuel = new Predicate( ) {
    public boolean evaluate(Object object) {
        Car car = (Car) input;
        return car.getFuel( ) > 0;
    }
}

Closure useAllFuel = new WhileFuel( hasFuel, drive );

Car car = new Car( );
car.setMakeModel( "Ford Escort" );
car.setFuel( 20 );
System.out.println( "Car before while closure: " + car );

useAllFuel.execute( car );
System.out.println( "Car after while closure: " + car );
```

The WhileClosure, useAllFuel, takes a Car object, executing a Closure and evaluating a Predicate after every execution. The state of the car is printed both before and after it is passed to the WhileClosure:

```
Car before while closure: Ford Escort with 20 gallons of fuel.
Car after while closure: Ford Escort with no fuel.
```

Discussion

If you need to execute a Closure a set number of times, you can also use a ForClosure, passing in an int that specifies the number of times an object is passed to the execute( ) method of a Closure. This example uses the same Closure defined in the Solution, but, this time, the drive Closure is only executed five times:

```
Closure driveSome = new ForClosure( 5, drive );

Car car = new Car();
car.setMakeModel( "Toyota Camry" );
car.setFuel( 20 );

System.out.println( "Car before for closure: " + car );

driveSome.execute( car );

System.out.println( "Car after for closure: " + car );
```

Since the driveSome Closure is called only five times, the Camry still has 15 gallons after the ForClosure is executed:

```
Car before for closure: Toyota Camry with 20 gallons of fuel.
Car after for closure: Toyota Camry with 15 gallons of fuel.
```

CHAPTER 5
Collections

5.0   Introduction

Java 2 Standard Edition (J2SE) introduced the Collections API—a dramatic improvement over Vector and Hashtable in Java 1.1. This new API provides Set, List, Map, and Iterator interfaces with various implementations addressing different needs for different applications. Despite the additions and improvements, there are still gaps in the Java's Collections API—functionality that is addressed by a supplemental library, Jakarta Commons Collections. Most of the features introduced in Jakarta Commons Collections are easily anticipated extensions of the Java 2 platform: a reversible Comparator or a Bag interface, for example. Other concepts in Commons Collections are innovative additions to the J2SE—predicated collections, self-validating collections, set operations, and lazy collections using transformers. Commons Collections 3.0 also introduces the concept of functors (see Chapter 4).

Java 5.0 (a.k.a. Tiger) has introduced a number of new language features and improvements to the Collections API. A Queue class and type-safe generics are two major additions that will become available to most programmers with the production-ready release of 5.0. Some recipes in this chapter introduce utilities that overlap the functionality of 5.0, and, if a recipe introduces a utility with an analog in 5.0, an effort has been made to identify any opportunity to achieve the same result with new 5.0 classes and features.

5.1   Obtaining Commons Collections

Problem

You need to use Jakarta Commons Collections because your application makes heavy use of Collection objects, and you wish to use some of the utilities provided by this component.

Solution

Commons Collections was introduced in Chapter 4. For instructions on obtaining Collections, see Recipe 4.1.

See Also

For more information about the Commons Collections project, see the project page at *http://jakarta.apache.org/commons/collections*. If you have questions about using Commons Collections, feel free to join the *commons-user@jakarta.apache.org* mailing list. Instructions for joining the user mailing list can be found in Recipe 1.2. For information on obtaining the source code for Commons Collections, see Recipe 4.2.

5.2 Using a Looping Iterator

Problem

You need to loop through the contents of a Collection.

Solution

Use a LoopingIterator to repeatedly iterate through the contents of a Collection. Pass an existing Collection to the constructor of LoopingIterator, and call iterator(). The following code uses a LoopingIterator to retrieve five items from a List with three items:

```
List drivers = new ArrayList();

drivers.add( "Chris" );
drivers.add( "Sean" );
drivers.add( "Kathy" );

LoopingIterator loopingIterator = new LoopingIterator( drivers );

for( int i = 1; i <= 5; i++ ) {
    String driver = (String) loopingIterator.next();
    System.out.println( "Driver for Day " + i + ": " + driver );
}
```

The previous example simulates the selection of a driver in a car pool with three drivers. Five drivers are selected, and the LoopingIterator returns the first item in the List on the fourth day:

```
Driver for Day 1: Chris
Driver for Day 2: Sean
Driver for Day 3: Kathy
Driver for Day 4: Chris
Driver for Day 5: Sean
```

Discussion

Keep in mind that a LoopingIterator never stops iterating; hasNext( ) always returns true in a LoopingIterator. If you are using a LoopingIterator with a while loop, be sure to code an exit condition. A LoopingIterator is appropriate for a situation in which a series of values must be repeatedly evaluated, or a loop of commands must be repeatedly executed. An application, for example, may have a series of components that need to be continuously updated, or a series of queues or buffers that need to be continuously tested or monitored—an event loop, for example.

The LoopingIterator also implements the Commons Collections interface ResettableIterator; this extension of the Iterator interface can be reset to start at the beginning of a Collection. When using a ResettableIterator, call reset( ) to jump back to the beginning of a Collection:

```
List items = new ArrayList( );

items.add( "Item 1" );
items.add( "Item 2" );
items.add( "Item 3" );

LoopingIterator iterator = new LoopingIterator( items );

// Print out two elements from the LoopingIterator
System.out.println( iterator.next( ) );
System.out.println( iterator.next( ) );

// Reset iterator to start of List
System.out.println( "Reset" );
iterator.reset( );

// Print out two elements from the LoopingIterator
System.out.println( iterator.next( ) );
System.out.println( iterator.next( ) );
```

This example iterates over the first two elements in a List before calling reset( ). After calling reset( ), the code calls next( ) twice, printing out the first two elements, as shown below:

```
Item 1
Item 2
Reset
Item 1
Item 2
```

See Also

Recipe 5.3 deals with another implementation of ResettableIterator, ArrayListIterator, which can be used to iterate over a subset of elements in an ArrayList.

5.3   Iterating Over an ArrayList

Problem

You need to iterate over a portion of an ArrayList. For example, you have an ArrayList with 30 elements, and you need to iterate from index 0 to index 20.

Solution

Use an ArrayListIterator to iterate through a specified region of an ArrayList. This implementation of Iterator is constructed with a reference to an ArrayList and two optional parameters that specify the start and end of an iteration. This example demonstrates the use of ArrayListIterator to iterate over the 3rd, 4th, and 5th elements of an ArrayList:

```
String[] strings = new String[] { "A", "B", "C", "D", "E", "F" };
List list = new ArrayList( Arrays.asList( strings ) );

Iterator iterator = new ArrayListIterator( list, 3, 6 );
while( iterator.hasNext() ) {
    int index = iterator.nextIndex();
    String element = (String) iterator.next();
    System.out.println( "Element at " + index + ": " + element );
}
```

ArrayListIterator also allows you to obtain the index of an element during an iteration. In the previous example, iterator.nextIndex() returns the index of the element returned by the subsequent call to iterator.next(). The code above iterates through three elements of the ArrayList, producing the following output:

```
Element at 3: D
Element at 4: E
Element at 5: F
```

Discussion

You can construct an ArrayListIterator with up to three arguments. The first argument is the ArrayList to be iterated over. The second optional argument specifies the inclusive start index, and the third optional argument specifies the exclusive end index. If only two parameters are supplied to the constructor, the ArrayListIterator will iterate until the end of the ArrayList is reached. The following code demonstrates the three constructors of ArrayListIterator:

```
String[] strings = new String[] { "A", "B", "C", "D", "E", "F" };
List list = new ArrayList( Arrays.asList( strings ) );

// Iterate over all elements
Iterator iterator1 = new ArrayListIterator( list );

// Iterate over "C", "D", "E", "F"
Iterator iterator2 = new ArrayListIterator( list, 2 );
```

```
// Iterate over "B", "C", "D"
Iterator iterator3 = new ArrayListIterator( list, 1, 4 );
```

ArrayListIterator implements the ResettableIterator interface, which provides one function: reset( ). The reset( ) method takes the iterator back to the beginning of an iteration. After a reset, a call to next( ) returns the first element that an ArrayListIterator has been configured to return—the element at the index specified in the constructor's optional second parameter. An ArrayListIterator also provides a way to set the current element: the set( ) method takes an object parameter and changes the contents of the underlying ArrayList. The following example demonstrates both the reset( ) and set( ) methods on ArrayListIterator:

```
String[] strings = new String[] { "A", "B", "C", "D", "E", "F" };
List list = new ArrayList( Arrays.asList( strings ) );

System.out.println( "Original List: " + Arrays.toString( list.toArray() ) );

ResettableIterator iterator = new ArrayListIterator( list, 2 );

// Retrieve an Element from the List
int index = iterator.nextIndex();
String element = (String) iterator.next();
System.out.println( "Element at " + index + ": " + element );

// Set the Current Element
iterator.set( "G" );
System.out.println( "Modifying index: " + index + " to G");

// Retrieve the Next Element from the List
index = iterator.nextIndex();
element = (String) iterator.next();
System.out.println( "Element at " + index + ": " + element );

// Set the Current Element
iterator.set( "H" );
System.out.println( "Modifying index: " + index + " to H");

// Reset the Iterator (Go to beginning of iteration)
iterator.reset();
System.out.println( "Reset" );

index = iterator.nextIndex();
element = (String) iterator.next();
System.out.println( "Element at " + index + ": " + element );

System.out.println( "Modified List: " + Arrays.toString( list.toArray() ) );
```

This example iterates through the ArrayList, modifying two elements before calling reset( ). The following output shows that after a reset( ), the first element returns the value, which was supplied to set( ):

```
Original List: {A,B,C,D,E,F}
Element at 2: C
```

```
Modifying index: 2 to G
Element at 3: D
Modifying index: 3 to H
Reset
Element at 2: G
Modified List: {A,B,G,H,E,F}
```

See Also

If you need to iterate over an array or an object array, use two related implementations of Iterator: ArrayIterator and ObjectArrayIterator. See the Commons Collections project page at *http://jakarta.apache.org/commons/collections* for more information about these Iterator implementations.

5.4   Filtering a Collection with a Predicate

Problem

You need to iterate through elements of a Collection that match a specified condition. Or, you have a Collection from which you need to remove elements not satisfying a condition.

Solution

Create a FilterIterator with a Predicate; if the Predicate returns true for an element, that element will be included in the Iterator. The FilterIterator decorates another Iterator and provides the ability to apply an arbitrary filter to a Collection. In the following example, EarthQuake beans are kept in an ArrayList that is filtered using the majorQuakePredicate and a FilterIterator:

```
import org.apache.commons.collection.Predicate;
import org.apache.commons.collection.iterators.FilterIterator;

List quakes = new ArrayList();

EarthQuake quake1 = new EarthQuake();
quake1.setLocation( "Chicago, IL" );
quake1.setIntensity( new Float( 6.4f ) );
quake1.setIntensity( new Float( 634.23f ) );
quake1.setTime( new Date() );
quakes.add( quake1 );

EarthQuake quake2 = new EarthQuake();
quake2.setLocation( "San Francisco, CA" );
quake2.setIntensity( new Float( 4.4f ) );
quake2.setIntensity( new Float( 63.23f ) );
quake2.setTime( new Date() );
quakes.add( quake2 );

Predicate majorQuakePredicate =
    new MajorQuakePredicate( new Float(5.0), new Float(1000.0) );
```

```
Iterator majorQuakes =
    new FilterIterator( quakes.iterator( ), majorQuakePredicate );

while( majorQuakes.hasMore( ) ) {
    EarthQuake quake = (EarthQuake) majorQuakes.next( );
    System.out.println( "ALERT! MAJOR QUAKE: "
        + quake.getLocation( ) + ": " + quake.getIntensity( ) );
}
```

An instance of MajorQuakePredicate is created, and it is passed to a FilterIterator. Quakes satisfying the criteria are returned by the FilterIterator and printed to the console:

```
ALERT! MAJOR QUAKE: Chicago, IL: 6.4
```

Discussion

The Solution uses a custom Predicate to select a subset of a Collection, filtering EarthQuake beans and alerting the user if a major earthquake is measured. An earthquake is classified by intensity on the Richter scale and the depth of the epicenter; this information is modeled by the EarthQuake bean defined in Example 5-1.

Example 5-1. An EarthQuake bean

```
package com.discursive.jccook.collections.predicates;

public class EarthQuake {
    private String location;
    private Float intensity;
    private Float depth;
    private Date time;

    public class EarthQuake( ) {}

    public String getLocation( ) { return location; }
    public void setLocation(String location) { this.location = location; }

    public Float getIntensity( ) { return intensity; }
    public void setInsensity(Float intensity) { this.intensity = intensity; }

    public Float getDepth( ) { return depth; }
    public void setDepth(Float depth) { this.depth = depth; }

    public Date getTime( ) { return time; }
    public void setTime(Date time) { this.time = time; }
}
```

An earthquake is considered major if it is above a five on the Richter scale and above a depth of 1000 meters. To test each EarthQuake object, a custom Predicate, MajorQuakePredicate, evaluates EarthQuake objects, returning true if an earthquake satisfies the criteria for a major earthquake. The Predicate defined in Example 5-2 encapsulates this decision logic.

Example 5-2. Major earthquake classification Predicate

```
package com.discursive.jccook.collections.predicates;

import org.apache.commons.collections.Predicate;

public class MajorQuakePredicate implements Predicate {
    private Float majorIntensity;
    private Float majorDepth;

    public MajorQuakePredicate(Float majorIntensity, Float majorDepth) {
        this.majorIntensity = majorIntensity;
        this.majorDepth = majorDepth;
    }

    public boolean evaluate(Object object) {
        private satisfies = false;

        if( object instanceof EarthQuake) {
            EarthQuake quake = (EarthQuake) object;
            if( quake.getIntensity().floatValue() > majorIntensity.floatValue() &&
                quake.getDepth().floatValue() < majorDepth.floatValue() ) {
                satisfies = true;
            }
        }
        return satisfies;
    }
}
```

If you want to create a Collection of elements that match a Predicate, you can remove elements from a Collection using CollectionUtils.filter(). CollectionUtils.filter() is destructive; it removes elements from a Collection. The following example demonstrates the use CollectionUtils.filter() to remove nonmatching elements from a Collection:

```
import org.apache.commons.collection.Predicate;
import org.apache.commons.collection.iterators.FilterIterator;

ArrayList quakes = createQuakes();

Predicate majorQuakePredicate =
    new MajorQuakePredicate( new Float(5.0), new Float(1000.0) );

CollectionUtils.filter( quakes, majorQuakePredicate );
```

After the execution of this code, quakes will only contain EarthQuake objects that satisfy the MajorQuakePredicate. If you don't want to alter or modify an existing Collection, use CollectionUtils.select() or CollectionUtils.selectRejected() to create a new Collection with matching or nonmatching elements. The following example demonstrates the use of CollectionUtils.select() and CollectionUtils.selectRejected() to select elements from a Collection leaving the original Collection unaffected:

```
import org.apache.commons.collection.Predicate;
import org.apache.commons.collection.iterators.FilterIterator;
```

```
ArrayList quakes = createQuakes( );

Predicate majorQuakePredicate =
    new MajorQuakePredicate( new Float(5.0), new Float(1000.0) );

Collection majorQuakes = CollectionUtils.select( quakes, majorQuakePredicate );
Collection minorQuakes =
    CollectionUtils.selectRejected( quakes, majorQuakePredicate );
```

The majorQuakes Collection contains EarthQuake objects satisfying the majorQuakePredicate, and the minorQuakes Collection contains EarthQuake objects not satisfying the majorQuakePredicate. The quakes List is not modified by select( ) or selectRejected( ).

See Also

Collections can be filtered via a combination of CollectionUtils and Predicate objects, or you can also select elements from a Collection using an XPath expression. Recipe 12.1 demonstrates the use on Commons JXPath to query a Collection.

5.5   Iterating Through Distinct Elements

Problem

You need to iterate over the unique elements in a Collection.

Solution

Use a UniqueFilterIterator to iterate over distinct elements contained in a Collection. UniqueFilterIterator wraps another instance of Iterator, keeping track of all the objects returned by that Iterator. When calling next( ) on a UniqueFilterIterator, only objects not yet encountered are returned. The following example demonstrates the use of UniqueFilterIterator to find unique elements in a List:

```
import org.apache.commons.collections.iterators.UniqueFilterIterator;

String[] medals = new String[] { "gold", "silver", "silver", "gold", "bronze" };
List medalsList = Arrays.asList( medals );

Iterator uniqueIterator = new UniqueFilterIterator( medalsList.iterator( ) );

while( uniqueIterator.hasNext( ) ) {
    System.out.println( "Unique Medal: " + uniqueIterator.next( );
}
```

UniqueFilterIterator iterates over a List of strings, returning one copy of each distinct element; UniqueFilterIterator uses the equals( ) and hashCode( ) methods to compare objects in the Collection passed to the constructor. Equal objects with equal hash codes are removed. As shown by the output produced by the example, the UniqueFilterIterator prints out only the three distinct medals in the medalsList: "gold," "silver," and "bronze":

```
Unique Medal: gold
Unique Medal: silver
Unique Medal: bronze
```

Discussion

The building blocks for UniqueFilterIterator have already been introduced. FilterIterator was introduced in Recipe 5.4, and UniquePredicate is a Predicate that keeps track of objects it has evaluated in a HashSet. A UniqueFilterIterator is the equivalent of a FilterIterator with a UniquePredicate. As the following code demonstrates, the example from the Solution can be implemented with a FilterIterator and a Predicate:

```
import org.apache.commons.collections.iterators.FilterIterator;
import org.apache.commons.collections.functors.UniquePredicate;

String[] medals = new String[] { "gold", "silver", "silver", "gold", "bronze" };
List medalsList = Arrays.asList( medals );

Iterator uniqueIterator =
    new FilterIterator( medalsList.iterator(), new UniquePredicate() );

while( uniqueIterator.hasNext() ) {
    System.out.println( "Unique Medal: " + uniqueIterator.next();
}
```

See Also

For more information about the UniquePredicate see Recipe 4.7.

5.6   Using a Bag

Problem

You need to find out how many times an object occurs within a Collection, and you need a Collection that lets you manipulate the cardinality of objects it contains.

Solution

Use a Bag. A Bag can store the same object multiple times while keeping track of how many copies it contains. For example, a Bag object can contain 20 copies of object "A" and 50 copies of object "B," and it can be queried to see how many copies of an object it contains. You can also add or remove multiple copies of an object—add 10 copies of "A" or remove 4 copies of "B." The following example creates a Bag and adds multiple copies of two String objects:

```
import org.apache.commons.collections.Bag;
import org.apache.commons.collections.bag.HashBag;

Bag bag = new HashBag();

bag.add( "TEST1", 100 );
bag.add( "TEST2", 500 );

int test1Count = bag.getCount( "TEST1" );
int test2Count = bag.getCount( "TEST2" );

System.out.println( "Counts: TEST1: " + test1Count + ", TEST2: " + test2Count );

bag.remove( "TEST1", 1 );
bag.remove( "TEST2", 10 );

int test1Count = bag.getCount( "TEST1" );
int test2Count = bag.getCount( "TEST2" );

System.out.println( "Counts: TEST1: " + test1Count + ", TEST2: " + test2Count );
```

This example put 100 copies of the String "TEST1" and 500 copies of the String "TEST2" into a HashBag. The contents of the Bag are then printed, and 1 instance of "TEST1" and 10 instances of "TEST2" are removed from the Bag:

```
Counts: TEST1: 100, TEST2: 500
Counts: TEST1: 99, TEST2: 490
```

Discussion

Bag has two implementations—HashBag and TreeBag—which use a HashMap and a TreeMap to store the contents of a Bag. The same design considerations apply to Bag that apply to Map. Use HashBag for performance and TreeBag when it is important to maintain the order that each distinct object was added to a Bag. A TreeBag returns unique objects in the order they were introduced to the Bag.

To demonstrate the Bag object, a system to track inventory is created using a Bag as an underlying data structure. An inventory management system must find out how many copies of a product are in stock, and a Bag is appropriate because it allows you to keep track of the cardinality of an object in a Collection. In Example 5-3, a record store tracks an inventory of albums, consisting of 200 Radiohead albums, 100 Kraftwerk albums, 500 Charlie Parker albums, and 900 ABBA albums.

Example 5-3. Using a Bag to track inventory

```
package com.discursive.jccook.collections.bag;

import java.text.NumberFormat;
import java.util.Collection;
```

Example 5-3. Using a Bag to track inventory (continued)

```java
import java.util.Iterator;
import java.util.Set;

import org.apache.commons.collections.Bag;
import org.apache.commons.collections.bag.HashBag;
import org.apache.commons.lang.StringUtils;

public class BagExample {
    Bag inventoryBag = new HashBag();

    // Define 4 Albums
    Album album1 = new Album( "Radiohead", "OK Computer" );
    Album album2 = new Album( "Kraftwerk", "The Man-Machine" );
    Album album3 = new Album( "Charlie Parker", "Now's the Time" );
    Album album4 = new Album( "ABBA", "ABBA - Gold: Greatest Hits" );

    public static void main(String[] args) {
        BagExample example = new BagExample();
        example.start();
    }

    private void start() {
        // Read our inventory into a Bag
        populateInventory();

        System.out.println( "Inventory before Transactions" );
        printAlbums( inventoryBag );
        printSeparator();

        // A Customer wants to purchase 500 ABBA, 2 Radiohead, and 150 Parker
        Bag shoppingCart1 = new HashBag();
        shoppingCart1.add( album4, 500 );
        shoppingCart1.add( album3, 150 );
        shoppingCart1.add( album1, 2 );
        checkout( shoppingCart1, "Customer 1" );

        // Another Customer wants to purchase 600 copies of ABBA
        Bag shoppingCart2 = new HashBag();
        shoppingCart2.add( album4, 600 );
        checkout( shoppingCart2, "Customer 2" );

        // Another Customer wants to purchase 3 copies of Kraftwerk
        Bag shoppingCart3 = new HashBag();
        shoppingCart3.add( album2, 3 );
        checkout( shoppingCart3, "Customer 3" );

        System.out.println( "Inventory after Transactions" );
        printAlbums( inventoryBag );

    }
```

Example 5-3. Using a Bag to track inventory (continued)

```java
    private void populateInventory() {
        // Adds items to a Bag
        inventoryBag.add( album1, 200 );
        inventoryBag.add( album2, 100 );
        inventoryBag.add( album3, 500 );
        inventoryBag.add( album4, 900 );
    }

    private void printAlbums( Bag albumBag ) {
        Set albums = albumBag.uniqueSet();
        Iterator albumIterator = albums.iterator();
        while( albumIterator.hasNext() ) {
            Album album = (Album) albumIterator.next();
            NumberFormat format = NumberFormat.getInstance();
            format.setMinimumIntegerDigits( 3 );
            format.setMaximumFractionDigits( 0 );
            System.out.println( "\t" +
                format.format( albumBag.getCount( album ) ) +
                " - " + album.getBand() );
        }
    }

    private void checkout( Bag shoppingCart, String customer ) {
        // Check to see if we have the inventory to cover this purchase
        if( inventoryBag.containsAll( (Collection) shoppingCart ) ) {
            // Remove these items from our inventory
            inventoryBag.removeAll( (Collection) shoppingCart );
            System.out.println( customer + " purchased the following items:" );
            printAlbums( shoppingCart );
        } else {
            System.out.println( customer + ", I'm sorry " +
                                "but we are unable to fill your order." );
        }
        printSeparator();
    }

    private void printSeparator() {
        System.out.println( StringUtils.repeat( "*", 65 ) );
    }
}
```

Albums are stored in the `inventoryBag` variable, which is populated by a call to `populateInventory()` method. The `printAlbums()` method demonstrates how a Bag's iterator will iterate through all of the distinct objects stored in a Bag, printing out the count for each album by calling `getCount()` on the `inventoryBag`. After populating and printing the store's inventory, the `start()` method models the behavior of three customers. Each customer creates a Bag instance, `shoppingBag`, which holds the `Album` objects she wishes to purchase.

When a customer checks out of the store, the `containsAll()` method is called to make sure that the `inventoryBag` contains adequate inventory to fulfill a customer's

---

order. If a customer attempts to buy 40 copies of an album, we create a Bag with 40 instances of the Album object, and containsAll( ) will only return true if the inventoryBag contains at least 40 matching albums. Certain that the order can be fulfilled, removeAll( ) reduces the number of albums in the inventoryBag by 40 and the customer's transaction is considered complete.

Each customer transaction is modeled by a Bag that is subtracted from the inventoryBag using the removeAll( ) method. Example 5-3 prints the inventory before and after the three customer transactions, summarizing the result of each:

```
Inventory before Transactions
    200 - Radiohead
    100 - Kraftwerk
    900 - ABBA
    500 - Charlie Parker
****************************************************************
Customer 1 purchased the following items:
    002 - Radiohead
    500 - ABBA
    150 - Charlie Parker
****************************************************************
Customer 2, I'm sorry but we are unable to fill your order.
****************************************************************
Customer 3 purchased the following items:
    003 - Kraftwerk
****************************************************************
Inventory after Transactions
    198 - Radiohead
    097 - Kraftwerk
    400 - ABBA
    350 - Charlie Parker
```

Technically speaking, Bag is not a real Collection implementation. The removeAll( ), containsAll( ), add( ), remove( ), and retainAll( ) methods do not strictly follow the contract defined by the Collection interface. Adhering to a strict interpretation of the Collection interface, removeAll( ) should remove all traces of an object from a collection, and containsAll( ) should not pay attention to the cardinality of an object in a collection. Calling removeAll( ) with a single Album object should clear the Bag of any references to the specified Album object, and containsAll( ) should return true if a collection contains even one instance of a specified object. In Bag, a call to removeAll( ) with three Album objects will remove only the specified number of each Album object. In Example 5-3, the checkout( ) method uses removeAll( ) to remove albums from the inventory. A call to containsAll( ) will only return true if a Bag contains a number greater than or equal to the cardinality specified in the Collection. In Example 5-3, the checkout( ) method uses containsAll( ) to see if there is sufficient inventory to satisfy an order. These violations should not keep you from using Bag, but keep these exceptions to the collection interface in mind if you are going to expose a Bag as a collection in a widely used API.

See Also

For more information about the bag data structure, look at a definition from the National Institute of Standards and Technology (NIST) at *http://www.nist.gov/dads/HTML/bag.html*.

5.7 Using a Buffer

Problem

You need a data structure that can act as a temporary staging area, i.e., a buffer.

Solution

Use Buffer from Jakarta Commons Collections. A *buffer* is an object that is defined by the algorithm used for element removal. Buffer objects can be priority queues, staging areas, message queues, or buffers for I/O. One of the simplest Buffer implementations is the UnboundedFifoBuffer, a first-in, first-out data structure with no size limit. The following example demonstrates the use of an UnboundedFifoBuffer:

```
import org.apache.commons.collections.Buffer;
import org.apache.commons.collections.buffer.UnboundedFifoBuffer;

// Create an Unbounded FIFO
Buffer buffer = new UnboundedFifoBuffer( );

// Add elements to the Buffer
buffer.add("A");
buffer.add("B");
buffer.add("D");

// Remove element from the buffer
String value = (String) buffer.remove( );

buffer.add("E");

value = (String) buffer.remove( );
```

This example creates an UnboundedFifoBuffer, adding three elements: "A," "B," and "D." When remove( ) is invoked, the buffer selects the item that was placed into the buffer first—the first-in is the first-out. The first call to remove( ) returns "A," and the second call returns "B."

Discussion

A FIFO buffer can be viewed as a kind of stack; instead of pop( ) returning the last item to be placed on the stack, remove( ) returns the bottom of the stack—the first item added to the Buffer. A Buffer throws a BufferUnderflowException if you try to remove( ) or get( ) an element from an empty Buffer. This data structure is useful if you need a temporary holding area between stages in a pipeline—a queue to hold objects as they wait to be processed by the next stage. An unbounded FIFO buffer has no size limit, and, as such, it could grow to a limitless size. In fact, if an application continued to fill an unbounded buffer, it would exhaust available memory. Figure 5-1 describes a FIFO buffer as a linear sequence of elements: items flow through this sequence from left to right.

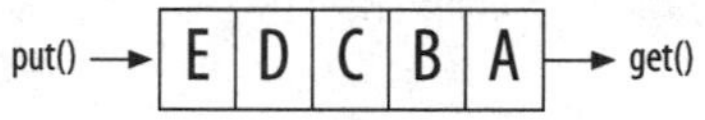

Figure 5-1. A FIFO buffer

In addition to UnboundedFifoBuffer, there is a bounded counterpart—BoundedFifoBuffer. BoundedFifoBuffer has a maximum size that cannot be exceeded; adding an object to a BoundedFifoBuffer already at maximum size will cause a BufferOverflowException. Example 5-4 demonstrates the use of a bounded buffer with a maximum size limit of two.

Example 5-4. Using a BoundedFifoBuffer

```
import org.apache.commons.collections.Buffer;
import org.apache.commons.collections.BufferOverflowException;
import org.apache.commons.collections.buffer.BoundedFifoBuffer;
...

// Create a Bounded FIFO with a max size of two
Buffer buffer = new BoundedFifoBuffer(2);

buffer.add( "One" );
buffer.add( "Two" );

// Adding a third element to this buffer will cause an exception
try {
    buffer.add( "Three" );
} catch( BufferOverflowException bue ) {
    System.out.println( "Buffer is Full!" );
}

// Remove an object... Buffer now contains one element.
Object removed = buffer.remove();

// Add another object
buffer.add( "Three" );

Object remove1 = buffer.remove();
Object remove2 = buffer.remove();

// This next remove() should cause a BufferUnderflowException
try {
    Object remove3 = buffer.remove();
```

Example 5-4. Using a BoundedFifoBuffer (continued)

```
} catch( BufferUnderflowException bue ) {
    System.out.println( "Buffer is Empty!" );
}
```

 Later recipes will demonstrate the use of Buffer objects in processing pipelines where it is important to provide a limit on how much memory a Buffer is able to consume.

See Also

A Buffer in Jakarta Commons Collections is analogous to a Queue in Java 5.0. The Queue interface is accompanied by a number of interfaces that provide almost identical behavior to the Buffer interface as defined in Jakarta Commons Collections 3.0. Queue contains some new methods, offer( ) and peek( ), which perform the same functions as add( ) and remove( ), with one difference: these new methods return false if there is any problem adding an object to a Queue. More information about queues and other changes to the Collections framework in Java 5.0 are available at: *http://java.sun.com/j2se/1.5.0/docs/guide/collections/changes5.html.*

5.8   Creating a Priority Queue

Problem

You need to prioritize objects: removing higher priority objects from a Collection before lower priority objects.

Solution

Use a PriorityBuffer to hold objects to be prioritized. Objects will be removed from this Buffer according to a priority generated with a Comparator. Whenever the remove( ) method is called on this Buffer implementation, a PriorityBuffer uses the Comparator to sort its contents, returning the element of greatest priority. Using a PriorityBuffer without a Comparator causes the buffer to prioritize objects by natural order, casting each object to Comparable and comparing objects with the compareTo( ) method; all objects must implement the Comparable interface if no Comparator is supplied. The following example demonstrates the use of a PriorityBuffer without supplying a Comparator:

```
import java.util.*;
import org.apache.commons.collections.Buffer;
import org.apache.commons.collections.buffers.PriorityBuffer;

// Create a PriorityBuffer with no Comparator
Buffer priority = new PriortyBuffer( );
priority.add( new Long( 2 ) );
```

```
    priority.add( new Long( 1 ) );
    priority.add( new Long( 20 ) );
    priority.add( new Long( 7 ) );
    priority.add( new Long( 18 ) );
    priority.add( new Long( 1 ) );

    // Print the results in priority order
    Iterator priorityIterator = priority.iterator();
    while( priorityIterator.hasNext() ) {
        Long value = (Long) priority.next();
        System.out.prinltn( "Value: " + value );
    }
```

The previous example removes values from the buffer based on a natural order, and the following output is produced:

```
Value: 20
Value: 18
Value: 7
Value: 2
Value: 1
Value: 1
```

Discussion

A `PriorityBuffer`, like all `Buffer` implementations, is defined by the logic to select which object to remove. If you've ever visited an emergency room, you are already familiar with the inner workings of the `PriorityBuffer`. When a patient enters the emergency room, his or her condition is evaluated by a nurse who then assigns a severity. When a doctor moves to the next patient, she chooses the next patient based on severity and how long each patient has been waiting. A patient with a critical, life-threatening condition will be treated before an individual with a headache—the critical patient has a higher priority in the `Buffer`.

The following example models an emergency waiting room with a `PriorityBuffer`. Assume that you have a `Patient` bean with `name`, `severity`, and `checkIn` properties, which is defined in Example 5-5. A patient's severity is a number from 0 to 10, 0 being the lowest severity and 10 being the highest. A critical patient would be assigned a priority of 10, and a patient with a bad cold would be assigned a severity of 0. A patient also has a `checkIn` time: this is the time he is admitted to the waiting room, and it is used as a tie-breaker to determine priority when two patients have the same severity.

Example 5-5. A Patient object

```
package com.discursive.jccook.collections.buffers;

public class Patient {
    private String name;
    private Integer severity;
    private Date checkIn;
```

Example 5-5. A Patient object (continued)

```
    public class Patient() {}

    public String getName() { return name; }
    public void setName(String name) { this.name = name; }

    public Integer getSeverity() { return severity; }
    public void setSeverity(Integer severity) { this.severity = severity; }

    public Date getCheckIn() { return checkIn; }
    public void setCheckIn(Date checkIn) { this.checkIn = checkIn; }
}
```

The `PatientPriorityComparator` in Example 5-6 prioritizes patients by severity of condition and time since check-in. A patient with a more severe condition takes priority over a patient with a less severe condition who has been waiting longer, and, if two patients have the same severity, the one who has been waiting longer gets a higher priority. If this `Comparator` is used to sort an array of `Patient` objects, the most critical patient would be at the last index, and the least critical would be at the first index.

Example 5-6. A Comparator to sort Patient objects by priority

```
package com.discursive.jccook.collections.buffers;

import java.util.Comparator;

public PatientPriorityComparator implements Comparator {

    public int compare(Object o1, Object o2) {
        int comparison = -1;

        if( o1 instanceof Patient &&
            o2 instanceof Patient ) {

            Patient p1 = (Patient) o1;
            Patient p2 = (Patient) o2;

            comparison = p1.getSeverity().compareTo( p2.getSeverity() );

            if( comparison == 0 ) {
                comparison =
                    p1.getCheckIn().compareTo( p2.getCheckIn() );
            }
        }
        return comparison;
    }
}
```

When using the `PriorityBuffer` with a `PatientPriorityComparator`, `Patient` objects are added to the `Buffer` and `remove( )` returns the `Patient` with the highest priority.

Using a PriorityBuffer means that you do not need to worry about constantly resorting a Collection by priority; this logic is completed automatically every time an object is removed from the Buffer. In other words, you are delegating responsibility to a Buffer; it takes care of the sorting and selecting on an as-needed basis.

Example 5-7 adds three Patient objects to a PriorityBuffer: John Doe 1 has an ear ache, John Doe 2 has a broken back, and Jane Doe 3 has a concussion. Both John 2 and Jane 3 have serious conditions, and, since John 2 checked in before Jane 3, John 2 has a higher priority than Jane 3. John 1's condition is not nearly as critical; therefore, his priority is much lower, and he is treated last.

Example 5-7. Using a prioritizing buffer

```
package com.discursive.jccook.collections.buffers;

public class WaitingRoomApp {

    public static void main(String[] args) {
        WaitingRoomApp example = new WaitingRoomApp( );
        example.start( );
    }

    public void start( ) {
        Buffer patients =
            new PriorityBuffer( new PatientPriorityComparator( ) );

        Patient johnDoe1 = new Patient( );
        johnDoe1.setName( "John Doe 1" );
        johnDoe1.setSeverity( new Integer( 7 ) );
        johnDoe1.setCheckIn( new Date( ) );
        patients.add( johnDoe1 );

        Patient johnDoe2 = new Patient( );
        johnDoe2.setName( "John Doe 2" );
        johnDoe2.setSeverity( new Integer( 9 ) );
        johnDoe2.setCheckIn( new Date( ) );
        patients.add( johnDoe2 );

        Patient janeDoe3 = new Patient( );
        janeDoe3.setName( "Jane Doe 3" );
        janeDoe3.setSeverity( new Integer( 9 ) );
        janeDoe3.setCheckIn( new Date( ) );
        patients.add( janeDoe3 );

        while( patients.size( ) > 0 ) {
            Patient patient = (Patient) patients.remove( );
            System.out.println( "Patient: " + patient.getName( ) );
        }
    }
}
```

As each Patient is treated, the patient's name is printed to the console:

```
Patient: John Doe 2
Patient: Jane Doe 3
Patient: John Doe 1
```

See Also

A PriorityBuffer in Jakarta Commons Collections is analogous to a PriorityQueue in Java 5.0. For information about PriorityQueue and other important changes to the Collections framework in Java 5.0, see *http://java.sun.com/j2se/1.5.0/docs/api/index.html*.

5.9   Using a Blocking Buffer

Problem

Your system needs to wait for input and act on an object the moment it is added to a Buffer. To achieve this, you need your application to block until input is received.

Solution

Use BlockingBuffer to decorate an instance of Buffer. When a process calls get( ) or remove( ) on a buffer decorated with BlockingBuffer, the decorated buffer does not return a value until it has an object to return. The following example creates a BlockingBuffer and a listener that calls remove( ). A BlockingBuffer can only be demonstrated by an example that deals with multiple threads, and the following code uses a Runnable implementation, BufferListener, which is defined in Example 5-8:

```
import java.util.*;
import org.apache.commons.collections.Buffer;
import org.apache.commons.collections.buffers.BlockingBuffer;
import org.apache.commons.collections.buffers.BoundedFifoBuffer;

// Create a Blocking Buffer
Buffer buffer = BlockingBuffer.decorate( new BoundedFifoBuffer() );

// Create Thread to continously remove() from the previous Buffer
BufferListener listener = new BufferListener(buffer);
Thread listenerThread = new Thread( listener );
listenerThread.start( );

buffer.add( "Hello World!" );
buffer.add( "Goodbye, Y'all." );
```

The previous example creates an instance of BufferListener—a Runnable object that calls remove( ) on a BoundedFifoBuffer decorated with BlockingBuffer. The listenerThread will block on a call to buffer.remove( ) within the run( ) method of BufferListener, an object that runs in a separate thread and waits for objects to be added to a BlockingBuffer.

Example 5-8. A BufferListener constantly calling remove()

```java
public class BufferListener implements Runnable {
    private Buffer buffer;

    public BufferListener(Buffer buffer) {
        this.buffer = buffer;
    }

    public void run() {
        while(true) {
            String message = (String) buffer.remove();
            System.out.println( message );
        }
    }
}
```

The two calls to buffer.add( ) causes BufferListener to print the strings added:

```
Hello World!
Goodbye, Y'all.
```

Discussion

A BlockingBuffer is used in a system that needs to act on a piece a data as soon as it is available, and this data structure comes in handy when there are a series of worker threads listening to buffers between components in a pipeline. BlockingBuffer allows you to build cascading pipelines, which automatically notify the next stage of available data. Think of this pattern as a stepped waterfall; water automatically flows down the steps, and each step is a Buffer. (See Figure 5-2.)

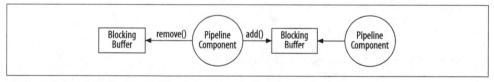

Figure 5-2. Using a BlockingBuffer to create a pipeline

Assume that you need to write a workflow application for a news publisher; the workflow consists of a pipeline: news stories are published as XML files, which are passed to a search indexer and then processed with an XSLT stylesheet. A news story is simply passed as a String containing an XML document. The following example creates a pipeline consisting of two BlockingBuffer instances terminated by an UnboundedFifoBuffer:

```java
import java.util.*;
import org.apache.commons.collections.Buffer;
import org.apache.commons.collections.buffers.BlockingBuffer;
import org.apache.commons.collections.buffers.UnboundedFifoBuffer;
```

```
// Create a Blocking Buffer for each stage, last stage not a blocking buffer
Buffer published = BlockingBuffer.decorate( new UnboundedFifoBuffer() );
Buffer indexed = BlockingBuffer.decorate( new UnboundedFifoBuffer() );
Buffer transformed = new UnboundedFifoBuffer();

// Create a Thread that will watch the published Buffer and index a news story
Indexer indexer = new Indexer(published, indexed);
Thread indexerThread = new Thread( indexer );
indexerThread.start( );

// Create a Thread that will watch the indexed Buffer and style a news story
Styler styler = new Styler(index, transformed);
Thread stylerThread = new Thread( styler );
stylerThread.start( );

String newsStory = getNewsStory( );

published.add( newsStory );
```

The previous example creates three buffers to hold the results of the stages of a pipeline—published, indexed, and transformed. Three Runnable objects are created to perform the task of processing each news story; the Indexer object listens to the published buffer and places its results in the indexed buffer, and the Styler object listens to the indexed buffer and places its results in the transformed buffer. The Indexer object implements Runnable and is constructed with two Buffer objects, inbound and outbound. The Indexer, as shown in Example 5-9, continuously calls remove( ) on a BlockingBuffer and waits until a story is available to process.

Example 5-9. An Indexer stage in a pipeline

```
public class Indexer implements Runnnable {
    private Buffer inbound;
    private Buffer outbound;

    public Indexer(Buffer inbound, Buffer outbound) {
        this.inbound = inbound;
        this.outbound = outbound;
    }

    public void run( ) {
        while(true) {
            String story = (String) inbound.remove( );
            String processedStory = processStory( story );
            outbound.add( processedStory );
        }
    }

    public String processedStory(String story) {
        // Run story through a search indexer
        return story;
    }
}
```

The Styler is omitted because it follows the exact same pattern. Every stage in this pipeline is a Runnable implementation running in a thread and listening to an inbound buffer by calling (and blocking) on inbound.remove( ). Using this mechanism allows your system to process information in parallel by running separate stages in separate threads, and there is no need for a controller to coordinate the actions of a complex system. A pipeline can be extended by simply adding another stage with an additional BlockingBuffer. This pattern is useful in a system that models a very complex workflow; instead of attempting to capture a complex symphony of coordination, break the system into autonomous stages that only know about inputs and outputs.

See Also

A BlockingBuffer in Jakarta Commons Collections is analogous to a BlockingQueue in Java 5.0. A BlockingQueue in Java 5.0 has an important feature that is missing in Commons Collections 3.0 implementation of BlockingBuffer: in Java 5.0's BlockingQueue, you can specify a timeout when adding and removing values from a queue.

5.10   Storing Multiple Values in a Map

Problem

You need to store multiple values for a single key in a Map. Instead of a one-to-one relationship between keys and values, you need a Map that provides one-to-many relationships between keys and values.

Solution

Use a MultiMap. A MultiMap maintains a collection of values for a given key. When a new key/value pair is added to a MultiMap, the value is added to the collection of values for that key. The MultiMap also provides a way to remove a specific key/value pair. The following example demonstrates the use of MultiMap:

```
import org.apache.commons.collections.MultiMap;
import org.apache.commons.collections.MultiHashMap;

MultiMap map = new MultiHashMap( );

map.put( "ONE", "TEST" );
map.put( "TWO", "PICNIC" );

map.put( "ONE", "HELLO" );
map.put( "TWO", "TESTIMONY" );

Set keySet = map.keySet( );
Iterator keyIterator = keySet.iterator( );
```

```
            while( keyIterator.hasNext() ) {
                Object key = keyIterator.next();

                System.out.print( "Key: " + key + ", " );

                Collection values = (Collection) map.get( key );
                Iterator valuesIterator = values.iterator();
                while( valuesIterator.hasNext() ) {
                    System.out.print( "Value: " + valuesIterator.next() + ". " );
                }

                System.out.print( "\n" );
            }
```

Each key in a `MultiMap` corresponds to a collection of values. This example produces
the following output while iterating through all values for each key:

```
Key: ONE, Value: TEST. Value: HELLO
Key: TWO, Value: PICNIC. Value: Testimony
```

Discussion

In a traditional `Map`, a key is removed with `map.remove()`; this method removes the
specified key from the map. In a `MultiMap`, a specific key/value pair can be removed
from a key's value collection. When removing a specific pair, the value is extracted
from a key's value collection. Example 5-10 demonstrates the use of a `MultiMap.`
`remove()` method.

Example 5-10. Using MultiMap.remove()

```
package com.discursive.jccook.collections.map;

import org.apache.commons.collections.*;
import java.util.*;

public class MultiMapExample {
    public static void main(String[] args) {
        MultiMapExample example = new MultiMapExample();
        example.start();
    }

    public void start() {
        MultiMap map = new MultiHashMap();

        map.put( "ONE", "TEST" );
        map.put( "ONE", "WAR" );
        map.put( "ONE", "CAR" );
        map.put( "ONE", "WEST" );

        map.put( "TWO", "SKY" );
        map.put( "TWO", "WEST" );
        map.put( "TWO", "SCHOOL" );
```

Example 5-10. Using MultiMap.remove() (continued)

```
            // At this point "ONE" should correspond to "TEST", "WAR", "CAR", "WEST"
            map.remove( "ONE", "WAR" );
            map.remove( "ONE", "CAR" );

            // The size of this collection should be two "TEST", "WEST"
            Collection oneCollection = (Collection) map.get("ONE");

            // This collection should be "TEST", "WEST", "SKY", "WEST", "SCHOOL"
            Collection values = map.values();
    }
}
```

The MultiMap is relevant when one object is associated with many different objects. A sensible example would be a MultiMap of people to the languages they speak fluently, and the following example demonstrates such a Map:

```
MultiMap languageAbility = new MultiHashMap();

languageAbility.put( "Tom", "French" );
languageAbility.put( "Chris", "Spanish" );
languageAbility.put( "Chris", "German" );
languageAbility.put( "John", "Arabic" );
languageAbility.put( "Tom", "Pashto" );

// What languages does Tom speak?
Collection languages = (Collection) languageAbility.get("Tom");
Iterator languageIterator = languages.iterator();
while( languageIterator.hasNext() ) {
    System.out.println( "Tom speaks " + languageIterator.next() );
}
```

If you had to locate people who were fluent in a given language, it would be equally as valid to use languages as keys and names as values. One could then query the MultiMap for a list of people who speak a certain language. If your system contains two collections of objects that have a many-to-many relationship, these relationships can be managed with two instances of MultiMap.

5.11   Retrieving a Key by a Value

Problem

You need a Map that allows you to access a value by a key and a key by a value.

Solution

BidiMap in Commons Collections provides an implementation of Map, which can be reversed if both the keys and values are unique; you can use a BidiMap to retrieve a value for a key or a key for a value. The following example demonstrates the use of a

BidiMap to access state names by state abbreviation and state abbreviations by state names:

```
BidiMap bidiMap = new DualHashBidiMap( );

bidiMap.put( "il", "Illinois" );
bidiMap.put( "az", "Arizona" );
bidiMap.put( "va", "Virginia" );

// Retrieve the key with a value via the inverse map
String vaAbbreviation = bidiMap.inverseBidiMap( ).get( "Virginia" );

// Retrieve the value from the key
String illinoisName = bidiMap.get( "il" );
```

DualHashBidiMap stores keys and values in two HashMap instances. One HashMap stores keys as keys and values as values, and the other HashMap stores the inverse—values as keys and keys as values.

Discussion

In Example 5-11, a BidiMap is used to store country names and country codes; an application stores ISO country codes and translates between ISO country codes and country names to present intelligible output—"us" is translated to "United States." Alternatively, when a user types in a name of a country, the application needs to be able to produce the country code for that country name—"United States" must be translated back to "us."

Example 5-11. Storing ISO country codes in a BidiMap

```
package com.discursive.jccook.collections.bidi;

import org.apache.commons.collections.BidiMap;
import org.apache.commons.collections.bidimap.DualHashBidiMap;

public class BidiMapExample {

    private BidiMap countryCodes = new DualHashBidiMap( );

    public static void main(String[] args) {
        BidiMapExample example = new BidiMapExample( );
        example.start( );
    }

    private void start( ) {
        populateCountryCodes( );

        String countryName = (String) countryCodes.get( "tr" );
        System.out.println( "Country Name for code 'tr': " + countryName );

        String countryCode =
            (String) countryCodes.inverseBidiMap( ).get("Uruguay");
        System.out.println( "Country Code for name 'Uruguay': " + countryCode );
```

Example 5-11. Storing ISO country codes in a BidiMap (continued)

```
        countryCode = (String) countryCodes.getKey("Ukraine");
        System.out.println( "Country Code for name 'Ukraine': " + countryCode );
    }

    private void populateCountryCodes() {
        countryCodes.put("to","Tonga");
        countryCodes.put("tr","Turkey");
        countryCodes.put("tv","Tuvalu");
        countryCodes.put("tz","Tanzania");
        countryCodes.put("ua","Ukraine");
        countryCodes.put("ug","Uganda");
        countryCodes.put("uk","United Kingdom");
        countryCodes.put("um","USA Minor Outlying Islands");
        countryCodes.put("us","United States");
        countryCodes.put("uy","Uruguay");
    }
}
```

The previous example makes sense because country codes and country names are both unique; there is only one entry for "Djibouti," "dj,"and no other country has an overlapping code because country codes are defined by an International Organization for Standardization (ISO) standard, ISO 3166. If you attempt to insert a duplicate key in a regular map, the existing entry with the same key would be replaced by the new value. In a BidiMap, if you insert a duplicate value, or a *duplicate key*, the entry holding this value is replaced by a new entry. The following example illustrates this concept:

```
private BidiMap bidiMap = new DualHashBidiMap();

// Insert initial content { "one:"red", "two":"green", "three":"blue" }
bidiMap.put("one","red");
bidiMap.put("two","green");
bidiMap.put("three","blue");

// replace "one" key entry
bidiMap.put("one","black");

// replace "green" value entry
bidiMap.put("five","green");

// Contents are now { "one":"black", "three":"blue", "five":"green" }
```

Changing key "one," value "black" replaces the original key "one," value "red" because the key is duplicated; this behavior is consistent with a normal implementation of Map. The difference in a BidiMap is that when adding key "five," value "green" to a BidiMap, the previous key "two," value "green" is replaced with a new entry because "green" is a duplicate value. A regular Map simply adds another entry, and getting the value of either the "five," or "two," key would return the value "green." Because "green" already occurs as a key in the inverse map, the entry corresponding to the "two," key is removed and replaced by a new entry. Bidirectional access to keys by value is only possible if keys and values form two unique sets.

There are three implementations of the BidiMap interface: DualHashBidiMap, DialTreeBidiMap, and TreeBidiMap. A DualHashBidiMap is the simplest option, storing keys and values in two separate instances of HashMap. When a value is requested by key, one HashMap is consulted, and when a key is requested by value, the inverse HashMap is consulted. The DualHashMap is likely to be your implementation of choice if it is not important to keep track of the insertion order; it has a straightforward implementation using the familiar HashMap.

If you need to preserve the order of insertion, a DualTreeBidiMap uses two separate TreeMap instances to hold the regular and inverse mappings. This implementation implements the SortedMap interface that keeps track of the order of insertion and provides subMap(), headMap(), and tailMap() methods. A third implementation, TreeBidiMap, implements BidiMap without maintaining two internal storage maps. Instead, TreeBidiMap stores nodes in a red-black tree, identifying each node as both a key and a value; it costs twice as much to put() into a TreeBidiMap, but this implementation comes in handy if you are worried about memory consumption—it does not need to store each key and value twice in two maps.

See Also

This example used ISO 3166 country codes, a list of every country and corresponding two letter country code. If you are writing an application for a worldwide audience, you may find the following list helpful: *http://www.iso.ch/iso/en/prods-services/iso3166ma/02iso-3166-code-lists/list-en1.html*.

5.12   Using a Case-Insensitive Map

Problem

You need to use a Map with String keys that will ignore the capitalization of a key when retrieving a value.

Solution

Use a CaseInsensitiveMap from the Commons Collections. This implementation of Map takes String keys and provides case-insensitive access. An entry with a key "Test" can be retrieved with the strings "TEST," "test," and "tEST." Here is a small example demonstrating the case insensitivity:

```
import java.util.*;
import org.apache.commons.collection.map.CaseInsensitiveMap;

Map grades = new CaseInsensitiveMap();
grades.put( "Fortney", "B-" );
```

```
grades.put( "Puckett", "D+" );
grades.put( "Flatt", "A-" );

String grade1 = (String) grades.get( "puckett" );
String grade2 = (String) grades.get( "FLATT" );
```

In this example, the grades are stored with a capitalized last name, and the results are retrieved with irregularly capitalized last names. This example returns the grades for "Puckett" and "Flatt" even though they were retrieved with "puckett" and "FLATT."

Discussion

Example 5-12 demonstrates the use of CaseInsensitiveMap to access state names by state abbreviations regardless of capitalization. This is useful when an application is requesting a state from a user in a form to capture an address. If a user enters "il," "IL," or "Il," you need to be able to return "Illinois."

Example 5-12. Using a CaseInsensitiveMap for U.S. states

```
package com.discursive.jccook.collections.insensitive;

import java.util.Map;
import org.apache.commons.collections.map.CaseInsensitiveMap;

public class CaseInsensitiveExample {

    Map states = new CaseInsensitiveMap();

    public static void main(String[] args) {
        CaseInsensitiveExample example = new CaseInsensitiveExample();
        example.start();
    }

    private void start() {
        states.put("IL", "Illinois");
        states.put("PA", "Pennsylvania");
        states.put("GA", "Georgia");
        states.put("AZ", "Arizona");

        String stateName = (String) states.get( "il" );
        System.out.println( "Value retrieved for 'il': " + stateName );

        stateName = (String) states.get( "IL" );
        System.out.println( "Value retrieved for 'IL': " + stateName );

        stateName = (String) states.get( "iL" );
        System.out.println( "Value retrieved for 'iL': " + stateName );

    }
}
```

Example 5-12 populates a CaseInsensitiveMap with state abbreviations and state names, and it retrieves the state name for three different capitalizations of "IL": "iL," "IL," and "il." For all three keys, the CaseInsensitiveMap returns the proper state name—"Illinois"—as illustrated by the output from the previous example:

```
Value retrieved for 'il': Illinois
Value retrieved for 'IL': Illinois
Value retrieved for 'iL': Illinois
```

See Also

If you are interested in how this class works, take a look at the source for CaseInsensitiveMap, and you will see that this implementation of Map extends the AbstractHashedMap class in the org.apache.commons.collections.map package. It would be just as easy to decorate a Map with a Transformer object to provide case insensitivity. Recipe 5.16 discusses the use of a Transformer to alter objects as they are stored in a Collection.

5.13   Creating Typed Collections and Maps

Problem

You need to guarantee that a Collection or a Map only contains objects of a certain type.

Solution

Use TypedCollection.decorate( ) to create a Collection that only accepts objects of a specified type. Supply an existing Collection along with the Class that all elements should be constrained to. TypedCollection will decorate this existing Collection, validating elements as they are added to a Collection. The following example creates a Collection that will only accept strings:

```
List existingList = new ArrayList( );
Collection typedCollection = TypedCollection.decorate( existingList, String.class );

// This will add a String
typedCollection.add( "STRING" );

// And, This will throw an IllegalArgumentException
typedCollection.add( new Long(28) );
```

Similarly, if you want to constrain keys and values to specified types, pass a Map to TypedMap.decorate( ) method, specifying a Class for both the key and the value. In the following example, typedMap only accepts String keys and Number values:

```
Map existingMap = new HashMap( );
Map typedMap = TypedMap.decorate( existingMap, String.class, Number.class );
```

```
// This will add a String key and a Double value
typedMap.put( "TEST", new Double( 3.40 ) );

// Both of these throw an IllegalArgumentException
typedMap.put( new Long(202), new Double( 3.40 ) );
typedMap.put( "BLAH", "BLAH" );
```

TypedCollection and TypedMap will decorate any existing Collection or Map and will throw an IllegalArgumentException if you try to add an incompatible type.

Discussion

A Map frequently contains keys and values with consistent types; for instance, an application that keeps track of Person objects by name most likely has a personMap with Person values and String keys. Rarely does a Map hold a wide diversity of types. Collections and Maps are not type-safe, and this lack of type safety means that unexpected objects may be cast to incompatible types, causing nasty ClassCastExceptions. It is unlikely that every time you call get( ) and cast the resulting object, you catch ClassCastException; and, in most systems, it is reasonable to assume that no one has put an incompatible type into a Map. But, if a Map plays a central role in a critical application, you may want an extra layer of validation; decorate your maps with TypedMap to ensure that a Map contains consistent types. There is little penalty for decorating a Map as such, and if someone writes code to insert invalid input, your application should fail immediately with an IllegalArgumentException.

If your application uses a TypedMap, it is easier to track down defects. If a ClassCastException is thrown when calling get( ), you then need to work backward to find out where the offending object was put into a Map. An alternative is to validate each object as it is added to a Map. If the put( ) method throws IllegalArgumentException, it will be easier to identify the offending code.

Java 5.0 adds the idea of generics—compile-time type safety for any number of objects including Collections and Maps. But, if you are stuck with an older version of the JDK, you can use Commons Collections to create a Collection that only accepts input of a certain type. TypedSet, TypedBag, TypedList, TypedMap, TypedBuffer, TypedSortedSet, TypedSortedBag, TypedSortedMap all provide the same decoration as TypedCollection, but they return a specific interface; for example, TypedList decorates and returns a List, and TypedSet decorates and returns a Set. Example 5-13 demonstrates the use of the TypedList decorator to return a List instead of a Collection.

Example 5-13. Using TypedList to decorate a list

```
package com.discursive.jccook.collections.typed;

import java.util.ArrayList;
import java.util.List;

import org.apache.commons.collections.list.TypedList;
```

Example 5-13. Using TypedList to decorate a list (continued)

```java
public class TypedListExample {

    private List hostNames;

    public static void main(String[] args) {
        TypedListExample example = new TypedListExample();
        example.start();
    }

    public void start() {
        // Make sure that items added to this
        hostNames = TypedList.decorate( new ArrayList(), String.class );

        // Add two String objects
        hostNames.add( "papp01.thestreet.com" );
        hostNames.add( "test.slashdot.org" );

        // Try to add an Integer
        try {
            hostNames.add( new Integer(43) );
        } catch( IllegalArgumentException iae ) {
            System.out.println( "Adding an Integer Failed as expected" );
        }

        // Now we can safely cast without the possibility of a ClassCastException
        String hostName = (String) hostNames.get(0);

    }
}
```

If a List decorated with TypedList encounters an invalid object, the add() method will throw an IllegalArgumentException.

 A Typed<X> decorated Collection will not be able to provide the compile-time type safety of Java 5.0's generics, but it will enforce a restriction on what it can accept—it is up to you to catch the runtime exception.

TypedMap allows you to constrain both the keys and values of a map. TypedMap.decorate() takes three parameters: the Map to decorate, the key Class, and the value Class. To create a Map that only constrains key types, pass in a null value for the value type. To create a Map that only validates the type of the value, pass in a null for the key type. Example 5-14 uses TypedMap.decorate() to create a Map that only accepts String keys and Number values.

Example 5-14. Decorating a map with TypedMap

```java
package com.discursive.jccook.collections.typed;

import java.util.HashMap;
import java.util.Map;

import org.apache.commons.collections.map.TypedMap;

public class TypedMapExample {

    private Map variables;

    public static void main(String[] args) {
        TypedMapExample example = new TypedMapExample( );
        example.start( );
    }

    public void start( ) {
        // Make sure that items added to this
        variables =
            TypedMap.decorate(  new HashMap( ), String.class, Number.class );

        // Add two String objects
        variables.put( "maxThreads", new Integer(200) );
        variables.put( "minThreads", new Integer(20) );
        variables.put( "lightSpeed", new Double( 2.99792458e8 ) );

        // Try to add a String value
        try {
            variables.put( "server", "test.oreilly.com" );
        } catch( IllegalArgumentException iae ) {
            System.out.println( "Adding an String value Failed as expected" );
        }

        // Try to add an Integer key
        try {
            variables.put( new Integer(30), "test.oreilly.com" );
        } catch( IllegalArgumentException iae ) {
            System.out.println( "Adding an Integer key Failed as expected" );
        }

        // Now we can safely cast without the possibility of a ClassCastException
        Number reading = (Number) variables.get("lightSpeed");

    }
}
```

See Also

Java 5.0 has added generics —a welcome addition. For more information about generics, look at the release notes for Java 5.0 at *http://java.sun.com/j2se/1.5.0/docs/relnotes/features.html#generics*.

For more information about the decorator design pattern, read the classic *Design Patterns: Elements of Reusable Object-Oriented Software*, by Erich Gamma et al., or take a look at this onJava.com article by Budi Kurniawan: *http://www.onjava.com/ pub/a/onjava/2003/02/05/decorator.html*, which deals with the decorator pattern as applied to Java Swing development, but this pattern also has relevance outside of a GUI development context.

This TypedCollection decorator is a specialized version of a PredicatedCollection. Type-safety is implemented through the use of an InstanceofPredicate, and the next recipe discusses the use of a PredicatedMap.

5.14   Constraining Map Values

Problem

You need to ensure that all values added to a Map satisfy a set of arbitrary conditions.

Solution

Decorate an existing Map with PredicatedMap from Commons Collections. Predicates add an inbound validation to a Map, validating keys or values any time an entry is added to a PredicatedMap. If a Predicate assigned to a key or value returns false, put( ) throws an IllegalArgumentException. The following example decorates a HashMap with PredicatedMap—two Predicates are created to validate the keys and the values:

```
import java.util.*;
import org.apache.commons.collections.map.PredicatedMap;
import org.apache.commons.collections.Predicate;
import org.apache.commons.collections.functors.EqualPredicate;
import org.apache.commons.collections.functors.InstanceofPredicate;
import org.apache.commons.collections.functors.OrPredicate;

// Create a Predicate that only accepts Strings
Predicate onlyStrings = new InstanceofPredicate( String.class );

// Create a Predicate that only allows "green" or "red"
Predicate onlyGreen = new EqualPredicate( "green" );
Predicate onlyRed = new EqualPredicate( "red" );
Predicate greenOrRed = new OrPredicate( onlyGreen, onlyRed );

// Created a Decorated Map - accepting String keys and "green" or "red" values
Map map = PredicatedMap.decorate( new HashMap(), onlyStrings, greenOrRed );

// All of these puts should work
map.put( "tony" , "green" );
map.put( "alice" , "red" );
map.put( "mike" , "red" );
map.put( "bobby" , "green" );
```

```
// All of these puts should throw an IllegalArgumentException
map.put( new Double(4.0) , "green" );
map.put( "alice" , "purple" );
map.put( new Long(32) , new Long(43) );
```

In the previous example, keys are validated by a simple InstanceofPredicate, which ensures that each key is a String. The values are validated with an OrPredicate, which combines two EqualPredicates; values are accepted if they are equal to the strings "green" or "red."

Discussion

A PredicatedMap can work with any Predicate no matter how simple or complex. Passing in a null value for either the key or value Predicate instructs the PredicatedMap not to validate keys or values. In the following example, a PredicatedMap decorates a HashMap to ensure that a Map contains valid Team values:

```
import org.apache.commons.collections.functors.AndPredicate;
import org.apache.commons.collections.map.PredicatedMap;

// Create the Predicates
ValidTeamPredicate validTeam = new ValidTeamPredicate( );
ValidCoachPredicate validCoach = new ValidCoachPredicate( );

// Tie two Predicates together into an AndPredicate
AndPredicate valuePredicate = new AndPredicate( validTeam, validCoach );

// Decorate a HashMap with a predicate on the value
Map teamMap = PredicatedMap.decorate( new HashMap( ), null, valuePredicate);

// Manufacture some teams
Team redSox = new Team( "Red Sox", new Coach( "Patrick", "Moloney") );
Team yankees= new Team( "Yankees", new Coach( "David", "McGarry") );
Team dodgers = new Team( "Dodgers", new Coach( "Nick", "Taylor") );
Team twins = new Team( null, new Coach( "Patrick", "Moloney") );
Team braves = new Team( "Braves", null );

// The following put calls should work fine
teamMap.put( "RedSox", redSox );
teamMap.put( "Yankees", yankees );
teamMap.put( "Dodgers", dodgers );

// This put should fail because the team name is null
try {
    teamMap.put( "Twins", twins);
} catch( IllegalArgumentException iae ) {
    System.out.println( "Twins put failed, as expected" );
}

// This put should fail because the coach is null
try {
    teamMap.put( "Braves", braves);
```

```
        } catch( IllegalArgumentException iae ) {
            System.out.println( "Braves put failed, as expected" );
        }
```

An application can assume that every team in teamMap has met the following requirements:

- Every Team object must have a non-null name property.
- Every Team object must have a non-null coach property, and this Coach object must have a first and last name.

The previous example uses two Predicate objects to validate both the team and the coach. These two custom predicates (ValidTeamPredicate and ValidCoachPredicate) are defined in Examples 5-15 and 5-16. These Predicate objects are passed to the PredicatedMap.decorate( ) method to decorate a Map with these conditions. The first Predicate, ValidTeamPredicate, validates a Team object to see if it has a non-null name property.

Example 5-15. A Predicate to validate a Team's name property

```
import org.apache.commons.collections.Predicate;

public class ValidTeamPredicate implements Predicate {

    public boolean evaluate(Object object) {
        Team team = (Team) object;
        return team.getName( ) != null;
    }

}
```

Example 5-16. Predicate to validate a Team's coach property

```
import org.apache.commons.collections.Predicate;

public class ValidCoachPredicate implements Predicate {

    public boolean evaluate(Object object) {
        boolean validCoach = false;
        Team team = (Team) object;
        if( team.getCoach( ) != null &&
            team.getCoach( ).getFirstName( ) != null &&
            team.getCoach( ).getLastName( ) != null ) {
            validCoach = true;
        }
        return validCoach;
    }

}
```

The second Predicate, ValidCoachPredicate, validates a Team object, checking to see if the coach property is non-null, and that the coach has a first and last name.

In Example 5-16, a Predicate is created by combining the ValidTeamPredicate and ValidCoachPredicate in an AndPredicate. A HashMap is then decorated with PredicatedMap.decorate( ), passing the AndPredicate in as the predicate to validate Map values. A few Team objects are created, all of which are valid with the exception of the Twins and the Braves, and, as expected, the Twins and Braves cause put( ) to throw an IllegalArgumentException.

5.15   Constraining List Contents

Problem

You need to constrain objects that can be added to a List.

Solution

Decorate a List using PredicatedList. The following example demonstrates the use of PredicatedList to create a List that only accepts even Integer objects:

```
import java.util.*;
import org.apache.commons.collections.list.PredicatedList;
import org.apache.commons.collections.Predicate;
import org.apache.commons.lang.ArrayUtils;

// Create a Predicate that only accepts even Integer objects
Predicate onlyEven = new Predicate() {
    public boolean evaluate(Object object) {
        Integer integer = (Integer) object;
        return( integer.intValue() % 2 == 0 );
    }
}

List list = PredicatedList.decorate( new ArrayList(), onlyEven );

list.add( new Integer(1) ); // Will throw IllegalArgumentException
list.add( new Integer(2) );
list.add( new Integer(3) ); // Will throw IllegalArgumentException
list.add( new Integer(4) );
```

In this example, attempting to add an Integer with an odd value causes an IllegalArgumentException, but adding an even number does not cause an exception to be thrown.

Discussion

A PredicatedList is very similar to a PredicatedMap; this decorator works with an existing List and adds inbound validation to a List. There is no limit to the complexity of the Predicate that can be used to provide inbound validation to a List.

See Also

PredicatedList and PredicatedMap are not the only Collection decorators available in the Jakarta Commons Collections. Any Collection interface in the following list can be decorated with a Predicate.

- PredicatedBag decorates a Bag.
- PredicatedBuffer decorates a Buffer.
- PredicatedCollection decorates a Collection.
- PredicatedList decorates a List.
- PredicatedMap decorates a Map.
- PredicatedSet decorates a Set.
- PredicatedSortedBag decorates a SortedBag.
- PredicatedSortedMap decorates a SortedMap.
- PredicatedSortedSet decorates a SortedSet

For more information about these utilities, see the Jakarta Commons Collections project page at *http://jakarta.apache.org/commons/collections*.

5.16   Transforming Collections

Problem

You need to perform a transformation using each element in a Collection.

Solution

Use CollectionUtils.transform(). Supply a Collection and a Transformer to this method, and this utility will pass each element in the Collection to that Transformer, returning a new Collection containing the results of each transformation. The following example demonstrates the use of transform() with a custom Transformer object:

```
import java.util.*;
import org.apache.commons.collections.Transformer;
import org.apache.commons.collections.CollectionUtils;
import org.apache.commons.lang.ArrayUtils;
import org.apache.commons.lang.StringUtils;

// Create a transformer that reverses strings.
Transformer reversingTransformer = new Transformer() {
    public Object transform(Object object) {
        String string = (String) object;
        return StringUtils.reverse( string );
    }
}
```

```
String[] array = new String[] { "Aznar", "Blair", "Chirac", "Putin", "Bush" };
List stringList = Arrays.asList( ArrayUtils.clone( array ) );

// Transform each element with a Transformer
CollectionUtils.transform( stringList, reversingTransformer );

System.out.println( "Original: " + ArrayUtils.toString( array ) );
System.out.println( "Transformed: " +
                    ArrayUtils.toString( stringList.toArray() ) );
```

This example creates a List of strings, transforming each element with a Transformer
that produces reversed strings. The List is transformed in-place, which means that
the contents of the List are replaced with the output from the transform( ) method
of the Transformer. As expected, the transformed List contains reversed strings:

```
Original: Aznar, Blair, Chirac, Putin, Bush
Transformed: ranzA, rialB, carihC, nituP, hsuB
```

CollectionUtils.transform( ) does not only apply to Lists; any object implementing the Collection interface can be used with this utility.

Discussion

Transformers are another form of functor that transforms one object into another,
leaving the original object unchanged. Transformer is a very straightforward interface, simply requiring the presence of a transform( ) method. The Transformer interface, like Predicate, is augmented by a number of useful built-in implementations,
which can combine the effects of multiple transformers. One of these Transformer
implementations is the ChainedTransformer, which allows you to create a linear
pipeline of transformations. The following example demonstrates the use of a
ChainedTransformer to transform the contents of a Collection:

```
import java.util.*;
import org.apache.commons.collections.Transformer;
import org.apache.commons.collections.finctors.ChainedTransformer;
import org.apache.commons.collections.CollectionUtils;
import org.apache.commons.lang.ArrayUtils;
import org.apache.commons.lang.StringUtils;

// Create a transformer that multiplies a number by 10
Transformer multiplyTransform = new Transformer() {
    public Object transform(Object object) {
        Integer integer = (Integer) object;
        return new Integer( integer.intValue() * 10 );
    }
}

// Create a transformer that subtracts 20 from a number
Transformer subtractTransform = new Transformer() {
    public Object transform(Object object) {
        Integer integer = (Integer) object;
        return new Integer( integer.intValue() - 20 );
```

```
        }
    }

    // Chain the transformers together
    Transformer transformChain = new ChainedTransformer(
        new Transformer[] { multiplyTransform, subtractTransform } );

    // Create a List of Integer objects
    int[] array = new int[] { 1, 2, 3, 4, 5, 6, 7, 8 };
    List intList = Arrays.asList( ArrayUtils.toObject( array ) );

    CollectionUtils.transform( intList, transformChain );

    System.out.println( "Original: " + ArrayUtils.toString( array ) );
    System.out.println( "Transformed: " +
                        ArrayUtils.toString( intList.toArray() ) );
```

Two transformers, multiplyTransform and subtractTransform, are defined as anonymous inner classes, which implement the Transformer interface. These two Transformers are combined in a ChainedTransformer. An array of int primitives is converted to an array of Integer objects using ArrayUtils.toObject( ). This object array is then converted to a List, which is transformed using CollectionUtils. transform( ). The transformation multiples each element by 10 and subtracts 20, producing the following output:

```
    Original: 1, 2, 3, 4, 5, 6, 7, 8
    Transformed: -10, 0, 10, 20, 30, 40, 50, 60
```

See Also

In addition to the ChainedTransformer, there are a number of other useful Transformer implementations that ship with Commons Collections. The ChainedTransformer and other Transformer implementations are discussed in depth in Chapter 4. For more information about the various implementations of Transformer, see the Commons Collections project (*http://jakarta.apache.org/commons/collections*).

5.17   Creating a Least Recently Used Cache

Problem

You need to present common data to many clients, and you want to cache this common data in a data structure of limited size, evicting the least recently used entry when the maximum size limit has been reached.

Solution

Use LRUMap—a fixed size map that uses the least recently used algorithm to evict entries once the maximum size has been reached. The least recently used algorithm evicts the element that has not been used for the longest amount of time. The following example demonstrates the use of an LRUMap to store stock quotes:

```
import java.util.Map;
import org.apache.commons.collections.map.LRUMap;

cache = new LRUMap( 5 );

// Populate the cache with 5 stock prices
cache.put( "MSFT", new Float( 0.03 ) );
cache.put( "TSC", new Float( 0.001 ) );
cache.put( "LU", new Float( 23.30 ) );
cache.put( "CSCO", new Float( 242.20 ) );
cache.put( "P", new Float( 10.23 ) );

// Now use some of the entries in the cache
Float cscoPrice  = (Float) cache.get( "CSCO" );
Float msPrice = (Float) cache.get( "MSFT" );
Float tscPrice = (Float) cache.get( "TSC" );
Float luPrice = (Float) cache.get( "LU" );
Float pPrice = (Float) cache.get( "P" );
Float msPrice2 = (Float) cache.get( "MSFT" );

// Add another price to the Map, this should kick out the LRU item.
cache.put( "AA", new Float( 203.20 ) );

// CSCO was the first price requested, it is therefore the
// least recently used.
if( !cache.containsKey("CSCO") ) {
    System.out.println( "As expected CSCO was discarded" );
}
```

Since the LRUMap created in this example can only hold five elements, the "CSCO" quote is evicted when "AA" is added to the map because it is the "least recently used."

Discussion

An LRUMap is appropriate when a system presents common data to a number of clients. For example, if a web site displays breaking news stories, objects representing these stories can be stored in a size-limited cache with an LRU eviction policy, such as LRUMap. Demand for objects that represent breaking news stories can be very time sensitive; many customers read the same story at the same time. Your application server has a size-limited LRUMap that holds 100 news stories, and, when a new story is added, the LRUMap evicts the stalest story in the Map.

See Also

The LRUMap is an ideal solution for a cache, but, if your application needs to make heavy use of caching, take a look at the following open source cache implementations—OSCache or JCS. For more information about OSCache, see the Open-Symphony OSCache project page (*http://www.opensymphony.com/oscache/*). The

Java Caching System (JCS) was an offshoot of the Jakarta Turbine project; for more information about JCS, see the JCS project page (*http://jakarta.apache.org/turbine/jcs/*).

5.18   Using a Lazy Map

Problem

You need a Map that can populate a value when its corresponding key is requested.

Solution

Decorate a Map with LazyMap. Attempting to retrieve a value with a key that is not in a Map decorated with LazyMap will trigger the creation of a value by a Transformer associated with this LazyMap. The following example decorates a HashMap with a Transformer that reverses strings; when a key is requested, a value is created and put into the Map using this Transformer:

```
import java.util.*;
import org.apache.commons.collections.Transformer;
import org.apache.commons.collections.map.LazyMap;
import org.apache.commons.lang.StringUtils;

// Create a Transformer to reverse strings - defined below
Transformer reverseString = new Transformer() {
    public Object transform( Object object ) {
        String name = (String) object;
        String reverse = StringUtils.reverse( name );
        return reverse;
    }
}

// Create a LazyMap called lazyNames, which uses the above Transformer
Map names = new HashMap( );
Map lazyNames = LazyMap.decorate( names, reverseString );

// Get and print two names
String name = (String) lazyNames.get( "Thomas" );
System.out.println( "Key: Thomas, Value: " + name );

name = (String) lazyNames.get( "Susan" );
System.out.println( "Key: Susan, Value: " + name );
```

Whenever get( ) is called, the decorated Map passes the requested key to a Transformer, and, in this case, a reversed string is put into a Map as a value. The previous example requests two strings and prints the following output:

```
Key: Thomas, Value: samohT
Key: Susan, Value: nasuS
```

Discussion

LazyMap works best when a key is a symbol or an abbreviation for a more complex object. If you are working with a database, you could create a LazyMap that retrieves objects by a primary key value; in this case, the Transformer simply retrieves a record from a database table using the supplied key. Another example that springs to mind is a stock quote; in the stock exchange, a company is represented as a series of characters: "YHOO" represents the company Yahoo!, Inc., and "TSC" represents TheStreet.com. If your system deals with a quote feed, use a LazyMap to cache frequently used entries. Example 5-17 uses a LazyMap to create a cache populated on demand, and it also demonstrates the LRUMap—a fixed-size implementation of the Map introduced in Recipe 5.17.

Example 5-17. Example using a LazyMap

```
package com.discursive.jccook.collections.lazy;

import java.net.URL;
import java.util.Map;

import org.apache.commons.collections.map.LRUMap;
import org.apache.commons.collections.map.LazyMap;

public class LazyMapExample {

    Map stockQuotes;

    public static void main(String[] args) throws Exception {
        LazyMapExample example = new LazyMapExample();
        example.start();
    }

    public void start() throws Exception {

        StockQuoteTransformer sqTransformer = new StockQuoteTransformer();
        sqTransformer.setQuoteURL( new URL("http://quotes.company.com") );
        sqTransformer.setTimeout( 500 );

        // Create a Least Recently Used Map with max size = 5
        stockQuotes = new LRUMap( 5 );

        // Decorate the LRUMap with the StockQuoteTransformer
        stockQuotes = LazyMap.decorate( stockQuotes, sqTransformer );

        // Now use some of the entries in the cache
        Float price = (Float) stockQuotes.get( "CSCO" );
        price = (Float) stockQuotes.get( "MSFT" );
        price = (Float) stockQuotes.get( "TSC" );
        price = (Float) stockQuotes.get( "TSC" );
        price = (Float) stockQuotes.get( "LU" );
        price = (Float) stockQuotes.get( "P" );
```

Example 5-17. Example using a LazyMap (continued)

```
        price = (Float) stockQuotes.get( "P" );
        price = (Float) stockQuotes.get( "MSFT" );
        price = (Float) stockQuotes.get( "LU" );

        // Request another price to the Map, this should kick out the LRU item.
        price = (Float) stockQuotes.get( "AA" );

        // CSCO was the first price requested, it is therefore the
        // least recently used.
        if( !stockQuotes.containsKey("CSCO") ) {
            System.out.println( "As expected CSCO was discarded" );
        }
    }
}
```

The Transformer in Example 5-17 is an object that takes a string and hits a URL using Jakarta HttpClient—a utility introduced in Chapter 11. Every time a new symbol is encountered, this Transformer creates another thread with a timeout and hits a "quote server" that is configured to return the latest price for that company's symbol. Example 5-18 defines a StockQuoteTransformer that retrieves a quote by passing a stock symbol as a URL parameter.

Example 5-18. A StockQuoteTransformer

```
package com.discursive.jccook.collections.lazy;

import java.net.URL;

import org.apache.commons.collections.Transformer;
import org.apache.commons.httpclient.HttpClient;
import org.apache.commons.httpclient.HttpURL;
import org.apache.commons.httpclient.methods.GetMethod;

public class StockQuoteTransformer implements Transformer {

    protected URL quoteURL;
    protected long timeout;

    public Object transform(Object symbol) {
        QuoteRetriever retriever = new QuoteRetriever( (String) symbol );

        try {
            Thread retrieveThread = new Thread( retriever );
            retrieveThread.start();
            retrieveThread.join( timeout );
        } catch( InterruptedException ie ) {
            System.out.println( "Quote request timed out.");
        }

        return retriever.getResult();
    }
```

Example 5-18. A StockQuoteTransformer (continued)

```
    public URL getQuoteURL( ) { return quoteURL; }
    public void setQuoteURL(URL url) { quoteURL = url; }

    public long getTimeout( ) { return timeout; }
    public void setTimeout(long l) { timeout = l; }

    public class QuoteRetriever implements Runnable {
        private String symbol;
        private Float result = new Float( Float.NaN );

        public QuoteRetriever(String symbol) {
            this.symbol = symbol;
        }

        public Float getResult( ) {
            return result;
        }

        public void run( ) {
            HttpClient client = new HttpClient( );
            try {
                HttpURL url = new HttpURL( quoteURL.toString( ) );
                url.setQuery( "symbol", symbol );

                GetMethod getMethod = new GetMethod( url.toString( ) );
                client.executeMethod( getMethod );
                String response = getMethod.getResponseBodyAsString( );

                result = new Float( response );
            } catch( Exception e ) {
                System.out.println( "Error retrieving quote" );
            }
        }
    }

    }
}
```

The point of this example is to demonstrate the power of decorating an LRUMap with LazyMap and to write a Transformer that can fetch a piece of data from another server, not that the StockQuoteTransformer uses Jakarta HttpClient.

See Also

For more information about Jakarta HttpClient, see Chapter 11. For more information about the LRUMap, see Recipe 5.17.

5.19   Counting Objects in a Collection

Problem

You need to count the number of times an object occurs in a `Collection`.

Solution

Use `CollectionUtils` methods `countMatches()` or `cardinality()`. `countMatches()` takes a `Collection` and a `Predicate`, returning the number of elements that satisfy that `Predicate`. `cardinality()` takes an `Object` and a `Collection`, returning the number of items equal to the supplied `Object`. The following example demonstrates the use of both methods to count the number of times an `Object` occurs in a `Collection`:

```
import java.util.*;
import org.apache.commons.collections.Predicate;
import org.apache.commons.collections.functors.EqualPredicate;
import org.apache.commons.collections.CollectionUtils;
import org.apache.commons.lang.ArrayUtils;

String[] array = new String[] { "A", "B", "C", "C", "B", "B" };
List stringList = Arrays.asList( array );

Predicate equalPredicate = new EqualPredicate("C");

int numberCs = CollectionUtils.countMatches( stringList, equalsPredicate );
int numberBs = CollectionUtils.cardinality( "B", stringList );

System.out.println( "List: " + ArraUtils.toString( array ) );
System.out.println( "Number of Cs: " + numberCs );
System.out.println( "Number of Bs: " + numberBs );
```

When used with the `EqualPredicate`, `countMatches()` performs the same function as `cardinality()`. This example produces the following output.

```
List: A, B, C, C, B, B
Number of Cs: 2
Number of Bs: 3
```

Discussion

`countMatches()` is not limited to counting the number of elements in a `Collection` equal to an object; this method can also be used to count objects that meet any arbitrary `Predicate`. For example, you could count the number of elements in a list that match a composite predicate or a custom predicate. The following example demonstrates the use of `countMatches()` to count the number of objects that match a custom predicate:

```
import java.util.*;
import org.apache.commons.collections.Predicate;
import org.apache.commons.collections.functors.EqualPredicate;
import org.apache.commons.collections.CollectionUtils;
import org.apache.commons.lang.ArrayUtils;
```

```
int[] array = new int[] { 1, 2, 3, 4, 5, 6, 7, 8, 9, 10 };
List intList = Arrays.asList( ArrayUtils.toObject( array ) );

Predicate isEvenPredicate = new Predicate() {
    public boolean evaluate(Object object) {
        Integer value = (Integer) object;
        return ( (value.intValue() % 2) == 0 );
    }
}

int numberEven = CollectionUtils.countMatches( intList, isEvenPredicate );

System.out.println( "List: " + ArrayUtils.toString( array ) );
System.out.println( "Number of Even Numbers: " + numberEven );
```

This example counts the number of even numbers in a Collection; the isEvenPredicate is an anonymous inner class that implements the Predicate interface. This Predicate is passed to CollectionUtils.countMatches( ), producing the following output:

```
List: 1, 2, 3, 4, 5, 6, 7, 8, 9, 10
Number of Even Numbers: 5
```

CollectionUtils can also return a frequency Map for every object in a Collection; calling CollectionUtils.getCardinalityMap( ) returns such a Map. The keys of this Map are the distinct objects in the Collection, and the values are Integer objects representing the number of times each object appears in the Collection. The following example demonstrates the creation of a frequency Map from a list of strings:

```
import java.util.*;
import org.apache.commons.collections.Predicate;
import org.apache.commons.collections.functors.EqualPredicate;
import org.apache.commons.collections.CollectionUtils;
import org.apache.commons.lang.ArrayUtils;

String[] array = new String[] { "Red", "Blue", "Blue", "Yellow", "Red", "Black" };
List stringList = Arrays.asList( arrays );

Map cardinalityMap = CollectionUtils.getCardinalityMap( stringList );

System.out.println( "List: " + ArrayUtils.toString( array ) );
System.out.println( "Cardinality Map:\n" + MapUtils.debugPrint( cardinalityMap ) );
```

A String array is converted to a List of strings, and a frequency Map is created. This Map is printed using MapUtils.debugPrint( ):

```
List: Red, Blue, Blue, Yellow, Red, Black
Cardinality Map:
{
    Red = 3
    Blue = 2
    Yellow = 1
    Black = 1
}
```

See Also

If you are interested in the cardinality of objects in a `Collection`, consider using a Bag. A Bag is a `Collection` that revolves around the cardinality of objects it contains. Bag objects are described in Recipe 5.6.

5.20   Performing Set Operations

Problem

You need to perform set operations to find the union, intersection, disjunction, and difference of two collections.

Solution

Use one of four `CollectionUtils` methods to perform set operations—union( ), intersection( ), disjunction( ), and subtract( ). Example 5-19 demonstrates the use of these four methods with two `Collections`.

Example 5-19. Using CollectionUtils union(), intersection(), disjunction(), and subtract()

```
import java.util.*;

String[] arrayA = new String[] { "1", "2", "3", "3", "4", "5" };
String[] arrayB = new String[] { "3", "4", "4", "5", "6", "7" };

List a = Arrays.asList( arrayA );
List b = Arrays.asList( arrayB );

Collection union = CollectionUtils.union( a, b );
Collection intersection = CollectionUtils.intersection( a, b );
Collection disjunction = CollectionUtils.disjunction( a, b );
Collection subtract = CollectionUtils.subtract( a, b );

Collections.sort( union );
Collections.sort( intersection );
Collections.sort( disjunction );
Collections.sort( subtract );

System.out.println( "A: " + ArrayUtils.toString( a.toArray() ) );
System.out.println( "B: " + ArrayUtils.toString( b.toArray() ) );
System.out.println( "Union: " + ArrayUtils.toString( union.toArray() ) );
System.out.println( "Intersection: " +
                    ArrayUtils.toString( intersection.toArray() ) );
System.out.println( "Disjunction: " +
                    ArrayUtils.toString( disjunction.toArray() ) );
System.out.println( "Subtract: " + ArrayUtils.toString( subtract.toArray() ) );
```

The previous example performs these four operations on two List objects, a and b, printing the results with ArrayUtils.toString( ):

```
A: {1,2,2,2,3,3,4,5}
B: {3,4,4,5,6,7}
Union: {1,2,2,2,3,3,4,4,5,6,7}
Intersection: {3,4,5}
Disjunction: {1,2,2,2,3,4,6,7}
Subtract: {1,2,2,2,3}
```

Discussion

Pay close attention to how these four functions deal with cardinality. These four set operations on CollectionUtils—union( ), intersection( ), disjunction( ), and subtraction( )—all respect the cardinality of objects in both Collections. Take, for example, the results of the union of a and b in the Solution; the union of a and b contains two "3" elements and two "4" elements. The cardinality of an element in a union is the maximum cardinality of the element in both Collections. On the other hand, the cardinality of an element in an intersection is the minimum cardinality of the element in both Collections; there is only one "3" element and one "4" element in the intersection of a and b.

Figure 5-3 illustrates each set operation with a Venn diagram. "A union B" is the combination of A and B, and "A intersection B" is the common overlap of A and B. "A subtract B" is all elements only in A, and "A disjunction B" is all elements in either A or B but not both.

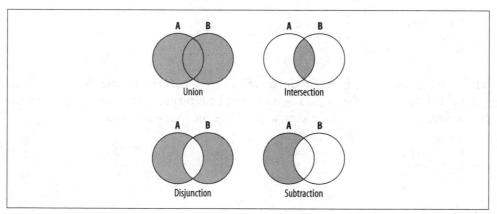

Figure 5-3. Venn diagrams for four set operations in CollectionUtils

5.21   Retrieving Map Values Without Casting

Problem

You need to retrieve a primitive double from a Map, but the value is stored as a Double object.

Solution

Use MapUtils.getDoubleValue( ) to retrieve a Double object from a Map as a double primitive. The following example demonstrates getDoubleValue( ):

```
import java.util.*;
import org.apache.commons.lang.ArrayUtils;
import org.apache.commons.collections.MapUtils;

Object[] mapArray = new Object[][] {
    { "A", new Double( 2.0 ) },
    { "B", new Double( 0.223242 ) },
    { "C", new Double( 2828e4 ) },
    { "D", "GARBAGE"} };

Map numberMap = ArrayUtils.toMap( mapArray );

double a = MapUtils.getDoubleValue( numberMap, "A" );
double b = MapUtils.getDoubleValue( numberMap, "B" );
double c = MapUtils.getDoubleValue( numberMap, "C" );
double d = MapUtils.getDoubleValue( numberMap, "D", new Double( Double.NaN ) );

System.out.println( "A = " + a );
System.out.println( "B = " + b );
System.out.println( "C = " + c );
System.out.println( "D = " + d );
```

This simple utility retrieves four doubles from numberMap; the fourth call to getDoubleValue( ) supplies a default double to be returned if the value's type cannot be converted to a double. This example produces the following output:

```
A = 2.0
B = 0.223242
C = 28280.0
D = NaN
```

Discussion

This utility is laughably simple, but if you are working with numbers, this utility can help you avoid casting and calling doubleValue( ). In addition to MapUtils. getDoubleValue( ), MapUtils also contains the MapUtils.getDouble( ) method, which simply returns a Double object. The following example demonstrates the various utility methods for obtaining primitives and their corresponding object types from a Map:

```
import java.util.*;
import org.apache.commons.collections.MapUtils;

Map map = new HashMap( );
map.put( "A", new Long( 3.4 ) );
map.put( "B", new Short( 33 ) );
map.put( "C", "BLAH" );

Number aNumber = MapUtils.getNumber( map, "A" );
Long aLong = MapUtils.getLong( map, "A" );

long a = MapUtils.getLongValue( map, "A" );
short b = MapUtils.getShortValue( map, "B" );
Byte c = MapUtils.getByte( map, "C", Byte.MAX_VALUE );
```

As shown in the previous example, MapUtils contains utility methods for working with bytes, shorts, and long, among other primitive types.

Table 5-1 details several related methods for Boolean, Double, and Number, which can retrieve objects and primitive values from a Map. While Table 5-1 deals with Boolean and Double, you should be aware that similar methods exist for all primitive types and corresponding objects.

Table 5-1. Methods on MapUtils

Return type	Signature
Boolean	getBoolean(Map map, Object key) getBoolean(Map map, Object key, Boolean default)
boolean	getBooleanValue(Map map, Object key) getBooleanBalue(Map map, Object key, boolean default)
Double	getDouble(Map map, Object key) getDouble(Map map, Object key, Double default)
double	getDoubleValue(Map map, Object key) getDoubleValue(Map map, Object key, double default)
Number	getNumber(Map map, Object key) getNumber(Map map, Object key, Number default)

CHAPTER 6

XML

6.0   Introduction

Extensible Markup Language (XML) went from a risky buzzword to a ubiquitous data format in a few short years, bringing with it an overwhelming array of tools, standards, APIs, and technologies. World Wide Web Consortium's (W3C) publication of the initial XML recommendation in 1998 redefined the way information is represented, stored, and exchanged, and it seems that a new standard involving XML is created every month: XSL, XML Query, XPointer, XPath, XLink, XHTML, SVG, MathML, XForms, XML Encryption, SOAP, XML-RPC, WSDL, XML Schema, RelaxNG, TREX, and the list continues. Such standards are accompanied by an almost endless series of standard APIs, such as SAX and DOM. To further complicate matters, Sun Microsystems has created a number of Java APIs to handle most everything XML, including JAXP, TrAX, JAXB, JAXM, JAX-RPC, JAXR, and SAAJ. It would take years to become an expert in each of these standards, tools, and APIs, and, because of this, most programmers focus on the tip of the iceberg: SAX, DOM, a little XPath, DTD, and XML Schema. This chapter focuses on parsing and data binding; reading a XML document and creating an XML document from a set of objects.

More than a few developers have noted that parsing a simple XML document with SAX or DOM can be an unreasonably complex task, especially if one is simply attempting to create a prototype. With SAX, you need to write a series of callback methods like `startElement()` and `endElement()`, and in DOM, you need to write a not-trivial amount of code to traverse a `Document` object. It isn't the case that you should never write a DOM or SAX parser; there are some systems that call for this level of control and complexity, and a thorough knowledge of SAX, DOM, and JDOM is essential knowledge for any developer. This chapter isn't looking to unseat the reigning standards; instead, this chapter simply introduces you to some tools that sit on top of standard parsers and do some parsing dirty work in specific situations. A very common task in any Java program is reading in an XML document and creating a set of objects, and Commons Digester and Commons Betwixt make this task as simple as it should be.

With almost a trillion different ways to parse or create a simple XML document, you can easily overlook a tool that might save days of programming time. Commons Digester, Commons Betwixt, Zeus, Quick, Apache XMLBeans, JAXB, XStream, JiBX, Exolab Castor, and others are all projects and products that deal with the simple task of serializing objects to XML and unmarshalling XML to objects. This field is crowded, and a number of these technologies have great promises and great flaws. Just as this chapter was not written to convince you to abandon SAX and DOM, this chapter was also not written to sell Digester or Betwixt over all other options. If you don't like what you see in this chapter, there are a variety of options, and while the abundance of choice is overwhelming, open source is about having options and choices. This chapter introduces you to two battle-tested options from Jakarta Commons—Jakarta Commons Digester and Jakarta Commons Betwixt.

Commons Digester makes the task of parsing XML exceedingly straightforward; with the Digester in hand, you can map an XML document to a series of objects using a simple set of rules and a small amount of Java code. If you use Digester with an XML rule set, it is possible to write a system that parses an XML document with three or four lines of compiled code and no hardcoded logic dealing with document structure. Commons Betwixt maps beans to XML documents and vice versa. The BeanWriter class can be used to serialize an object as an XML document, and the BeanReader can be used to read an XML document. The XML produced by Betwixt can be customized with an XML document that controls such things as whether properties are to be serialized as attributes or elements, how Collections are handled, or how property names are converted to element or attribute names.

For more information about XML data binding, pick up a copy of Brett McLaughlin's *Java & XML Data Binding* (O'Reilly) or *Java & XML* (O'Reilly). For more information about XML, see the W3C at *http://www.w3c.org*. For a list of technologies, take a look at Ronald Bourret's *XML Data Binding Resources* (*http://www.rpbourret.com/ xml/XMLDataBinding.htm*).

6.1   Obtaining Jakarta Commons Digester

Problem

You need to use Jakarta Commons Digester to quickly parse an XML document into a set of objects.

Solution

You must download the latest version of Commons Digester and place the Commons Digester JAR in your project's classpath. Following the steps outlined in Recipe 1.1, download Commons Digester 1.5 instead of Commons Lang. Uncompress the distribution archive and place *commons-digester.jar* in your classpath. Commons Digester depends on Commons BeanUtils, Commons Logging, and Commons Collections. To download dependencies, see Recipes 3.2, 5.1, and 7.9.

Discussion

Commons Digester started as a part of Jakarta Struts, and it was moved to the Jakarta Commons project by way of the Commons Sandbox in early 2001. Digester is the mechanism Struts uses to read XML configuration; *struts-config.xml* is the main configuration point for Jakarta Struts, and it is converted to a set of objects using the Digester. The Digester's most straightforward application is the mapping of an XML document to a set of Java objects, but, as shown in this chapter and Chapter 12, Digester can also be used to create a simple XML command language and search index. Digester is a shortcut for creating a SAX parser. Almost anything you can do with a SAX parser can be done with Jakarta Commons Digester.

If you have a Maven project that needs to use Commons Digester, add a dependency on Commons Digester 1.5 with the following section in *project.xml*:

```
<dependencies>
  <dependency>
    <id>commons-digester</id>
    <version>1.5</version>
  </dependency>
  ....other dependencies...
</dependencies>
```

See Also

For more information about Commons Digester, see the Commons Digester project page at *http://jakarta.apache.org/commons/digester*. For information about using the Digester to create a Lucene index, see Chapter 12.

6.2 Turning XML Documents into Objects

Problem

You need to parse an XML document into an object graph, and you would like to avoid using either the DOM or SAX APIs directly.

Solution

Use the Commons Digester to transform an XML document into an object graph. The Digester allows you to map an XML document structure to an object model in an external XML file containing a set of rules telling the Digester what to do when specific elements are encountered. In this recipe, the following XML document containing a description of a play will be parsed into an object graph:

```
<?xml version="1.0"?>

<plays>
  <play genre="tragedy" year="1603" language="english">
    <name>Hamlet</name>
    <author>William Shakespeare</author>
    <summary>
      Prince of Denmark freaks out, talks to ghost, gets into a
      crazy nihilistic funk, and dies in a duel.
    </summary>
    <characters>
      <character protagonist="false">
        <name>Claudius</name>
        <description>King of Denmark</description>
      </character>
      <character protagonist="true">
        <name>Hamlet</name>
        <descr>
          Son to the late, and nephew of the present king
        </descr>
      </character>
      <character protagonist="false">
        <name>Horatio</name>
        <descr>
          friend to Hamlet
        </descr>
      </character>
    </characters>
  </play>
</plays>
```

This XML document contains a list of play elements describing plays by William Shakespeare. One play element describes "Hamlet"; it includes a name, author, and summary element as well as a characters element containing character elements describing characters in the play. After parsing a document with Digester, each play element will be represented by a Play object with a set of properties and a List of Character objects:

```
public class Play {
    private String genre;
    private String year;
    private String language;
    private String name;
    private String author;
    private String summary;
    private List characters = new ArrayList();

    // accessors omitted for brevity
```

```
        // Add method to support adding elements to characters.
        public void addCharacter(Character character) {
            characters.add( character );
        }
    }

    public class Character {
        private String name;
        private String description;
        private boolean protagonist;

        // accessors omitted for brevity
    }
```

The Digester maps XML to objects using a set of rules, which can be defined either in an XML file, or they can be constructed programmatically by creating instances of Rule and adding them to an instance of Digester. This recipe uses an XML file to create a set of rules that tell the Digester how to translate an XML document to a List of Play objects:

```
<?xml version="1.0"?>

<digester-rules>
  <pattern value="plays/play">
    <object-create-rule classname="xml.digester.Play"/>
    <set-next-rule methodname="add" paramtype="java.lang.Object"/>
    <set-properties-rule/>
    <bean-property-setter-rule pattern="name"/>
    <bean-property-setter-rule pattern="summary"/>
    <bean-property-setter-rule pattern="author"/>

    <!-- Nested Pattern for Characters -->
    <pattern value="characters/character">
      <object-create-rule classname="xml.digester.Character"/>
      <set-next-rule methodname="addCharacter"
                     paramtype="xml.digester.Character"/>
      <set-properties-rule/>
      <bean-property-setter-rule pattern="name"/>
      <bean-property-setter-rule pattern="descr"
                                 propertyname="description"/>
    </pattern>

  </pattern>
</digester-rules>
```

This mapping document (or rule sets) can be explained in very straightforward language. It is telling Digester how to deal with the document, "When you see an element matching the pattern *plays/play*, create an instance of xml.digester.Play, set some properties, and push it on to a Stack (object-create-rule). If you encounter an element within a play element that matches *characters/character*, create an instance of xml.digester.Character, set some properties, and add it to the Play object." The following code creates an instance of Digester from the XML rule sets shown previously, producing a plays List, which contains one Play object:

```
import org.apache.commons.digester.Digester;
import org.apache.commons.digester.xmlrules.DigesterLoader;

List plays = new ArrayList();

// Create an instance of the Digester from the XML rule set
URL rules = getClass().getResource("./play-rules.xml");
Digester digester = DigesterLoader.createDigester(rules);

// Push a reference to the plays List on to the Stack
digester.push(plays);

// Parse the XML document
InputStream input = getClass().getResourceAsStream("./plays.xml");
Object root = digester.parse(input);

// The XML document contained one play "Hamlet"
Play hamlet = (Play) plays.get(0);
List characters = (List) hamlet.getCharacters();
```

Discussion

Digester is simple, but there is one concept you need to understand: Digester uses a Stack to relate objects to one another. In the previous example, set-next-rule tells the Digester to relate the top of the Stack to the next-to-top of the Stack. Before the XML document is parsed, a List is pushed onto the Stack. Every time the Digester encounters a play element, it will create an instance of Play, push it onto the top of the Stack, and call add() with Play as an argument on the object next to the top of the stack. Since the List is next to the top of the Stack, the Digester is simply adding the Play to the playList. Within the pattern element matching *plays/play*, there is another pattern element matching *characters/character*. When an element matching *characters/character* is encountered, a Character object is created, pushed onto the top of the Stack, and the addCharacter() method is called on the next to top of the Stack. When the Character object is pushed onto the top of the Stack, the Play object is next to the top of the Stack; therefore, the call to addCharacter() adds a Character to the List of Character objects in the Play object.

Digester can be summed up as follows: define patterns to be matched and a sequence of actions (rules) to take when these patterns are encountered. Digester is essentially short-hand for your own SAX parser, letting you accomplish the same task without having to deal with the complexity of the SAX API. If you look at the source for the org.apache.commons.digester.Digester class, you see that it implements org.xml.sax.helpers.DefaultHandler and that a call to parse() causes Digester to register itself as a content handler on an instance of org.xml.sax. XMLReader. Digester is simply a lightweight shell around SAX, and, because of this, you can parse XML just as fast with the Digester as with a system written to the SAX API.

Digester rule sets can be defined in an external XML document, or programmatically in compiled Java code, but the general rules are the same. The following code recreates the rule set defined in the previous XML rule set:

```
import org.apache.commons.digester.BeanPropertySetterRule;
import org.apache.commons.digester.Digester;
import org.apache.commons.digester.ObjectCreateRule;
import org.apache.commons.digester.Rules;
import org.apache.commons.digester.SetNextRule;
import org.apache.commons.digester.SetPropertiesRule;

Digester digester = new Digester( );

Rules rules = digester.getRules( );

// Add Rules to parse a play element
rules.add( "plays/play", new ObjectCreateRule("xml.digester.Play"));
rules.add( "plays/play", new SetNextRule("add", "java.lang.Object") );
rules.add( "plays/play", new SetPropertiesRule( ) );
rules.add( "plays/play/name", new BeanPropertySetterRule("name") );
rules.add( "plays/play/summary", new BeanPropertySetterRule("summary") );
rules.add( "plays/play/author", new BeanPropertySetterRule("author") );

// Add Rules to parse a character element
rules.add( "plays/play/characters/character", new
           ObjectCreateRule("xml.digester.Character"));
rules.add( "plays/play/characters/character",
           new SetNextRule("addCharacter", "xml.digester.Character"));
rules.add( "plays/play/characters/character", new SetPropertiesRule( ) );
rules.add( "plays/play/characters/character/name",
           new BeanPropertySetterRule("name") );
rules.add( "plays/play/characters/character/description",
           new BeanPropertySetterRule("description") );
```

While this is perfectly acceptable, think twice about defining Digester rule sets programmatically. Defining rule sets in an XML document provides a very clear separation between the framework used to parse XML and the configuration of the Digester. When your rule sets are separate from compiled code, it will be easier to update and maintain logic involved in parsing; a change in the XML document structure would not involve changing code that deals with parsing. Instead, you would change the model and the mapping document. Defining Digester rule sets in an XML document is a relatively new Digester feature, and, because of this, you may find that some of the more advanced capabilities of Digester demonstrated later in this chapter are not available when defining rule sets in XML.

See Also

More information about Digester XML rule sets can be found in the package document for org.apache.commons.digester.xmlrules (*http://jakarta.apache.org/commons/digester/apidocs/index.html*).

6.3   Namespace-Aware Parsing

Problem

You need to parse an XML document with multiple namespaces.

Solution

Use Digester to parse XML with multiple namespaces, using digester.setNamespaceAware(true), and supplying two RuleSet objects to parse elements in each namespace. Consider the following document, which contains elements from two namespaces: *http://discursive.com/page* and *http://discursive.com/person*:

```
<?xml version="1.0"?>

<pages xmlns="http://discursive.com/page"
       xmlns:person="http://discursive.com/person">
  <page type="standard">
    <person:person firstName="Al" lastName="Gore">
      <person:role>Co-author</person:role>
    </person:person>
    <person:person firstName="George" lastName="Bush">
      <person:role>Co-author</person:role>
    </person:person>
  </page>
</pages>
```

To parse this XML document with the Digester, you need to create two separate sets of rules for each namespace, adding each RuleSet object to Digester with addRuleSet(). A RuleSet adds Rule objects to an instance of Digester. By extending the RuleSetBase class, and setting the namespaceURI in the default constructor, the following class, PersonRuleSet, defines rules to parse the *http://discursive.com/person* namespace:

```
import org.apache.commons.digester.Digester;
import org.apache.commons.digester.RuleSetBase;

public class PersonRuleSet extends RuleSetBase {
    public PersonRuleSet() {
        this.namespaceURI = "http://discursive.com/person";
    }

    public void addRuleInstances(Digester digester) {
        digester.addObjectCreate("*/person", Person.class);
```

```
        digester.addSetNext("*/person", "addPerson");
        digester.addSetProperties("*/person");
        digester.addBeanPropertySetter("*/person/role", "role");
    }
}
```

PersonRuleSet extends RuleSetBase, which is an implementation of the RuleSet interface. RuleSetBase adds support for namespaces with a protected field namespaceURI.
The constructor of PersonRuleSet sets the namespaceURI field to *http://discursive.com/
person*, which tells the Digester to apply these rules only to elements and attributes
in the *http://discursive.com/person* namespace. PageRuleSet extends RuleSetBase and
provides a set of rules for the *http://discursive.com/page* namespace:

```
import org.apache.commons.digester.Digester;
import org.apache.commons.digester.RuleSetBase;

public class PageRuleSet extends RuleSetBase {
    public PageRuleSet( ) {
        this.namespaceURI = "http://discursive.com/page";
    }

    public void addRuleInstances(Digester digester) {
        digester.addObjectCreate("*/page", Page.class);
        digester.addSetNext("*/page", "addPage");
        digester.addSetProperties("*/page");
        digester.addBeanPropertySetter("*/page/summary", "summary");
    }
}
```

Both RuleSet implementations instruct the Digester to create a Page or a Person
object whenever either element is encountered. The PageRuleSet instructs the
Digester to create a Page object when a page element is encountered by using a wild-
card pattern—*/page*. Both PageRuleSet and PersonRuleSet use digester.addSetNext( )
to add the objects just created to the next object in the Stack. In the following code,
an instance of Pages is pushed onto the Digester Stack, and both RuleSet implementations are added to a Digester using addRuleSet( ):

```
import org.apache.commons.digester.Digester;
import org.apache.commons.digester.ObjectCreateRule;
import org.apache.commons.digester.RuleSetBase;
import org.apache.commons.digester.Rules;
import org.apache.commons.digester.SetNextRule;

Pages pages = new Pages( );

Digester digester = new Digester( );
digester.setNamespaceAware(true);
digester.addRuleSet( new PageRuleSet( ) );
digester.addRuleSet( new PersonRuleSet( ) );

digester.push(pages);
```

```
InputStream input = getClass( ).getResourceAsStream("./content.xml");
digester.parse(input);

Page page = (Page) pages.getPages( ).get(0);
System.out.println(page);
```

Because the PageRuleSet adds each Page object to the next object on the Stack, the Pages object has an addPage( ) method that accepts a Page object.

Discussion

Each of the RuleSet implementations defined a set of rules in compiled Java code. If you prefer to define each set of rules in an XML file, you may use the FromXmlRuleSet instead of the RuleSetBase, as follows:

```
import org.apache.commons.digester.Digester;
import org.apache.commons.digester.xmlrules.FromXmlRuleSet;

Pages pages = new Pages( );

Digester digester = new Digester( );
digester.setNamespaceAware(true);

// Add page namespace
digester.setRuleNamespaceURI("http://discursive.com/page");
URL pageRules = getClass( ).getResource("./page-rules.xml");
digester.addRuleSet( new FromXmlRuleSet( pageRules ) );

// Add person namespace
digester.setRuleNamespaceURI("http://discursive.com/person");
URL personRules = getClass( ).getResource("./person-rules.xml");
digester.addRuleSet( new FromXmlRuleSet( personRules ) );

digester.push(pages);

InputStream input = getClass( ).getResourceAsStream("./content.xml");
digester.parse(input);

Page page = (Page) pages.getPages( ).get(0);
System.out.println(page);
```

Calling digester.setRuleNamespaceURI( ) associates the Rules contained in each FromXmlRuleSet with a specific namespace. In the Solution, the RuleSetBase protected field namespaceURI was used to associate RuleSet objects with namespaces. In the previous example, the namespace is specified by calling setRuleNamespaceURI( ) before each FromXmlRuleSet is added to the digester because there is no access to the protected member variable, namespaceURI, which FromXmlRuleSet inherits from

RuleSetBase. *person-rules.xml* contains an XML rule set for parsing the *http://discursive.com/person* namespace:

```
<?xml version="1.0"?>

<!DOCTYPE digester-rules PUBLIC
        "-//Jakarta Apache //DTD digester-rules XML V1.0//EN"
        "http://jakarta.apache.org/commons/digester/dtds/digester-rules.dtd">

<digester-rules>
  <pattern value="*/page">
    <object-create-rule classname="com.discursive.jccook.xml.bean.Page"/>
    <set-next-rule methodname="addPage"/>
    <set-properties-rule/>
    <bean-property-setter-rule pattern="summary" name="summary"/>
  </pattern>
</digester-rules>
```

page-rules.xml contains an XML rule set for parsing the *http://discursive.com/page* namespace:

```
<?xml version="1.0"?>

<!DOCTYPE digester-rules PUBLIC
        "-//Jakarta Apache //DTD digester-rules XML V1.0//EN"
        "http://jakarta.apache.org/commons/digester/dtds/digester-rules.dtd">

<digester-rules>
  <pattern value="*/person">
    <object-create-rule classname="com.discursive.jccook.xml.bean.Person"/>
    <set-next-rule methodname="addPerson"/>
    <set-properties-rule/>
    <bean-property-setter-rule pattern="role"/>
  </pattern>
</digester-rules>
```

See Also

For more information relating to the use of namespaces in the Digester, refer to the Javadoc for the org.apache.commons.digester package at *http://jakarta.apache.org/commons/digester/apidocs*.

6.4   Creating a Simple XML Command Language

Problem

You would like to capture commands in an XML document, and create a framework to execute these commands.

Solution

Write a custom implementation of Rule, and create a rule set that instructs Commons Digester to invoke these rules when specific elements are parsed. Consider the example of a system that sends an encrypted email. The following XML document contains instructions for the primitive encryption of an email:

```xml
<?xml version="1.0"?>

<operations xmlns="http://discursive.com/textmanip">
  <email to="tobrien@discursive.com"
         from="root@discursive.com">
    <replace search="o" replace="q"/>
    <replace search="d" replace="z"/>
    <lower/>
    <reverse/>
  </email>
</operations>
```

The email tag surrounds three elements—replace, lower, and reverse. The system that executes these commands receives a message as a String and runs this String through three stages before sending an email to *tobrien@discursive.com*. When the parser encounters the replace element, it replaces all occurrences of the contents of the search attribute with the contents of the replace attribute. When the parser encounters a lower element, it translates all characters to lowercase; and when the parser encounters a reverse element, it reverses the String. When the parser encounters the end of the email element, the result of these four operations is sent to the recipient specified in the to attribute of the email element.

```java
import org.apache.commons.digester.Digester;

// Message object that holds text to manipulate
Message message = new Message();
message.setText( "Hello World!" );

System.out.println( "Initial Message: " + message.getText() );

// XML Document with set of commands
InputStream encrypt = getClass().getResourceAsStream("./encrypt.xml");

// Create Custom Rules (or Commands)
Digester digester = new Digester();
digester.addRule( "*/email", new EmailRule() );
digester.addRule( "*/lower", new LowerRule() );
digester.addRule( "*/reverse", new ReverseRule() );
digester.addRule( "*/replace", new ReplaceRule() );
digester.push( message );

// Parse the XML document - execute commands
digester.parse( encrypt );

System.out.println("Resulting Message: " + message.getText() );
```

The Message object is a bean with one String property: text. This Message object is pushed onto the Digester's Stack and is acted upon by each of the commands in the XML document *encrypt.xml*, shown previously. This code is executed, and the following output is produced showing that the original message has been passed through two replace commands, a lowercase command, and a reverse command:

```
Intial Message: Hello World!
Resulting Message: !zlrqw qlleh
```

This example defines three new extensions of Rule: EmailRule, LowerRule, ReverseRule, and ReplaceRule. Each of these rules will retrieve and operate upon the root object from the Digester; this "root" object is the bottom of the Stack, and, in this case, the Message object pushed onto the Digester before parsing. These rules are assigned to patterns; for example, the previous code associates the EmailRule with the */email pattern and the LowerRule with the */lower pattern. The Rule object defines a series of callback methods to handle different stages of parsing an element—begin( ), body( ), end( ), and finish( ). The LowerRule from the previous example overrides one method, and manipulates the Message that which is on the top of the Digester Stack:

```
package com.discursive.jccook.xml.bean;

import org.apache.commons.digester.Rule;
import org.apache.commons.lang.StringUtils;


public class LowerRule extends Rule {
    public LowerRule() { super(); }

    public void body(String namespace, String name, String text)
            throws Exception {
        Message message = (Message) digester.getRoot();
        String lower = StringUtils.lowerCase( message.getText() );
        message.setText( lower );
    }
}
```

LowerRule uses StringUtils from Commons Lang to translate the text property of the Message object to lowercase. If you need to write a Rule that can access attributes, you would override the begin( ) method. The following class, ReplaceRule, extends Rule and overrides the begin( ) method:

```
package com.discursive.jccook.xml.bean;

import org.apache.commons.digester.Rule;
import org.apache.commons.lang.StringUtils;
import org.xml.sax.Attributes;

public class ReplaceRule extends Rule {
    public ReplaceRule() { super(); }
```

```
        public void begin(Attributes attributes) throws Exception {
            Message message = (Message) digester.getRoot();

            String repl = attributes.getValue("search");
            String with = attributes.getValue("replace");
            String text = message.getText();

            String translated =
                StringUtils.replace( text, repl, with );
            message.setText( translated );
        }
    }
```

ReplaceRule reads the search and replace attributes, using StringUtils to replace all occurrences of the search String in the text property of Message with the replace String. The EmailRule demonstrates a more complex extension of the Rule object by overriding begin( ) and end( ):

```
import org.apache.commons.digester.Rule;
import org.apache.commons.net.smtp.SMTPClient;
import org.xml.sax.Attributes;

public class EmailRule extends Rule {
    private String to;
    private String from;

    public EmailRule() { super(); }

    public void begin(Attributes attributes) throws Exception {
        to = attributes.getValue( "to" );
        from = attributes.getValue( "from" );
    }

    public void end( ) throws Exception {
        Message message = (Message) digester.getRoot();

        SMTPClient client = new SMTPClient();
        client.connect("www.discursive.com");
        client.sendSimpleMessage(from, to, message.getText() );
    }
}
```

The email element encloses the four elements that control the primitive message encryption, and the end of this element tells this rule to send an email to the address specified in the to attribute recorded in begin( ). EmailRule uses the SMTPClient from Commons Net to send a simple email in end( ).

Discussion

The Rule class defines four methods that you can override to execute code when XML is parsed—begin( ), body( ), end( ), and finish( ). begin( ) provides access to an element's attributes; body( ) provides access to the element's namespace, local name, and body text; end( ) is called when the end of an element is encountered; and finish( ) is called after end( ) and can be used to clean up data or release resources, such as open network connections or files. When using the Digester in this manner, you are using a technique much closer to writing a SAX parser; instead of dealing with a single startElement, Digester registers itself as a content handler with an XMLReader and delegates to Rule objects associated with a given pattern. If you are simply dealing with attributes, elements, and text nodes, Commons Digester can be a very straightforward alternative to writing a SAX parser.

See Also

This recipe uses StringUtils to manipulate text. For more information about StringUtils, see Chapter 2. An email message is sent from the EmailRule using the SMTPClient from Commons Net. For more information about Commons Net, see Chapter 10.

6.5   Variable Substitution and XML Parsing

Problem

You need to parse XML that contains references to variables, and you need to replace these references with variable values at parse time.

Solution

Use Commons Digester's MultiVariableExpander and the VariableSubstitutor to expand variable references in an XML document during a parse.

 This recipe explores a feature of Commons Digester—variable substitution—which is available only with a prerelease version of Digester, 1.6-dev. To follow the example in this recipe, you must download a nightly snapshot distribution from *http://cvs.apache.org/builds/jakarta-commons/nightly/*. Use nightly distributions of Commons components at your own risk; these distributions may contain unresolved bugs.

The following XML document contains four variable references—*${email.to}*, *${order.id}*, *${user.name}*, and *${product.name}*—all of which need to be replaced with values before the XML is parsed by the Digester:

```
<?xml version="1.0"?>

<email to="${email.to}" from="ceo@xyzblah.com">
  <subject>Purchase Confirmation: ${order.id}</subject>
  <priority>High</priority>
  <message>
    Dear ${user.name}, we appreciate your business. As CEO
    of Big Software Company, Inc., I would like to
```

```
            personally thank you for helping us become filthy rich.
            Your purchase of ${product.name} helped me purchase an
            even larger boat for myself.  Thanks again.
        </message>
    </email>
```

This document represents a purchase confirmation message, and your system needs to unmarshall the above message to the following class, Email:

```
public class Email {
    private String to;
    private String from;
    private String subject;
    private String priority;

    // accessors omitted for brevity.
}
```

The following XML rule set is similar to the rule set defined in Recipe 6.2. When the parser hits an email element, an instance of Email is created and properties are populated:

```
<?xml version="1.0"?>

<digester-rules>
  <pattern value="email">
    <object-create-rule classname="com.discursive.jccook.xml.bean.Email"/>
    <set-next-rule methodname="add" paramtype="java.lang.Object"/>
    <set-properties-rule/>
    <bean-property-setter-rule pattern="subject"/>
    <bean-property-setter-rule pattern="priority"/>
    <bean-property-setter-rule pattern="message"/>
  </pattern>
</digester-rules>
```

This difference between this recipe and Recipe 6.2 is that our XML document contains variables to be replaced at parse time. The following code creates a Map that contains variables referenced in the XML document being parsed. This code creates the variable Map, reads the XML rule set from *email-rules.xml*, and parses the XML document *email.xml*:

```
import org.apache.commons.digester.Digester;
import org.apache.commons.digester.Substitutor;
import org.apache.commons.digester.substitution.MultiVariableExpander;
import org.apache.commons.digester.substitution.VariableSubstitutor;
import org.apache.commons.digester.xmlrules.DigesterLoader;

// Read the Digester XML rule set and create Digester
URL rules = getClass().getResource("./email-rules.xml");
Digester digester = DigesterLoader.createDigester(rules);

// Create object to push onto Digester Stack
List emails = new ArrayList();
digester.push( emails );
```

```
// Create Map of variables
Map vars = new HashMap( );
vars.put("email.to", "ldavid@hbo.com");
vars.put("user.name", "Tim");
vars.put("order.id", "1RR2E223WVVS" );
vars.put("product.name", "Foundation" );

// Create an expander with the Map that matches ${var}
MultiVariableExpander expander = new MultiVariableExpander( );
expander.addSource("$", vars);

// Create a substitutor with the expander
Substitutor substitutor = new VariableSubstitutor(expander);
digester.setSubstitutor(substitutor);

// Parse XML document
InputStream input = getClass( ).getResourceAsStream("./email.xml");
digester.parse( input );

// Retrieve Email object
Email email = (Email) emails.get(0);
System.out.println( "Email Subject: " + email.getSubject() );
System.out.println( "Email To: " + email.getTo() );
```

Variable substitution is performed by a VariableSubstitutor that has been configured with a MultiVariableExpander. The MultiVariableExpander retrieves variables
from a Map, and, in this example, the addSource( ) method is called with a $ marker.
This means that variables are referenced by surrounding a variable name with ${ and
}–${variable}. The previous example produces the following output, which demon-
strates the substitution of variables:

```
Email Subject: Purchase Confirmation: 1RR2E223WVVS
Email To: ldavid@hbo.com
```

Discussion

Variable substitution is part parsing, part templating, and can be valuable when you
need to specify a set of default properties on a bean that need to be parameterized for
different situations. The example in this recipe was an email message confirming a
purchase from an e-commerce system, but there are other situations where an object
may need to be personalized with a user identifier or a username.

See Also

For more information about other new features planned for Digester 1.6, see the current development Javadoc for the Digester at *http://jakarta.apache.org/commons/
digester/apidocs/index.html*.

6.6   Obtaining Jakarta Commons Betwixt

Problem

You need to use Jakarta Commons Betwixt to serialize and deserialize beans to and from XML documents.

Solution

You must download the latest version of Commons Betwixt, and place the Commons Betwixt JAR in your project's classpath. Following the steps outlined in Recipe 1.1, download Commons Betwixt 0.5 instead of Commons Lang. Uncompress the distribution archive and place *commons-betwixt.jar* in your classpath. Commons Betwixt depends on Commons Digester, Commons BeanUtils, Commons Logging, and Commons Collections. To download dependencies, see Recipes 3.2, 5.1, 6.1, and 7.9.

Discussion

Betwixt allows you to translate from beans to XML and vice versa. Beans are serialized to XML documents using a `BeanWriter`, and they are read from XML using a `BeanReader`. The structure of the XML can be automatically generated or customized using an XML document to bind properties to elements or attributes.

If you have a Maven project that needs to use Commons Betwixt, add a dependency on Commons Betwixt 0.5 with the following section in *project.xml*:

```
<dependencies>
  <dependency>
    <id>commons-betwixt</id>
    <version>0.5</version>
  </dependency>
  ....other dependencies...
</dependencies>
```

See Also

For more information about Commons Betwixt, see the Commons Betwixt project page at *http://jakarta.apache.org/commons/betwixt*.

6.7   Turning Beans into XML Documents

Problem

You need to create an XML document from a bean.

Solution

Use Commons Betwixt BeanWriter to transform a bean to an XML document. The following code turns an instance of the Play object from Recipe 6.2 into an XML document:

```
import org.apache.commons.betwixt.io.BeanWriter;

Play play = new Play( );

// populatePlay populates all properties and nested Character objects
populatePlay( play );

// Write XML document
BeanWriter beanWriter = new BeanWriter( );
beanWriter.enablePrettyPrint( );
beanWriter.write( play );

System.out.println( beanWriter.toString( ) );
```

A BeanWriter instance is created, indentation is enabled with a call to enablePrettyPrint( ), and the Play object is written to an XML document with beanWriter.write( ). The previous example prints an XML document with structure similar to the XML document parsed in Recipe 6.2 with the exception of the genre, year, and language elements. The following XML document is produced by the call to beanWriter.write( ):

```
<Play>
  <author>William Shakespeare</author>
  <characters>
    <character>
      <description>King of Denmark</description>
      <name>Claudius</name>
      <protagonist>false</protagonist>
    </character>
    <character>
      <description>
        Son to the late, and nephew of the present
        king
      </description>
      <name>Hamlet</name>
      <protagonist>true</protagonist>
    </character>
    <character>
      <description>friend to Hamlet</description>
      <name>Horatio</name>
      <protagonist>false</protagonist>
    </character>
  </characters>
  <genre>tragedy</genre>
  <language>english</language>
  <name>Hamlet</name>
  <summary>
```

```
        Prince of Denmark (Hamlet) freaks out, talks to
        father's ghost, and finally dies in a duel.
      </summary>
      <year>1603</year>
    </Play>
```

Discussion

Using the BeanWriter is an easy way to create XML documents from beans, and if you don't have a preference for the layout of the resulting XML document, it is the easiest way to serialize an object to XML. The BeanWriter offers some control over the appearance of the XML it generates. setEndOfLine( ) takes a String that is used as a line termination sequence. setWriteEmptyElements( ) controls the way in which an empty element is written by Betwixt. If setWriteEmptyElements( ) is passed true, an element will be written to the XML document even if there are no child nodes or attributes. setIndent( ) takes a String that is used as an indentation string when pretty printing—indented output—is enabled using the enablePrettyPrint( ) method on BeanWriter.

When Betwixt encounters the List of Character objects, it creates an element characters, which holds individual character elements created by using introspection on the Character class. This behavior is configurable, and you can instruct Betwixt to omit the characters elements in favor of multiple character child elements. Such a customization is demonstrated in the Discussion of Recipe 6.8.

BeanWriter can also be used to write an XML document to an OutputStream or a Writer by passing a Writer or an OutputStream to the BeanWriter constructor. The following code uses a BeanWriter to write an XML document to *test.dat*:

```
import org.apache.commons.betwixt.io.BeanWriter;

Play play = new Play( );
populatePlay( play );

// Open a File Writer
Writer outputWriter = new FileWriter("test.dat");

// Pass FileWriter to BeanWriter
BeanWriter beanWriter = new BeanWriter( outputWriter );
beanWriter.setEndOfLine( "\r\n" );
beanWriter.setIndent( "\t" );
beanWriter.enablePrettyPrint( );
beanWriter.write( play );

// Close FileWriter
outputWriter.close( );
```

Since the previous example contains a call to setEndOfLine( ), enablePrettyPrint( ), and setIndent( ), *test.dat* will have DOS-style line termination and Betwixt will use the tab character for indentation.

See Also

By default, BeanWriter writes every bean property of Play as an element. Recipe 6.8 shows you how to customize the XML generated by Betwixt.

6.8   Customizing XML Generated from an Object

Problem

You are trying to create an XML document from a Java object, and you want to customize the layout and structure of the generated XML document.

Solution

Use a Betwixt mapping file to customize the output of the BeanWriter. Below is an example of a mapping file for the Play class, which was introduced in Recipe 6.2. When Betwixt serializes or deserializes an object to or from XML, it will search for a resource, *<classname>.betwixt*, in the same package as the class to be written or read. The following XML document—*Play.betwixt*—is stored in the same package as the Play class, and it customizes the XML output from Betwixt:

```
<info primitiveTypes="element">
  <element name="play">
    <attribute name="genre" property="genre"/>
    <attribute name="year" property="year"/>
    <attribute name="language" property="language"/>
    <addDefaults/>
  </element>
</info>
```

This file tells Betwixt that genre, year, and language shall be stored as XML attributes, and that the remaining bean properties are to be written as XML elements. The following code is used to create a customized XML document from an instance of Play:

```
import org.apache.commons.betwixt.io;

Play play = (Play) plays.get(0);

BeanWriter beanWriter = new BeanWriter();
beanWriter.enablePrettyPrint();
beanWriter.write( play );

logger.debug( beanWriter.toString() );
```

Betwixt creates the following XML document, which stores the genre, year, and language properties as attributes of the play element. The differences between this XML document and the XML document in Recipe 6.7 are emphasized:

```
<play genre="tragedy" year="1603" language="english">
  <author>William Shakespeare</author>
```

```
<characters>
  <character protagonist="false">
    <description>King of Denmark</description>
    <name>Claudius</name>
  </character>
  <character protagonist="true">
    <description>Son to the late, and nephew of the present king</description>
    <name>Hamlet</name>
  </character>
  <character protagonist="false">
    <description>friend to Hamlet</description>
    <name>Horatio</name>
  </character>
</characters>
<name>Hamlet</name>
<summary>Prince of Denmark (Hamlet) freaks out, talks to father's ghost, and
  finally dies in a duel.</summary>
</play>
```

Discussion

The previous example wrote the protagonist property of the Character class as an attribute of the character element. This customization was accomplished by putting a *Character.betwixt* resource in the same package as the Character class. *Character.betwixt* is shown here:

```
<info primitiveTypes="element">
  <element name="character">
    <attribute name="protagonist" property="protagonist"/>
    <addDefaults/>
  </element>
</info>
```

In addition to customizing the structure on an XML document, a Betwixt mapping file can also be used to change the names of elements and attributes in an XML document. The following mapping file—another version of *Character.betwixt*—writes the description property of Character as a bio element:

```
<info primitiveTypes="element">
  <element name="character">
    <attribute name="protagonist" property="protagonist"/>
    <element name="bio" property="description"/>
    <addDefaults/>
  </element>
</info>
```

In this recipe, Betwixt has wrapped all character elements in a characters element. If you prefer character elements to be child elements of play, you can tell the XMLIntrospector used by BeanWriter to omit elements wrapping collections with the following code:

```
import org.apache.commons.betwixt.io.BeanWriter;
import org.apache.commons.betwixt.XMLIntrospector;
```

```
Play play = (Play) plays.get(0);

BeanWriter beanWriter = new BeanWriter();
beanWriter.enablePrettyPrint();

// Configure XML Introspector to omit collection elements
XMLIntrospector introspector = beanWriter.getXMLIntrospector();
introspector.setWrapCollectionsInElement(false);

beanWriter.write( play );

logger.debug( beanWriter.toString() );
```

The previous code creates an XML document without the characters element:

```
<play genre="tragedy" year="1603" language="english">
  <author>William Shakespeare</author>
  <character protagonist="false">
    <description>King of Denmark</description>
    <name>Claudius</name>
  </character>
  <character protagonist="true">
    <description>Son to the late, and nephew of the present king</description>
    <name>Hamlet</name>
  </character>
  <character protagonist="false">
    <description>friend to Hamlet</description>
    <name>Horatio</name>
  </character>
  <name>Hamlet</name>
  <summary>Prince of Denmark (Hamlet) freaks out, talks to father's ghost, and
    finally dies in a duel.</summary>
</play>
```

Betwixt also allows for the customization of element and attribute names; for example, if your class contains the property maximumSpeed, it can be written as an attribute named maximum-speed or MAXIMUM_SPEED, using the HyphenatedNameMapper strategy. The same property could also be written as an element named MaximumSpeed, using the CapitalizeNameMapper strategy. Different naming strategies can be used for elements and attributes by passing instances of NameMapper to setElementNameMapper() and setAttributeNameMapper() on an XMLIntrospector. The following code demonstrates the setting of both the attribute and element NameMapper on a BeanWriter's XMLIntrospector:

```
import org.apache.commons.betwixt.io.BeanWriter;
import org.apache.commons.betwixt.XMLIntrospector;
import org.apache.commons.betwixt.strategy.CapitalizeNameMapper;
import org.apache.commons.betwixt.strategy.HyphenatedNameMapper;

BeanWriter beanWriter = new BeanWriter();

// Set NameMappers on XMLIntrospector
XMLIntrospector introspector = beanWriter.getXMLIntrospector();
```

```
introspector.setElementNameMapper( new CapitalizeNameMapper() );
introspector.setAttributeNameMapper( new HyphenatedNameMapper() );

beanWriter.write( object );
```

See Also

For more information about possible customizations in Betwixt, see the "Binding Beans" section of the user guide at *http://jakarta.apache.org/commons/betwixt/guide/binding.html*.

6.9   Turning XML Documents into Beans

Problem

You need to convert an XML document into a Bean.

Solution

Use Betwixt's BeanReader to parse an XML document and create an instance of the appropriate bean. Register bean classes with the BeanReader, and parse an XML document loaded from an InputStream, InputSource, or Reader. The following XML document will be parsed into the Play and Character beans introduced in Recipe 6.2:

```
<play genre="tragedy" year="1603" language="english">
  <author>William Shakespeare</author>
  <character protagonist="false">
    <description>King of Denmark</description>
    <name>Claudius</name>
  </character>
  <character protagonist="true">
    <description>Son to the late, and nephew of the present king</description>
    <name>Hamlet</name>
  </character>
  <character protagonist="false">
    <description>friend to Hamlet</description>
    <name>Horatio</name>
  </character>
  <name>Hamlet</name>
  <summary>Prince of Denmark (Hamlet) freaks out, talks to father's ghost, and
    finally dies in a duel.</summary>
</play>
```

This XML document was created with BeanWriter, using the customized format from Recipe 6.8. To read this XML document with BeanReader, the Play class will need to be registered with BeanReader and the XMLIntrospector must have the same settings as the XMLIntrospector used when writing the document with BeanWriter. The following code instantiates and configures a `BeanReader` to read this customized XML for the Play object:

```
import org.apache.commons.betwixt.io.BeanReader;

InputStream customPlay =
    getClass( ).getResourceAsStream("./customized-play.xml");
BeanReader beanReader = new BeanReader( );
beanReader.getXMLIntrospector( ).setWrapCollectionsInElement(false);
beanReader.registerBeanClass(Play.class);

Play play = (Play) beanReader.parse( customPlay );
```

Discussion

Betwixt uses Commons Digester to parse XML, and the `BeanReader` object is an extension of the `Digester`. `BeanReader` creates a Digester rule set using introspection and the Betwixt mapping files available on the classpath. Digester, as introduced in the first half of this chapter, is a quick way to parse an XML document; all that is required to parse XML with the Digester is a rule set and a little bit of code. Betwixt is built-upon Digester, and the `BeanReader` further reduces the amount of work required to parse XML to a bean. Instead of completing the process demonstrated in Recipe 6.2, you can simply write a few, very manageable, *.betwixt* files using `BeanReader` to read the XML documents and `BeanWriter` to write the XML documents.

When Betwixt is adding `Character` objects to the characters `List` on a `Play` object, it's calling the `addCharacter( )` method on the `Play` object. Without this `addCharacter( )` object, Betwixt would not be able to populate this `List`. Betwixt automatically recognizes a plural property name such as `characters`, `characterList`, or `characterSet`, and it attempts to call the corresponding `addCharacter( )` method. For more information about the algorithm Betwixt uses to recognize composite properties, see "Using Adder Methods for Composite Properties" in the Betwixt user guide (*http://jakarta.apache.org/commons/betwixt/guide/binding.html*).

See Also

For more information about reading beans with Betwixt, see "Reading Beans" in the Betwixt user guide (*http://jakarta.apache.org/commons/betwixt/guide/reading.html*).

## CHAPTER 7

Application Infrastructure

7.0   Introduction

The plumbing of an application—command-line parsing, configuration, and logging—can be viewed as application infrastructure. This chapter introduces a few tools to help applications work with configuration, arguments, and log files: Commons CLI for command-line parsing, Commons Configuration for reading application configuration from properties files and XML documents, Commons Logging, and Log4J.

7.1   Obtaining Commons CLI

Problem

You need to use Commons CLI (Command-Line Interface) to parse an application's command-line arguments.

Solution

Download Commons CLI 1.0. Following the steps outlined in Recipe 1.1, download "Commons CLI 1.0" instead of Commons Lang. The Commons CLI archive—*cli-1.0.zip*—contains a file named *commons-cli-1.0.jar*; place this JAR file in your classpath, and you are ready to use Commons CLI in your application.

Discussion

Commons CLI provides a standard mechanism for parsing command-line arguments. Contained in the `org.apache.commons.cli` package, CLI provides a set of classes that can parse command-line arguments containing optional arguments, arguments with parameters, and short and long arguments. As shown in this chapter, CLI also provides a mechanism for printing out usage information.

See Also

For more information about Commons CLI, see the Commons CLI project page (*http://jakarta.apache.org/commons/cli*).

For C developers, see the getopt and argp in the GNU C Library. For more information, see the section "Parsing Program Arguments" in the GNU C Library manual (*http://www.gnu.org/software/libc/manual/html_node/index.html*).

7.2   Parsing a Simple Command Line

Problem

You need to parse a simple command line containing optional and required arguments.

Solution

Use the Jakarta Commons CLI to parse program arguments. Populate an `Options` object to configure command-line parsing. Pass the `Options` class and a `String[]` of arguments to a `CommandLineParser`, which parses and returns a `CommandLine` object capturing the supplied options and parameters.

For the purposes of this recipe, assume that you are attempting to parse a command line with three optional arguments: -h, -v, and -f <filename>. -h prints out a simple help message with usage information and available command-line options, -v runs the program with verbose logging, and -f sends the output of the application to a file. To parse this command line, your main( ) method would resemble the following code:

```java
import org.apache.commons.cli.CommandLineParser;
import org.apache.commons.cli.BasicParser;
import org.apache.commons.cli.Options;
import org.apache.commons.cli.CommandLine;

public static void main(String[] args) throws Exception {

    // Create a Parser
    CommandLineParser parser = new BasicParser();
    Options options = new Options();
    options.addOption("h", "help", false, "Print this usage information");
    options.addOption("v", "verbose", false, "Print out VERBOSE information" );
    options.addOption("f", "file", true, "File to save program output to");

    // Parse the program arguments
    CommandLine commandLine = parser.parse( options, args );

    // Set the appropriate variables based on supplied options
    boolean verbose = false;
    String file = "";
```

```
    if( commandLine.hasOption('h') ) {
        System.out.println( "Help Message")
        System.exit(0);
    }

    if( commandLine.hasOption('v') ) {
        verbose = true;
    }

    if( commandLine.hasOption('f') ) {
        file = commandLine.getOptionValue('f');
    }
}
```

Discussion

The Options object tells the CommandLineParser to expect three arguments: -h, -v, and -f. The first argument to options.addOption( ) is the short name or abbreviation of the option, and the second argument is the long name of the argument. When the long name of an option is specified, either may be used as program arguments. For example, a command line specifying short-name arguments, -h -v -f test.xml, is equivalent to a command line specifying long-name arguments, --help --version --file test.xml, and both short- and long-name arguments may be mixed in the same command line. The third argument to options.addOption( ) specifies whether the option takes a parameter; in the previous example, only the file option expects a parameter. The fourth parameter is a String containing a description of the option for a user.

An Options object may be configured using the options.addOption( ), or an Option object can be created and added to the Options object. The following code is equivalent to the call to options.addOption( ) in the previous example, which adds the help option:

```
Option helpOption = new Option("h", "Prints this usage information");
helpOption.setLongOpt( "help" );
options.addOption( helpOption );
```

Both the Options object and the args String[] are passed to parser.parse( ), which returns a CommandLine object. CommandLine captures the supplied program arguments, and provides access to the supplied options and arguments. commandLine. hasOption('h') checks for the presence of the optional help choice, and commandLine. getOptionValue('f') retrieves the filename argument for the file option.

See Also

In this recipe, BasicParser, an implementation of CommandLineParser, is used to parse command lines. This implementation allows for mixed short- and long-name options: -f test.xml --help. If you are developing an application that needs to parse arguments using POSIX Conventions, use org.apache.commons.cli.PosixParser instead of BasicParser. If you need to parse arguments using the less strict GNU conventions, use the org.apache.commons.cli.GNUParser.

For background about the differences between POSIX and GNU standards, see Section 4.6 of the "GNU Coding Standards" (*http://www.gnu.org/prep/standards_18.html*). For information about POSIX syntax guidelines, see Section 12.2, "Utility Syntax Guidelines" of "The Single UNIX Specification Version 3" (*http://www.unix-systems.org/online.html*), also known as IEEE Standard 1003.1 and ISO/IEC 9945.

7.3   Parsing a Complex Command Line

Problem

You need to parse a command line with two exclusive options.

Solution

Store mutually exclusive Option objects in an OptionGroup, and add this OptionGroup to an Options object using the addOptionGroup( ) method. Assume you are working with the following program argument specification: -h, -v, and -f <filename> | -m <email>. -h and -v are both optional and only one of -f or -m can be specified. If both -m and -f are supplied as program arguments, an exception is thrown. In the following example, the -f and -m options are added to an OptionGroup, which is then added to the Options object used to parse the program arguments:

```
import org.apache.commons.cli.CommandLineParser;
import org.apache.commons.cli.BasicParser;
import org.apache.commons.cli.Options;
import org.apache.commons.cli.OptionBuilder;
import org.apache.commons.cli.OptionGroup;
import org.apache.commons.cli.CommandLine;

public static void main(String[] args) throws Exception {

    // Create a Parser
    CommandLineParser parser = new BasicParser();
    Options options = new Options();
    options.addOption("h", "help", false, "Print this usage information");
    options.addOption("v", "verbose", false, "Print out VERBOSE information" );

    OptionGroup optionGroup = new OptionGroup();
    optionGroup.addOption( OptionBuilder.hasArg(true).create('f') );
    optionGroup.addOption( OptionBuilder.hasArg(true).create('m') );
    options.addOptionGroup( optionGroup );

    // Parse the program arguments
    CommandLine commandLine = parser.parse( options, args );

    // ... do important stuff ...
}
```

If the user supplies both -f and -m at the same time, the `CommandLineParser` will throw an `AlreadySelectedException`.

Discussion

In the Solution, the -f and -m options were created using the `OptionBuilder` class. This utility lets you build an `Option` object by chaining a series of method calls. For example, the following code creates a required option, "b," which takes an argument:

```
Option option = OptionBuilder.hasArgs(true).isRequired(true).create('b');
```

`OptionGroup` objects are a good way to enforce the structure of command-line options. If you were parsing the command line with a `StringTokenizer` and keeping track of all of the specified options that may or may not have parameters, this could involve 30 or 40 lines of code just to manage this validation process. By using the Jakarta Commons CLI, you delegate this complexity and cut down on the amount of code you need to maintain.

See Also

What happens if a user specifies two options from an `OptionGroup`? Does the application just fail catastrophically from a `RuntimeException`? Usually, if a program has a problem parsing command-line arguments, it will print out a helpful usage message. "Printing Usage Information" demonstrates the use of CLI to automatically create a usage message.

7.4   Printing Usage Information

Problem

You need to provide the user with a formatted list of available options.

Solution

Pass an `Options` object to a `HelpFormatter` and print a usage message. Example 7-1 creates the same `Options` object from Recipe 7.3. If the help option is specified, or if there is a problem parsing the program arguments, the `printUsage()` method is called to print usage information to `System.out`.

Example 7-1. Printing usage information with HelpFormatter

```
import org.apache.commons.cli.CommandLineParser;
import org.apache.commons.cli.BasicParser;
import org.apache.commons.cli.Options;
import org.apache.commons.cli.OptionBuilder;
import org.apache.commons.cli.OptionGroup;
import org.apache.commons.cli.CommandLine;
import org.apache.commons.cli.HelpFormatter;
```

Example 7-1. Printing usage information with HelpFormatter (continued)

```java
public class SomeApp {
    private static final String USAGE = "[-h] [-v] [-f <file> | -m <email>]";
    private static final String HEADER =
        "SomeApp - A fancy and expensive program, Copyright 2010 Blah.";
    private static final String FOOTER =
        "For more instructions, see our website at: http://www.blah123.org";

    public static void main(String[] args) throws Exception {

        // Create a Parser
        CommandLineParser parser = new BasicParser();
        Options options = new Options();
        options.addOption("h", "help", false, "Print this usage information");
        options.addOption("v", "verbose", false, "Print out VERBOSE information" );

        OptionGroup optionGroup = new OptionGroup();
        optionGroup.addOption( OptionBuilder.hasArg(true).withArgName("file")
                                      .withLongOpt("file").create('f') );
        optionGroup.addOption( OptionBuilder.hasArg(true).withArgName("email")
                                      .withLongOpt("email").create('m') );
        options.addOptionGroup( optionGroup );
           // Parse the program arguments
        try {
            CommandLine commandLine = parser.parse( options, args );

            if( commandLine.hasOption('h') ) {
                printUsage( options );
                System.exit(0);
            }

                // ... do important stuff ...
        } catch( Exception e ) {
            System.out.println( "You provided bad program arguments!" );
            printUsage( options );
            System.exit(1);
        }
    }

    private static void printUsage(Options options) {
        HelpFormatter helpFormatter = new HelpFormatter();
        helpFormatter.setWidth( 80 );
        helpFormatter.printHelp( USAGE, HEADER, options, FOOTER );
    }
}
```

When this application is executed and the parser encounters an unexpected program argument, the following output is produced:

```
You provided bad program arguments!
usage: [-h] [-v] [-f <file> | -m <email>]
SomeApp - A fancy and expensive program, Copyright 2010 Blah.
 -f,--file <file>
```

```
 -h,--help              Print this usage information
 -m,--email <email>
 -v,--verbose           Print out VERBOSE information
For more instructions, see our website at: http://www.blah123.org
```

Discussion

If an exception is thrown during parser.parse( ), the application will print an error message and call printUsage( ), which creates a HelpFormatter object and sets the display width to 80 characters. helpFormatter.printHelp( ) prints to standard out and takes five parameters, including the Options object, which contains configuration for the CommandLineParser. The first parameter specified a usage string, which is an abbreviated specification of the program arguments: -h, -v, and -f <file> | -m <email>. The second argument is a header to print before the list of available options. The third parameter is the same Options object passed to the CommandLineParser. HelpFormatter will use this Options object to print out the short name, long name, and description of each option. The fourth parameter is a footer to display after the list of options.

7.5   Obtaining Commons Configuration

Problem

You need to use Commons Configuration to access configuration stored in properties files and XML documents.

Solution

Commons Configuration 1.0 is not yet released, but you may download a nightly build from *http://cvs.apache.org/builds/jakarta-commons/nightly/commons-configuration/*. As Commons Configuration approaches a 1.0 release, a full binary release may also be available. Once Commons Configuration is released, you should be able to download a JAR by following the steps outlined in Recipe 1.1 and downloading "Commons Configuration 1.0" instead of Commons Lang. The Commons Configuration archive contains a JAR file named *commons-configuration-1.0-rc1.jar*, which should be placed in your classpath.

Discussion

Commons Configuration is designed to provide access to application configuration in the form of properties files, XML documents, JNDI resources, or data from a JDBC Datasource. Commons Configuration also allows you to create a hierarchical or multileveled configuration allowing for default settings to be selectively overridden by local configuration. Commons Configuration also provides typed access to single- and multivalued configuration parameters.

See Also

For more information about the Commons Configuration project, see the Commons Configuration project page at *http://jakarta.apache.org/commons/configuration*.

7.6 Configuring Applications with Properties Files

Problem

You need to access configuration parameters as typed objects. In other words, you have configuration parameters that may be numbers or lists of strings, and you want to access them as typed objects instead of first retrieving them as String objects from a Properties object.

Solution

Use the PropertiesConfiguration from Commons Configuration in the org.apache.commons.configuration package. This class loads a properties file and provides access to numbers, arrays, and lists. The following properties file contains three properties: speed is a floating-point number, names is a comma-separated list of strings, and correct is a boolean value:

```
speed=23.332
names=Bob,Gautam,Jarret,Stefan
correct=false
```

This properties file is stored in *test.properties* in the working directory of an application, which needs access to all three properties as a float, List, and boolean. The following code creates a PropertiesConfiguration and accesses each property:

```
import org.apache.commons.configuration.Configuration;
import org.apache.commons.configuration.PropertiesConfiguration;

Configuration config = new PropertiesConfiguration( "test.properties" );

float speed = config.getFloat("speed"));
List names = config.getList("names"));
boolean correct = config.getBoolean("correct");
```

Discussion

Passing a String to the constructor of PropertiesConfiguration will load configuration properties from a file named *test.properties*. Properties are then referenced by the key of the property in the properties file. This recipe demonstrates a modest improvement upon the existing Properties class that ships with the J2SE. The methods provided by the Configuration interface enable you to retrieve properties with a specific type, throwing a `NumberFormatException`, `ClassCastException`, and `NoSuchElementException` if there is a problem finding or parsing a property value.

See Also

For a full list of the methods provided by the `Configuration` interface, see the Commons Configuration JavaDoc at *http://jakarta.apache.org/commons/configuration/apidocs*.

7.7   Configuring Applications with XML

Problem

You need to configure an application with an XML document.

Solution

Use an implementation of `XMLConfiguration` to load configuration parameters from an XML document. The following XML document contains configuration information that is loaded with a `DOMConfiguration` object:

```
<?xml version="1.0" encoding="ISO-8859-1" ?>

<engine-config>
    <start-criteria>
        <criteria type="critical">
            Temperature Above -10 Celsius
        </criteria>
        <criteria>
            Fuel tank is not empty
        </criteria>
    </start-criteria>
    <name>
        <first>Tom</first>
        <last>Payne</last>
    </name>
    <horsepower>42</horsepower>
</engine-config>
```

A `DOMConfiguration` object uses the Xerces XML parser to parse an entire XML document into a DOM Document object. Subsequent calls to methods on the `Configuration` interface cause the `DOMConfiguration` object to traverse nodes in the Document. The code to read in this XML configuration with `DOMConfiguration` follows:

```
import org.apache.commons.configuration.Configuration;
import org.apache.commons.configuration.DOMConfiguration;

String resource = "com/discursive/jccook/configuration/global.xml";
Configuration config = new DOMConfiguration(resource);

// Retrieve a list of all Criteria elements
List startCriteria = config.getList("start-criteria.criteria");
```

```
// Retrieve the value of the first criteria element
String firstCriteria = config.getString("start-criteria.criteria(0)");

// Retrieve the type attribute of the first criteria element
String firstCriteriaType = config.getString("start-criteria.criteria(0)[@type]");

// Retrieve the horsepower as an int
int horsepower = config.getInt("horsepower");
```

Discussion

Passing a String to the constructor of DOMConfiguration loads an XML document from the classpath as a resource. If you need to load XML configuration from a file, pass a File object to the DOMConfiguration constructor. Configuration parameters are retrieved using methods from the Configuration interface, and parameters are referenced using a syntax that resembles XPath. Subelements are referenced by appending a period and the subelement name to the name of an element; in this example, name.first references the subelement first of the element name. Attributes are referenced by prefixing an attribute name with an @ and surrounding the reference with brackets; in this example, start-critera.criteria(0)[@type] references the type attribute of the criteria element. Specific elements in a list of elements are referenced by surrounding the index with parentheses; start-criteria.criteria(0) references the first criteria element.

DOMConfiguration will only work if the Xerces XML parser is available in your classpath. If Xerces is not available, you may use another implementation of XMLConfiguration, DOM4JConfiguration, which is written to parse an XML document using DOM4J. To use the DOM4JConfiguration, make sure that DOM4J is in your classpath, and interchange DOM4JConfiguration with DOMConfiguration from the previous example.

See Also

For more information about downloading the Xerces XML parser, see the Xerces project page at *http://xml.apache.org/xerces*.

For more information about downloading DOM4J, see the DOM4J project page at *http://www.dom4j.org*.

7.8   Using Composite Configuration

Problem

Your application calls for a multilayered configuration where a set of default properties can be selectively overridden by local or user configuration preferences.

Solution

Create a *configuration.xml* file that contains references to multiple properties files, and pass this file to a ConfigurationFactory. A ConfigurationFactory will then return a Configuration implementation that obtains configuration parameters from multiple properties file.

Table 7-1 lists configuration properties for an application. A global configuration layer defines default values for configuration parameters. A local configuration layer allows you to customize the behavior of a system at a particular site, and the user configuration layer refines configuration parameters for a specific user. When an application retrieves the value of "name," the user layer's value of "Sean" overrides the global layer's value of "Default User."

Table 7-1. Three layers of configuration

Property	Global	Local	User
threads.max	50	30	
threads.min	20		1
timeout	15.52		
interactive	TRUE		
color	red		black
speed	50	55	75
name	Default User		Sean

Properties are stored in three separate files shown in Examples 7-2 (*global.properties*), 7-3 (*local.properties*), and 7-4 (*user.properties*).

Example 7-2. global.properties

```
threads.max=50
threads.min=2
timeout=15.52
interactive=true
color=red
speed=50
name=Default User
```

Example 7-3. local.properties

```
# Overrides Global Props
threads.max=30
speed=55
```

Example 7-4. user.properties

```
# Overrides Local Props
threads.min=1
color=black
```

Example 7-4. user.properties (continued)

```
speed=5000
name=Sean
```

A *configuration.xml* file provides a configuration for the ConfigurationFactory. This file is stored as a resource in the classpath, and the URL for this resource is passed to the setConfigurationURL() method of ConfigurationFactory. The following *configuration.xml* will create a Configuration object, which locates properties from properties files using the override order defined in the XML document. *user. properties* overrides *local.properties*, which overrides *global.properties*:

```xml
<?xml version="1.0" encoding="ISO-8859-1" ?>

<configuration>
    <properties fileName="user.properties"/>
    <properties fileName="local.properties"/>
    <properties fileName="global.properties"/>
</configuration>
```

The following code passes the URL of the *configuration.xml* resource to a ConfigurationFactory, and a Configuration instance is returned, which resolves application configuration parameters according to the rules outlined above:

```java
import org.apache.commons.configuration.Configuration;
import org.apache.commons.configuration.ConfigurationFactory;

// Configure Factory
ConfigurationFactory factory = new ConfigurationFactory();
URL configURL = this.getClass().getResource("configuration.xml");
factory.setConfigurationURL( configURL );

Configuration config = factory.getConfiguration();

// Print out properties
System.out.println( "Timeout: " + config.getFloat("timeout"));
System.out.println( "Max Threads: " + config.getString("threads.max"));
System.out.println( "Name: " + config.getString("name"));
System.out.println( "Speed: " + config.getInt("speed"));
```

This code executes and prints the value of four properties to the console. The timeout property is retrieved from *global.properties*, the threads.max property is retrieved from *local.properties*, and both speed and name are retrieved from *user.properties*:

```
Timeout: 15.52
Max Threads: 30
Name: Sean
Speed: 75
```

Discussion

The *configuration.xml* file instructs the ConfigurationFactory to create a Configuration implementation based on multiple properties files. In the previous example, when the application retrieves a property, there is no parameter signifying the source of the property. There is no mechanism for obtaining the source of a configuration property; in other words, there is no way for our application to see which properties file a particular value was obtained from, and there is no mechanism for enumerating the properties in a single properties file. The *configuration.xml* file "configures" the ConfigurationFactory to create a Configuration—complexity is hidden from the application and the source of configuration can be changed with no effect to this example.

A *configuration.xml* file can also instruct a ConfigurationFactory to use a mixture of properties files and XML documents. The following *configuration.xml* instructs the ConfigurationFactory to create a Configuration instance that looks for properties from a properties file and an XML document:

```
<?xml version="1.0" encoding="ISO-8859-1" ?>

<configuration>
    <properties fileName="test.properties"/>
    <dom4j fileName="test.xml"/>
</configuration>
```

With this configuration, a Configuration instance will attempt to locate a property with a matching key in *test.properties* before it attempts to locate the matching property in *test.xml*. See Recipe 7.7 for more information about retrieving configuration from XML documents.

See Also

In addition to properties files and XML documents, Commons Configuration can also be instructed to resolve configuration properties from a JNDI tree using org. apache.commons.configuration.JNDIConfiguration. For more information on accessing properties in a JNDI tree using Commons Configuration, see the "Configuration Overview" page on the Commons Configuration project site (*http://jakarta.apache. org/commons/configuration/overview.html*).

7.9   Obtaining Commons Logging

Problem

You need to use Commons Logging to develop a system that works under various logging frameworks, including Sun's logging framework and Apache Log4J.

Solution

Download Commons Logging 1.0.3. Following the steps outlined in Recipe 1.1, download "Commons Logging 1.0.3" instead of Commons Lang. The Commons Logging archive—*commons-logging-1.0.3.zip*—will contain a file named *commons-logging.jar*. Place this JAR file in your classpath, and you will be ready to use Commons Logging.

Discussion

Commons Logging was created for developers who need to create components or libraries that may need to operate in environments with different logging frameworks, including Apache Log4J and the built-in logging framework introduced in Java 1.4. Using Commons Logging, a component like Commons BeanUtils or Commons Digester can write log messages to an abstracted Log interface, and Commons Logging can deal with passing these log messages to whichever logging framework is available. Commons Logging is used in almost every Jakarta Commons component.

If you have a Maven project that needs to use Commons Logging, add a dependency on Commons Logging 1.0.3 with the following section in *project.xml*:

```
<dependencies>
  <dependency>
    <id>commons-logging</id>
    <version>1.0.3</version>
  </dependency>

    ....other dependencies...
</dependencies>
```

See Also

For more information about Commons Logging, see the Commons Logging project site (*http://jakarta.apache.org/commons/logging*).

7.10   Using an Abstract Logging Interface

Problem

You are writing a reusable library, and you do not know where or how your code will execute. You need to write log messages to an abstracted logging interface because you cannot count on the presence of Log4J or JDK 1.4 logging.

Solution

Write messages to the Jakarta Commons Logging Log interface, and rely on Commons Logging to decide which concrete logging framework to use at runtime. The following code uses the Log interface to log trace, debug, info, warning, error, and fatal messages:

```
import org.apache.commons.logging.LogFactory;
import org.apache.commons.logging.Log

Log log = LogFactory.getLog( "com.discursive.jccook.SomeApp" );
```

```
if( log.isTraceEnabled( ) ) {
    log.trace( "This is a trace message" );
}

if( log.isDebugEnabled( ) ) {
    log.debug( "This is a debug message" );
}

log.info( "This is an informational message" );

log.warn( "This is a warning" );

log.error( "This is an error" );

log.fatal( "This is fatal" );
```

LogFactory.getInstance( ) returns an implementation of the Log interface, which corresponds to an underlying concrete logging framework. For example, if your system is configured to use Apache Log4J, a Log4JLogger is returned, which corresponds to the Log4J category *com.discursive.jccook.SomeApp*.

Discussion

The developers of a reusable library can rarely predict where and when such a library will be used, and since there are a number of logging frameworks currently available, it makes sense to use Commons Logging when developing reusable components such as Jakarta Commons components. When LogFactory.getInstance( ) is called, Commons Logging takes care of locating and managing the appropriate logging framework by testing a number of system properties and libraries available on the classpath. For the developer of a small reusable component, the complexity ends at the calls to the Log interface; the burden of configuring the underlying logging framework is shifted to the developer integrating this library into a larger system.

See Also

Recipe 7.11 details the algorithm Commons Logging uses to identify the appropriate concrete logging framework to use at runtime.

7.11   Specifying a Logging Implementation

Problem

You are using a component that writes log messages with Commons Logging, and you need to configure the underlying logging implementation.

Solution

If the system property *org.apache.commons.logging.Log* is not set, Commons Logging will use Apache Log4J if it is available in the classpath. To explicitly configure Commons Logging to use Log4J, set the *org.apache.commons.logging.Log* property to `org.apache.commons.logging.impl.Log4JLogger` with the following statement:

```
System.setProperty( "org.apache.commons.logging.Log",
                    "org.apache.commons.logging.impl.Log4JLogger" );
```

If the system property *org.apache.commons.logging.Log* is not set and Apache Log4J is not available on the classpath, Commons Logging will then use the built-in JDK 1.4 logging framework. To explicitly configure Commons Logging to use the JDK 1.4 logging framework, set the *org.apache.commons.logging.Log* property to `org.apache.commons.logging.impl.Jdk14Logger`.

If neither Apache Log4J nor the JDK 1.4 logging framework is available on the classpath and the *org.apache.commons.logging.Log* system property is not set, Commons Logging uses a basic logging implementation named `SimpleLog`. To explicitly configure Commons Logging to use `SimpleLog`, set the *org.apache.commons.logging.Log* property to `org.apache.commons.logging.impl.SimpleLog`.

Discussion

To summarize, Commons Logging performs the following steps when choosing an underlying logging implementation:

1. Checks the *org.apache.commons.logging.Log* system property. If this property is set, use the class specified in this property.
2. Checks for the presence of Log4J in the classpath. If Log4J is present, use a `Log4JLogger` instance.
3. Checks for the presence of the JDK 1.4 logging framework. If JDK 1.4 is present, use a `JDK14Logger` instance.

If neither Log4J nor JDK 1.4 is available, use `SimpleLog`.

See Also

For more information about the configuration of Apache Log4J, see Recipes 7.13 and 7.14. For more information about the configuration of the JDK 1.4 logging framework, see Sun's documentation of this framework at *http://java.sun.com/j2se/1.4.2/docs/guide/util/logging/*.

`SimpleLog` is a very simple logger that can be used when an application does not need a complex logging framework. For more information about configuring `SimpleLog` via system properties, read the Commons Logging JavaDoc at *http://jakarta.apache.org/commons/logging/api/index.html*.

7.12 Obtaining Apache Log4J

Problem

You need to use Apache Log4J to print statements to a log file for informational or debugging purposes.

Solution

Download Apache Log4J 1.2.8 from the Binary Downloads page (*http://logging.apache.org/site/binindex.cgi*) of the Apache Logging Services project. On this page you will find two links to *Jakarta-log4j-1.2.8.tar.gz* and *Jakarta-log4j-1.2.8.zip*. Once this archive is uncompressed, you will find a *log4j-1.2.8.jar* file in the *dist/lib* directory. Put this JAR file in your classpath and you will be ready to use Log4J in your application.

Discussion

Log4J (formerly known as Jakarta Log4J) is a highly configurable logging framework providing hierarchical loggers, various log destinations, and log formats. Messages are written to Log4J Logger objects, which represent a specific category in a hierarchy of log categories; for example, the *com.discursive.Blah* category is a child of the *com.discursive* category. All messages sent to a child category are sent to each ancestor in a tree of Logger categories. A category can be assigned an Appender and a Layout; an Appender controls where a message is sent, and a Layout defines the formatting and contents of a message. Log4J ships with a number of Appender implementations, including SMTPAppender, RollingFileAppender, SocketAppender, SyslogAppender, and NTEventLogAppender. Log4J also ships with a number of Layout implementations, including XMLLayout, PatternLayout, HTMLLayout, and DateLayout.

See Also

For more information about the Apache Logging Services project, see the Logging Services project page at *http://logging.apache.org*. For more information about the Apache Log4J project, see the Log4J project page at *http://logging.apache.org/log4j/docs/*.

7.13 Configuring Log4J with a Properties File

Problem

You need to use Log4J, and you would like to configure it with a properties file.

Solution

Use the BasicConfigurator to read a *log4j.properties* file resource from the classpath. The following code configures Log4J from a resource named *log4j.properties*, and logs two messages:

```
import org.apache.log4j.PropertyConfigurator;
import org.apache.log4j.Logger;

URL log4Jresource = this.getClass().getResource("log4j.properties");
PropertyConfigurator.configure( log4Jresource );

Logger log = Logger.getLogger( "com.discursive.SomeApp" );
log.info( "This is a log message" );
log.error( "This is an error message" );
```

The *log4j.properties* file contains a basic Log4J configuration that sets the root category logging level to WARN and the application's logging level to DEBUG:

```
# All logging output sent to standard out and a file
# WARN is default logging level
log4j.rootCategory=WARN, STDOUT, FILE

# Application logging level is DEBUG
log4j.logger.com.discursive=DEBUG

# Configure the Standard Out Appender
log4j.appender.STDOUT=org.apache.log4j.ConsoleAppender
log4j.appender.STDOUT.layout=org.apache.log4j.PatternLayout
log4j.appender.STDOUT.layout.ConversionPattern=%5p (%F:%L) %m%n

# Configure a rolling file appender
log4j.appender.FILE=org.apache.log4j.RollingFileAppender
log4j.appender.FILE.File=output.log
log4j.appender.FILE.MaxFileSize=2000KB
log4j.appender.FILE.MaxBackupIndex=5
log4j.appender.FILE.layout=org.apache.log4j.PatternLayout
log4j.appender.FILE.layout.ConversionPattern=%d %-5p %c - %m%n
```

This example prints a single info message to the console with the following format:

```
 INFO (Sample.java:24) This is a log message
ERROR (Sample.java:25) This is an error message
```

The rootCategory is configured to send all log messages to the console and a RollingFileAppender. A file named *output.log* contains the following content after this code has been executed:

```
2004-06-14 00:12:22,324  INFO Sample - This is a log message
2004-06-14 00:12:22,326 ERROR Sample - This is an error message
```

Discussion

`PropertyConfigurator.configure( )` takes a URL referencing a resource to be loaded from the classpath. This properties file is read and Log4J is configured to send all messages to both the console and a file. Content is written to a file using a `RollingFileAppender`, which writes to a file until it reaches a configurable maximum size (2 MB). Once this size has been reached, a `RollingFileAppender` will move the existing *output.log* file to a file named *output.log.1* and create a new *output.log* file. As configured in the previous example, the `RollingFileAppender` will keep five backup log files, moving *output.log.1* to *output.log.2* and *output.log* to *output.log.1* the next time a log file's maximum size has been reached.

The Solution configures the default logging level to be `WARN`, meaning that all log messages lower on the level hierarchy will not be sent to appenders. Log4J has five default levels, and they are listed in order of importance: `DEBUG`, `INFO`, `WARN`, `ERROR`, and `FATAL`. If a category is configured with a logging level of `ERROR`, only `ERROR` and `FATAL` messages are sent to appenders, and if a category is configured with a logging level of `DEBUG`, all logging messages are sent to appenders. If you are only interested in the debugging output from your own program, set the `rootCategory` to a high logging level, and override that level for your application's classes. `log4j.logger.com.discursive=DEBUG` overrides the `rootCategory`'s logging level for every topic at or below the `com.discursive` logging category.

See Also

The properties file shown in the Solution should be used as a starting point for Log4J configuration. For more information about various implementations of `Appender` or syntax for `ConversionPattern`, see the Log4J API documentation at *http://logging. apache.org/log4j/docs/api/index.html*.

7.14   Configuring Log4J with XML

Problem

You need to configure Log4J with an XML document.

Solution

Use the `DOMConfigurator` to configure Log4J with an XML document. The following code configures Log4J from a resource named *log4j.xml*, and logs two messages:

```
import org.apache.log4j.DOMConfigurator;
import org.apache.log4j.Logger;

URL log4Jresource = this.getClass( ).getResource("log4j.xml");
DOMConfigurator.configure( lof4Jresource );
```

```
Logger log = Logger.getLogger( "com.discursive.SomeApp" );
log.info( "This is a log message" );
log.error( "This is an error message" );
```

The *log4j.xml* file contains a basic Log4J configuration, which sets the root category logging level to WARN, and the application's logging level to DEBUG. This XML document configures Log4J exactly the way that Log4J was configured by the previous example; log messages are sent to both the console and a RollingFileAppender:

```xml
<?xml version="1.0" encoding="UTF-8" ?>
<configuration configDebug="true">

    <appender name="STDOUT" class="org.apache.log4j.ConsoleAppender">
        <layout class="org.apache.log4j.PatternLayout">
            <param name="ConversionPattern" value="%5p (%F:%L) %m%n"/>
        </layout>
    </appender>

    <appender name="FILE" class="org.apache.log4j.RollingFileAppender">
            <param name="File" value="output.log" />
            <param name="MaxFileSize" value="2000KB" />
            <param name="MaxBackupIndex" value="5" />
            <layout class="org.apache.log4j.PatternLayout">
              <param name="ConversionPattern" value="%d %-5p %c - %m%n"/>
            </layout>
    </appender>

    <category name="com.discursive">
      <priority value="DEBUG" />
    </category>

    <root>
       <priority value="WARN"/>
       <appender-ref ref="STDOUT" />
       <appender-ref ref="FILE" />
    </root>

</configuration>
```

This configuration will produce the same output as the previous recipe. The only difference between this recipe and the last is that XML is used to configure Log4J.

See Also

For more information about Log4J, see the Log4J project page at *http://logging.apache.org/log4*.

## CHAPTER 8

Math

8.0   Introduction

In recent years, Java has lost its reputation as a language suffering from serious performance problems. Although the debate still rages on and various benchmarks show conflicting results, improvements to the JVM, the compiler, and a more intelligent garbage collector have boosted performance to levels on par with C++. Java has never been the traditional language-of-choice for scientific computing, numerical methods, or high-performance computing, but, as performance improves, there are fewer reasons to avoid using Java for numerical computing. It is no longer inconceivable to consider Java when implementing systems involving complex mathematics, and Jakarta Commons contains two projects that provide some very basic math capabilities: Commons Lang and Commons Math.

The first four recipes in this chapter deal with math utilities found in Commons Lang. This includes a class that represents fractions, finding the minimum and maximum values in an array, representing a range of numbers, and convenient ways to retrieve different random variables. Commons Lang was introduced in Chapter 1, and instructions for downloading and installing Commons Lang can be found in Recipe 1.1. The remainder of this chapter deals with Jakarta Commons Math. Recipes involving Commons Math deal with complex numbers, the calculation of univariate statistics, solving a system of linear equations, and establishing a relationship between two independent variables. Instructions for downloading and installing Commons Math can be found in Recipe 8.5.

8.1   Using Fractions

Problem

You need to work with fractions supplied by the user, such as 3 4/5 and 134/21. Your application needs to parse, multiply, and reduce fractions.

Solution

Use Jakarta Commons Lang's `Fraction` class to parse and manipulate fractions. The following code demonstrates the parsing of a `String` containing a fraction:

```
import org.apache.commons.lang.math.Fraction;

String userInput = "23 31/37";
Fraction fraction = Fraction.getFraction( userInput );
double value = fraction.doubleValue();
```

The `String` "23 31/37" is converted to a double value of 23.837837. A `Fraction` object is created by calling the `Fraction.getFraction()` method, and double value of the `Fraction` object is obtained with `fraction.doubleValue()`.

Discussion

The `Fraction` class provides a number of operations that can be used to simplify the following expression to an improper fraction. The following code evaluates the expression in Figure 8-1 using `Fraction`:

```
import org.apache.commons.lang.math.Fraction;

Fraction numer1 = Fraction.getFraction( 3, 4 );
Fraction numer2 = Fraction.getFraction( 51, 3509 );

Fraction numerator = numer1.multiplyBy( numer2 );
Fraction denominator = Fraction.getFraction( 41, 59 );

Fraction fraction = numerator.divideBy( denominator );
Fraction result = fraction.reduce();

System.out.println( "as Fraction: " + result.reduce().toString() );
System.out.println( "as double: " + result.doubleValue() );
```

$$\left(\frac{\frac{3}{4} \times \frac{51}{3509}}{\frac{41}{59}} \right)$$

Figure 8-1. Expression to be evaluated with Fraction

The previous example creates an instance of `Fraction` by calling the static `getFraction(int numerator, int denominator)` method. `Fraction` objects are then multiplied and divided with the `multiplyBy()` and `divideBy()` methods of `Fraction`. And, the final call to `reduce()` reduces the `Fraction` to the smallest possible denominator. This example executes and prints the following output to the console:

```
Expression as Fraction: 9027/575476
Expression as double: 0.015686145034719084
```

An improper fraction is a fraction such that X/Y > 1 (i.e., "135/23" or "3/2"). Fraction provides the ability to convert improper fractions to proper fractions as demonstrated in the following example:

```
import org.apache.commons.lang.math.Fraction;

String userInput = "101/99";
String properString = Fraction.getFraction(userInput).toProperString( );
// properString is now "1 2/99"
```

Fraction does not automatically reduce contents, and it is important to call reduce( ) before performing any arithmetic with the Fraction class to reduce the risk of overflow. For example, Fraction. getFraction(10000, 100000).pow(6) should equal 1.0E-6, but, because Fraction simply multiplies each numerator and denominator without reducing the fraction, the result of this statement will be 1.0. When raised to the power of 6, the Fraction object quickly becomes Fraction.getFraction(Integer.MAX_VALUE, Integer.MAX_VALUE) or 1.0. Call reduce( ) liberally or you may have occasion to curse this Fraction class.

Table 8-1 lists a sampling of methods available on the Fraction class.

Table 8-1. Methods on Commons Lang Fraction

Method	Description
abs( )	Returns the absolute value of a Fraction
add(Fraction fraction)	Adds two Fraction objects together
subtract(Fraction fraction)	Subtracts the parameter from the current Fraction
multiplyBy(Fraction fraction)	Multiplies the parameter by the current Fraction
divideBy(Fraction fraction)	Divides the current Fraction by the parameter
reduce( )	Reduces the Fraction to the smallest denominator
negate( )	Returns $-1 *$ Fraction
invert( )	Swaps the numerator and denominator
getNumerator( )	Returns the numerator
getDenominator( )	Returns the denominator
getProperNumerator( )	Returns the proper numerator
getProperWhole( )	Returns the proper whole number
pow( )	Raises a Fraction to the specified power

See Also

For more information about downloading Commons Lang, see Recipe 1.1.

8.2 Finding the Maximum and Minimum in an Array

Problem

You need to retrieve the maximum and minimum values from a double[], float[], long[], int[], short[], or byte[].

Solution

Use Commons Lang NumberUtils.max( ) and NumberUtils.min( ) to retrieve the minimum or maximum values from an array of primitives. The following code retrieves the minimum and maximum values from a double[]:

```
import org.apache.commons.lang.math.NumberUtils;

double[] array = {0.2, 0.4, 0.5, -3.0, 4.223, 4.226};

double max = NumberUtils.max( array ); // returns 4.226
double min = NumberUtils.min( array ); // returns -3.0
```

Discussion

NumberUtils.min( ) and NumberUtils.max( ) both accept double[], float[], long[], int[], short[], and byte[]. If the array is empty or null, both NumberUtils.min( ) and NumberUtils.max( ) will return an IllegalArgumentException.

Jakarta Commons Math also contains a class that can find the minimum and maximum value in a double[]. The following example uses the Max and Min classes from Commons Math to evaluate a double[]:

```
import org.apache.commons.math.stat.univariate.rank.Max;
import org.apache.commons.math.stat.univariate.rank.Min;

double[] array = {0.2, 0.4, 0.5, -3.0, 4.223, 4.226};

Max maximum = new Max( );
Min minimum = new Min( );

double max = maximum.evaluate( array, 0, array.length );
double min = minimum.evaluate( array, 0, array.length );
```

8.3 Using Number Ranges

Problem

You need to define a range of acceptable values for a variable, and test to see if that variable is within those boundaries.

Solution

Use an implementation of Range, an interface that defines a simple numerical range. There are a number of different implementations for different types: NumberRange, DoubleRange, FloatRange, IntRange, and LongRange. The following example demonstrates the use of DoubleRange to verify that a variable is within a valid range. A DoubleRange is created with minimum and maximum values, and a value is tested by DoubleRange using a method named containsDouble( ):

```
import org.apache.commons.lang.math.DoubleRange;
import org.apache.commons.lang.math.Range;

Range safeSpeed = new DoubleRange( 0.0, 65.0 );

double currentSpeed = getCurrentSpeed( );
if( !safeSpeed.containsDouble( currentSpeed ) ) {
    System.out.println( "Warning, current speed is unsafe." );
}
```

Discussion

Additionally, one can also test to see if another Range is contained within a Range, or if a Range overlaps another Range. The following example demonstrates the use of containsRange( ) to determine if a Range is entirely contained within another Range:

```
import org.apache.commons.lang.math.Range;
import org.apache.commons.lang.math.IntRange;
import org.apache.commons.lang.math.NumberUtils;

double recordHigh = getRecordHigh( );
double recordLow = getRecordLow( );

IntRange recordRange = new IntRange( recordLow, recordHigh );

int todayTemp = getTodaysMaxTemp( );
IntRange daysRange = new IntRange( NumberUtils.min( todayTemp ),
                                   NumberUtils.max( todayTemp ) );

if( !recordRange.containsRange( todayTemp ) ) {
    System.out.println( "Today is a record temperature day!" );
}
```

The previous code creates a Range, recordRange, from the record high and low temperatures. It then creates daysRange, which is a Range of the current day's high and low temperatures. If dayRange is not entirely contained within the recordRange, then the current day contains a record temperature and recordRange.containsRange(daysRange) will return false. containsRange( ) returns true if every value in the containing range occurs in the contained range, and overlapsRange( ) returns true if two Range objects share any common value. NumberUtils is used to retrieve the maximum and minimum values from the todayTemp array.

In another example, a Range object is used to ascertain the state of an element from a temperature measurement. Elemental Gold (Au) melts at 1337.33 Kelvin and boils at 3129.15 Kelvin. The following code is used to read the temperature from a thermometer and print the current state of the element:

```
import org.apache.commons.lang.math.Range;
import org.apache.commons.lang.math.DoubleRange;

double melting = 1337.33;
double boiling = 3129.15

// State ranges for element Au
Object[] stateRanges =
    new Object[][]{{"solid" , new DoubleRange( 0.0, melting )},
                   {"liquid", new DoubleRange( melting, boiling )},
                   {"gas", new DoubleRange( boiling,Double.INFINITY) };

// Read measurement from thermometer
double temp = themometer.getReading( );
String state = "unknown";

// Test the state
for( int i = 0; i < stateRanges.length; i++ ) {
    DoubleRange stateRange = (DoubleRange) stateRanges[i][1];
    if( stateRange.contains( temp ) ) {
        state = (String) stateRanges[i][0];
    }
}

System.out.println( "The substance is in a " + state + " state." );

// If the temperature is a temperate 293 K, this line would print
// "The Gold is in a solid state."
```

The ranges in this example overlap; the solid range ends at melting, and the liquid range begins at melting. Because each Range is tested in a defined order, each Range object in this example is lower- and upper-bound inclusive. If the temp variable has the same value as melting, the program will indicate solid state, and if the temp variable has the same value as boiling, this program will signify the liquid state.

See Also

For more information about downloading Commons Lang, see Recipe 1.1.

8.4   Generating Random Variables

Problem

J2SE 1.4 includes a java.lang.Math class that provides a mechanism to get a random double value between 0.0 and 1.0, but you need to create random boolean values, or random int variables between zero and a specified number.

Solution

Generate random variables with Commons Lang RandomUtils, which provides a mechanism to generate random int, long, float, double, and boolean variables. The following code generates a random integer between zero and the value specified in the parameter to nextInt( ):

```
import org.apache.commons.lang.math.RandomUtils;

// Create a random integer between 0 and 30
int maxVal = 30;
int randomInt = RandomUtils.nextInt( maxVal );
```

Or, if your application needs a random boolean variable, create one with a call to the static method nextBoolean( ):

```
import org.apache.commons.lang.math.RandomUtils;

boolean randomBool = RandomUtils.nextBoolean( );
```

Discussion

A frequent argument for not using a utility like RandomUtils is that the same task can be achieved with only one line of code. For example, if you need to retrieve a random integer between 0 and 32, you could write the following code:

```
int randomInt = (int) Math.floor( (Math.random( ) * (double) maxVal) );
```

While this statement may seem straightforward, it does contain a conceptual complexity not present in RandomUtils.nextInt(maxVal). RandomUtils.nextInt(maxVal) is a simple statement: "I need a random integer between 0 and maxVal"; the statement without RandomUtils is translated to a more complex statement:

> I'm going to take a random double between 0.0 and 1.0, and multiply this number by maxVal, which has been cast to a double. This result should be a random double between 0.0 and maxVal, which I will then pass to Math.floor( ) and cast to an int.

While the previous statement does achieve the same task as RandomUtils, it does so by rolling-up multiple statements into a single line of code: two casts, a call to floor( ), a call to random( ), and a multiplication. You may be able to instantly recognize this pattern as code that retrieves a random integer, but someone else may have a completely different approach. When you start to use some of the smaller utilities from

Jakarta Commons systemwide, an application will tend toward greater readability; these small reductions in conceptual complexity quickly add up.

8.5 Obtaining Commons Math

Problem

You need to use Jakarta Commons Math to work with complex numbers, matrices, statistics, or linear equations.

Solution

Download Jakarta Commons Math and put the necessary JAR files in your classpath. Because Commons Math has not yet been released, you will need to download the latest nightly snapshot of Commons Math from *http://cvs.apache.org/builds/ jakarta-commons/nightly/commons-math/*. Once you have downloaded the latest nightly build, uncompress the distribution, and place the *commons-math-1.0-RC1. jar* file in your classpath.

Discussion

Jakarta Commons Math was created to provide some more advanced mathematical capabilities under an Apache-style license. Commons Math provides classes to work with complex numbers, utilities to calculate statistics, a matrix implementation, special functions, continued fractions, root-finding, interpolation, and bivariate regression. Commons Math depends on Commons Collections 3.0, Commons Lang 2.0, and Commons Logging 1.0.3. To obtain these dependencies, see Recipes 1.1, 5.1, and 7.9.

 By the time this book is published, Commons Math 1.0 may be released. Make sure you look at the Commons Math project page (*http://jakarta.apache.org/commons/math*) and check for a release before downloading.

While the previous four recipes demonstrated classes and utilities available in Jakarta Commons Lang, the next five recipes demonstrate classes and utilities from Jakarta Commons Math. Simpler math utilities, which have wide application, will frequently be included in Commons Lang, and more complex utilities will be added to Commons Math. As both components continue to evolve, you may notice some overlap between the feature-set of Commons Lang and Commons Math.

See Also

Commons Math is a relatively new math library primarily motivated by licensing and community issues; all established math libraries were covered under a GPL or LGPL license. The Jakarta Commons community saw an opportunity to create a library, and through the hard work of a few dedicated developers in Commons, a very useful math library will soon be released. That being said, if you need a more mature math library, and your project can use LGPL components, look at the Colt Distribution from CERN (*http://hoschek.home.cern.ch/hoschek/colt/*).

For the authoritative cookbook of mathematics, pick up a copy of *Numerical Recipes in C++* or *Numerical Recipes in C* (Cambridge University Press). These classic tomes contain a huge library of code and examples, but be forewarned, the mathematics will quickly intimidate the faint of math. More information about this indispensable text can be found at the Numerical Recipes website (*http://www.nr.com/*). Unlike all the components described throughout this book, the code and examples from both of these books is covered under a very restrictive license described at *http://www.numerical-recipes.com/infotop.html#distinfo*.

8.6 Calculating Simple Univariate Statistics

Problem

You need to calculate univariate statistics such as mean, median, variance, minimum and maximum.

Solution

Use Commons Math's StatUtils to calculate simple univariate statistics. The following example uses StatUtils to calculate simple statistics for a double[ ]:

```
import org.apache.commons.math.stat.StatUtils;

double[] values = new double[] { 2.3, 5.4, 6.2, 7.3, 23.3 };

System.out.println( "min: " + StatUtils.min( values ) );
System.out.println( "max: " + StatUtils.max( values ) );
System.out.println( "mean: " + StatUtils.mean( values ) );
System.out.println( "product: " + StatUtils.product( values ) );
System.out.println( "sum: " + StatUtils.sum( values ) );
System.out.println( "variance: " + StatUtils.variance( values ) );
```

This code executes and prints a few simple statistics to the console, as follows:

```
min: 2.3
max: 23.3
mean: 8.9
product: 13097.61036
sum: 44.5
variance: 68.25500000000001
```

Discussion

StatUtils delegates these calculations to functors in the `org.apache.commons.math.stat.univariate.moment`, `org.apache.commons.math.stat.univariate.rank`, and `org.apache.commons.math.stat.univariate.summary` packages. The following example uses the individual classes from these packages to recreate the previous example, and it adds some measures not available in StatUtil:

```
import org.apache.commons.math.stat.univariate.moment.*;
import org.apache.commons.math.stat.univariate.rank.*;
import org.apache.commons.math.stat.univariate.summary.*;

// Measures from previous example
Min min = new Min();
Max max = new Max();
Mean mean = new Mean();
Product product = new Product();
Sum sum = new Sum();
Variance variance = new Variance();

System.out.println( "min: " + min.evaluate( values ) );
System.out.println( "max: " + max.evaluate( values ) );
System.out.println( "mean: " + mean.evaluate( values ) );
System.out.println( "product: " + product.evaluate( values ) );
System.out.println( "sum: " + sum.evaluate( values ) );
System.out.println( "variance: " + variance.evaluate( values ) );

// New measures
Percentile percentile = new Percentile();
GeometricMean geoMean = new GeometricMean();
Skewness skewness = new Skewness();
Kurtosis kurtosis = new Kurtosis();

System.out.println( "80 percentile value: " +
                    percentile.evaluate( values, 80.0 ) );
System.out.println( "geometric mean: " + geoMean.evaluate( values ) );
System.out.println( "skewness: " + skewness.evaluate( values ) );
System.out.println( "kurtosis: " + kurtosis.evaluate( values ) );
```

The previous example adds percentile, geometric mean, standard deviation, skewness, and kurtosis to the available univariate statistics. The previous example produces the following output:

```
min: 2.3
max: 23.3
mean: 8.9
product: 13097.61036
sum: 44.5
variance: 68.25500000000001
80 percentile value: 20.099999999999998
geometric mean: 6.659450778469037
standard dev: 8.261658429153314
skewness: 1.9446683453691376
kurtosis: 4.102348153299074
```

See Also

If you need a formal definition of a specific moment, rank, or summary, see Math-World (*http://mathworld.wolfram.com*), an invaluable mathematical reference site from Wolfram, the makers of Mathematica.

8.7 Solving a System of Linear Equations

Problem

You need to find the values of x, y, and z that satisfy the system of linear equations shown in Figure 8-2.

$$3x + 20y + 89z = 1324$$
$$4x + 40y + 298z = 2999$$
$$7x - 21y + 0.42z = 2039$$

Figure 8-2. A system of linear equations

Solution

Use the `RealMatrix` and `RealMatrixImpl` from Commons Math. Represent this system of linear equations as matrices in the *Ax=B* form, as shown in Figure 8-3. Place the coefficients of *A* in a `RealMatrix`, and put *B* in a `double[]`. Call the `solve()` method on `RealMatrix` to retrieve a `double[]` of values for x, y, and z that satisfy this system of equations.

$$\begin{bmatrix} 3 & 20 & 89 \\ 4 & 40 & 298 \\ 7 & 21 & 0.42 \end{bmatrix} \begin{bmatrix} x \\ y \\ z \end{bmatrix} = \begin{bmatrix} 1324 \\ 2999 \\ 2039 \end{bmatrix}$$

Figure 8-3. System of linear equations in Ax=B form

The following example takes the coefficients and constants from Figure 8-3 and uses a `RealMatrix` to solve this system:

```
import org.apache.commons.math.linear.RealMatrix;
import org.apache.commons.math.linear.RealMatrixImpl;
import org.apache.commons.lang.ArrayUtils;

double[][] coefficients = { { 3.0, 20.0, 89.0 },
                            { 4.0, 40.0, 298.0 },
                            { 7.0, 21.0, 0.42 } };
double[] values = { 1324, 2999, 2039 };
```

```
RealMatrix matrix = new RealMatrixImpl( );
matrix.setData( coefficients );

double[] answers = matrix.solve( values );

System.out.println( "Answers: " + ArrayUtils.toString( answers ) );
```

This example solves this system of equations and prints out the values of x, y, and z using Commons Lang `ArrayUtils` to print a `double[]`:

```
Answers: {400.4839095455532,-36.59139305646149,9.599731825759218}
```

Using Commons Math, we find that the following values satisfy this system of equations: $x = 400$, $y = -36$, and $z = 9.6$.

Discussion

To solve these equations, a `double[][]` of coefficients is created to represent a 3×3 matrix, and a `double[]` of constants is created. The `RealMatrix` interface is implemented by `RealMatrixImpl`, which stores a matrix as a `double[][]`; to populate this `double[][]`, pass the `double[][]`, coefficients, to the `setData( )` method of `RealMatrixImpl`. To solve the system, the values `double[]` is passed to `matrix.solve( )`, and a `double[]` containing x, y, and z is returned.

This method will not work for every matrix; there are systems of linear equations that are unsolvable. For example, if one attempts to find values for the system of equations from Figure 8-4, an `InvalidMatrixException` will be thrown stating that the matrix is singular. Additionally, if the number of rows in *B* does not equal the number of columns in *A*, `solve( )` will throw an `InvalidMatrixException`.

$$x + y + z = 1$$
$$x + y - z = 35$$
$$x - y + z = 23$$

Figure 8-4. An unsolvable system of equations

See Also

For more information about solving systems of linear equations (or, for that matter, information about anything), see Wikipedia (*http://en.wikipedia.org/wiki/System_of_linear_equations*). `RealMatixImpl` uses a process known as LU decomposition to solve this system of equations. For more information about LU decomposition, see the JavaDoc for the `org.apache.commons.math.linear` package (*http://jakarta.apache.org/commons/math/apidocs/index.html*).

8.8   Arithmetic with Complex Numbers

Problem

You need to perform arithmetic with complex numbers. For example, given the complex numbers *A*, *B*, *C*, and *E* and two equations shown in Figure 8-5, you need to find the real part of *F* and the imaginary part of *D*.

$$(A+B)/C=D$$
$$D*xE=F$$
$$Answer = Re(F)/Im(D)$$

Figure 8-5. Expressions evaluated with the Complex object

Solution

Use Commons Math `Complex` and `ComplexMath` classes to represent complex numbers and perform arithmetic using complex numbers. Use the `ComplexFormat` class to print the real and imaginary parts of a complex number. The following example demonstrates the use of the `Complex` class to calculate *D* and *F* from Figure 8-5 using arbitrary values for *A*, *B*, *C*, and *E*:

```
import org.apache.commons.math.complex.Complex;
import org.apache.commons.math.complex.ComplexFormat;

Complex a = new Complex(2, 3);
Complex b = new Complex(4, 5);
Complex c = new Complex(0.3, 2);
Complex e = new Complex(4, 4);

Complex sum = a.add( b );
Complex d = c.divide( sum );
Complex f = e.multiply( d.conjugate() );

System.out.println( "D is: " + ComplexFormat.formatComplex( d ) );
System.out.println( "F is: " + ComplexFormat.formatComplex( f ) );

double realF = f.getReal();
double imD = d.getImaginary();
double answer = realF / imD;

System.out.println( "Answer Re(F)/Im(D): " +
        NumberFormat.getInstance().format( answer ) );
```

The variables a, b, c, and e are created using arbitrary values, and an intermediate `Complex` object sum is calculated by adding b to a—a.add(b). d is calculated by dividing this intermediate sum by c: c.divide(sum). f is calculated by multiplying e times the complex conjugate of d: e.multiply(d.conjugate()). The final answer is calculated by taking the real part of f (f.getReal()) and dividing that by the imaginary part of d: d.getImaginary( ). The previous example performs complex arithmetic and prints the following to the console:

```
D is: 0.18 + 0.1i
F is: 1.1 + 0.33i
Answer Re(F)/Im(D): 11.417
```

Discussion

The previous example used the ComplexFormat class to create a String representation of a Complex object. This class allows you to print out the complex number *N* in the format *Re(N) + Im(N)i*. This class also has a constructor that takes a String to use instead of "i." In electrical engineering, where "i" is frequently used to refer to current, complex impedance is represented using a "j" instead of an "i." To print a complex number using a "j", write the following code:

```
Complex impedance = new Complex( 1.0, 2.0 );
ComplexFormat format = new ComplexFormat("j");
System.out.println( "Impedance: " + format.format( impedance ) );
```

The previous code prints the following output to the console:

```
Impedance: 1.0 + 2.0j
```

The Complex object contains simple arithmetic methods such as add( ), subtract( ), multiply( ), divide( ), conjugate( ), and negate( ). More advanced methods are available as static methods on the ComplexMath class. ComplexMath includes trigonometric methods such as sin( ), sinh( ), cos( ), and tan( ), as well as methods to calculate logarithms and to take the square root of a Complex object.

See also

For more information about the ComplexMath utility, see the Commons Math Java-Doc at *http://jakarta.apache.org/commons/math/apidocs/index.html*.

8.9 Establishing Relationships Between Variables

Problem

You need to establish a relationship between two independent variables. These variables could be temperature versus energy use or the number of news channels versus stress-related ailments; you need to measure the correlation between two variables.

Solution

Add data points to an instance of Commons Math SimpleRegression. This class will calculate the slope, slope confidence, and a measure of relatedness known as R-square. The SimpleRegression class performs a least squares regression with one independent variable; adding data points to this model refines parameters to the equation $y = ax + b$. The following code uses SimpleRegression to find a relationship between two series of values *[0, 1, 2, 3, 4, 5]* and *[0, 1.2, 2.6, 3.2, 4, 5]*:

```
import orgorg.apache.commons.math.stat.multivariate.SimpleRegression;

SimpleRegression sr = new SimpleRegression( );

// Add data points
sr.addData( 0, 0 );
sr.addData( 1, 1.2 );
sr.addData( 2, 2.6 );
sr.addData( 3, 3.2 );
sr.addData( 4, 4 );
sr.addData( 5, 5 );

// Print the value of y when line intersects the y axis
System.out.println( "Intercept: " + sr.getIntercept() );

// Print the number of data points
System.out.println( "N: " + sr.getN() );

// Print the Slope and the Slop Confidence
System.out.println( "Slope: " + sr.getSlope() );
System.out.println( "Slope Confidence: " + sr.getSlopeConfidenceInterval() );

// Print RSquare a measure of relatedness
System.out.println( "RSquare: " + sr.getRSquare() );
```

This example passes six data points to SimpleRegression and prints the slope, number of data points, and R-square from SimpleRegression:

```
Intercept: 0.238
N: 6
Slope: 0.971
Slope Confidence: 0.169
RSquare: 0.985
```

Discussion

R-square is the square of something called the Pearson's product moment correlation coefficient, which can be obtained by calling getR( ) on SimpleRegression. R-square is a determination of correlation between two series of numbers. The parameters to the addData( ) method of SimpleRegression are a corresponding x and y value in two sets of data. If R-square is 1.0, the model shows that as x increases linearly, y increases linearly. In the previous example, R-square is 0.98, and this demonstrates that the (x,y) data points added to SimpleRegression have a strong linear relationship.

If R-square is −1.0, x increases linearly as y decreases linearly. A value of 0.0 shows that the relationship between x and y is not linear. The following example demonstrates two series of numbers with no relationship:

```
import org.apache.commons.math.stat.multivariate.SimpleRegression;

SimpleRegression sr = new SimpleRegression( );
sr.addData( 400, 100 );
sr.addData( 300, 105 );
sr.addData( 350, 70 );
sr.addData( 200, 50 );
sr.addData( 150, 300 );
sr.addData( 50, 500 );

// Print RSquare a measure of relatedness
System.out.println( "RSquare: " + sr.getRSquare( ) );
```

The data points added to this `SimpleRegression` are all over the map; x and y are unrelated, and the R-square value for this set of data points is very close to zero:

```
Intercept: 77.736
N: 12
Slope: 0.142
Slope Confidence: 0.699
RSquare: 0.02
```

The (x,y) data points supplied to the previous example have no linear correlation. This doesn't prove that there is no relationship between x and y, but it does prove that the relationship is not linear.

See Also

For more information about least squares, the technique used by `SimpleRegression`, see Wikipedia (*http://en.wikipedia.org/wiki/Least_squares*). More information about R and R-square can also be found on Wikipedia (*http://en.wikipedia.org/wiki/Pearson_product-moment_correlation_coefficient*).

8.10 Estimating the Amount of Time Left in a Process

Problem

You are running a program that takes a long time to execute, and you need to present the user with an estimated time until completion.

Solution

Use Commons Math's `SimpleRegression` and Commons Lang's `StopWatch` to create a `ProcessEstimator` class that can be used to predict when a particular program will be finished. Your program needs to process a number of records, and this program could take a few hours to finish. You would like to provide some feedback, and, if you are confident that each record will take roughly the same amount of time, you can use SimpleRegression's slope and intercept to estimate the time when all records will be processed. Example 8-1 defines the ProcessEstimator class that combines the power of StopWatch and ProcessEstimator to estimate the time remaining in a process.

Example 8-1. ProcessEstimator to estimate time of program execution

```
package com.discursive.jccook.math.timeestimate;

import org.apache.commons.lang.time.StopWatch;
import org.apache.commons.math.stat.multivariate.SimpleRegression;

public class ProcessEstimator {

    private SimpleRegression regression = new SimpleRegression();
    private StopWatch stopWatch = new StopWatch();

    // Total number of units
    private int units = 0;

    // Number of units completed
    private int completed = 0;

    // Sample rate for regression
    private int sampleRate = 1;

    public ProcessEstimator( int numUnits, int sampleRate ) {
        this.units = numUnits;
        this.sampleRate = sampleRate;
    }

    public void start() {
        stopWatch.start();
    }

    public void stop() {
        stopWatch.stop();
    }

    public void unitCompleted() {
        completed++;

        if( completed % sampleRate == 0 ) {
            long now = System.currentTimeMillis();
            regression.addData( units - completed, stopWatch.getTime() );
        }
    }
}
```

Example 8-1. ProcessEstimator to estimate time of program execution (continued)

```
    public long projectedFinish( ) {
        return (long) regression.getIntercept( );
    }

    public long getTimeSpent( ) {
        return stopWatch.getTime( );
    }

    public long projectedTimeRemaining( ) {
        long timeRemaining = projectedFinish() - getTimeSpent( );
        return timeRemaining;
    }

    public int getUnits( ) {
        return units;
    }

    public int getCompleted( ) {
        return completed;
    }

}
```

ProcessEstimator has a constructor that takes the number of records to process and the sample rate to measure progress. With 10,000 records to process and a sample of 100, the SimpleRegression will add a data point of units remaining versus time elapsed after every 100 records. As the program continues to execute, projectedTimeRemaining( ) will return an updated estimation of time remaining by retrieving the y-intercept from SimpleRegression and subtracting the time already spent in execution. The y-intercept from SimpleRegression represents the y value when x equals zero, where x is the number of records remaining; as x decreases, y increases, and y represents the total time elapsed to process all records.

The ProcessEstimationExample in Example 8-2 uses the ProcessEstimator to estimate the time remaining while calling the performLengthyProcess( ) method 10,000 times.

Example 8-2. An example using the ProcessEstimator

```
package com.discursive.jccook.math.timeestimate;

import org.apache.commons.lang.math.RandomUtils;

public class ProcessEstimationExample {

    private ProcessEstimator estimate;

    public static void main(String[] args) {
        ProcessEstimationExample example = new ProcessEstimationExample( );
        example.begin( );
    }
```

Example 8-2. An example using the ProcessEstimator (continued)

```
    public void begin( ) {
        estimate = new ProcessEstimator( 10000, 100 );
        estimate.start( );

        for( int i = 0; i < 10000; i++ ) {
            // Print status every 1000 items
            printStatus(i);
            performLengthyProcess( );
            estimate.unitCompleted( );
        }

        estimate.stop( );

        System.out.println( "Completed " + estimate.getUnits( ) + " in " +
                Math.round( estimate.getTimeSpent( ) / 1000 ) + " seconds." );
    }

    private void printStatus(int i) {
        if( i % 1000 == 0 ) {
            System.out.println( "Completed: " + estimate.getCompleted( ) +
                                " of " + estimate.getUnits( ) );

            System.out.println( "\tTime Spent: " +
                                 Math.round( estimate.getTimeSpent( ) / 1000) +
                                 " sec" + ", Time Remaining: " +
                        Math.round( estimate.projectedTimeRemaining( ) / 1000) +
                                 " sec" );
        }
    }

    private void performLengthyProcess( ) {
        try {
            Thread.sleep(RandomUtils.nextInt(10));
        } catch( Exception e ) {}
    }
}
```

After each call to performLengthyProcess( ), the unitCompleted( ) method on ProcessEstimator is invoked. Every 100th call to unitComplete( ) causes ProcessEstimator to update SimpleRegression with the number of records remaining and the amount of time spent so far. After every 1000th call to performLengthyProcess( ), a status message is printed to the console as follows:

```
Completed: 0 of 10000
    Time Spent: 0 sec, Time Remaining: 0 sec
Completed: 1000 of 10000
    Time Spent: 4 sec, Time Remaining: 42 sec
Completed: 2000 of 10000
    Time Spent: 9 sec, Time Remaining: 38 sec
Completed: 3000 of 10000
    Time Spent: 14 sec, Time Remaining: 33 sec
Completed: 4000 of 10000
```

```
    Time Spent: 18 sec, Time Remaining: 28 sec
Completed: 5000 of 10000
    Time Spent: 24 sec, Time Remaining: 23 sec
Completed: 6000 of 10000
    Time Spent: 28 sec, Time Remaining: 19 sec
Completed: 7000 of 10000
    Time Spent: 33 sec, Time Remaining: 14 sec
Completed: 8000 of 10000
    Time Spent: 38 sec, Time Remaining: 9 sec
Completed: 9000 of 10000
    Time Spent: 43 sec, Time Remaining: 4 sec
Completed 10000 in 47 seconds.
```

As shown above, the output periodically displays the amount of time you can expect the program to continue executing. Initially, there is no data to make a prediction with, so the ProcessEstimator returns zero seconds, but, as the program executes the performLengthyProcess( ) method 10,000 times, a meaningful time remaining is produced.

Discussion

The previous example used a method that sleeps for a random number of milliseconds between 1 and 10, and this value is selected using the RandomUtils class described in Recipe 8.4. It is easy to predict how long this process is going to take because, on average, each method call is going to sleep for five milliseconds. The ProcessEstimator is inaccurate when the amount of time to process each record takes a steadily increasing or decreasing amount of time, or if there is a block of records that takes substantially more or less time to process. If the amount of time to process each record does not remain constant, then the relationship between records processed and time elapsed is not linear. Because the ProcessEstimator uses a linear model, SimpleRegression, a nonconstant execution time will produce inaccurate predictions for time remaining. If you are using the ProcessEstimator, make sure that it takes roughly the same amount of time to process each record.

See Also

This recipe refers to the StopWatch class from Commons Lang. For more information about the StopWatch class, see Recipe 1.19.

## CHAPTER 9

Templating

9.0 Introduction

Systems designed without clear separation between presentation and application logic quickly become chores to maintain. Trivial look-and-feel updates in such applications take days or weeks, and trying to extend such a coupled architecture can introduce unmanageable risks and code that is impossible to unit test. To minimize the possibility of creating such disasters, avoid coupling presentation and application logic through the use of a good templating engine. Maintain clear separation between presentation and application logic from the beginning—be orthogonal. Don't print out HTML, XML, or SQL from Java code, use a templating engine.

The simplest example of templating is Java's `MessageFormat`. A simple message, such as `Hello {0}, I speak {1}`, can be parameterized using the `MessageFormat` class. A more complex templating example is found in applications that use Jakarta Velocity or FreeMarker to avoid mixing Java with HTML or textual output. Throughout this spectrum of complexity, the concept of templating remains the same; a template with references to variables is merged with a context containing these variables. There are many ways to decouple the rigors of logic from the prettiness of presentation, and after reading this chapter, you will have a range of options for different situations.

This chapter touches upon Jakarta Velocity, Jakarta Commons JEXL, and a technology outside of the Apache Software Foundation named FreeMarker. Templating engines are frequently used in web application, and this chapter ends with instructions for integrating these engines into a J2EE web application. Separating HTML or textual content into a separate file allows you to give graphic designers and business users a larger role in customizing and creating content for the enduser. With a templating engine, you can dramatically reduce the time and effort it takes to make simple changes. But, by far, the largest benefit of a templating engine is that it allows programmers to do more programming and graphic designers to do more designing by reducing needless coupling of presentation markup and compiled application logic.

Common Templating Problems in Applications

Server-side Java has won a fair amount of attention over the past five years, but developers seldom consider using templating engines when writing a standalone Java application. Consider the following code, which prints a formatted report for a bank customer:

```
System.out.println( "*****************************" );
System.out.println( "******* BANK STATEMENT *******" );
System.out.println( "*****************************" );
Account[] accounts = AccountUtil.getAccounts("1232");
double total = 0.0;
for( int i = 0; i < accounts.length; i++ ) {
    System.out.println( "Account: " +
        accounts[i].getBalance() );
    total += accounts[i].getBalance();
}
System.out.println( "Total: " + total );
System.out.println( "*****************************" );
```

In this example, textual content is mixed with Java code, and a programmer must be involved in any change to the look and feel of the report. If this report were generated using an external template, a nonprogrammer could be trained to change the report, or the customers could customize the output of this program by modifying a template with straightforward syntax.

Consider another common problem: generating an XML document. There are seemingly thousands of ways to create an XML document: using DOM or JDOM to create a Document object, serializing an object with Jakarta Commons Betwixt, and using Exolab's Castor are a few of these possibilities. Some of these techniques are explained in Chapter 6, but here is an example of how not to generate an XML document:

```
System.out.println("<?xml version=\"1.0\"?>");
System.out.println("<Config>");
System.out.println("<Property name=\"" + name + "\"\n" +
                "value=\"" + value + "\"/>");
System.out.println("</Config>");
```

Avoid this practice at all costs. Here are a few red flags from the previous two examples:

Mixed languages

Nesting an XML document into a Java class by way of printing out String literals is unreadable. When you need to mentally decode heavily escaped XML nested in Java, you are asking yourself to do too much at once. You will also end up with mixed context, an XML element starting within a pair of parentheses, and ending in another. In this fugue of forward and back slashes, one misplaced slash produces an invalid XML document, or one overlooked NullPointerException causes a catastrophe. You are asking your brain to compile two strands of code with intertwined and overlapping syntax. While your compiler might not complain, your system will be difficult to maintain. Code that is difficult to comprehend is even more difficult to maintain.

Escaped characters in compiled code

Escaping characters in String literals quickly becomes an annoyance, especially if the strings to be encoded contain back slashes and double quotes. I accept that the String *c:\temp\blah.txt*, must be written as c:\\temp\\blah.txt, but I don't enjoy doing it. How confusing is a literal \"c:\\temp\\\"? Avoid this entirely by using a templating engine or externalizing strings in properties files.

Mixing presentation with conditional or iterative logic

A previous example printed each account balance in a for loop. A common trick in JSP is to create a while loop with JSP scriptlets, surrounding the code to be executed with <% while(i < 4) { %> and <% } %>. Templating languages such as Velocity or even JSP 2.0 with JSTL support conditional and iterative operations without asking you to mix languages.

There are other opportunities for using a template in an application. These include code generation, creating SQL scripts, and interacting with an interpreted language via generated scripts. The list continues, and it proves that templating isn't just for making web pages.

Templating in Web Applications

Examine the JSP code below (the variable names have been changed to protect the innocent). Take this code and multiply it by 100 or 200 pages. Now, what happens when you want to move from PostgreSQL to Oracle? Do you do a global search and replace on the driver class name and the JDBC URL? Or, even worse, what happens when someone asks you to translate the entire site to Chinese in two weeks? It would be easier to learn Chinese in two weeks than it would be to internationalize this code. The offending JSP is:

```
<% ResultSet rs;
   try {
     Class.forName( "org.postgresql.Driver" );
     String dbURL = "jdbc:postgresql://192.168.0.1/dbname";
     Connection dbCon =
         DriverManager.getConnection( dbURL, "system", "");

     PreparedStatement ps =
         dbCon.prepareStatement( "select * from Offer " +
                               "where id = ?" );
     ps.setString( 1, request.getAttribute("id") );
     rs = ps.executeQuery();
       rs.next();
   } catch( Exception e ) {
       %><%= Something bad happened, Call Jack (800) 232-2233 %>
<% } %>
```

```
<jsp:include page="header.html" />

Hello <%= rs.getString("name") %>,

I would like to inform you of a good offer.
<%= rs.getString("offerText") %>

There are a few things I would like to tell you.
<ul>
  <% Thing[] things = OfferUtil.getThings( rs.getString("id") );
     for( int i = 0; i < things.length; i++ ) { %>
     <li><%= things[i].getText( )%></li>
  <% } %>
</ul>

<jsp:include page="footer.html" />
```

 This is real code from a real system, and it was written by a whole team of programmers who didn't find anything terribly wrong with this style. If you were raised on JSP like this, you might not recognize some of the problems. What is wrong with the previous example? Four different "languages" are combined in one file (Java, SQL, HTML, and JSP); the page starts off with JSP scriptlets, then the example contains Java code that prints out HTML and generates SQL statements. Lastly, this particular JSP page forgets to close the connection it created to the database—something that could easily create a resource leak under a heavy load. Make it simpler, use a templating engine (or upgrade to JSP 2.0) and never write a line of Java in a JSP again.

Velocity, JEXL, and FreeMarker are remedies for the coupling issues demonstrated in the previous examples. Each of these tools can be integrated into any application in a matter of minutes. In this chapter, you will learn techniques for separating presentation logic from behavioral (or business) logic. At the end of the chapter, I will briefly explain how you can integrate all of these utilities into a J2EE web application.

9.1   Obtaining Commons JEXL

Problem

You need to use Jakarta Commons JEXL to evaluate a simple expression that contains references to variables and object properties.

Solution

You must download the latest version of Commons JEXL, and place the Commons JEXL JAR in your project's classpath. Follow the steps outlined in Recipe 1.1, downloading Commons JEXL 1.0 instead of Commons Lang.

Commons JEXL depends on Commons Logging 1.0.3, which can be downloaded from the same location as Commons JEXL.

Discussion

Commons JEXL is an expression language interpreter influenced by the expression language features of JSP 2.0; JEXL is an extended version of JSP 2.0 EL that does not depend on the Servlet API. This means that it can be integrated into any application that needs to use an expression language.

 JEXL is similar to EL with one major difference. The JSP 2.0 EL implementation project in Jakarta Commons, Commons EL, is covered by a Java Specification Request (JSR), which was developed under the Java Community Process (JCP). Because of this, EL is bound to implement the JSP specification—no more and no less. On the other hand, JEXL is free to extend and improve upon the standard.

If you have a Maven project, which needs to use Commons JEXL, add a dependency on Commons JEXL 1.0 with the following section in *project.xml*:

```
<dependencies>
  <dependency>
    <id>commons-jexl</id>
    <version>1.0</version>
  </dependency>

  ....other dependencies...
</dependencies>
```

See Also

For more information about downloading Commons Logging 1.0.3, see Recipe 7.9.

To learn more about Commons JEXL, visit the Jakarta Commons JEXL web site (*http://jakarta.apache.org/commons/jexl/*).

If you have questions about how to use Jakarta Commons JEXL, you can join the *commons-user@jakarta.apache.org* mailing list. Refer to Recipe 1.2 for instructions on joining the Commons User mailing list.

For more information about the Java Community Process, see the JCP home at *http://www.jcp.org/en/home/index*.

9.2   Using an Expression Language

Problem

You need to parameterize text messages with variables and bean properties.

Solution

Use Commons JEXL to evaluate an expression containing references to bean properties. To reference properties of an object, create an expression using the bean property syntax introduced in Chapter 3. Surround each property reference with curly braces and a leading $, as in the following example:

```
${opera.name} was composed by ${opera.composer} in ${opera.year}.
```

Use the following code to "merge" an instance of the Opera bean with the above expression:

```
import org.apache.commons.jexl.Expression;
import org.apache.commons.jexl.ExpressionFactory;
import org.apache.commons.jexl.JexlContext;
import org.apache.commons.jexl.JexlHelper;

Opera opera = new Opera();
opera.setName("The Magic Flute");
opera.setComposer("Mozart");
opera.setYear(1791);

String expr =
    "${opera.name} was composed by ${opera.composer} in " +
    "${opera.year}.";

Expression e = ExpressionFactory.createExpression( expr );
JexlContext jc = JexlHelper.createContext();
jc.getVars().put("opera", opera);
String message = (String) e.evaluate(jc);

System.out.println( message );
```

This code puts an instance of the Opera bean in a JexlContext and evaluates the expression, producing the following output:

```
The Magic Flute was composed by Mozart in 1791.
```

Discussion

The previous example creates and populates an instance of the Opera bean: opera. An Expression object is then created by passing a String containing a JEXL expression to ExpressionFactory.createExpression(). A JexlContext is created with a call to JexlHelper.createContext(). This context contains a map-like structure that holds named variables, and the Opera object is added to the JexlContext under the name opera. Once an Expression and a JexlContext are created and populated, expression. evaluate() merges the expression with the context, and a message is generated. A JEXL expression evaluates to an Object, but, in this case, the expression evaluates to a String object, and the results of the evaluation are cast to a String.

This simple example sets the stage for a majority of recipes in this chapter; most templating engines involve the pattern established by the previous example. First, there is a template—in this case, a `String` that contains expressions that are to be replaced by bean properties. Second, a collection of named variables are put into a context. Lastly, the template is merged with the variables in the context.

This chapter makes heavy use of expressions in templating engines, and this is a logical time to introduce the concept of the syntax used to create expressions. If you are familiar with JavaServer Pages (JSPs) you may know about a tag library called the JavaServer Pages Standard Tag Library (JSTL), which is a set of standard JSP tag libraries that make creating JSP pages much easier. Along with JSTL came something called EL, which is an expression language you can use in JSTL tags and in JSP 2.0. In general, JEXL can do everything that JSP EL can do, and more. Table 9-1 lists expressions that are valid in both JSP 2.0 EL and Jakarta Commons JEXL.

Table 9-1. Simple Commons JEXL and JSP 2.0 EL expressions

EL expression	Evaluates to
`${true}`	true
`${1}`	The integer 1
`${'Hello'}`	The String "Hello"
`${'blah' == 'blah'}`	true
`${var == true}`	true if the variable named var is a Boolean true
`${x.a < 352}`	true if x.getA( ) is a number less than 352
`${ball.color == 'Green'}`	true if ball.getColor( ) equals "Green"
`${x == 2 || y == 4}`	true if x equals 2 or if y equals 4
`${thing.color.name}`	Retrieves the value of thing.getColor().getName( )
`${thing.shapes["circle"]}`	Retrieves the object stored under the key "circle" on the Map shapes, which is a bean property of thing
`${thing.someList[55]}`	Retrieves the object at index 54 of a List, someList, which is a bean property of thing
`${empty var}`	Evaluates to true if var is null or empty
`${!(y < 4)}`	true if y is not less than 4

See Also

For more information about JSP 2.0 Expression Language, see Hans Bergsten's article on *onJava.com* called "JSP 2.0: The New Deal, Part 1" (*http://www.onjava.com/pub/a/onjava/2003/11/05/jsp.html*) or his book *JavaServer Pages* (O'Reilly).

9.3   Invoking Methods in an Expression

Problem

You are trying to print out a message that contains data returned by a method.

Solution

Commons JEXL can evaluate any method that is made available to the interpreter. The following expression invokes the language( ) method on an Opera bean. The acts property of Opera is a List, and this expression invokes the size( ) method on this List to obtain the number of acts in the Opera:

```
${opera.name} was composed by ${opera.composer} in ${opera.year}.
This opera has ${opera.acts.size()}, and it is performed in ${opera.language()}
```

The following code creates and populates an expression and a context, merging the two to create a message:

```
import org.apache.commons.jexl.Expression;
import org.apache.commons.jexl.ExpressionFactory;
import org.apache.commons.jexl.JexlContext;
import org.apache.commons.jexl.JexlHelper;

Opera opera = new Opera();
opera.setName("The Magic Flute");
opera.setComposer("Mozart");
opera.setYear(1791);
opera.acts( new ArrayList(2) );

String expr =
    "${opera.name} was composed by ${opera.composer} in ${opera.year}.";
    "This opera has ${opera.acts.size()} acts, and it is performed in " +
    "${opera.language()}";

Expression e = ExpressionFactory.createExpression( expr );
JexlContext jc = JexlHelper.createContext();
jc.getVars().put("opera", opera);
String message = (String) e.evaluate(jc);

System.out.println( message );
```

The following message is printed to the console:

```
The Magic Flute was composed by Mozart in 1791.  This opera has
2 acts, and it is performed in German.
```

Discussion

This code is almost the same as the previous recipe, but you will notice that the expression contains a direct call to the opera.language( ) method and a call to the size( ) method on the acts property of opera.

Because JEXL is not governed by the Java Community Process (JCP), JEXL is free to extend the feature set of EL. Table 9-2 presents valid JEXL expressions that are actually *invalid* JSP 2.0 EL expressions.

Table 9-2. Extended capabilities of JEXL expression language

JEXL expression	Evaluates to
`${object.function()}`	Accessing any function on an object, this evaluates to the return value from this function.
`${"Wolfgang" +` `  " " + "Mozart"}`	JEXL supports string concatenation. This expression evaluates to "Wolfgang Mozart."
`${"Cow".size()}`	In JEXL you can get the size of a string like this. This expression evaluates to 3.
`${hashMap.size()}`	On a map, JEXL will return the number of keys.
`${arrayList.size()}`	Returns the size of a list.

See Also

For more information about Commons JEXL's improvements on JSP 2.0 EL, see the Commons JEXL page (*http://jakarta.apache.org/commons/jexl/*).

9.4   Externalizing Logic with an Expression Language

Problem

You need to capture application logic in an external file.

Solution

Use an external properties file to store expressions used in an application. For this recipe, imagine yourself creating a system to sort `Ball` objects based on a set of arbitrary criteria. Instead of hard-coding criteria in a series of Java if-else clauses, create a framework with loads sorting criteria from a properties file containing boolean JEXL expressions. For instance, the first line in this properties file would be:

```
Hvy-Green-Basket = ball.color == 'Green' && (ball.weight > 1000)
```

This translates to "If the ball's color is Green and the weight is over 1000, put this ball into the Heavy Green basket." The name of each property is the name of the basket into which a `Ball` matching the criteria is placed. The contents of the criteria file are:

```
Hvy-Green-Basket = ball.color == 'Green' && (ball.weight > 1000)
Sm-Yellow-bin = ball.color == 'Yellow' && (ball.weight < 100)
Transparent-Bin = ball.isTransparent()
Lrg-Yellow-Basket = ball.color == 'Yellow' &&(ball.weight >= 100)
Misc-Bin = true
```

Each criterion is applied to each Ball object in the order it appears in the criteria file. The heavy green sorting criteria is applied first, and each criterion is evaluated until the last criterion is reached. The last criteria always evaluates to true—similar to a switch-case control statement, the "Misc-bin" is the default. The following code reads this criteria file and evaluates each JEXL expression in order to sort a collection of Ball objects:

```
import org.apache.commons.jexl.Expression;
import org.apache.commons.jexl.ExpressionFactory;
import org.apache.commons.jexl.JexlContext;
import org.apache.commons.jexl.JexlHelper;

// Load in our criteria properties
Properties criteria = new Properties();
criteria.load( getClass().getResourceAsStream("criteria.txt") );

Set binNames = criteria.getKeys();

// Load our ball objects into a List
List balls = getBalls();
Iterator ballsIter = balls.iterator();
while( ballsIter.hasNext() ) {
    Ball ball = (Ball) ballsIter.next();

    // Iterate through every rule, until you find a match...
    Iterator binIter = binName.iterator();
    while( ruleIter.hasNext() ) {

        // Get the name of the basket
        String basket = (String) binIter.next();

        // Get the expression corresponding to this bin.
        String expr = conditions.get( bin );
        Expression e = ExpressionFactory.createExpression( expr );

        // Populate the context with the current Ball object
        JexlContext jc = JexlHelper.createContext();
        jc.getVars().put("ball", ball);

        // Evaluate the Expression.
        Boolean result = (Boolean) e.evaluate(jc);

        // If the expression evaluated to true, add this Ball to the bin.
        if( result.booleanValue() == true ) {
            sendBall( ball, basket );
        }
    }
}
```

The result of the Expression evaluation is a Boolean value, and, if the Boolean result is true, the matching Ball is sent to the specified basket.

Discussion

Using this technique, as the number of criteria increases, the code to implement this sorting algorithm remains unchanged. The behavior of the system can be altered by changing the criteria file; compiled code is left untouched. The code in this Solution section is longer than a series of if-else clauses to implement these criteria in code, but, as the number of sorting criteria increases, you will be glad you took the extra time to create a general solution without hard coding system behavior in Java code.

This was the first example that involved something more than printing out a pretty message for human consumption. JEXL has been used to create a "language" for sorting criteria; if a client wants to change the rules, you can now train someone familiar with simple logic statements to change a system to meet changing requirements.

See Also

This recipe demonstrated a system that uses a simple set of rules to categorize balls. For more information about a serious open source Rule Engine for Java named JESS, take a look at *http://herzberg.ca.sandia.gov/jess/index.shtml*. If you are interested in Rule Engines, take a look at JSR 94: Java Rule Engine API (*http://jcp.org/en/jsr/detail?id=94*) or Ernest Friedman-Hill's "Jess in Action" (Manning).

9.5   Obtaining Jakarta Velocity

Problem

You need to use Jakarta Velocity to create templates that can reference variables and object properties and contain limited conditional and iterative control structures.

Solution

You must download the latest version of Jakarta Velocity, and place the Velocity JAR in your project's classpath. Follow the steps outlined in Recipe 1.1, downloading Jakarta Velocity 1.4 instead of Commons Lang.

Discussion

After downloading the Velocity 1.4 binary release, unzip or untar the archive, and put both the *velocity-1.4.jar* and *velocity-dep-1.4.jar* into your project's classpath. If you have a Maven project that needs to use Jakarta Velocity, add a dependency on Jakarta Velocity with the following section in *project.xml*:

```
<dependencies>
  <dependency>
    <id>velocity</id>
```

```
    <version>1.4</version>
  </dependency>

  ....other dependencies...
</dependencies>
```

See Also

To learn more about Velocity, visit the Jakarta Velocity web site (*http://jakarta. apache.org/velocity/*).

If you have questions about how to use Jakarta Velocity, you can join the *velocity-user@jakarta.apache.org* mailing list. Refer to Recipe 1.2 for instructions on joining a user mailing list. To join the Velocity user mailing list, see the Velocity section of the Jakarta mailing lists page (*http://jakarta.apache.org/site/mail2.html#Velocity*).

9.6   Using a Simple Templating Language

Problem

You need to produce a parameterized message using a template stored in a file.

Solution

Use Jakarta Velocity and store your template in the filesystem. Jakarta Velocity is a straightforward templating engine with a lightweight syntax similar to the expression language introduced in Recipe 9.2. The following Velocity template is used to create an email:

```
#set( $customer = $subscription.customer )
#set( $magazine = $subscription.magazine )

$customer.firstName,

Your subscription to ${magazine.title} on
$subscription.endDate.  If you are interested in renewing your subscription, please
click on the following URL, and enter your password:

${magazine.baseUrl}/renew?cust=${customer.id}
```

This template references a Subscription bean bound to the name subscription. This Subscription object has a customer property and a magazine property, and both of these properties are assigned to a local template variable using the #set directive. To render a Velocity template, the engine is initialized using Velocity.init( ), a VelocityContext is created and populated, and the template is read with a FileReader. The following code renders this template:

```
import org.apache.velocity.VelocityContext;
import org.apache.velocity.app.Velocity;
```

```
// Initialize Velocity
Velocity.init( );

// Create a context and put our subscription object into the context
VelocityContext context = new VelocityContext( );
context.put("subscription", testSubscription( ));

// Create a Reader to read our velocity template.
Reader reader = new FileReader( new File("renew.vm") );

// Evaluate our template and write the result to a StringWriter
StringWriter writer = new StringWriter( );
Velocity.evaluate(context, writer, "test", reader);

System.out.println( writer.toString( ) );
```

The template is loaded from the filesystem in a file named *renew.vm*, and the following output is printed to the console:

> *Tim,*
>
> Your subscription to *Science World* expires on *July 20, 2003*. If you are interested in renewing your subscription, please click on the following URL, and enter in your password.
>
> http://www.scienceworld.com/renew?cust=22324

Discussion

In the previous example, Velocity is used as a singleton—a single instance of the VelocityEngine in one Java Virtual Machine. The Velocity engine has a number of configuration options, but, in this example, the Velocity engine is configured with a default set of properties through a call to Velocity.init( ). The template is stored on the filesystem, and the template is read using a FileReader. The output of the template evaluation is written to a StringWriter. To merge a template with a context, Velocity.evaluate( ) is passed the following parameters: a VelocityContext, a Writer to hold the output, a name for logging purposes, and a Reader to read the template.

Velocity syntax is very simple, and it is similar to the expression language used in JSP 2.0 EL and Commons JEXL. If you want to print out the value of a bean property, use ${bean.property} or ${bean.getProperty( )}; Velocity can handle both bean properties and methods. In addition to the basic expression syntax, Velocity also supports a number of directives and control loops, which are explored in Recipe 9.7

The one directive used in the previous example is #set, which assigns a variable for use later in the script; #set($customer = $subscription.customer) assigns the customer property of the subscription object to the variable $customer. Table 9-3 lists some sample Velocity references that demonstrate referencing bean properties and invoking methods.

Table 9-3. Sample Velocity references

Velocity reference	Evaluates to
`${sub}`	The value of "sub" in the `VelocityContext`.
`${sub.endDate}`	The value of `sub.getEndDate( )`.
`${sub.setProp("Val")}`	The return type of `setProp( )` is void, this reference does not evaluate to a value, but it does invoke the setter with one argument.
`$!{customer.firstName}`	If `customer.getFirstName( )` returns a `null` reference, this evaluates to an empty `String`. This is called a quiet reference.
`${customer.firstName}`	If `customer.getFirstName( )` returns a `null`, this evaluates to the `String` "null."

See Also

Velocity has a number of configuration options that allow you to configure logging, character encoding, and the behavior of directives. For more information about configuring Velocity, see "Velocity Configuration Key and Values" in the Velocity Developer's Guide (*http://jakarta.apache.org/velocity/developer-guide.html*).

9.7 Writing Templates with Conditionals and Loops

Problem

Your template needs to iterate over a list of objects and highlight objects if a specific property meets a certain criteria.

Solution

Use a Velocity template with the #foreach and #if directives. The following Velocity template uses a #foreach to loop through a List of Airport beans and an #if to check for the location of an airport relative to the supplied $countryCode:

```
The World's Busiest Airports

<table>
  <tr>
    <td>Rank</td><td>Code</td><td>Name</td><td>Passengers</td>
    <td>${countryCode} Domestic</td>
  </tr>
  #foreach( $airport in $airports )
    <tr>
      <td>$velocityCount</td>
      <td>$airport.code</td>
      <td>$airport.name</td>
      <td>$airport.passengers</td>
      #if( $airport.countryCode == $countryCode )
        <td>Y</td>
```

```
    #else
      <td>N</td>
    #end
  </tr>
#end
</table>
```

To render this template, a List of Airport objects and a countryCode String is created and put into a VelocityContext. The $countryCode reference is used to test the countryCode property of every Airport object in the List; if the countryCode property matches, a Y is placed in the last column. The following code initializes the Velocity engine, creates a VelocityContext, and renders the template:

```
import org.apache.velocity.Velocity;
import org.apache.velocity.app.VelocityContext;

// Initialize Velocity with default properties
Velocity.init( );

// Create a List to hold our Airport objects
List airports = new ArrayList( );
airports.add( new Airport(1, "ATL", "Hartsfield Atlanta", 76876128, "US" ) );
airports.add( new Airport(2, "ORD", "Chicago O'Hare", 66501496, "US" ) );
airports.add( new Airport(3, "LHR", "London Heathrow", 63338649, "UK" ) );
airports.add( new Airport(4, "HND", "Tokyo-Haneda", 61079478, "JP" ) );
airports.add( new Airport(5, "LAX", "Los Angeles", 56198447, "US" ) );
airports.add( new Airport(6, "DFW", "Dallas/Fort Worth", 52826304, "US" ) );

// Create a context and put a List into the context, and a country code
VelocityContext context = new VelocityContext( );
context.put( "airports", airports );
context.put( "countryCode", "US" );

// Create a Reader to read our velocity template.
Reader reader = new FileReader( new File("renew.vm") );

// Evaluate our template and write the result to a StringWriter
StringWriter writer = new StringWriter( );
Velocity.evaluate(context, writer, "test", reader);

System.out.println( writer.toString( ) );
```

This code produces the following output after merging the Velocity template with a VelocityContext:

```
The World's Busiest Airports

Rank  Code  Name                 Passengers  US Domestic
1     ATL   Hartsfield Atlanta   76876128         Y
2     ORD   Chicago O'Hare       66501496         Y
3     LHR   Heathrow             63338649         N
4     HND   Tokyo-Haneda         61079478         N
5     LAX   Los Angeles          56198447         Y
6     DFW   Dallas/Fort Worth    52826304         Y
```

Discussion

The #foreach directive can iterate over arrays, Enumerations, Lists, and Sets; each element is exposed as a local reference specified in the parameter to #foreach. A #foreach block is terminated by #end. The #foreach directive also exposes a local reference $velocityCount, which holds the index of the current row, and, if you need to create a table with alternating row colors, use the velocityCount variable with the #if directive:

```
#foreach( $widgets in $theToolbox )
  #if( $velocityCount % 2 == 0 )
    #set( $bgColor = '#DDD' )
  #else
    #set( $bgColor = '#CCC' )
  #end
  <tr color="${bgColor}">
    <td>Some Data</td>
  </tr>
#end
```

The #if directive takes a boolean expression, and renders the content contained in the #if block if this expression evaluates to true. Like #foreach, an #if block is also terminated by #end. The #if directive can also be followed by an #elseif block or an #else block, as shown in the following example:

```
#if( $variable == "TEST" )
  This is a test.
#elseif( $variable == "SERIOUS" )
  The condition is Serious.
#elseif( $variable == "MAJOR" )
  The condition is Major.
#else
  The condition is Nominal
#end
```

The #foreach directive can be used to iterate over a Set of keys from a Map. To access each element in a Map, use the bracket notation shown in the following example:

```
#set( $keys = someMap.keySet() )

#foreach( $key in $keys )
  $key: $someMap[$key]
#end
```

See Also

For information about the relational and logical operators supports by Velocity, see the Velocity Template Language (VTL) Reference Guide (*http://jakarta.apache.org/velocity/vtl-reference-guide.html*).

9.8   Using Macros in a Templating Engine

Problem

You need to reuse portions of a template to standardize the display of common elements such as an address or a name.

Solution

Use Velocity Macro definitions to reuse logic to print out both names and addresses. Velocity macros are like subroutines that take a set of parameters and perform common tasks. In the following Velocity template, two macros, #name and #address, handle the printing of names and addresses:

```
#set( $volunteer = $appointment.volunteer )
#set( $location = $appointment.location )
#set( $org = $appointment.organization )

## Define the "name" macro
#macro( name $object )$!object.firstName $!object.lastName#end

## Define the "address" macro
#macro( address $object )
$!object.address.street1
$!object.address.street2
$!object.address.city, $!object.address.state $!object.address.zipcode
#end

#name( $volunteer ),

Thank you for volunteering to help serve food at the $location.name next week.  This
email is a reminder that you are scheduled to help out from $appointment.startTime to
$appointment.endTime on $appointment.date.  The address of the shelter is:

#address( $location )

If you need directions to the shelter click the following URL:

    ${org.baseUrl}directions?location=${location.id}

Also, if you are unable to help out on $appointment.date, please let us know by
sending an email to ${org.email} or by filling out the form at this URL:

    ${org.baseUrl}planschange?appointment=${appointment.id}

Thanks again,

#name( $org.president )

#address( $org )
```

In the following code, the template shown previously is loaded from a classpath resource organize.vm, and an Appointment object is placed in a VelocityContext:

```
import org.apache.velocity.VelocityContext;
import org.apache.velocity.app.VelocityEngine;
import org.apache.velocity.runtime.RuntimeConstants;

// Create and initialize a VelocityEngine setting a configuration property
VelocityEngine vEngine = new VelocityEngine( );
vEnging.setProperty( RuntimeConstants.VM_CONTEXT_LOCALSCOPE, Boolean.TRUE );
vEngine.init( );

// Create a test Appointment
Appointment appointment = testAppointment( );

// Create a Velocity Context and give it the appointment
VelocityContext context = new VelocityContext( );
context.put("appointment", appointment);

// Prepare a StringWriter that will hold the contents of
// our template merge
StringWriter writer = new StringWriter( );

// Get a stream to read in our velocity template.  The
// organize.vm file is loaded from the classpath and is stored
// in the same package as the current class.
InputStream templateStream = getClass( ).getResourceAsStream("organize.vm");
Reader reader = new InputStreamReader( templateStream );

// Evaluate the template
vEngine.evaluate(context, writer, "test", reader);

// Print out the results of the template evaluation
System.out.println( "organize: " + writer.toString( ) );
```

The template is merged with a VelocityContext, and the following output is produced:

```
John S.,

Thank you for volunteering to help serve food at the Boston Homeless Veterans Shelter
next week.  This email is a reminder that you are scheduled to help out from 9:00 AM
to 2:00 PM on Monday, September 12, 2003.  The address of the shelter is:

    17 Court Street
    Boston, MA 01260

If you need directions to the shelter click the following URL:

    http://www.organize.com/directions?location=2342

Also, if you are unable to help out on September 12th, please let us know by sending
an email to organize@helpout.com or by filling out the form at this URL:

    http://www.organize.com/planschange?appointment=29932422
```

Thanks again,

Brishen R.
201 N. 2nd Street
Jersey City, NJ 20213

Discussion

A macro definition is started with the #macro directive and ended with #end; the same macro is invoked by calling #<macro_name>(<parameters>). Velocity macros must be defined before they are referenced, using the following syntax:

```
#macro(<name> <arguments>)
    <Macro Body>
#end
```

Macro parameters are not typed as are method parameters in Java; there is no mechanism to check that an Address object is passed to the #address macro, throwing an exception if an inappropriate object is encountered. To successfully render this Velocity template, verify that an Address is sent to the #address macro and a Person is sent to the #name macro.

In the previous example, an instance of VelocityEngine is created and the RuntimeConstants.VM_CONTEXT_LOCALSCOPE property is set to true. This property corresponds to the velocimacro.context.localscope, which controls the scope of references created by #set directives within macros. When this configuration property is set to true, references created in the body of a macro are local to that macro.

The Velocity template in the Solution expects a single reference $appointment to an Appointment bean. Each Appointment has a volunteer property of type Person, and every Organization has a president property of type Person. These Person objects, ${appointment.volunteer} and ${appointment.organization.president}, are passed to the #name macro that prints out the first and last name. Two Address objects, ${appointment.location.address} and ${appointment.organization.address}, are passed to the #address macro that prints a standard U.S. mailing address.

A macro can contain any directive used in Velocity; the following macro uses nested directives to print out a list of numbers in HTML. #numberList allows you to specify a range with $low and $high; values in $numbers within this range will be printed bold:

```
#macro( numberList $numbers $low $high )
    <ul>
     #foreach( $number in $numbers )
       #if( ($number > $low) && ($number < $high) )
           <li><b>$number</b> - In Range!</li>
       #else
         <li>$number</li> - Out of Range!</li>
       #end
     #end
    </ul>
#end
```

The macro defined above would be called by the following Velocity template. Note the presence of comments, which are preceded by two hashes (##):

```
#set( $squares = [1, 4, 9, 16, 25, 36, 49, 64, 81, 100] )

## Print out a list of numbers highlighting numbers
## between 25 and 75
#numberList( $squares, 25, 75 )
```

See Also

If your system has a large number of Velocity templates, you can create a set of files to hold common macros, which will be made available to every Velocity template using the velocimacro.library property. For more information, see the Velocity User Guide (*http://jakarta.apache.org/velocity/user-guide.html#Velocimacros*).

9.9   Invoking Methods in a Template

Problem

You need to invoke methods from a Velocity template.

Solution

Use Velocity to access public methods on an object in the VelocityContext. Bind an object to the VelocityContext and reference methods on these objects in a Velocity template. The following template, available on the classpath at *scripting/velocity/results.vm*, invokes the average( ), min( ), and max( ) methods on a StatUtil object bound to the reference $stat:

```
** Aggregate Statistics

Average: $stat.average( $results.scores )%
Lowest: $stat.min( $results.scores )%
Highest: $stat.max( $results.scores )%

** Scores:
#foreach( $student in $results.students )
    #score( $student 50 )
#end

More results are available here:
http://www.test.com/detail?test={results.id}
```

The StatUtil object, which is bound to $stat, computes basic statistics on integer arrays. This class definition is:

```
public class StatUtil {
    public int average(int[] array) {
        int sum = 0.0;
        for( int i = 0; i < array.length; i++ ) {
```

```
            sum += array[i];
        }
        return( sum / array.length );
    }

    public int min(int[] array) {
        int min = Integer.MAX_VALUE;
        for( int i = 0; i < array.length; i++) {
            if( array[i] < min) { min = array[i]; }
        }
        return( min );
    }

    public int max(int[] array) {
        int max = Integer.MIN_VALUE;
        for( int i = 0; i < array.length; i++) {
            if( array[i] > max) { max = array[i]; }
        }
        return( max );
    }
}
```

The template shown above is loaded from the classpath, and a StatUtil object is added to the VelocityContext. The VelocityEngine is configured to load templates from the classpath, and the template is merged with a call to mergeTemplate( ):

```
import org.apache.velocity.VelocityContext;
import org.apache.velocity.app.VelocityEngine;

// The following lines of code tell the Velocity Engine
// where to find our shared Macros, 2. Load everything from
// Classpath.
VelocityEngine vEngine = new VelocityEngine();
vEngine.setProperty("velocimacro.library", "scripting/velocity/macros.vm");
vEngine.setProperty("resource.loader","class");
vEngine.setProperty("class.resource.loader.description", "Classpath Loader");
vEngine.setProperty("class.resource.loader.class",
        "org.apache.velocity.runtime.resource.loader.ClasspathResourceLoader");
vEngine.init();

// Put the test results and the StatUtil object into the context
VelocityContext context = new VelocityContext();
context.put("results", testResults());
context.put("stat", new StatUtil());

// Since we've configured our VelocityEngine to load our
// templates from the classpath, we can call mergeTemplate and
// let the VelocityEngine take care of reading our template.
StringWriter writer = new StringWriter();
vEngine.mergeTemplate("scripting/velocity/results.vm", context, writer);

// Print out the results
System.out.println( "results: " + writer.toString() );
```

When the template is merged with a VelocityContext containing student results and a StatUtil object, the following output is produced:

```
Here is the student performance on Test #3: The Geography of Upper Mongolia.

** Aggregate Statistics

Average:      84.3%

** Scores:
Tim O.        40.2%    FAIL
Susan P.      90.6%    PASS
Steven R.     80.4%    PASS
Kofi A.       78.0%    PASS
Rock P.       85.1%    PASS

More results are available here:
http://www.tests.com/detail?testId=2324223
```

Discussion

Note that the #score macro is absent from this template. The #score macro encapsulates presentation logic to translate a number grade to a printed letter grade. This macro is stored in a separate file made available as a classpath resource stored in *scripting/velocity/macros.vm*:

```
#macro( score $student $passingGrade )
    #if( $student.score >= $passingGrade )
      Student: ${student.name} Score: ${student.score}% PASS
    #else
      Student: ${student.name} Score: ${student.score}% FAIL
    #end
#end
```

The VelocityEngine is configured to load both the #score macro and the template from the classpath by setting the resource.loader, class.resource.loader. description, and class.resource.loader.class. The #score macro is loaded from a macro library, and the location of this library is specified in the velocimacro.library configuration property. Velocity has built-in resource loaders to load resources from the filesystem, the classpath, a database, or a JAR file. The following configuration configures two resource loaders for a VelocityEngine—a filesystem resource loader and a classpath resource loader. When a resource is loaded, the VelocityEngine attempts to locate the resource in the filesystem, and, if the resource is not found, it searches the classpath. Using this configuration, you can create an application with default templates in the classpath, which can be overridden by customized templates on the filesystem. The file resource loader is also configured to cache file resources in memory, checking for a modification every 600 seconds:

```
resource.loader = file, class

file.resource.loader.description = Customized Templates
file.resource.loader.class = \ org.apache.velocity.runtime.resource.loader.
FileResourceLoader
file.resource.loader.path = custom/templates
file.resource.loader.cache = true
file.resource.loader.modificationCheckInterval = 600

class.resource.loader.description = Default Templates
class.resource.loader.class = \ org.apache.velocity.runtime.resource.loader.
ClasspathResourceLoader
```

Instead of configuring a VelocityEngine in Java code, the name of this properties file can be passed to the init( ) method:

```
VelocityEngine engine = new VelocityEngine( );
engine.init( "conf/velocity.properties" );
```

See Also

If you need to format dates and numbers, take a look at the VelocityTools project, which provides a few ready-made utilities, such as DateTool, NumberTool, and MathTool (*http://jakarta.apache.org/velocity/tools/index.html*).

Velocity's simplicity can be both a blessing and a curse. In this last example, note that the student scores were all stored as integer values. Velocity's numeric comparisons only work with integers values. Try to evaluate ${var < 37.4} in a Velocity template and you will have inconsistent results. Velocity is simple is by design. If you are looking for a more complex templating engine, the next few recipes introduce another templating engine named FreeMarker.

9.10   Obtaining FreeMarker

Problem

You need to use FreeMarker to write templates that can reference variables, object properties, and DOM Node objects.

Solution

You must download the latest version of FreeMarker, and place the FreeMarker JAR in your project's classpath. Go to the FreeMarker download page at *http://www. freemarker.org/freemarkerdownload.html*, and download the FreeMarker 2.3 distribution. After you untar and unzip the distribution, you will find a *freemarker.jar* file in the *lib* directory; place this file in your project's classpath.

Discussion

If you have a Maven project that needs to use FreeMarker, add a dependency on FreeMarker with the following section in *project.xml*:

```
<dependencies>
  <dependency>
    <id>freemarker</id>
    <version>2.3</version>
  </dependency>

  ....other dependencies...
</dependencies>
```

See Also

To learn more about FreeMarker, visit the FreeMarker web site (*http://www. freemarker.org/*).

To participate in the FreeMarker community, join the FreeMarker users or developers list (*http://sourceforge.net/mail/?group_id=794*).

9.11   Using a Complex Scripting Engine

Problem

You need to find a templating engine that supports number formatting, date formatting, and comparison of double values. In addition, you are looking for a templating engine that gives you more control over whitespace and line breaks.

Solution

Use FreeMarker, a templating engine with a large built-in feature set that includes support for date and number formatting and intelligent handling of whitespace. The following FreeMarker template creates a summary report for a college course:

```
<#assign student = enrollment.student >
<#assign course = enrollment.course >
<#assign exams = enrollment.exams >
<#-- This macro assigns a variable named final -->
<@final exams=exams/>

${student.firstName} ${student.lastName},

Here is a summary of your performance in ${course.dept} ${course.num} ${course.name}.

Class:         ${course.name}
Professor:     ${course.professor}
Section:       ${enrollment.section?string("000")}
```

```
Exam, Date, Score, Weight, Grade
------------------------------------------------
<#list exams as exam>
  <@compress single_line=true>
    <#assign score = exam.score >
    ${exam.name},
    ${exam.date?date?string.short},
    #{exam.score; m1M1},
    ${exam.weight},
    <@letter score=score/>
  </@compress>

</#list>

Final Grade:  ${final; m1M1} <@letter score=final/>
Your final grade has been submitted to the Registrar.

<#macro final exams>
    <#local num = 0>
    <#local dem = 0>
    <#list exams as exam>
        <#local num = num + (exam.score * exam.weight)/>
        <#local dem = dem + exam.weight>
    </#list>
    <#assign final = num / dem>
</#macro>

<#macro letter score>
    <#if (score >= 90)> A
    <#elseif (score >= 80)> B
    <#elseif (score >= 70)> C
    <#elseif (score >= 60)> D
    <#else> F
    </#if>
</#macro>
```

To merge this template with data, populate a Map with named attributes and pass this Map to the template.process( ) method. The following code creates a Configuration object that loads a FreeMarker template, *template.ftl*, from the classpath. An Enrollment object is added to the root Map, and the output of the template merge is written to a StringWriter:

```
import freemarker.template.Configuration;
import freemarker.cache.ClassTemplateLoader;
import freemarker.template.ObjectWrapper;
import freemarker.template.Template;

StringWriter writer = new StringWriter( );

// Create a Configuration object for FreeMarker
Configuration cfg = Configuration.getDefaultConfiguration( );
cfg.setTemplateLoader(new ClassTemplateLoader(getClass( )));
cfg.setObjectWrapper(ObjectWrapper.BEANS_WRAPPER);
```

```
// The root Map serves as a Context for our template engine
Map root = new HashMap();
root.put("enrollment", testEnrollment());

// A template is processed with a Map and output is sent to a Writer.
Template template = cfg.getTemplate("template.ftl");
template.process(root, writer);
System.out.println("output: \n" + writer.toString());
```

The template is rendered, and the following output is printed to the console:

```
Stefan Winz,

Here is a summary of your performance in ECON 201 Macroeconomics.

Class:        Macroeconomics
Professor:    Dr. Stephen H. Jones
Section:       002

Exam, Date, Score, Weight, Grade
-----------------------------------------------
T01, 01/10/03,    93.4, 1.00, A
T02, 01/27/03,    85.5, 1.50, B
Mid, 02/15/03,    98.0, 2.00, A+
T03, 03/31/03,    71.5, 1.00, C-
T04, 04/10/03,    88.5, 1.50, B+
Fin, 05/05/03,    95.0, 4.00, A

Final Grade:    91        A-

Your final grade has been submitted to the Registrar.  Have a great Summer!
```

Discussion

In the template for this recipe, three objects are retrieved from an Enrollment object: a course property, a student property, and a List of Exam objects. Three variables—course, student, and exam—are created with the <#assign> directive, <#assign variable = expression >. Properties are referenced as they were referenced in JEXL and Velocity; ${enrollment.student} is used to access the student property on the enrollment. A student's final course grade is calculated in a macro by calling <@final exams=exams/>. This macro assigns a global template variable, final, which is formatted to one decimal place with the expression ${final; m1M1}.

At first glance, a FreeMarker template looks very similar to a Velocity template, but there are several interesting features not available in Velocity:

Formatting dates and numbers
    Our date object was formatted with the expression ${exam.date?date?string. short}. ?date instructs the engine to take only the day, month, and year portion of the date, and ?string.short tells FreeMarker to use the locale's short-date format (12/31/04). You can also specify your own date format using the same syntax you

would use in `SimpleDateFormat`. The expression `${exam.date?string("MM-dd-yyyy hh:mm:ss")}` would output a string similar to "12-31-2004 04:23:22."

Comparing dates and numbers

FreeMarker can compare dates and numbers, both integer and floating point.

Macros with named parameters

Macros can be invoked with named parameters. For example, the `@letter` macro can be invoked with named parameters: `<@letter team="Boston Celtics" score="34"></@letter>`.

Here are some other interesting FreeMarker features not available in Velocity:

- Namespaces for variables and macros
- "Built-in" functions for basic types
- Access to XML document objects
- Improved looping
- Local macro variables
- Built-in XML and HTML escaping

 Velocity has a very large user base, and it is the right tool for a simple job. FreeMarker has some very useful features "out of the box," while Velocity requires developers to install supporting utilities or write these "extensions" from scratch. Some developers will prefer a templating language that is simple by design, and others need a tool that is substantially more complex. There is a case to be made for simplicity. If you working on a large team, where you have content authors who need to create and maintain your templates, you may want to use a technology like Velocity that embraces simplicity. Open source communities benefit from healthy cross-pollination of ideas and competition, and FreeMarker was developed as an alternative to Jakarta Velocity; they even have a feature comparison page (*http://www.freemarker.org/ fmVsVel.html*).

See Also

It is beyond the scope of this book to drill into the details of every FreeMarker feature listed in this recipe. If you are interested in learning more about FreeMarker, take a look at the online documentation (*http://www.freemarker.org/docs/index.html*).

If you are using Jakarta Velocity and wish to migrate your templates to FreeMarker, the FreeMarker team has written a utility, code named "US Cavalry," which will automatically translate your VTL templates to FTL templates. To obtain "US Cavalry," see *http://www.freemarker.org/usCavalry.html*.

9.12 Accessing XML Documents from a Templating Engine

Problem

You need to reference XML nodes from a template.

Solution

Use FreeMarker and parse an XML document with the `NodeModel` class. A `NodeModel` is an object that allows access to an XML document as a hierarchy of named elements and attributes from a FreeMarker template. `NodeModel` has a `public static` method `parse()`, which parses an XML document and returns a `NodeModel` to be added to your context `Map`. The following code parses an XML document and passes a `NodeModel` to a template:

```
import freemarker.template.Configuration;
import freemarker.cache.ClassTemplateLoader;
import freemarker.template.ObjectWrapper;
import freemarker.template.Template;
import freemarker.ext.dom.NodeModel;

// Create a File Object for our XML data
File composers = new File("composers.xml");
NodeModel nodeModel = NodeModel.parse( composers );

Map root = new HashMap();
root.put("doc", nodeModel);

// A template is processed with a Map and output is sent to a Writer.
Template template = cfg.getTemplate("composerTable.ftl");
template.process(root, writer);
System.out.println("output: \n" + writer.toString());
```

A `File` object refers to an XML document, and `NodeModel.parse()` is used to parse this document to a `NodeModel` object, which is then placed in the root `Map`—the context with which the FreeMarker template will be merged. The XML document contains information about the lives of great classical composers, and the structure of this document is shown here:

```
<?xml version="1.0"?>

<composers>
  <composer>
    <name>Bach, Johann Sebastian</name>
    <born date="3/21/1685">
      <location>Eisenbach</location>
    </born>
    <notes>Bach wrote intense and complex fugues.</notes>
    <link>http://www.bachfaq.org/</link>
```

```
    </composer>
    <composer>
      <name>Mozart, Wolfgang Amadeus</name>
      <born date="1/27/1756">
        <location>Salzburg</location>
      </born>
      <notes>Wrote first symphony at age 8.</notes>
      <link>http://www.mozartproject.org/</link>
    </composer>
    <composer>
      <name>Hendrix, Jimi</name>
      <born date="11/27/1942">
        <location>Seattle</location>
      </born>
      <notes>Hendrix set his guitar on fire in Monterey</notes>
      <link>http://www.jimihendrix.com/</link>
    </composer>
  </composers>
```

The NodeModel object is exposed to the template as doc, and the #list directive is used to iterate through each composer element. A reference to a child element link of the composer element is ${composer.link}, and a reference to the date attribute of the born element is preceded by @–${composer.born.@date}. The FreeMarker template, which references elements and attributes through a NodeModel, is:

```
<#list doc.composers.composer as composer>
  <p>
    <a href="${composer.link}">${composer.name}</a><br/>
    Born on ${composer.born.@date} in ${composer.born.location}<br/>
    Notes: ${composer.notes}
  </p>
</#list>
```

Discussion

In addition to simple access to elements and attributes, FreeMarker also allows you to use XPath expressions if Apache Xalan is available on the classpath. If you have Xalan, you can use XPath with the same syntax you would use if you were trying to access a map. Instead of someMap["key"], you would use someElement["<XPath>"]. Here is a quick example, which uses an XPath expression to iterate through every composer's "born" element:

```
<#list doc["composers/composer/born"] as birth>
  <p>Born: ${birth.date}, ${birth.location}  ${birth?parent.name}</p>
</#list>
```

FreeMarker also includes a number of built-ins for NodeModel objects; in the previous template, ?parent returns the parent element of the element represented by the birth node. Table 9-4 lists a number of built-ins for XML nodes; ?children returns all of the child nodes of a given node, and ?ancestors gives every node above this node in an XML document.

Table 9-4. FreeMarker built-ins for NodeModel objects

Expression	Evaluates to
${composers?children}	A sequence of all child nodes. This example would return 3 composer nodes.
${composer?parent}	If called on a composer node, this would return the composers node.
${composer?root}	This would return the doc node, which is the topmost node in this document.
${link?ancestors}	If this corresponded to the link element for Jimi Hendrix, this would return a sequence of [${composers.composer[3]}, ${composers}]. This returns an array of all ancestors starting with ${link?parent} and ending at ${link.root}.
${link?node_name}	This would return "link." This returns the name of the element or attribute in question.
${link?node_type}	This would return "element." It could return "attribute," "element," "text," "comment," "entity," and a few other types corresponding to Node types in the DOM API.

See Also

For more detail about referencing XML elements through NodeModel and the use of XPath expressions in FreeMarker, see the "Learning by Example" section of Imperative XML Processing (*http://www.freemarker.org/docs/xgui_imperative_learn.html*).

FreeMarker also offers syntax for declarative processing of XML—assigning macros to handle elements in an XML document. For more information about FreeMarker declarative XML processing, see the FreeMarker online documentation (*http://www.freemarker.org/docs/xgui_declarative_basics.html*).

9.13   Using Velocity in a Web Application

Problem

You are sick of writing JSP and having to wait for pages to compile. You would like to find a way to use Velocity instead of JSP.

Solution

Configure your web application to use the VelocityViewServlet to render your Velocity templates. Download the latest version of the VelocityView project from *http://jakarta.apache.org/site/binindex.cgi*; it is listed under "Velocity Tools 1.1." Put the velocity and velocity-tools jars in the *WEB-INF/lib* directory, and configure your web application to render templates ending in **.vm* with the VelocityViewServlet. Add the following servlet and servlet-mapping elements to your *web.xml* file as follows:

```
<!-- Define Velocity template compiler -->
<servlet>
  <servlet-name>velocity</servlet-name>
  <servlet-class>
    org.apache.velocity.tools.view.servlet.VelocityViewServlet
  </servlet-class>
```

```
    <load-on-startup>10</load-on-startup>
  </servlet>

  .....other servlets.....

  <!-- Map *.vm files to Velocity -->
  <servlet-mapping>
    <servlet-name>velocity</servlet-name>
    <url-pattern>*.vm</url-pattern>
  </servlet-mapping>
```

All requests ending in *.vm* are processed by the VelocityViewServlet, which locates the appropriate Velocity template in the document root of your web application. Attributes from the request, session, and application scope will be available as variables in the VelocityContext.

To test this configuration, create a simple Velocity template in the document root of your web application named *index.vm*, start your servlet container, and attempt to render the template by loading *http://<server>/<web-app>/index.vm* in a browser. If everything is set up correctly, you should see the rendered template. If the configuration is not correct, you will see the source for your Velocity template.

Discussion

JSP compilation is an annoyance, especially if you are constantly altering and debugging JSP—all that waiting around adds up over the course of a long project. Using Velocity can help improve performance; the simplicity and elegance of Velocity makes parsing and executing a template fast and efficient. If you are looking for a viable alternative to JSP, try Velocity as your view layer, and you might be surprised.

Velocity can be a refreshing break from JSP, and almost any web application framework will work with Velocity. If you are working with an existing web application, there is no need to stop using JSP in lieu of Velocity; you can use both technologies in the same web application. Templates ending in *.jsp* will be rendered by the existing JSP servlet, and templates ending in *.vm* will be rendered by the VelocityViewServlet.

See Also

VelocityTools also contains a project named VelocityStruts, which provides tools to integrate Velocity with Jakarta Struts. The VelocityStruts project has tools that duplicate the functionality of the Struts JSP tag libraries—a FormTool corresponds to the html tag library, a MessageTool duplicates the bean:message tag, a TilesTool provides access to the Struts tiles plug-in. It is possible to introduce Velocity into an existing Struts application by simply adding the servlet and servlet-mapping to *web.xml*, as shown above. Configure the VelocityViewServlet, and configure an Action to forward to a velocity template; configure the struts tools by following the directions on the VelocityStruts user guide (*http://jakarta.apache.org/velocity/tools/struts/userguide.html*).

9.14   Using FreeMarker in a Web Application

Problem

You would like to use FreeMarker templates in a web application.

Solution

FreeMarker ships with a FreemarkerServlet, which can be configured to render your FreeMarker templates. To configure this servlet, add the following servlet and servlet-mapping elements to your *web.xml* file:

```
<servlet>
  <servlet-name>freemarker</servlet-name>
  <servlet-class>freemarker.ext.servlet.FreemarkerServlet</servlet-class>
  <init-param>
    <param-name>TemplatePath</param-name>
    <param-value>/</param-value>
  </init-param>
  <init-param>
    <param-name>NoCache</param-name>
    <param-value>true</param-value>
  </init-param>
  <init-param>
    <param-name>ContentType</param-name>
    <param-value>text/html</param-value>
  </init-param>
  <load-on-startup>1</load-on-startup>
</servlet>

<servlet-mapping>
  <servlet-name>freemarker</servlet-name>
  <url-pattern>*.ftl</url-pattern>
</servlet-mapping>
```

Discussion

If your application contains custom JSP tag libraries, these tag libraries can be used from a FreeMarker template. To see how a JSP tag library can be used in FreeMarker, take a look at the following JSP page, which references an app tag library with a TLD file in */WEB-INF/app-taglib.tld*:

```
<%@page language="java"%>
<%@taglib uri="/WEB-INF/app-taglib.tld" prefix="app"%>

<p>
 This is an HTML page with a taglib in it.
</p>

<app:printStuff var="test" mode="fast"/>
```

The app tag library has a printStuff tag, which takes the parameters var and mode. The same tag can be used in a FreeMarker template by assigning a reference to

JspTaglibs["/WEB-INF/app-taglib.tld"] in an `<#assign>` directive. The tag can then be used with a call to `<@app.printStuff/>`:

```
<#assign app=JspTaglibs["/WEB-INF/app-taglib.tld"]>

<p>
 This is an HTML page with a taglib in it.
</p>

<@app.printStuff var="test" mode="fast"/>
```

That couldn't be much simpler.

See Also

This is a valuable piece of functionality if you are using a framework like Struts, which depends on JSP tag libraries. For more details about using FreeMarker with Struts, see "Using FreeMarker with Servlets" (*http://fmpp.sourceforge.net/freemarker/pgui_misc_servlet.html*).

9.15   Writing Templates in Eclipse

Problem

You are writing a fair amount of Velocity and FreeMarker templates, and you are looking for a tool that can do some syntax highlighting, validation, and code completion.

Solution

If you are writing Velocity templates, use the Velocity UI for Eclipse. To get this plug-in, point your Eclipse Update Manager at *http://veloedit.sourceforge.net/updates/*.

If you are writing FreeMarker templates, use the FreeMarker Eclipse plug-in. To get this plug-in, point your Eclipse Update Manager at *http://www.freemarker.org/eclipse/update*.

See Also

The FreeMarker project maintains templates, plug-ins, and modes for Eclipse, Emacs, jEdit, KWrite, TextPad 4, and Vim. These tools are described on the FreeMarker site at *http://freemarker.org/editors.html*.

The Velocity project has pointers to templates, plug-ins, and modes for IntelliJ IDEA, Eclipse, UltraEdit, JEdit, TextPad, and Emacs. These tools are described on the Velocity site at *http://jakarta.apache.org/velocity/devtools.html*.

For more information about Eclipse, see Steve Holzner's *Eclipse* (O'Reilly) and *Eclipse Cookbook* (O'Reilly).

## CHAPTER 10

I/O and Networking

10.0   Introduction

If you've ever had to copy a File or copy the contents of an InputStream to an OutputStream, you've probably wondered why Java goes out of its way to make things difficult. Java I/O is not a terribly complex subject, but it does have a knack for turning simpler tasks into complex nests of heavily wrapped Readers and streams. Jakarta Commons IO fills a few gaps in Java's I/O and networking capabilities by providing utilities and methods to copy streams, copy files, touch files, recursively delete directories, and safely close Readers and streams. If you are working with Reader, Writer, InputStream, or OutputStream, you should take a look at IOUtils and CopyUtils; they may save you a few lines of tedious code.

Commons IO also provides a set of simple FilenameFilter implementations, which can be used to selectively list files or directories. In addition to Commons IO's FilenameFilter implementations, Jakarta ORO's GlobFilenameFilter and Perl5FilenameFilter are presented to introduce you to more complex filters involving expressions. ORO is a subproject of Jakarta that provides support for Perl 5 regular expressions and glob expressions. A glob expression is commonly used when listing files in a directory; for example, the expression, *.xml, is a glob expression that matches every file that ends in .xml. While Java 1.4 provides support for regular expressions, there are subtle differences between the regular expression syntax supported by Java 1.4 and the regular expression syntax supported in Perl 5. You can learn more about the differences between Perl5 regular expressions supported by ORO and regular expressions supported by Java 1.4 by reading the ORO project page at *http://jakarta.apache.org/oro*. Take a look at Jakarta ORO if your application needs to work with globs and complex regular expressions.

Commons Net contains simple clients for common protocols, such as FTP, POP3, and SMTP. Using Commons Net, you can retrieve or transfer files to an FTP server with a very small amount of code. Sun provides a very capable set of classes to send and retrieve mail using POP and SMTP, but the javax.mail API brings a certain amount of complexity and overhead that might not make sense for an application sending a simple email message. Commons Net provides a lightweight SMTP client, which can be used to send a simple email message in a few lines of code without introducing the complexity of javax.mail. Commons Net also contains a very straightforward POP3 client, which can be used to check a POP mailbox for incoming messages. In addition to FTP, POP, and SMTP, Commons Net contains simple clients for Trivial File Transfer Protocol (TFTP), Telnet, Finger, and NNTP.

10.1 Obtaining Commons IO

Problem

You need to use Jakarta Commons IO.

Solution

You must download the latest version of Commons IO, and place the Commons IO JAR in your project's classpath. Following the steps outlined in Recipe 1.1, download Commons IO 1.0 instead of Commons Lang.

Discussion

Commons IO contains a few utilities for simplifying a number of common I/O tasks. CopyUtils and IOUtils in the org.apache.commons.io package provide a suite of static utility methods for working with streams and readers. org.apache.commons.io. FileUtils provides static utility methods to help with common File operations, such as touching a file, recursive deletion of directories, and reading files. The org.apache. commons.io.filefilter package contains implementations of FilenameFilter, such as SuffixFileFilter, which accepts files with a specified name suffix.

If you have a Maven project, which needs to use Commons IO, add a dependency on Commons IO 1.0 with the following section in *project.xml*:

```
<dependencies>
  <dependency>
    <id>commons-io</id>
    <version>1.0</version>
  </dependency>
  ....other dependencies...
</dependencies>
```

See Also

For more information about the Commons IO project, see the project page at *http:// jakarta.apache.org/commons/io*. If you have questions about using Commons IO, please feel free to join the *commons-user@jakarta.apache.org* mailing list. Instructions for joining the user mailing list can be found in Recipe 1.2.

10.2   Copying Streams, byte[], Readers, and Writers

Problem

You need to copy a stream, byte[], Reader, or Writer. For example, you need to copy the content from an InputStream or Reader to a Writer, or you need to copy a String to an OutputStream.

Solution

Use CopyUtils from Commons IO to copy the contents of an InputStream, Reader, byte[], or String to an OutputStream or a Writer. The following code demonstrates the use of CopyUtils to copy between an InputStream and a Writer:

```
import org.apache.commons.io.CopyUtils;

try {
    Writer writer = new FileWriter( "test.dat" );
    InputStream inputStream =
        getClass( ).getResourceAsStream("./test.resource");
    CopyUtils.copy( inputStream, writer );
    writer.close( );
    inputStream.close( );
} catch (IOException e) {
    System.out.println( "Error copying data" );
}
```

The previous example reads *test.resource* using an InputStream, which is copied to a FileWriter using CopyUtils.copy( ).

Discussion

If you need to copy information from a Reader or InputStream to a String, use IOUtils.toString( ). The following example opens an InputStream from a URL and copies the contents to a String:

```
import org.apache.commons.io.IOUtils;

URL url = new URL( "http://www.slashdot.org" );
try {
    InputStream inStream = url.openStream( );
    String contents = IOUtils.toString( inStream );
    System.out.println( "Slashdot: " + contents );
} catch ( IOException ioe ) {
    // handle this exception
}
```

Because CopyUtils uses a 4 KB buffer to copy between the source and the destination, you do *not* need to supply buffered streams or readers to the copy( ) method. When using CopyUtils.copy( ), make sure to flush( ) and close( ) any streams, Readers, or Writers passed to copy( ).

10.3   Closing Streams, Readers, and Writers

Problem

You need to close an InputStream, OutputStream, Reader, or Writer, and you want to avoid catching an IOException in a finally block.

Solution

Use IOUtils.closeQuietly( ) to close an InputStream, OutputStream, Reader, or Writer without having to test for null or deal with an IOException. The following code demonstrates the use of closeQuietly( ) to avoid a nasty try/catch within a finally block:

```
import org.apache.commons.io.IOUtils
import org.apache.commons.io.CopyUtils

Reader reader = null;
String result = "":

try {
    File file = new File( "test.dat" );
    reader = new FileReader( file );
    result = CopyUtils.toString( reader );
} catch( IOException ioe ) {
    System.out.println( "Unable to copy file test.dat to a String." );
} finally {
    IOUtils.closeQuietly( reader );
}
```

Discussion

It is always a good idea to close streams, readers, and writers in finally blocks because you can guarantee that a system will release I/O resources even if an exception is thrown. A call to close( ) releases resources associated with the stream, but because close( ) can throw an IOException, you need to either surround your call to close( ) with a try/catch block, or declare that your method throws an IOException. This problem is best illustrated by the following code, which closes a Reader and Writer without the help of IOUtils:

```
Reader reader = null;
Writer writer = null;
String result = "":
```

```
try {
    File file = ew File("test.dat");
    reader = new FileReader( file );
    writer = new StringWriter();
    CopyUtils.copy( reader, writer );
    result = writer.toString();
} catch( IOException ioe ) {
    System.out.println( "A serious problem has happened" );
} finally {
    try {
        if( reader != null ) {
            reader.close();
        }
    } catch( IOException ioe ) {
        System.out.println( "There has been a problem closing the reader." );
    }
    try {
        if( writer != null ) {
            writer.close();
        }
    } catch( IOException ioe ) {
        System.out.println( "There has been a problem closing the writer." );
    }
}
```

The code within the finally block is as tedious to read as it is to write. To avoid a NullPointerException, both the Reader and Writer need to be compared with null, and both Reader and Writer need separate try/catch blocks to avoid a situation where a Writer remains open because of a problem closing the Reader. Another variation on this theme is to surround the entire example with a single try/catch for IOException:

```
try {
    Reader reader = null;
    Writer writer = null;
    String result = "":

    try {
        File file = new File("test.dat");
        reader = new FileReader( file );
        writer = new StringWriter();
        CopyUtils.copy( reader, writer );
        result = writer.toString();
    } finally {
        if( reader != null ) {
            reader.close();
        }
        if( writer != null ) {
            writer.close();
        }
    }
} catch( IOException ioe ) {
    System.out.println( "There was an I/O exception." );
}
```

While this looks manageable, the try/catch for IOException has been expanded to cover the entire example, just to avoid catching an exception in a finally block. In the previous sample, when an IOException was thrown, the exception was handled within a few lines of its origin, making it easier to provide meaningful context in an exception message. Expanding the scope of a try/catch block and introducing a nested try/catch/finally is an overly complex solution for what should be a relatively straightforward task—closing a Reader and a Writer. There is a more subtle problem with this second approach, as well; if an IOException is thrown by reader. close( ) in the finally block, writer.close( ) may never be executed—a possible resource leak.

IOUtils.closeQuietly( ) allows you to ignore this dilemma entirely if you accept the assumption that a problem closing a stream can be safely ignored. If there is a problem closing an InputStream, OutputStream, Reader, or Writer, it is unlikely that you will be able to take any corrective action in a finally block. IOUtils.closeQuietly( ) takes a reference to an InputStream, OutputStream, Reader, or Writer, tests for null, and swallows any IOException that may be thrown in the process of closing a stream or reader.

See Also

This recipe used CopyUtils, which was demonstrated in Recipe 10.2.

10.4   Printing a Human-Readable File Size

Problem

You need to display the size of a file in kilobytes, megabytes, or gigabytes. Instead of displaying file sizes as 1,073,741,824 bytes, you want an approximate, human-readable size, such as 1 GB.

Solution

Use FileUtils.byteCountToDisplaySize( ) to produce a String containing an approximate, human-readable size. The following code passes the number of bytes in the file *project.xml* to FileUtils.byteCountToDisplaySize( ):

```
import org.apache.commons.io.FileUtils;

try {
    File file = new File("project.xml");
    long bytes = file.length( );
    String display = FileUtils.byteCountToDisplaySize( bytes );
    System.out.println("File: project.xml");
    System.out.println("  bytes: " + bytes );
    System.out.println("  size: " + display );
```

```
    } catch( IOException ioe ) {
        System.out.println( "Error reading file length." );
    }
```

This code prints out the number of bytes in the *project.xml* file, and the human-readable size "2 KB":

```
File: project.xml
  bytes: 2132
   size: 2 KB
```

Discussion

FileUtils contains three static variables—FileUtils.ONE_KB, FileUtils.ONE_MB, and FileUtils.ONE_GB—which represent the number of bytes in a kilobyte, megabyte, and gigabyte. FileUtils.byteCountToDisplaySize() divides the number of bytes by each constant until it finds a constant that can divide the number of bytes, discarding the remainder to create a human-readable value. For example, the value 2,123,022 is divided by FileUtils.ONE_GB, which returns a value of less than 1.0. The value is then divided by FileUtils.ONE_MB, which returns 2—the value used in the human-readable size "2 MB."

 FileUtils.byteCountToDisplaySize() will not round the size of a file; a 2.9 MB file will have a display size of 2 MB. The byte count is divided by ONE_KB, ONE_MB, or ONE_GB, and the remainder is discarded.

10.5 Copying Files, Strings, and URLs

Problem

You need to copy a file to another file, or you need to copy a file to a directory.

Solution

Use FileUtils.copyFile() and FileUtils.copyFileToDirectory(). The following code copies the file *test.dat* to *test.dat.bak*:

```
import org.apache.commons.io.FileUtils;

try {
    File src = new File( "test.dat" );
    file dest = new File( "test.dat.bak" );

    FileUtils.copyFile( src, dest ) {
} catch( IOException ioe ) {
    System.out.println( "Problem copying file." );
}
```

You may also use FileUtils.copyFileToDirectory( ) to copy a file to a directory. The following code copies the file *test.dat* to the directory *./temp*:

```
try {
    File src = new File( "test.dat" );
    File dir = new File( "./temp" );

    FileUtils.copyFileToDirectory( src, dir );
} catch( IOException ioe ) {
    System.out.println( "Problem copying file to dir.");
}
```

Discussion

Quite often you need to write the contents of a String to a file. FileUtils.writeStringToFile( ) provides a quick way to write textual content stored in a String to a File, without opening a Writer. The following code writes the contents of the data String to the file *temp.tmp*:

```
try {
  String string = "Blah blah blah";
  File dest = new File( "test.tmp" );

  FileUtils.writeStringToFile( dest, string, ? );
}
```

Another common task is storing the contents of a URL in a File. FileUtils.copyURLToFile( ) takes a URL object and stores the contents in a file. The following code stores the contents of the *New York Times* front page in a file *times.html*:

```
try {
    URL src = new URL( "http://www.nytimes.com" );
    File dest = new File( "times.html" );

    FileUtils.copyURLToFile( src, dest );
} catch( IOException ioe ) {
    System.out.println( "Error copying contents of a URL to a File." );
}
```

10.6   Deleting Directories Recursively

Problem

You need to delete a directory and everything it contains. You need a recursive delete—the equivalent of a Unix rm -r.

Solution

Use `FileUtils.deleteDirectory()` to remove a directory and everything below it. The following example deletes the *temp* directory:

```
import org.apache.commons.io.FileUtils;

try {
    File dir = new File( "temp" );
    FileUtils.deleteDirectory( dir );
} catch( IOException ioe ) {
    System.out.println( "Error deleting directory." );
}
```

This code will delete every file and directory in the *temp* directory and, once the directory is empty, `deleteDirectory()` will remove the *temp* directory itself.

Discussion

You can also "clean" a directory with the `cleanDirectory()` method. When cleaning a directory, the contents of the directory are erased, but the directory itself is not deleted. The following example cleans the *temp* directory, emptying it of all files and subdirectories:

```
import org.apache.commons.io.FileUtils;

try {
    File dir = new File( "temp" );
    FileUtils.cleanDirectory( dir );
} catch( IOException ioe ) {
    System.out.println( "Problem cleaning a directory" );
}
```

10.7   Obtaining the Size of a Directory

Problem

You need to know the size of everything contained within a directory.

Solution

Use the `sizeOfDirectory()` method on `FileUtils`. The following example returns the size of the *temp* directory:

```
File dir = new File( "temp" );
long dirSize = FileUtils.sizeOfDirectory();
```

If *temp* contains a number files, `FileUtils.sizeOfDirectory()` will return the sum of the size of every file in *temp*. If *temp* contains subdirectories, this method will recursively call `sizeOfDirectory()` on each subdirectory to obtain the size of each subdirectory, and it will return the sum of these sizes.

10.8   Touching a File

Problem

You need to perform the equivalent of the Unix touch command; you want to create a file or update a file's modified timestamp.

Solution

Use the touch( ) method from FileUtils. To use touch( ), pass it a File object; if the File does not exist, touch( ) will create a new file. If the file exists, the timestamp of the file will be updated to the current time. The following code demonstrates the touch( ) method on the file *testFile.txt*:

```
import org.apache.commons.io.FileUtils;

try {
    File testFile = new File( "testFile.txt" );

    // If testFile didn't already exists, create it
    // If testFile already exists, update the modified timestamp
    FileUtils.touch( testFile );
} catch( IOException ioe ) {
    System.out.println( "Error touching testFile" );
}
```

If *testFile.txt* does not exist, the file will be created by the call to touch( ). If *testFile.txt* does exist, the last modified timestamp will be updated to the current time after the call to touch( ).

10.9   Filtering Files

Problem

You need to select all the files in a directory ending in *.xml*, or you need to select only files (not subdirectories) contained in a directory. In other words, you need to filter a list of files.

Solution

Use one of the many implementations of IOFileFilter in the org.apache.commons.io.filefilter package. This package contains various implementations of FileFilter and FilenameFilter, which can be used to filter the contents of a directory. The following example uses SuffixFileFilter to return an array of filenames that end in *.xml*:

```
import java.io.FilenameFilter;
import org.apache.commons.io.filefilter.SuffixFileFilter;
import org.apache.commons.lang.ArrayUtils;
```

```
File rootDir = new File(".");
FilenameFilter fileFilter = new SuffixFileFilter(".xml");
String[] xmlFiles = rootDir.list( fileFilter );
System.out.println( "*** XML Files" );
System.out.println( ArrayUtils.toString( xmlFiles ) );
```

This code searches for all files ending in *.xml* in the current directory. Running this in the root of the example project matches one file, *project.xml*, producing the following output:

```
*** XML Files
{project.xml}
```

Discussion

The `org.apache.commons.io.filefilter` package contains a number of implementations of `FilenameFilter` and `FileFilter`. `PrefixFileFilter` and `SuffixFileFilter` let you match files and directories by a prefix or suffix. `NameFileFilter` matches a file or a directory to a specific name. `DirectoryFileFilter` accepts only directories. `AndFileFilter`, `OrFileFilter`, and `NotFileFilter` allow for the logical combination of filters. The following example uses a combination of the file filters in this package to list *.htm* or *.html* files in a directory:

```
import org.apache.commons.io.filefilter.AndFileFilter;
import org.apache.commons.io.filefilter.DirectoryFileFilter;
import org.apache.commons.io.filefilter.IOFileFilter;
import org.apache.commons.io.filefilter.NotFileFilter;
import org.apache.commons.io.filefilter.OrFileFilter;
import org.apache.commons.io.filefilter.SuffixFileFilter;
import org.apache.commons.lang.ArrayUtils;

IOFileFilter htmlFilter =
    new OrFileFilter( new SuffixFileFilter("htm"),
                      new SuffixFileFilter("html") );
IOFileFilter notDirectory = new NotFileFilter( DirectoryFileFilter.INSTANCE );
FilenameFilter fileFilter = new AndFileFilter( htmlFilter, notDirectory );

String[] htmlFiles = rootDir.list(fileFilter);
System.out.println( "*** HTML Files" );
System.out.println( ArrayUtils.toString( htmlFiles ) );
```

This example combines two `SuffixFileFilter` instances in an `OrFileFilter` to match *.htm* or *.html* files. Wrapping a `DirectoryFileFilter` with a `NotFileFilter` creates a filter that will accept files and reject directories. Combining these two filters in an `AndFileFilter` creates a filter to list files with either suffix. Every filter defined in the `org.apache.commons.io.filefilter` package is an implementation of the `IOFileFilter`, which implements both the `java.io.FileFilter` and `java.io.FilenameFilter` interfaces.

10.10 Measuring Stream Traffic

Problem

You need to keep track of the number of bytes read from an InputStream or written to an OutputStream.

Solution

Use a CountingInputStream or CountingOutputStream to keep track of the number of bytes written to a stream. The following example uses a CountingOutputStream to keep track of the number of bytes written to a FileOutputStream:

```
import org.apache.commons.io.IOUtils;
import org.apache.commons.io.output.CountingOutputStream;
import java.io.*;

File test = new File( "test.dat" );
CountingOutputStream countStream = null;

try {
    FileOutputStream fos = new FileOutputStream( test );
    countStream = new CountingOutputStream( fos );
    countStream.write( "Hello".getBytes() );
} catch( IOException ioe ) {
    System.out.println( "Error writing bytes to file." );
} finally {
    IOUtils.closeQuietly( countStream );
}

if( countStream != null ) {
    int bytesWritten = countStream.getCount();
    System.out.println( "Wrote " + bytesWritten + " bytes to test.dat" );
}
```

This previous example wrapped a FileOutputStream with a CountingOutputStream, producing the following console output:

```
Wrote 5 bytes to test.dat
```

Discussion

CountingInputStream wraps an InputStream and getCount( ) provides a running tally of total bytes read. The following example demonstrates CountingInputStream:

```
import org.apache.commons.io.IOUtils;
import org.apache.commons.io.output.CountingOutputStream;
import java.io.*;

File test = new File( "test.dat" );
CountingInputStream countStream = null;
```

```
try {
    FileInputStream fis = new FileInputStream( test );
    countStream = new CountingOutputStream( fis );
    String contents = IOUtils.toString( countStream );
} catch( IOException ioe ) {
    System.out.println( "Error reading bytes from file." );
} finally {
    IOUtils.closeQuietly( countStream );
}

if( countStream != null ) {
    int bytesRead = countStream.getCount();
    System.out.println( "Read " + bytesRead + " bytes from test.dat" );
}
```

10.11 Splitting an OutputStream

Problem

You need to send the same output to two OutputStreams.

Solution

Use Commons IO TeeOutputStream to send the same data to two instances of OutputStream. When data is written to a TeeOutputStream, that data is sent to the two instances of OutputStream passed to its constructor. The following example demonstrates the use of TeeOutputStream to write the same String to two instances of FileOutputStream:

```
import org.apache.commons.io.IOUtils;
import org.apache.commons.io.output.TeeOutputStream;

File test1 = new File("split1.txt");
File test2 = new File("split2.txt");
OutputStream outStream = null;

try {
    FileOutputStream fos1 = new FileOutputStream( test1 );
    FileOutputStream fos2 = new FileOutputStream( test2 );
    outStream = new TeeOutputStream( fos1, fos2 );

    outStream.write( "One Two Three, Test".getBytes() );
    outStream.flush();
} catch( IOException ioe ) {
    System.out.println( "Error writing to split output stream" );
} finally {
    IOUtils.closeQuietly( outStream );
}
```

Flushing or closing a TeeOutputStream will flush or close both of the OutputStream instances it contains. After this example is executed, two files, *split1.txt* and *split2.txt*, will contain the same text.

10.12 Obtaining Jakarta ORO

Problem

You need to use Jakarta ORO to finds files by a glob or regular expression.

Solution

Download Jakarta ORO 2.0.8 from *http://jakarta.apache.org/site/binindex.cgi*. Once you have downloaded and uncompressed the archive distribution, place the *jakarta-oro-2.0.8.jar* in your classpath.

Discussion

Jakarta ORO provides support for Perl regular expressions, AWK expressions, and glob expressions. Before Java 1.4 introduced the java.util.regex package and regular expression support in the String class, Jakarta ORO and Jakarta RegExp gave developers a way to use regular expressions in Java. Now that Java 1.4 supports regular expressions, ORO still remains relevant for developers who need specific support for Perl5 extended regular expressions.

If you have a Maven project that needs to use Jakarta ORO, add a dependency on Jakarta ORO 2.0.8 with the following section in *project.xml*:

```
<dependencies>
  <dependency>
    <id>oro</id>
    <version>2.0.8</version>
  </dependency>
  ....other dependencies...
</dependencies>
```

See Also

For more information about ORO, see the Jakarta ORO project at *http://jakarta.apache.org/oro*. For more information about the regular expression syntax supported by Jakarta ORO, see the package summary for the org.apache.oro.test.regex package at *http://jakarta.apache.org/oro/api/org/apache/oro/text/regex/package-summary.html*.

10.13 Using Globs and Perl5 Regular Expressions to List Files

Problem

You need to get a list of files that match either a glob or regular expression.

Solution

Use Perl5FilenameFilter or GlobFilenameFilter from Jakarta ORO to select all files matching an expression. Both of these classes implement the FileFilter and FilenameFilter interface, and both can be passed to the listFiles() method on a File object. The following example uses GlobFilenameFilter to list XML files in the *./dataDir* directory:

```
import org.apache.oro.io.GlobFilenameFilter;

File dataDir = new File("./dataDir");
FilenameFilter xmlFilter = new GlobFilenameFilter( "*.xml" );
File[] xmlFiles = dataDir.listFiles( xmlFilter );
```

To find all files matching a Perl regular expression, use the Perl5FilenameFilter. The following example returns files starting with "dev" and ending with ".tld" by passing a regular expression to the constructor of Perl5FilenameFilter:

```
File dataDir = new File("./dataDir");
FilenameFilter regexFilter = new Perl5FilenameFilter( "^dev.*.tld$" );
File[] tldFiles = dataDir.listFiles( regexFilter );
```

10.14 Obtaining Commons Net

Problem

You need to use Commons Net to write a simple FTP, SMTP, or POP3 client.

Solution

Download the latest version of Commons Net, and place the Commons Net JAR in your project's classpath. Following the steps outlined in Recipe 1.1, download Commons Net 1.2.2 instead of Commons Lang.

Discussion

Jakarta Commons Net contains some simple clients for commonly used network protocols, such as FTP, TFTP, Telnet, NNTP, POP3, and SMTP. Protocols are supported by collections of classes in packages dedicated to these protocols. For example, FTP is supported by a set of classes in the org.apache.commons.net.ftp package, including `FTPClient` and `FTPFile`; and SMTP is supported by classes in the `org.apache.commons.net.smtp` package, including `SMTPClient`.

If you have a Maven project that needs to use Commons Net, add a dependency on Commons Net 1.2.2 with the following section in *project.xml*:

```
<dependencies>
  <dependency>
    <id>commons-net</id>
    <version>1.2.2</version>
  </dependency>
  ....other dependencies...
</dependencies>
```

See Also

For more information about Commons Net, see the Commons Net project page at *http://jakarta.apache.org/commons/net*.

10.15 Writing an FTP Client

Problem

You need to write a program to interact with an FTP server.

Solution

Use Commons Net `FTPClient` to communicate with an FTP server. The following example retrieves the contents of the file *c64bus.gif* from *ftp.ibibilio.org*:

```
import org.apache.commons.io.IOUtils;
import org.apache.commons.net.ftp.FTPClient;

FTPClient client = new FTPClient();
OutputStream outStream = null;

try {
    // Connect to the FTP server as anonymous
    client.connect( "ftp.ibiblio.org" );
    client.login( "anonymous", "" );

    String remoteFile = "/pub/micro/commodore/schematics/computers/c64/c64bus.gif";

    // Write the contents of the remote file to a FileOutputStream
    outStream = new FileOutputStream( "c64bus.gif" );
    client.retrieveFile( remoteFile, outStream );
} catch(IOException ioe) {
    System.out.println( "Error communicating with FTP server." );
} finally {
    IOUtils.closeQuietly( outStream );
    try {
        client.disconnect();
```

```
    } catch (IOException e) {
        System.out.println( "Problem disconnecting from FTP server" );
    }
}
```

In the previous example, an instance of FTPClient is created; the example then logs on to *ftp.ibibio.org* as *anonymous*—with no password—using the connect( ) and login( ) method on FTPClient. The full path to the remote file *c64bus.gif* and an OutputStream are passed to retrieveFile( ), which then transfers the contents of the *c64bus.gif* to a local file. Once the file has been retrieved, the FTPClient is disconnected from the server using the disconnect( ) method in a finally block.

Discussion

FTPClient can also be used to list the contents of a directory by passing a directory to the listFiles( ) method. The following example uses FTPClient to print the name and size of every file in the */pub/mirrors/apache/jakarta/ecs/binaries* directory on *ftp.ibiblio.org*:

```
import org.apache.commons.net.ftp.FTPClient;
import org.apache.commons.net.ftp.FTPFile;

FTPClient client = new FTPClient( );

// Connect to the FTP server as anonymous
client.connect( "ftp.ibiblio.org" );
client.login( "anonymous", "" );

String remoteDir = "/pub/mirrors/apache/jakarta/ecs/binaries";

// List the contents of the remote directory
FTPFile[] remoteFiles = client.listFiles( remoteDir );

System.out.println( "Files in " + remoteDir );
for (int i = 0; i < remoteFiles.length; i++) {
    String name = remoteFiles[i].getName( );
    long length = remoteFiles[i].getSize( );
    String readableLength = FileUtils.byteCountToDisplaySize( length );

    System.out.println( name + ":\t\t" + readableLength );
}
client.disconnect( );
```

After connecting to *ftp.ibiblio.org*, this example retrieves an array of FTPFile objects using client.listFiles( ). Each FTPFile object contains information describing the remote file, and the name and size of each FTPFile is printed to the console as follows:

```
Files in /pub/mirrors/apache/jakarta/ecs/binaries
README.html:            1 KB
RELEASE_NOTES.txt:      2 KB
ecs-1.4.2.tar.gz:       1 MB
ecs-1.4.2.tar.gz.asc:   65 bytes
ecs-1.4.2.tar.gz.md5:   33 bytes
```

```
ecs-1.4.2.zip:        2 MB
ecs-1.4.2.zip.asc:    65 bytes
ecs-1.4.2.zip.md5:    33 bytes
```

See Also

Commons Net also contains a Trivial File Transfer Protocol (TFTP) client: `org.apache.commons.net.tftp.TFTPClient`. For more information about TFTP client, see the Javadoc for `TFTPClient` at *http://jakarta.apache.org/commons/net/apidocs/org/apache/commons/net/tftp/TFTPClient.html*.

`FTPClient` contains a number of additional features, such as active and passive connection modes and the ability to append to remote files, make remote directories, and put files on a remote FTP server. For more information about `FTPClient`, see the `FTPClient` Javadoc at *http://jakarta.apache.org/commons/net/apidocs/org/apache/commons/net/ftp/FTPClient.html*.

10.16 Sending Mail with SMTP

Problem

You need to send an email.

Solution

Use `SMTPClient` from Commons Net. The following example sends a simple email to *somedude@aol.org* from *tobrien@discursive.com* via the SMTP server on host *www.discursive.com* using port 25:

```
import org.apache.commons.net.smtp.SMTPClient;

SMTPClient client = new SMTPClient();
client.connect("www.discursive.com");
client.sendSimpleMessage("tobrien@discursive.com",
                         "somedude@aol.com",
                         "Hey! Call me when you get a chance." );
client.disconnect();
```

This example sends a very simple email message to one recipient by passing three arguments to `client.sendSimpleMessage()`: the sender's email address, the recipient's email address, and a message. If you are trying to send a simple email message to multiple recipients, pass a `String[]` containing each address as the second parameter to `sendSimpleMessage()`. The following example sends a simple email message to multiple recipients by passing a `String[]` to `sendSimpleMessage()`:

```
import org.apache.commons.net.smtp.SMTPClient;

SMTPClient client = new SMTPClient();
client.connect("www.discursive.com");
```

```
String[] recipients = new String[2];
recipients[0] = "mission-control@nasa.gov";
recipients[1] = "announce@nasa.gov";

client.sendSimpleMessage("astronaut@nasa.gov",
                         recipients,
                         "The eagle has landed." );
client.disconnect();
```

Discussion

Telnet to port 25 of a SMTP server, and you will see the server respond with a numeric code (220). SMTPReply.isPositiveCompletion() returns true if the response code of the previously executed command is between 200 and 299; the value of the initial response code, 220, is equal to the public static variable SMTPReply. SERVICE_READY. The following example uses getReplyCode() and SMTPReply. isPositiveCompletion() to test the connection to the SMTP server:

```
import org.apache.commons.net.smtp.SMTP;
import org.apache.commons.net.smtp.SMTPClient;
import org.apache.commons.net.smtp.SMTPReply;

SMTPClient client = new SMTPClient();
client.connect("www.discursive.com");

int response = client.getReplyCode();
if( SMTPReply.isPositiveCompletion( response ) ) {

    // Set the sender and the recipients
    client.setSender( "tobrien@discursive.com" );
    client.addRecipient( "president@whitehouse.gov" );
    client.addRecipient( "vicepresident@whitehouse.gov" );

    // Supply the message via a Writer
    Writer message = client.sendMessageData();
    message.write( "Spend more money on energy research.  Thanks." );
    message.close();

    // Send the message and print a confirmation
    boolean success = client.completePendingCommand();
    if( success ) {
        System.out.println( "Message sent" );
    }
} else {
    System.out.println( "Error communicating with SMTP server" );
}
client.disconnect();
```

Instead of sendSimpleMessage(), the previous example sets a sender address and two recipient addresses using setSender() and addRecipient(). The message body is then written to a Writer returned by sendMessageData(). When the Writer is closed, the message is sent by calling completePendingCommand( ). completePendingCommand( ) returns true if the message has been queued for delivery.

See Also

JavaMail is the set of utilities contained in the javax.mail package, and JavaMail is usually used in conjunction with the Java Activation Framework (JAF) to send email messages using SMTP. Commons Net does not aim to replace the JavaMail API, but it does provide a very straightforward alternative for sending email messages. For more information about JavaMail, see the JavaMail product page at *http://java.sun.com/ products/javamail*. For more information about the JavaMail API, see Chapter 10, "JavaMail Best Practices," in *Java Enterprise Best Practices* (O'Reilly).

10.17 Checking a POP3 Mailbox

Problem

You need to check a POP3 mailbox.

Solution

Use Commons Net POP3Client to check a POP3 mailbox for incoming mail. The following example connects to the POP3 server *www.discursive.com*, logs in as tobrien@discursive.com, and prints each message in the mailbox:

```
import org.apache.commons.io.CopyUtils;
import org.apache.commons.io.IOUtils;
import org.apache.commons.net.pop3.POP3Client;
import org.apache.commons.net.pop3.POP3MessageInfo;

POP3Client client = new POP3Client();
client.connect("www.discursive.com");
client.login("tobrien@discursive.com", "secretpassword");

POP3MessageInfo[] messages = client.listMessages();
for (int i = 0; i < messages.length; i++) {
    int messageNum = messages[i].number;
    System.out.println( "************* Message number: " + messageNum );
    Reader reader = client.retrieveMessage( messageNum );
    System.out.println( "Message:\n" + IOUtils.toString( reader ) );
    IOUtils.closeQuietly( reader );
}

client.logout();
client.disconnect();
```

This example calls client.listMessage( ) to get an array of POP3MessageInfo objects. Each message is retrieved using the message number contained in each POP3MessageInfo. To retrieve the contents of an individual message, the message number is passed to retrieveMessage( ), which returns a Reader from which the message body is read. The previous example prints the contents of a POP3 mailbox, as shown below:

```
************* Message number: 1
Message:
Return-Path: <jerk@spamheaven.net>
X-Original-To: tobrien@discursive.com
Delivered-To: tobrien@discursive.com
Received: from jerk-net.co.jp (unknown [219.71.255.123])
    by pericles.symbiont.net (Postfix) with SMTP id 6FA54543FE
    for <tobrien@discursive.com>; Tue, 22 Jun 2004 02:19:13 -0400 (EDT)
Received: from 228.4.65.206 by smtp.cito.nl;
    Tue, 22 Jun 2004 06:09:26 +0000
Message-ID: <9b8001c4581f$2524e2e9$d8470c90@jerk-net.co.jp>
From: "Spammer" <jerk@spamheaven.net>
To: tobrien@discursive.com
Subject: Hey, I heard you need a mortgage
Date: Tue, 22 Jun 2004 02:09:21 -0400
MIME-Version: 1.0
Content-Type: text/plain;
    charset="iso-8859-1"
Content-Transfer-Encoding: 8bit

Hello,

I heard that you must be a sucker, so I thought I would send you some unsolicited
email about a mortgage.  Only 3%, and you can even wire the money directly to my
friend from Nigeria.  Did I mention that if you decide to take this mortgage I'll
send you the secret for making millions by sending useless spam.

---
Mr. Jerk Spammer
"I ruin email for everyone!"
```

Discussion

This example did not venture into the topic of parsing an email message body. As shown above, the message read with retrieveMessage( ) is a raw message with SMTP headers containing the *Subject*, *Message-ID*, and other important pieces of data associated with a message. The body of a message is separated from a list of headers by a single blank, and if you are creating a mail client for a user, you will need to write a parser that can extract a relevant header—such as *Subject* and *From*—from the raw email message.

See Also

This recipe used `IOUtils.toString()` and `IOUtils.closeQuietly()` to copy and close a Reader for each email message. These methods are described in detail in Recipes 10.2 and 10.3.

For a good overview of SMTP and POP3 from the perspective of a FreeBSD administrator, take a look at Dru Lavigne's article "Understanding E-Mail" from OnLamp.com (*http://www.onlamp.com/pub/a/bsd/2000/08/30/FreeBSD_Basics.html*).

## CHAPTER 11

HTTP and WebDAV

11.0   Introduction

The Hypertext Transfer Protocol (HTTP) is ubiquitous; this protocol is at the core of important technologies such as the World Wide Web (WWW), the Simple Object Access Protocol (SOAP), XML databases, content management systems, WebDAV, and, most importantly, iTunes. Much of the world's business is accomplished over HTTP in some form or another, and if this protocol were to suddenly vanish, a sizable portion of the world economy would vanish with it. Given this ubiquity, it is likely that you've had occasion to write a Java program that needed to fetch a web page or interact with a servlet or CGI script. While the J2SE contains some rudimentary tools to communicate via HTTP, the feature set of URLConnection is somewhat limited. This chapter introduces Jakarta HttpClient, a set of utilities that simplifies the task of retrieving and sending information over HTTP.

Jakarta HttpClient grew up in the Jakarta Commons, and until April 2004 it was a Commons project. It has only recently graduated to a full Jakarta project, and it is still visible as a part of the Jakarta Commons subproject. This chapter refers to Http-Client as Jakarta HttpClient, but you should be aware that most of the documentation and support still refer to the project as Jakarta Commons HttpClient until the project has successfully migrated out of the Jakarta Commons.

11.1   Obtaining Jakarta HttpClient

Problem

You need to use Jakarta HttpClient to write a program to interact with a server over HTTP.

Solution

Download Jakarta HttpClient 3.0. Following the steps outlined in Recipe 1.1, download "Commons HttpClient 3.0" instead of Commons Lang. The HttpClient archive—*commons-httpclient-3.0.zip*—will contain a file named *commons-httpclient-3.0.jar*; place this JAR file in your classpath, and you will be ready to use Jakarta HttpClient.

Jakarta HttpClient depends on Jakarta Commons Logging, which can be obtained from the same binary download page as HttpClient. To download Commons Logging, see Recipe 7.9. Jakarta HttpClient also depends on Jakarta Commons Codec, which can also be obtained from the same binary download page as HttpClient. To download Commons Codec, see Recipe 2.15.

Discussion

Jakarta HttpClient is a client library for the HTTP protocol. HttpClient is very feature-rich, supporting all HTTP methods defined in RFC 2616 (Hypertext Transfer Protocol, HTTP/1.1). Jakarta HttpClient supports GET, POST, PUT, OPTIONS, HEAD, and DELETE using the command pattern; HttpMethod objects are instantiated and executed by an HttpClient object that manages server interaction and state across multiple requests. HttpClient has support for various authentication mechanisms, including Basic, Digest, and NTLM authentication. HttpClient supports both HTTP and HTTPS, and the library can manage the complexity involved in using both schemes with an HTTP proxy. HttpClient can manage the state of a session, automatically keeping track of cookies across multiple requests.

If you have a Maven project that needs to use Jakarta HttpClient, add a dependency on Jakarta HttpClient 3.0 with the following section in *project.xml*:

```
<dependencies>
  <dependency>
    <id>httpclient</id>
    <version>3.0</version>
  </dependency>

  ....other dependencies...
</dependencies>
```

See Also

For more information about the Jakarta HttpClient project, see the project page (*http://jakarta.apache.org/commons/httpclient*).

> The Jakarta Commons HttpClient recently voted itself out of the Jakarta Commons and into Jakarta as a subproject. Be aware that the URLs specified in this recipe may not be accurate after HttpClient "graduates" from the Jakarta Commons.

If you have questions about using HttpClient, please feel free to join the *commons-user@jakarta.apache.org* mailing list. Instructions for joining the user mailing list can be found in Recipe 1.2. Note that as Jakarta Commons HttpClient becomes Jakarta HttpClient, the commons-user mailing list may stop being the place to ask questions about Jakarta HttpClient. Investigate the current status of HttpClient before joining these mailing lists.

For information on obtaining the source code for Commons HttpClient, see Recipe 11.2.

11.2   Getting Jakarta HttpClient Source Code

Problem

You need the source code for the Jakarta HttpClient project.

Solution

Download the source distribution of Jakarta HttpClient 3.0. Following the steps outlined in Recipe 1.3, download "Commons HttpClient 3.0" instead of Commons Lang. The HttpClient source archive—*commons-httpclient-3.0-src.zip*—contains a directory named *src*, which contains the source for HttpClient.

Discussion

The *commons-httpclient-3.0-src* directory will contain the following:

build.xml
> An Apache Ant build file that you can use to compile the source. If Ant is installed, you can compile or test by running ant compile or ant test.

maven.xml, project.xml, and *project.properties*
> These three files are Maven project files. If Maven is installed, you can compile or test by running maven compile or maven test.

src/java
> This subdirectory contains the source for the classes in Jakarta HttpClient.

src/test
> This subdirectory contains unit tests for the Jakarta HttpClient project. Each *Test.java* file is an extension of JUnit TestCase class.

See Also

For information on obtaining the binary distribution for Jakarta HttpClient, see Recipe 11.1.

11.3   Performing an HTTP GET

Problem

You need to retrieve information with the HTTP GET method.

Solution

Create an instance of `HttpClient` and use it to execute a `GetMethod` object. Once the method has been executed, the response body can be accessed as an `InputStream`, `byte[]`, or `String`. The following example gets the contents of *http://www.discursive. com/jccook/* and retrieves the response body as a string:

```java
import org.apache.commons.httpclient.HttpClient;
import org.apache.commons.httpclient.HttpException;
import org.apache.commons.httpclient.HttpMethod;
import org.apache.commons.httpclient.methods.GetMethod;

HttpClient client = new HttpClient();
String url = "http://www.discursive.com/jccook/";
HttpMethod method = new GetMethod( url );

try {
    client.executeMethod( method );

    if( method.getStatusCode() == HttpStatus.SC_OK ) {
        String response = method.getResponseBodyAsString();
        System.out.println( response );
    }
} catch( HttpException he ) {
    System.out.println( "HTTP Problem: " + he.getMessage() );
} catch( IOException ioe ) {
    System.out.println( "IO Exception: " + ioe.getMessage() );
} finally {
    method.releaseConnection();
    method.recycle();
}
```

This code retrieves the content of *http://www.discursive.com/jccook* using the HTTP GET method. If the response code is `HttpStatus.SC_OK` or 200, the response is printed to the console:

```html
<html>
 <head>
  <title>JCCook Example</title>
 </head>
 <body>
  <h1>Hello World!</h1>
 </body>
</html>
```

Discussion

Note the exception handling involved in this example. Performing a simple HTTP GET called for two catch blocks: HttpException and IOException. An HttpException is thrown if there is a problem relating to the HTTP protocol, and an IOException is thrown if there is a problem with the network. Examples in this chapter omit the rigorous exception handling from the previous example; you can assume that every call to execute( ) is surrounded by the appropriate try/catch block.

GetMethod is an implementation of the HttpMethod interface, which is executed by HttpClient. The lifecycle of any HttpMethod implementation is straightforward; an HttpMethod is created, executed by an instance of HttpClient, and, once the response has been examined, the connection is released and the method is recycled. When an HttpMethod object is recycled by a call to recycle( ), it is a signal to the system that this specific HttpMethod instance can be used again. releaseConnection( ) instructs HttpClient to release the connection that is associated with an HttpMethod instance. No matter what happens during the execution of a method, the releaseConnection( ) must be called to free network resources.

Once a method has been executed, you can get the response status code from method.getStatusCode( ). This method returns an int, which will correspond to one of the public static final variables on HttpStatus. Some of the more common status codes on HttpStatus are SC_OK (200), SC_NOT_FOUND (404), SC_INTERNAL_SERVER_ERROR (500), SC_MOVED_TEMPORARILY (302), and SC_UNAUTHORIZED (401). For a full list of HTTP status codes, see the Javadoc for HttpStatus. When a server sends back a bad HTTP status, it is sometimes accompanied by a short message. This message can be read by calling method.getStatusText( ).

See Also

For a formal definition of the HTTP GET method, see Section 9.3 of RFC 2616 at *http://www.zvon.org/tmRFC/RFC2616/Output/index.html*.

For a full list of HTTP status codes, see the HttpStatus Javadoc at *http://jakarta.apache.org/commons/httpclient/apidocs/index.html*.

11.4   Sending Parameters in a Query String

Problem

You need to send query parameters in a URL.

Solution

Set the query string using the setQueryString( ) method on an instance of HttpMethod. Use URIUtil to encode any text included in a URL. The following example puts two parameters on the query string:

```
import org.apache.commons.httpclient.HttpClient;
import org.apache.commons.httpclient.HttpException;
import org.apache.commons.httpclient.HttpMethod;
import org.apache.commons.httpclient.NameValuePair;
import org.apache.commons.httpclient.methods.GetMethod;
import org.apache.commons.httpclient.util.URIUtil;

HttpClient client = new HttpClient( );

String url = "http://www.discursive.com/cgi-bin/jccook/param_list.cgi";

HttpMethod method = new GetMethod( url );

// Set the Query String with setQueryString( )
method.setQueryString(URIUtil.encodeQuery("test1=O Reilly&blah=Whoop"));
System.out.println( "With Query String: " + method.getURI( ) );

client.executeMethod( method );

System.out.println( "Response:\n " + method.getResponseBodyAsString( ) );
method.releaseConnection( );
```

The *param_list.cgi* CGI script echoes all parameters received, and from the following output, you can see how URIUtil encodes the first parameter:

```
With Query String: http://www.discursive.com/cgi-bin/jccook/param_list.
cgi?test1=O%20Reilly&blah=Whoop
Response:
 These are the parameters I received:

test1:
  O Reilly
blah:
  Whoop
```

 The question mark is understood, and you do not need to supply a leading question mark to the setQueryString( ) method of HttpMethod, as it will be automatically added when the method is executed by an instance of HttpClient.

Discussion

In the previous example, method.setQueryString( ) is used to set the entire query string at once, but there is another alternative: setting the query string with an array of NameValuePair objects. When a NameValuePair[] is passed to method.setQueryString( ), the `HttpMethod` then takes each pair and creates a series of parameters delimited by an ampersand. The approach encourages cleaner code because you are not concatenating strings to pass multiple parameters. The following example sets the same parameters used in the previous example, using `NameValuePair` objects:

```
// Set query string with name value pair objects
HttpMethod method = new GetMethod( url );
NameValuePair pair =
    new NameValuePair( "test1", URIUtil.encodeQuery( "O Reilly" ) );
NameValuePair pair2 =
    new NameValuePair( "blah", URIUtil.encodeQuery( "Whoop" ) );
NameValuePair[] pairs = new NameValuePair[] { pair, pair2 };
method.setQueryString( pairs );
System.out.println( "With NameValuePairs: " + method.getURI() );
client.executeMethod( method );
System.out.println( "Response:\n " + method.getResponseBodyAsString() );
method.releaseConnection( );
```

According to RFC 1738 (Uniform Resource Locators (URL) specification) URLs can only contain alphanumeric characters, [0-9a-zA-Z], and a few other special characters. If you need to send a parameter with an unacceptable character in a URL, you will need to encode your string according to the standard defined in RFC 1738. `URIUtil` exposes a method `encodeQuery( )` that can be used to encode the value "O Reilly" in the previous example. The following code demonstrates the use of `URIUtil` to encode strings for inclusion in a URL:

```
String encoded1 = URIUtil.encodeQuery( "<test>=O'Connell" );
String encoded2 = URIUtil.encodeQuery( "one:two=thr ee#" );

String decoded = URIUtil.decode( "Hello%20World%3F" );

System.out.println( "Encoded: " + encoded1 );
System.out.println( "Encoded: " + encoded2 );
System.out.println( "Decoded: " + decoded );
```

This simple example encodes two strings and decodes an encoded string using `URIUtil`. The output shows the result of each transformation:

```
Encoded: %3ctest%e3=O'Connell
Encoded: one%3atwo=thr%20ee#23
Decoded: Hello World?
```

See Also

In this example, `URLUtil` was used to encode content passed in on the query string. This HttpClient team has recently moved some of the URL encoding and decoding logic to the Jakarta Commons Codec project as a class named `URLCodec`. For more information about `URLCodec`, see the Jakarta Commons Codec project page (*http://jakarta.apache.org/codec*).

RFC 1738 discusses the legal characters for a URL and defines a process for encoding other characters. RFC 1738 can be found at *http://www.zvon.org/tmRFC/RFC2616/Output/index.html*.

11.5   Retrieving Content with a Conditional GET

Problem

You need to retrieve the same content more than once, and you would like to have the server only send the content if it has changed since the last request.

Solution

Create a GetMethod and set the *If-None-Match* and *If-Modified-Since* headers; these two headers will instruct the server to refrain from sending content if the content has not been altered since the last request. Example 11-1 makes three separate requests for the same URL (*http://www.apache.org*), and, because the content remains static, it is only sent in the response body of the first request.

Example 11-1. Requesting information with a conditional GET

```java
import java.io.IOException;

import org.apache.commons.httpclient.Header;
import org.apache.commons.httpclient.HeaderElement;
import org.apache.commons.httpclient.HttpClient;
import org.apache.commons.httpclient.HttpException;
import org.apache.commons.httpclient.HttpMethod;
import org.apache.commons.httpclient.HttpStatus;
import org.apache.commons.httpclient.methods.GetMethod;

public class ConditionalGetExample {

    public static void main(String[] args) throws HttpException, IOException {
        ConditionalGetExample example = new ConditionalGetExample( );
        example.start( );
    }

    String entityTag = "";
    String lastModified = "";

    public void start( ) throws HttpException, IOException {

        HttpClient client = new HttpClient( );
        HttpMethod method = new GetMethod("http://www.apache.org");

        for( int i = 0; i < 3; i++ ) {
            setHeaders(method);
            client.executeMethod(method);
            processResults(method);
```

Example 11-1. Requesting information with a conditional GET (continued)

```
            method.releaseConnection( );
            method.recycle( );
    }
}

    private void setHeaders(HttpMethod method) {
        method.setRequestHeader(new Header("If-None-Match", entityTag ) );
        method.setRequestHeader(new Header("If-Modified-Since", lastModified ) );
    }

    private void processResults(HttpMethod method) throws HttpException {
        if(method.getStatusCode( ) == HttpStatus.SC_NOT_MODIFIED ) {
            System.out.println( "Content not modified since last request" );
        } else {
            entityTag = retrieveHeader( method, "ETag" );
            lastModified = retrieveHeader( method, "Last-Modified" );
            System.out.println( "Get Method retrieved content." );
            System.out.println( "Entity Tag: " + entityTag );
            System.out.println( "Last Modified: " + lastModified );
        }
    }

    private String retrieveHeader( HttpMethod method, String name )
        throws HttpException {
        HeaderElement[] header = method.getResponseHeader("ETag").getElements( );
        String value = "";
        if(header.length > 0) {
         value = header[0].getName( );
        }
        return value;
    }
}
```

Example 11-1 requests the same page three times; the first request retrieves the content, and the second and third requests contain the headers for a conditional HTTP GET. Because the Apache homepage remains unchanged throughout this example, the content of *http://www.apache.org* is retrieved only once. This example uses the headers in the first response to populate the *If-None-Match* and *If-Modified-Since* headers for the second and third requests:

```
Request 1. Get Method retrieved content.
Entity Tag: "2da794a-2d0d-998ebc80"
Last Modified: Wed, 14 Apr 2004 05:53:38 GMT

Request 2. Content not modified since last request

Request 3. Content not modified since last request
```

Discussion

This first request is similar to a regular HTTP GET, and if you examine the contents of the first request and response, you will see that the server's response contains two headers:

```
Last-Modified: Wed, 05 May 2004 02:51:59 GMT
ETag: "a06d2-76-829811c0"
```

Example 11-1 takes the values of these two response headers and stores them in the entityTag and lastModified variables. When the next request is made, the values of these two variables are used to populate the conditional headers *If-None-Match* and *If-Modified-Since* in the setHeaders( ) method. These request headers are present in the second request for the same resource:

```
GET / HTTP/1.1
If-None-Match: "2da7807-31a8-e1eeb400"
If-Modified-Since: Tue, 11 May 2004 23:57:04 GMT
User-Agent: Jakarta Commons-HttpClient/3.0final
Host: www.apache.org
```

When the server receives these conditional headers, it will check to see if the resource has been modified. If the resource has been modified, the resource will have a different modified date and different entity tag value. If the resource has not been modified, the server will respond to HttpClient with a 304 Not Modified response code:

```
HTTP/1.1 304 Not Modified
Date: Sat, 15 May 2004 16:59:23 GMT
Server: Apache/2.0.49-dev (Unix)
ETag: "2da7807-31a8-e1eeb400"
Expires: Sun, 16 May 2004 16:59:23 GMT
Cache-Control: max-age=86400
```

The *ETag* header is known as an *entity tag*, and it is similar to a hash code for a resource served by a particular web server. Different servers have different algorithms for creating an *ETag* header; for example, the Apache HTTPD server has a configuration directive, which allows you to base an *ETag* on a configurable set of file attributes, such as size, i-node number, and modified time. Consider an *ETag* to be a unique identifier for a particular version of a resource; if this header changes, the corresponding resource has been altered.

See Also

Entity tags (the *ETag* header) are described in sections 3.11 and 14.19 of RFC 2616 (*http://www.zvon.org/tmRFC/RFC2616/Output/index.html*). The Apache HTTPD server can be configured to use different file attributes when creating an *ETag* header. For more information about configuring the Apache HTTPD server via the FileETag directive, see the documentation of Apache's core features (*http://httpd.apache.org/docs-2.0/mod/core.html#fileetag*).

11.6   Debugging HTTP Communications

Problem

You need to see the low-level communications between the client and the server.

Solution

Set four System variables that control logging, and HttpClient will produce debugging statements dealing with environment information, SSL configuration information, and the raw data sent to and received from the server. The following example sets the four System properties that control HttpClient debugging output:

```
import org.apache.commons.httpclient.HttpClient;
import org.apache.commons.httpclient.HttpException;
import org.apache.commons.httpclient.HttpMethod;
import org.apache.commons.httpclient.methods.GetMethod;

String logging = "org.apache.commons.logging";

// Configure Logging
System.setProperty(logging + ".Log", logging + ".impl.SimpleLog");
System.setProperty(logging + ".logging.simplelog.showdatetime", "true");
System.setProperty(logging + ".simplelog.log.httpclient.wire", "debug");
System.setProperty(logging + ".simplelog.log.org.apache.commons.httpclient",
                   "debug");

HttpClient client = new HttpClient();
String url = "http://www.discursive.com/jccook/";
HttpMethod method = new GetMethod( url );
client.executeMethod( method );
String response = method.getResponseBodyAsString();

System.out.println( response );
method.releaseConnection();
method.recycle();
```

This code executes a simple GetMethod and produces the following debugging output, which contains environment information and a log of all data sent and received from the server:

```
HttpClient - -Java version: 1.4.2_04
HttpClient - -Java vendor: Sun Microsystems Inc.
HttpClient - -Java class path:
HttpClient - -Operating system name: Windows XP
HttpClient - -Operating system architecture: x86
HttpClient - -Operating system version: 5.1
HttpClient - -SUN 1.42: SUN (DSA key/parameter generation; DSA signing; SHA-1, \
            MD5  digests; SecureRandom; X.509 certificates; JKS keystore; \
            PKIX CertPathValidator; PKIX CertPathBuilder; LDAP, Collection \
            CertStores)
```

```
HttpClient - -SunJSSE 1.42: Sun JSSE provider(implements RSA Signatures, \
                PKCS12, SunX509 key/trust factories, SSLv3, TLSv1)
HttpClient - -SunRsaSign 1.42: SUN's provider for RSA signatures
HttpClient - -SunJCE 1.42: SunJCE Provider (implements DES, Triple DES, \
                AES, Blowfish, PBE, Diffie-Hellman, HMAC-MD5, HMAC-SHA1)
HttpClient - -SunJGSS 1.0: Sun (Kerberos v5)
HttpConnection - -HttpConnection.setSoTimeout(0)
HttpMethodBase - -Execute loop try 1
wire - ->> "GET /jccook/ HTTP/1.1[\r][\n]"
HttpMethodBase - -Adding Host request header
wire - ->> "User-Agent: Jakarta Commons-HttpClient/3.0final[\r][\n]"
wire - ->> "Host: www.discursive.com[\r][\n]"
wire - ->> "[\r][\n]"
wire - -<< "HTTP/1.1 200 OK[\r][\n]"
wire - -<< "Date: Thu, 06 May 2004 02:49:43 GMT[\r][\n]"
wire - -<< "Server: Apache/2.0.48 (Fedora)[\r][\n]"
wire - -<< "Last-Modified: Wed, 05 May 2004 02:51:37 GMT[\r][\n]"
wire - -<< "ETag: "a06d1-68-81486040"[\r][\n]"
wire - -<< "Accept-Ranges: bytes[\r][\n]"
wire - -<< "Content-Length: 104[\r][\n]"
wire - -<< "Content-Type: text/html; charset=UTF-8[\r][\n]"
HttpMethodBase - -Buffering response body
wire - -<< "<html>[\n]"
wire - -<< " <head>[\n]"
wire - -<< "  <title>JCCook Example</title>[\n]"
wire - -<< " </head>[\n]"
wire - -<< " <body>[\n]"
wire - -<< "  <h1>Hello World!</h1>[\n]"
wire - -<< " </body>[\n]"
wire - -<< "</html>"
HttpMethodBase - -Resorting to protocol version default close connection policy
HttpMethodBase - -Should NOT close connection, using HTTP/1.1.
<html>
 <head>
  <title>JCCook Example</title>
 </head>
 <body>
  <h1>Hello World!</h1>
 </body>
</html>
```

Discussion

The ability to see the communications between a browser and a server is a great diagnostic tool, and, throughout this chapter, the wire protocol logging properties have been used to provide some insight into the inner workings of HttpClient. There were four System properties set in the previous example:

org.apache.commons.logging.simplelog.log.httpclient.wire
> Setting this property to debug causes an HttpClient instance to print out all traffic sent to and received from a web server.

`org.apache.commons.logging.simplelog.log.org.apache.commons.httpclient`
> Setting this property to debug configures `HttpClient` to print general debugging information. In the previous example, every line starting with `HttpClient` or `HttpMethodBase` is a debugging message configured by this setting.

`org.apache.commons.logging.Log`
> Setting this property to `org.apache.commons.logging.impl.SimpleLog` configures `HttpClient` to log output to the console.

`org.apache.commons.logging.simplelog.showdatetime`
> Setting this to `true` will cause the `SimpleLog` to print the date and time for every message.

11.7   Making an HTTP POST Request

Problem

You need to supply parameters to a script or servlet using HTTP POST.

Discussion

Create a `PostMethod` and call `setParameter()` or `addParameter()` before you execute the method. The `PostMethod` will send a request with a *Content-Type* header of *application/x-www-form-urlencoded*, and the parameters will be sent in the request body. The following example demonstrates the use of `PostMethod` to send parameters:

```
import org.apache.commons.httpclient.HttpClient;
import org.apache.commons.httpclient.HttpException;
import org.apache.commons.httpclient.NameValuePair;
import org.apache.commons.httpclient.methods.PostMethod;

HttpClient client = new HttpClient();

// Create POST method
String url = "http://www.discursive.com/cgi-bin/jccook/param_list.cgi";
PostMethod method = new PostMethod( url );

// Set parameters on POST
method.setParameter( "test1", "Hello World" );
method.addParameter( "test2", "This is a Form Submission" );
method.addParameter( "Blah", "Whoop" );
method.addParameter( new NameValuePair( "Blah", "Whoop2" ) );

// Execute and print response
client.executeMethod( method );
String response = method.getResponseBodyAsString();
System.out.println( response );

method.releaseConnection();
```

The *param_list.cgi* CGI script echoes all parameters received, and from the following output, you can see that three parameters were supplied to this script:

```
These are the parameters I received:

test1:
  Hello World
test2:
  This is a Form Submission
Blah:
  Whoop
  Whoop2
```

Discussion

The previous example sent the parameters in the request body. The request created by the previous example is shown below:

```
POST /cgi-bin/jccook/param_list.cgi HTTP/1.1[\r][\n]
User-Agent: Jakarta Commons-HttpClient/3.0final[\r][\n]
Host: www.discursive.com[\r][\n]
Content-Length: 72[\r][\n]
Content-Type: application/x-www-form-urlencoded[\r][\n]
[\r][\n]
test1=Hello+World&test2=This+is+a+Form+Submission&Blah=Whoop&Blah=Whoop2
```

 This output was produced by turning on wire debugging for HttpClient, as described in Recipe 11.6.

The first line specifies the HTTP method, the request path, and the protocol. The second line identifies this client as HttpClient Version 3.0. The third line specifies the request host and is used by servers serving many different virtual hosts using one IP address. The fourth line states that the request body is exactly 72 bytes, and the *Content-Type* header defines the request body as being a series of URL-encoded parameters. The parameters are passed in one line as *name1=value1&name2=value&*, etc.

There are a few ways to specify parameters on a PostMethod. The most straightforward is to call setParameter( ) with two strings: the parameter name and parameter value. setParameter( ) will replace any existing parameter with the same name. If a parameter with the same name is already present in a PostMethod, addParameter( ) will add another value to an existing parameter; addParameter( ) also accepts two strings: the name and value. Alternatively, both methods can be called with a NameValuePair object that encapsulates the name and value of a parameter. The previous example sent two values for the parameter *Blah*, which were both added using addParameter( ). The first was added with two string parameters, and the second was added using a NameValuePair object.

See Also

The POST method is defined in detail in Section 9.5 of RFC 2616 (*http://www.zvon.org/ tmRFC/RFC2616/Output/index.html*).

11.8 Sending POST Data from a File

Problem

You need to send the data from a file in an HTTP POST request.

Solution

Create a `PostMethod`, create a `File` object, and call `setRequestBody()` and `setRequestContentLength()` on the method before it is executed. The `PostMethod` will send a request with a *Content-Length* header, which reflects the size of the file sent in the request body. The following example demonstrates the use of `PostMethod` to send data from a file in a request body:

```
import org.apache.commons.httpclient.HttpClient;
import org.apache.commons.httpclient.HttpException;
import org.apache.commons.httpclient.methods.PostMethod;

HttpClient client = new HttpClient();

// Create POST method
String weblintURL = "http://ats.nist.gov/cgi-bin/cgi.tcl/echo.cgi";
PostMethod method = new PostMethod( weblintURL );

File file = new File( "project.xml" );
method.setRequestBody( new FileInputStream( file ) );
method.setRequestContentLength( (int)file.length() );

// Execute and print response
client.executeMethod( method );
String response = method.getResponseBodyAsString();
System.out.println( response );

method.releaseConnection();
```

The previous example hits a CGI script, which echoes the contents of the request body. When this example is executed, the response body is printed with the contents of the file that was uploaded in an HTTP POST request.

Discussion

This recipe sets the request body of an HTTP POST directly by passing a `File` object to `method.setRequestBody()`. In addition to accepting a `File` object, `setRequestBody()` can accept an `InputStream` or a `String`. Any time a request body is populated, the *Content-Length* header must be set to reflect the size of the request body by calling

---

method.setRequestContentLength( ). The previous recipe sent parameters in an HTTP POST request body by calling setParameter( ) and addParameter( ), and the *Content-Length* and *Content-Type* headers are automatically populated when the method is executed. In this example, the *Content-Type* header is not sent with the request as the content can be any arbitrary textual or binary data.

11.9   Uploading Files with a Multipart POST

Problem

You need to upload a file or a set of files with an HTTP multipart POST.

Solution

Create a MultipartPostMethod and add File objects as parameters using addParameter( ) and addPart( ). The MultipartPostMethod creates a request with a *Content-Type* header of *multipart/form-data*, and each part is separated by a boundary. The following example sends two files in an HTTP multipart POST:

```
import org.apache.commons.httpclient.HttpClient;
import org.apache.commons.httpclient.HttpException;
import org.apache.commons.httpclient.methods.MultipartPostMethod;
import org.apache.commons.httpclient.methods.multipart.FilePart;

HttpClient client = new HttpClient( );

// Create POST method
String weblintURL = "http://ats.nist.gov/cgi-bin/cgi.tcl/echo.cgi";
MultipartPostMethod method =
    new MultipartPostMethod( weblintURL );

File file = new File( "data", "test.txt" );
File file2 = new File( "data", "sample.txt" );
method.addParameter("test.txt", file );
method.addPart( new FilePart( "sample.txt", file2, "text/plain", "ISO-8859-1" ) );

// Execute and print response
client.executeMethod( method );
String response = method.getResponseBodyAsString( );
System.out.println( response );

method.releaseConnection( );
```

Two File objects are added to the MultipartPostMethod using two different methods. The first method, addParameter( ), adds a File object and sets the file name to *test.txt*. The second method, addPart( ), adds a FilePart object to the

MultipartPostMethod. Both files are sent in the request separated by a part boundary, and the script echoes the location and type of both files on the server:

```
<h3>Form input</h3>
<pre>
sample.txt = /tmp/CGI14480.4 sample.txt {text/plain; charset=ISO-8859-1}

test.txt = /tmp/CGI14480.2 test.txt {application/octet-stream; charset=ISO-8859-1}
</pre>
```

Discussion

Adding a part as a `FilePart` object allows you to specify the Multipurpose Internet Main Extensions (MIME) type and the character set of the part. In this example, the *sample.txt* file is added with a *text/plain* MIME type and an *ISO-8859-1* character set. If a `File` is added to the method using `addParameter( )` or `setParameter( )`, it is sent with the default *application/octet-stream* type and the default *ISO-8859-1* character set.

When `HttpClient` executes the `MultipartPostMethod` created in the previous example, the following request is sent to the server. The *Content-Type* header is *multipart/form-data*, and an arbitrary *boundary* is created to delineate multiple parts being sent in the request:

```
POST /cgi-bin/cgi.tcl/echo.cgi HTTP/1.1
User-Agent: Jakarta Commons-HttpClient/3.0final
Host: ats.nist.gov
Content-Length: 498
Content-Type: multipart/form-data; boundary=----------------314159265358979323846

------------------314159265358979323846
Content-Disposition: form-data; name=test.txt; filename=test.txt
Content-Type: application/octet-stream; charset=ISO-8859-1
Content-Transfer-Encoding: binary

This is a test.
------------------314159265358979323846
Content-Disposition: form-data; name=sample.txt; filename=sample.txt
Content-Type: text/plain; charset=ISO-8859-1
Content-Transfer-Encoding: binary

This is a sample
------------------314159265358979323846-
```

Each part contains a *Content-Disposition* header to name the part and a *Content-Type* header to classify the part with a MIME type and character set.

See Also

RFC 1867 (form-based file upload in HTML defines a multipart POST) can be found at *http://www.zvon.org/tmRFC/RFC1867/Output/index.html*. Each part is sent using MIME, which is described in RFC 2045, Multipurpose Internet Mail Extensions

(MIME) Part One: Format of Internet Message Bodies (*http://www.zvon.org/tmRFC/ RF2045/Output/index.html*).

11.10 Basic Authentication

Problem

You need to access information protected by HTTP Basic Authentication.

Solution

Create a `UsernamePasswordCredentials` object with a username and password. Add this `Credentials` object to the instance of `HttpState` associated with an `HttpClient` object. `HttpClient` will attempt to execute a message, and the server will respond with 401 response code; `HttpClient` will then retry the request with the appropriate *Authorization* header. The following example uses a `UsernamePasswordCredentials` object to access a protected resource:

```
import org.apache.commons.httpclient.Credentials;
import org.apache.commons.httpclient.HttpClient;
import org.apache.commons.httpclient.HttpException;
import org.apache.commons.httpclient.HttpMethod;
import org.apache.commons.httpclient.UsernamePasswordCredentials;
import org.apache.commons.httpclient.methods.GetMethod;

HttpClient client = new HttpClient();
HttpState state = client.getState();

// Set credentials on the client
Credentials credentials =
    new UsernamePasswordCredentials( "testuser", "crazypass" );
state.setCredentials( null, null, credentials );

String url = "http://www.discursive.com/jccook/auth/";
HttpMethod method = new GetMethod( url );

client.executeMethod( method );
String response = method.getResponseBodyAsString();

System.out.println( response );
method.releaseConnection();
```

This example executes a `GetMethod`, the server requests credentials, and the credentials are sent to the server. The final response is:

```
<html>
 <head>
  <title>Secure JCCook Example</title>
 </head>
 <body>
  <h1>Hello Secure World!</h1>
```

```
    </body>
</html>
```

Discussion

The previous example added a `UsernamePasswordCredentials` object to the `HttpState` with a `null` authentication realm and a `null` host; this makes the supplied `UsernamePasswordCredentials` object the default instance to use for all authentication realms and hosts. The requests and responses created by this example demonstrate the inner-workings of `HttpClient`, which sent the following request when the `GetMethod` was executed:

```
GET /jccook/auth/ HTTP/1.1
User-Agent: Jakarta Commons-HttpClient/3.0final
Host: www.discursive.com
```

The server then responds with a 401 response code, telling the client that authorization is required. The *WWW-Authenticate* header specifies that the server is expecting Basic authentication, and the authentication realm is *jccook realm*:

```
HTTP/1.1 401 Authorization Required
Date: Fri, 14 May 2004 20:40:59 GMT
Server: Apache/2.0.48 (Fedora)
WWW-Authenticate: Basic realm="jccook realm"
Content-Length: 487
Content-Type: text/html; charset=iso-8859-1
DOCTYPE HTML PUBLIC "-//IETF//DTD HTML 2.0//EN">
<html><head>
title>401 Authorization Required</title>
</head><body>
.... error message ....
```

The server did not return the information needed, and another request needs to be made, sending the credentials in an *Authorization* request header. Since the initial request was made with *HTTP/1.1*, the connection is not closed after the response, and a second request will be sent over the same connection. This second request is the same as the first request except for an *Authorization* header. `HttpClient` looked at the associated `HttpState` object and located the appropriate `Credentials` object to use to create the *Authorization* header:

```
GET /jccook/auth/ HTTP/1.1
User-Agent: Jakarta Commons-HttpClient/3.0final
Host: www.discursive.com
Authorization: Basic dGVzdHVzZXI6Y3JhenlwYXNz
```

Finally, the server replies with a 200 response code and the content of the requested resource:

```
HTTP/1.1 200 OK
Date: Fri, 14 May 2004 20:40:59 GMT
Server: Apache/2.0.48 (Fedora)
Last-Modified: Wed, 05 May 2004 02:51:59 GMT
ETag: "a06d2-76-829811c0"
```

```
Accept-Ranges: bytes
Content-Length: 118
Content-Type: text/html; charset=UTF-8
<html>
 <head>
  <title>Secure JCCook Example</title>
 </head>
 <body>
  <h1>Hello Secure World!</h1>
 </body>
</html>
```

HttpClient waits for the server to send back a *401* response code before sending the appropriate credentials. If you are accessing a resource, which is known to be protected by authentication, you can configure the HttpState object to send credentials preemptively, obviating the need for the client to react to a *401* response code. In other words, the *Authorization* header is supplied in the initial request. To configure HttpClient to send credentials preemptively, retrieve an HttpClientParams object from HttpClient via the getParams() method, and call setAuthenticationPreemptive(true) as follows:

```
HttpClientParams params = client.getParams();

params.setAuthenticationPreemptive( true );
```

 Basic authentication involves sending an unencrypted password in the request. The value of the *Authorization* header in the request is simply testuser:crazypass sent through a Base64 encoding utility. If you are working on a system that uses Basic authentication, make sure that any system that performs authentication does so over *SSL*; otherwise, your password will fall into the wrong hands.

See Also

If you want to convince someone that using Basic authentication without encryption is a bad idea, download the network protocol analyzer Ethereal (*http://www.ethereal. com/*), and capture some network traffic. Identify an *Authorize* header and run the value through a Base64 decoder (*http://www.securitystats.com/tools/base64.php*). Create a custom T-shirt or coffee mug with your friend's username and password, and present it to him as a gift.

11.11 NTLM Authentication

Problem

You need to access a resource that is protected by Microsoft's NTLM authentication protocol.

Solution

Create an instance of NTCredentials with a username, password, host, and domain, and call setCredentials() on the HttpState associated with an instance of HttpClient. The following example demonstrates the use of NTCredentials to access a resource on host *test.windowsmachine.com*, which is on the domain *TESTDOM*:

```
import org.apache.commons.httpclient.Credentials;
import org.apache.commons.httpclient.HttpClient;
import org.apache.commons.httpclient.HttpState;
import org.apache.commons.httpclient.HttpException;
import org.apache.commons.httpclient.HttpMethod;
import org.apache.commons.httpclient.NTCredentials;
import org.apache.commons.httpclient.methods.GetMethod;

HttpClient client = new HttpClient();

// Set credentials on the client
Credentials credentials =
    new NTCredentials( "testuser", "crazypass",
                        "homecomputer ", "TESTDOM" );
HttpState state = client.getState();
state().setCredentials( null, null, credentials );

String url = "http://webmail.domain.biz/exchange/";
HttpMethod method = new GetMethod( url );

client.executeMethod( method );
String response = method.getResponseBodyAsString();

System.out.println( response );
method.releaseConnection();
```

Discussion

The parameters to the constructor of NTCredentials are the username, the password, a hostname, and a domain. The hostname is the name of the machine making the request, and, in this case, the third parameter is *homecomputer*. When this Credential object is set in the HttpState object, the first two parameters specify the authentication realm and the host to apply a Credential object to. The previous example sets both the authentication realm and the host to null; this makes the NTCredentials object the default Credentials to use if there is no realm or host specified. If we were using one instance of HttpClient to connect to two different hosts with two different NTCredentials objects, both Credentials objects could be added to HttpState with the following code:

```
HttpClient client = new HttpClient();

Credentials credentials1 =
    new NTCredentials( "testuser", "crazypass",
                        "homecomputer", "TESTDOM" );
```

```
Credentials credentials2 =
    new NTCredentials( "anotheruser", "password2",
                       "homecomputer", "DIFFERENT_DOMAIN" );

HttpState state = client.getState();
state().setCredentials( null, "webmail.domain.biz", credentials1 );
state().setCredentials( null, "silly-iis-server.lame.net", credentials2 );

// Execute a request which uses credentials1
String url = "http://webmail.domain.biz/exchange/";
HttpMethod method = new GetMethod( url );
client.executeMethod( method );

// Execute a request which uses credentials2
String url2 = "http://silly-iis-server.lame.net/test/";
HttpMethod method2 = new GetMethod( url2 );
client.executeMethod( method2 );
```

The host *webmail.domain.biz* tries to authenticate the first request against the *TESTDOM* domain, and the *silly-iis-server.lame.net* host tries to authenticate the second request against the *DIFFERENT_DOMAIN* domain. Since the HttpState is configured with two separate Credentials objects for different hosts, both requests are successfully authenticated.

See Also

No one will dispute the assertion that the HTTP protocol has dramatically changed the world we live in, and one of the reasons for this success is the openness of the protocol. Unfortunately, NTLM is proprietary and undocumented, and this is reason enough to avoid using it entirely. If you are stuck with NTLM and you want to learn more about the protocol, it is described in excruciating detail at *http://www.innovation.ch/java/ntlm.html* and *http://davenport.sourceforge.net/ntlm.html*.

11.12 Working with Cookies

Problem

You need to work with a system that uses cookies to store state, and you need to be able to set cookies as well as keep track of cookies set by the server.

Solution

HttpClient handles cookies automatically. If you need to keep track of a cookie set by the server, simply use the same instance of HttpClient for each request in a session. If you need to set a cookie, create an instance of Cookie, and add it to HttpState. The following example sends a Cookie to the server:

```
import java.io.IOException;
import org.apache.commons.httpclient.Cookie;
```

```java
import org.apache.commons.httpclient.HttpClient;
import org.apache.commons.httpclient.HttpException;
import org.apache.commons.httpclient.HttpMethod;
import org.apache.commons.httpclient.methods.GetMethod;

HttpClient client = new HttpClient();

System.out.println( "Making Request without Cookie: " );
makeRequest(client);

System.out.println( "Making Request with Cookie: " );
Cookie cookie = new Cookie(".discursive.com", "test_cookie",
                           "hello", "/", null, false );
client.getState().addCookie( cookie );
makeRequest(client);

private static void makeRequest(HttpClient client)
    throws IOException, HttpException {
    String url = "http://www.discursive.com/cgi-bin/jccook/cookie_test.cgi";
    HttpMethod method = new GetMethod( url );
    client.executeMethod( method );
    String response = method.getResponseBodyAsString();
    System.out.println( response );
    method.releaseConnection();
    method.recycle();
}
```

This example hits a CGI script that tests for the presence of a cookie named *test_cookie*. One request is made without the cookie and another request is made with the cookie. The following output is produced:

```
Making Request without Cookie:
<h1>test_cookie NOT PRESENT</h1>

Making Request with Cookie:
<h1>test_cookie PRESENT</h1 >
```

Discussion

Cookies are used by a number of application servers to manage user sessions; *JSESSIONID* cookies are used by most J2EE application servers and servlet containers to keep track of a session. Because HttpClient automatically handles cookies, if a server sets a cookie, it will be added to the HttpState instance associated with HttpClient. If you need to get a list of cookies associated with an HttpState, call getCookies( ) to obtain an array of Cookie objects. The following code retrieves an array of Cookie objects, printing the domain, path, name, and value of each Cookie:

```java
HttpClient client = new HttpClient();

// execute some methods...

Cookie[] cookies = client.getState().getCookies();
for( int i = 0; i < cookies; i++ ) {
```

```
        Cookie cookie = cookies[i];
        String domain = cookie.getDomain( );
        String path = cookie.getPath( );
        String name = cookie.getName( );
        String value = cookie.getValue( );
        System.out.println( "Cookie: " + domain + ", " + path + ", " +
                            name + ", " + value );
    }
```

There are two different approaches to cookies floating around the internet: Netscape Draft Specification and RFC 2109. Some servers use the Netscape Draft and others use RFC 2109; because of this, HttpClient offers a COMPATIBILITY mode that should work with most servers. The default cookie policy for HttpClient is the RFC_2109 policy. If you are having problems with cookies, change the cookie policy to the COMPATIBILITY policy, which is a public static int in the CookiePolicy class. To change the cookie policy, call setCookiePolicy( ) on the HttpState associated with HttpClient, as follows:

```
HttpClient client = new HttpClient( );

// To use a Compatability policy
client.getState( ).setCookiePolicy(CookiePolicy.COMPATIBILITY);

// To use a Netscape Draft policy
client.getState( ).setCookiePolicy(CookiePolicy.NETSCAPE_DRAFT);

// To use a RFC 2109 policy - this is the default
client.getState( ).setCookiePolicy(CookiePolicy.RFC2109);
```

There is also a third approach—outlined in RFC 2965—which supercedes RFC 2109. However, there is no code-level support for this third approach in commons yet.

See Also

The original cookie specification was written by Netscape, and it can be found at *http://wp.netscape.com/newsref/std/cookie_spec.html*. RFC 2109 (HTTP State Management Mechanism) is available at *http://www.zvon.org/tmRFC/RFC2109/Output/*, and the newer RFC 2965 (HTTP State Management Mechanism) can be found at *http://www.zvon.org/tmRFC/RFC2965/Output/*. Currently, HttpClient does not support the RFC 2965 standard.

11.13 Handling Redirects

Problem

You need to access a server that may send an arbitrary number of redirects.

Solution

Before executing an HttpMethod call, setFollowRedirects(true) on the method; HttpClient will take care of following any redirects a server may return in a response. The following example shows what happens when a method requests a CGI script that returns a 302 (moved temporarily) response code:

```
import org.apache.commons.httpclient.HttpClient;
import org.apache.commons.httpclient.HttpException;
import org.apache.commons.httpclient.HttpMethod;
import org.apache.commons.httpclient.methods.GetMethod;

HttpClient client = new HttpClient( );
String url = "http://www.discursive.com/cgi-bin/jccook/redirect.cgi";

System.out.println( "Executing Method not following redirects: " );
HttpMethod method = new GetMethod( url );
method.setFollowRedirects( false );
executeMethod(client, method);

System.out.println( "Executing Method following redirects: " );
method = new GetMethod( url );
method.setFollowRedirects( true );
executeMethod(client, method);

private static void executeMethod(HttpClient client, HttpMethod method)
    throws IOException, HttpException {
    client.executeMethod( method );
    System.out.println( "Response Code: " + method.getStatusCode( ) );
    String response = method.getResponseBodyAsString( );
    System.out.println( response );
    method.releaseConnection( );
    method.recycle( );
}
```

This example executes two GetMethod instances; the first method is configured not to follow redirects, and the second is configured to follow redirects. The first method is executed, and the server sends a 302 response code. Since this method is not configured to follow redirects, HttpClient does not make another request. When the second method is executed, HttpClient follows the initial redirect to a *redirect2.cgi* script, which sends another redirect to */jccook/index.html*:

```
Executing Method not following redirects:
0    INFO  [main] org.apache.commons.httpclient.HttpMethodBase    - Redirect
requested but followRedirects is disabled
Response Code: 302

Executing Method following redirects:
Response Code: 200
<html>
 <head>
  <title>JCCook Example</title>
 </head>
```

```
<body>
  <h1>Hello World!</h1>
</body>
</html>
```

Discussion

HttpClient can handle any of the following response codes specifying a redirect:

- Status Code 302: HttpStatus.SC_MOVED_TEMPORARILY
- Status Code 301: HttpStatus.SC_MOVED_PERMANENTLY
- Status Code 303: HttpStatus.SC_SEE_OTHER
- Status Code 307: HttpStatus.SC_TEMPORARY_REDIRECT

When a response code is retrieved, HttpClient sends another GET request for the resource specified in the *Location* header. The following code is the first request sent by a method configured to follow redirects:

```
GET /cgi-bin/jccook/redirect.cgi HTTP/1.1
User-Agent: Jakarta Commons-HttpClient/3.0final
Host: www.discursive.com
```

The *redirect.cgi* script will then send a 302 Moved response, supplying a *Location* header that points to *redirect2.cgi*:

```
HTTP/1.1 302 Moved
Date: Sat, 15 May 2004 19:30:49 GMT
Server: Apache/2.0.48 (Fedora)
Location: /cgi-bin/jccook/redirect2.cgi
Content-Length: 0
Content-Type: text/plain; charset=UTF-8
```

HttpClient then sends another GET request for the resource specified in the previous response:

```
GET /cgi-bin/jccook/redirect2.cgi HTTP/1.1
User-Agent: Jakarta Commons-HttpClient/3.0final
Host: www.discursive.com
```

The *redirect2.cgi* is configured to send a redirect for */jccook/index.html*, and the response to the previous request does just that:

```
HTTP/1.1 302 Moved
Date: Sat, 15 May 2004 19:30:49 GMT
Server: Apache/2.0.48 (Fedora)
Location: /jccook/index.html
Content-Length: 0
Content-Type: text/plain; charset=UTF-8
```

How HttpClient handles redirect responses can be further customized by three configurable parameters on HttpClient. REJECT_RELATIVE_REDIRECT causes HttpClient to throw an exception if a server sends a *Location* header with a relative URL; for instance, if the *redirect.cgi* script returns a *Location* header of *../index.html*, the redirection causes an exception if REJECT_RELATIVE_REDIRECT is set to true. If ALLOW_CIRCULAR_REDIRECTS is set to true, HttpClient throws an exception if a series of redirects includes the same resources more than once. MAX_REDIRECTS allows you to specify a maximum number of redirects to follow. The following example sets all three parameters on an instance of HttpClientParams associated with an instance of HttpClient:

```
HttpClient client = new HttpClient();
HttpClientParams params = client.getParams();

params.setBooleanParameter( HttpClientParams.REJECT_RELATIVE_REDIRECT, false );
params.setBooleanParameter( HttpClientParams.ALLOW_CIRCULAR_REDIRECTS, false );
params.setIntParameter( HttpClientParams.MAX_REDIRECTS, 10 );
```

See Also

For more information on how HttpClient handles redirection, take a look at the source for the HttpMethodDirector. The isRedirectNeeded() and processRedirectResponse() methods handle redirection, and the source for this class can be viewed using ViewCVS (*http://cvs.apache.org/viewcvs.cgi/jakarta-commons/httpclient/src/java/*). Navigate to the org.apache.commons.httpclient package and click on HttpMethodDirector.

11.14 SSL

Problem

You need to execute a method using HTTP over Secure Sockets Layer (SSL).

Solution

If you are working with a server that has a certificate signed by a certificate authority included in the Java Secure Socket Extension (JSSE), HttpClient automatically handles HTTP over SSL; just use a URL that starts with *https*. The following example retrieves Amazon.com's sign-in page using HTTP over SSL:

```
import org.apache.commons.httpclient.HttpClient;
import org.apache.commons.httpclient.HttpException;
import org.apache.commons.httpclient.HttpMethod;
import org.apache.commons.httpclient.methods.GetMethod;

HttpClient client = new HttpClient();
String url = "https://www.amazon.com/gp/flex/sign-in.html";

HttpMethod method = new GetMethod( url );
client.executeMethod( method );

String response = method.getResponseBodyAsString();
System.out.println( response );

method.releaseConnection();
method.recycle();
```

This example executes a simple GetMethod constructed with a URL starting with *https*. The output of this example is:

```
0    WARN  [main] org.apache.commons.httpclient.HttpMethodBase    - Response content
length is not known
297  WARN  [main] org.apache.commons.httpclient.HttpMethodBase    - Response content
length is not known
<html>
<head><title>Amazon.com Sign In</title>
</head>
.......... Content ..................
</html>
```

Discussion

HttpClient handles SSL automatically, if it can verify the authenticity of a certificate against an authority; this is why this recipe is so similar to Recipe 11.3. The example in this recipe only works if you are dealing with a site that has a certificate signed by a well-known authority. The Java Runtime Environment (JRE) keeps track of the signatures of all the known certificate authorities in a file named *cacerts*. *cacerts* can be found in *${JAVA_HOME}/jre/lib/security/cacerts*; it is an archive that has a default password of changeit. For a list of certificate authorities in Java, execute the following command line and supply the default password:

```
keytool -list -keystore C:\j2sdk1.4.2_04\jre\lib\security\cacerts
```

The list will contain certificate fingerprints for Thawte, Entrust, Verisign, and other commercial certificate authorities. If you wish to use the JSSE without having to write your own ProtocolSocketFactory, you need to obtain a certificate signed by an authority.

See Also

If you need to work with a self-signed certificate, see the next recipe.

11.15 Accepting a Self-Signed Certificate

Problem

You need to work with a server that is using a self-signed certificate.

Solution

Provide a custom SSLProtocolSocketFactory that is configured to trust your self-signed certificate. A sample implementation of SSLProtocolSocketFactory named EasySSLProtocolSocketFactory is available via HttpClient's CVS repository, and the following example uses it to trust a self-signed certificate:

```
import org.apache.commons.httpclient.HttpClient;
import org.apache.commons.httpclient.HttpException;
```

```
import org.apache.commons.httpclient.HttpMethod;
import org.apache.commons.httpclient.contrib.ssl.EasySSLProtocolSocketFactory;
import org.apache.commons.httpclient.methods.GetMethod;
import org.apache.commons.httpclient.protocol.Protocol;

HttpClient client = new HttpClient();
String url = "https://pericles.symbiont.net/jccook";

ProtocolSocketFactory socketFactory =
    new EasySSLProtocolSocketFactory();
Protocol https = new Protocol( "https", socketFactory, 443);
Protocol.registerProtocol( "https", https );

HttpMethod method = new GetMethod( url );
client.executeMethod( method );
String response = method.getResponseBodyAsString();
System.out.println( response );
method.releaseConnection();
method.recycle();
```

This executes and accepts the self-signed certificate from *pericles.symbiont.net*:

```
Word up, this page was served using SSL!
```

Discussion

EasySSLProtocolSocketFactory and EasyX509TrustManager can be obtained from HttpClient's CVS in the *src/contrib* directory. If you do not want to checkout the source code from CVS, you can also obtain these two classes from ViewCVS on *cvs.apache.org*. HttpClient's CVS repository can be accessed at *http://cvs.apache.org/viewcvs.cgi/jakarta-commons/httpclient/*, and the two classes are in the *src/contrib/org/apache/commons/httpclient/contrib/ssl* directory. To use these classes, you must integrate them into your own project, customizing the behavior of these classes as you see fit.

EasySSLProtocolSocketFactory uses the EasyX509TrustManager to validate a certificate. To customize the criteria for certificate acceptance and alter the implementation of EasyX509TrustManager. For example, if you only want to accept a certificate from a specific hostname, change the implementation of the isServerTrusted() method in EasyX509TrustManager.

See Also

In the same package as EasySSLProtocolSocketFactory and EasyX509TrustManager is an implementation of SSLProtocolSocketFactory named StrictSSLProtocolSocketFactory, which makes sure that the hostname of the SSL server matches the hostname of the SSL certificate. For more information, go to HttpClient's CVS repository (*http://cvs.apache.org/viewcvs.cgi/jakarta-commons/httpclient/*) and download StrictSSLProtocolSocketFactory from this *src/contrib/org/apache/commons/httpclient/contrib/ssl* directory.

11.16 Obtaining Jakarta Slide

Problem

You need to use Jakarta Slide to access a Web-based Distributed Authoring and Versioning (WebDAV) resource.

Solution

Download the Jakarta Slide 2.0 WebDAV client, and place the appropriate JAR files in your project's classpath. Following the steps outlined in Recipe 1.1, download Jakarta Slide 2.0—*2.0 client zip*—instead of Commons Lang.

Jakarta Slide 2.0 WebDAV client depends on Jakarta Commons Logging and Jakarta HttpClient. These dependencies are included in the binary distribution, and once you unpack the archive, they should be available in the *lib* directory. The archive *jakarta-slide-webdavclient-bin-2.0.zip* will contain a JAR file named *jakarta-slide-webdavclient-2.0.jar*; add this JAR and the dependencies to your classpath, and you will be ready to use Jakarta Slide to access WebDAV resources.

Discussion

WebDAV, defined in RFC 2518, is an extension of HTTP/1.1, which supports distributed and collaborative authoring of content. Using a WebDAV client you can read, modify, copy, move, lock, and unlock resources, and you can read, enumerate, and modify properties associated with resources and collections of resources. Resources made available with WebDAV can be mounted as filesystems in Windows XP/2000, Mac OS X, and Linux, and the DAV protocol can be thought of as defining a filesystem built on top of HTTP/1.1. The WebDAV protocol is at the core of a number of distributed version control and content management systems.

Jakarta Slide extends Jakarta HttpClient implementing `HttpMethod` for the methods introduced by the WebDAV protocol. For example, the `LockMethod` in the `org.apache.webdav.lib.methods` package is an instance of `HttpMethod` from Jakarta HttpClient, and just as WebDAV is an extension of HTTP/1.1, Jakarta Slide is an extension of Jakarta HttpClient. When dealing with authentication, cookie management, or redirects, you can configure Jakarta Slide the same way you would configure Jakarta HttpClient; to use Slide, you must create an instance of `HttpClient`.

See Also

For more information about the Jakarta Slide project, see the project page at *http://jakarta.apache.org/slide*.

It is far beyond the scope of this book to fully describe WebDAV, and attempting to do so in one or two recipes would not do it justice. WebDAV, like the protocol it extends, has the potential to transform the way people think about content creation, file sharing, and version control. To learn more about WebDAV, see the following resources:

- RFC 2518 (HTTP Extensions for Distributed Authoring—WEBDAV) at *http://www.zvon.org/tmRFC/RFC2518/Output/index.html*.

- *http://www.webdav.org* is a hub for the WebDAV community. If you are interested in learning about WebDAV and a number of related specifications, see *http://www.webdav.org/specs/*. For a list of software products that support WebDAV, see *http://www.webdav.org/projects/*.

- Subversion is a great replacement for CVS from the Tigris community. You can configure Apache 2.0 to expose a Subversion repository via the WebDAV/DeltaV protocol using mod_dav_svn. For more information about Subversion and mod_dav_svn, see *http://subversion.tigris.org* or *Version Control with Subversion* by Ben Collins-Sussman, Brian W. Fitzpatrick, and C. Michael Pilato (O'Reilly).

If you would like to set up your own WebDAV resource, I recommend installing the Apache HTTP Server with mod_dav. More information about installing "The Number One HTTP Server on the Internet" can be found at *http://httpd.apache.org/*. Information about configuring mod_dav can be found at *http://httpd.apache.org/docs-2.0/mod/mod_dav.html*. The Jakarta Tomcat 5.0 distribution is bundled with a web application that exposes a resource using a WebDAV servlet. To download and install Jakarta Tomcat 5.0, see *http://jakarta.apache.org/tomcat/*.

11.17 Connecting to WebDAV Resources

Problem

You need to connect to a WebDAV resource and list the contents of a collection. As with most WebDAV resources, you need to supply authentication information.

Solution

Create an instance of WebdavResource, passing in a URL and a UsernamePasswordCredential object. List the contents of a WebDAV collection by calling the listWebdavResources() method. The following example demonstrates the use of WebdavResource to list the contents of a WebDAV collection:

```
import org.apache.commons.httpclient.Credentials;
import org.apache.commons.httpclient.HttpClient;
import org.apache.commons.httpclient.HttpException;
import org.apache.commons.httpclient.UsernamePasswordCredentials;
import org.apache.commons.lang.StringUtils;
import org.apache.commons.lang.time.FastDateFormat;
import org.apache.webdav.lib.WebdavResource;

HttpClient client = new HttpClient();
```

```
String url = "http://www.discursive.com/jccook/dav/";
Credentials credentials =
    new UsernamePasswordCredentials("davuser", "davpass");

// List resources in top directory
WebdavResource resource = new WebdavResource(url, credentials);
WebdavResource[] resources = resource.listWebdavResources();
System.out.println( "type  name              size     type" +
                    "               modified");
System.out.println( "-------------------------------------------" +
                    "-------------------------");
for( int i = 0; i < resources.length; i++ )    {
    WebdavResource item = resources[i];
    String type;
    if( item.isCollection() ) {
        type = "dir";
    } else {
        type = "file";
    }
    System.out.print( StringUtils.rightPad( type, 6 ) );
    System.out.print( StringUtils.rightPad( item.getName(), 15 ) );
    System.out.print( StringUtils.rightPad( item.getGetContentLength() + "", 8 ) );
    System.out.print( StringUtils.rightPad( item.getGetContentType(), 23 ) );
    Date lastMod = new Date( item.getGetLastModified() );
    System.out.print(
        StringUtils.rightPad(
            FastDateFormat.getInstance().format( lastMod ), 25 ));
    System.out.print( "\n" );
}
```

The program connects to a WebDAV resource using the credentials supplied to the
constructor of WebdavResource. It lists the contents of a collection and produces the
following output:

```
type  name          size    type                  modified
---------------------------------------------------------------------
file  test.html     14      text/html             5/6/04 12:16 AM
file  index.html    14      text/html             5/5/04 11:59 PM
dir   test          0       httpd/unix-directory  5/6/04 12:01 AM
```

Discussion

Jakarta Slide is built on top of Jakarta HttpClient, but you will notice that this recipe
did not involve the execution of an HttpMethod. This is because WebdavResource manages the complexity of working with an instance of HttpClient behind the scenes.
The only trace of HttpClient is the UsernamePasswordCredentials object that is passed
to the constructor of WebdavResource. Because Jakarta Slide is built on top of Jakarta
HttpClient, almost any feature of Jakarta HttpClient translates directly to Jakarta
Slide. If you need to access a WebDAV repository over SSL with a self-signed certificate, or if you need to alter the cookie policy, you can use the same facilities that are
available to you when you are using HttpClient directly.

11.18 Modifying a WebDAV Resource

Problem

You need to modify a WebDAV resource.

Solution

Use the putMethod( ) on WebdavResource, and be sure to lock and unlock the resource before and after modification. The following example demonstrates the use of lockMethod( ), putMethod( ), and unlockMethod( ) to modify a resource:

```
import org.apache.commons.httpclient.Credentials;
import org.apache.commons.httpclient.HttpClient;
import org.apache.commons.httpclient.HttpException;
import org.apache.commons.httpclient.UsernamePasswordCredentials;
import org.apache.webdav.lib.WebdavResource;

String url = "http://www.discursive.com/jccook/dav/test.html";
Credentials credentials =
    new UsernamePasswordCredentials("davuser", "davpass");

// List resources in top directory
WebdavResource resource = new WebdavResource(url, credentials);

// Lock the Resource for 100 seconds
boolean locked = resource.lockMethod( "tobrien", 100 );

if( locked ) {
    try {
        // Read content as a String
        String resourceData = resource.getMethodDataAsString( );

        // Modify a resource
        System.out.println( "*** Modifying Resource");
        resourceData = resourceData.replaceAll( "test", "modified test" );
        resource.putMethod( resourceData );
    } finally {
        // Unlock the resource
        resource.unlockMethod( );
    }
}

// Close the resource
resource.close( );
```

Discussion

lockMethod( ) accepts an owner and a timeout; the owner is the owner of the lock, and the timeout is the timeout of the lock in number of seconds. When locking a resource, the lockMethod( ) will return a boolean value: true if the lock was granted and false if the lock was not granted. The resource.putMethod( ) was called with a

String object, but it can also be invoked when a byte[], InputStream, or File. putMethod( ) returns a boolean value: true if the put was successful; otherwise, false. The unlockMethod( ) unlocks the resource and makes it available for other clients to lock, modify, and unlock.

See Also

Section 7 of RFC 2518 (HTTP Extensions for Distributed Authoring—WEBDAV) discusses the various types of write locks available in WebDAV. This RFC is available at *http://www.zvon.org/tmRFC/RFC2518/Output/chapter7.html*.

The Slide recipes in this chapter are only meant as a brief introduction to WebDAV. If you would like to learn more about how to work with properties, create collections, and search a WebDAV repository, please see the Jakarta Slide project page at *http://jakarta.apache.org/slide*.

CHAPTER 12
Searching and Filtering

12.0 Introduction

XPath is a popular way to select nodes from an XML document. If you are working with a single XML document or a series of XML documents in an XML Database—such as Apache Xindice—XPath is used to query, address, and filter XML content. Jakarta Commons JXPath allows you to use an XPath query to address objects in a collection or properties of a bean. JXPath is an unconventional application of an XML standard to Java objects, which allows you to quickly select objects from a Collection without the need for an Iterator and a comparison. For example, if you had a List of Person objects with an age property, you could select all of the people older than 10 by passing the expression */person[@age > 10]* to a JXPathContext. JXPath implements a large subset of the XPath specification, and JXPath expressions can be applied to a wide array of objects, beans, Document Object Model (DOM) Documents, collections, and maps. This chapter shows you how to use Commons JXPath to search and filter objects in a collection.

A system will frequently need to search for and identify occurrences of text in a large set of documents. To accomplish this, you will use a tool, such as Jakarta Lucene, to create a searchable index of terms. For example, if you've used an IDE, such as Eclipse, you may find yourself searching for all of the occurrences of the text "testVariable" in your workspace. Eclipse can quickly perform any number of complex searches, and when it does, it is using Jakarta Lucene to index and search every file. Jakarta Lucene is a very efficient search engine that can be used to search a set of documents for terms and phrases and analyze the frequency of terms within a set of documents. Lucene offers a complex query syntax, which allows for compound queries and term matching using proximity and wildcards. This chapter combines Lucene with Commons Digester to create a tool to search a set of XML documents.

12.1 Obtaining Commons JXPath

Problem

You need to use Jakarta Commons JXPath to select objects from a `Collection` using XPath syntax.

Solution

You must download the latest version of Commons JXPath, and place the Commons JXPath JAR in your project's classpath. Following the steps outlined in Recipe 1.1, download Commons JXPath 1.2 instead of Commons Lang.

Discussion

Commons JXPath provides a mechanism for evaluating XML Path Language (XPath) expressions against objects and various data structures in Java. This unconventional application of XPath to objects enables a developer to traverse, address, and filter specific nodes or locations in a complex object graph. This chapter details a few of the ways in which JXPath can be used to search, select, and filter objects.

If you have a Maven project that needs to use Commons JXPath, add a dependency on Commons JXPath 1.2 with the following section in *project.xml*:

```
<dependencies>
  <dependency>
    <id>commons-jxpath</id>
    <version>1.2</version>
  </dependency>
  ....other dependencies...
</dependencies>
```

See Also

For more information about Commons JXPath, see the Commons JXPath project page at *http://jakarta.apache.org/commons/jxpath*. For more information about XPath, see the official W3C XPath recommendation at *http://www.w3.org/TR/xpath*.

12.2 Querying an Object Graph with XPath

Problem

You need to retrieve nested bean properties using an XPath expression. You need to perform an XPath query on an object graph.

Solution

Use Commons JXPath to evaluate an XPath expression against an object graph. JXPath treats nested bean properties as if they were nested elements in an XML document; using JXPath, the expression *a/b/c* is the equivalent of getA().getB().getC(). Create a JXPathContext by passing an object to JXPathContext.newContext(), and retrieve the value of a nested property by passing an XPath expression to the getValue() method on JXPathContext. The following example creates an object graph rooted on a League object and retrieves nested properties using two XPath expressions:

```
import org.apache.commons.jxpath.JXPathContext;

// Create an Object graph
League league = new League();

Team team = new Team();
league.getTeams().add( team );

team.setCoach( new Person( "Coach Bob" ) );
team.getPlayers().add( new Person( "Player Charlie" );
team.getPlayers().add( new Person( "Player Ted" );
team.getPlayers().add( new Person( "Player Bart" );

Team team2 = new Team();
league.getTeams().add( team2 );

team2.setCoach( new Person( "Coach Susan" );
team2.getPlayers().add( new Person( "Player Jim" );

// Query for the coach of a specific player.
JXPathContext context = JXPathContext.newContext( league );
System.out.println( "** Retrieve the first name of Ted's coach");
String xpath = "teams/players[firstName = 'Player Ted']/../coach/firstName";
Object value = context.getValue( xpath );
System.out.println( value );

// Query for the players of a specific coach
context = JXPathContext.newContext( league );
System.out.println( "** Retrieve the players on Coach Susan's team");
value = context.getValue( "teams/coach[firstName = 'Coach Susan']/../players" );
System.out.println( value );
```

This example creates a League with two Team objects stored in a List. Each Team object has a coach property of type Person, and a players property, which is a List of Person objects. A JXPathContext is created by passing league to JXPathContext.newContext(), and two XPath queries are executed by passing query strings to getValue(). The first XPath query returns the firstName of Ted's coach, and the second XPath query returns the players List of the team Susan coaches. This example produces the following output:

```
Retrieve the first name of Ted's coach
Coach Bob
Retrieve the players on Coach Susan's team
[com.discursive.jccook.xml.jxpath.Person@173831b]
```

Discussion

XPath is generally used by select nodes in an XML document, and you may have used it to transform XML with Extensible Stylesheet Language Transformations (XSLT). In this example, XPath is used in a somewhat unconventional manner as a query to filter and select objects based on the values of deeply nested properties. The first query—*teams/players[firstname = 'Player Ted']/../coach/firstName*—is evaluated using the League object as the current node, and if one were to evaluate the XPath expressions *self()* or ., you would retrieve the League object passed to newContext(). When the previous example retrieved the first name of Ted's coach, JXPath iterated through the team List, and located the matching Player and Coach object. The execution of the first XPath expression in the previous example is equivalent to the following code, which iterates through the Team and Player lists:

```
String firstName = null;

Iterator teamIterator = league.getTeams().iterator();
while( teamIterator.hasNext() ) {
    Team team = (Team) teamIterator.next();
    Iterator playerIterator = team.getPlayers().iterator();
    while( playerIterator.hasNext() ) {
        Player player = (Player) playerIterator.next();
        if( player.getFirstName().equals( "Player Ted" ) ) {
            firstName = team.getCoach().getFirstName();
        }
    }
}
```

The ability to filter a complex object graph with a simple expression can help you avoid writing tedious code to iterate through doubly nested collections to compare property values.

See Also

Commons JXPath can also be used to reference objects at a specific index in a List or an array, or objects by a known key in a Map. Recipe 12.4 demonstrates how to use JXPath to reference items in a Map, and Recipe 12.3 demonstrates the use of JXPath to reference an item at a specific index in a List.

12.3 Search a Collection of Simple Objects

Problem

You need to select objects from a Collection using XPath predicates.

Solution

Use Jakarta Commons JXPath to select objects from a Collection using predicates in XPath expressions. The iterate( ) method on JXPathContext takes an XPath expression and returns an Iterator that contains each node satisfying that expression. The following example uses simple XPath predicates to select Person objects from a List by age, first name, and position:

```
import org.apache.commons.jxpath.JXPathContext;

// Create a List of Person objects
List people = new ArrayList( );
people.add(new Person("Ahmad", "Russell", 28 );
people.add(new Person("Tom", "Russell", 35 );
people.add(new Person("Ahmad", "Abuzayedeh", 33 );

// Select all people older than 30
System.out.println( "** People older than 30");
JXPathContext context = JXPathContext.newContext( people );
Iterator iterator = context.iterate(".[@age > 30]");
printPeople(iterator);

// Select all people with a first name of 'Ahmad'
context = JXPathContext.newContext( people );
System.out.println( "** People with first name 'Ahmad'" );
iterator = context.iterate(".[@firstName = 'Ahmad']");
printPeople(iterator);

// Select the second person from the List
context = JXPathContext.newContext( people );
System.out.println( "** Third Person in List" );
Person p = (Person) context.getValue(".[2]");
System.out.println( "Person: " + p.getFirstName() + " " + p.getLastName() +
                    ", age: " + p.getAge() );

// A method to print out the result of each iteration.
private void printPeople(Iterator iterator) {
    while( iterator.hasNext( ) ) {
        Person p = (Person) iterator.next( );
        System.out.println( "Person: " + p.getFirstName() +
            " " + p.getLastName() + ", age: " + p.getAge() );
    }
}
```

A JXPathContext is created by passing a List to newContext( ), and each expression is evaluated through a call to context.iterate( ). Three expressions are evaluated, and the results of each expression are printed in the printPeople( ) method:

```
** People older than 30
Person: Tom Russell, age: 35
Person: Ahmad Abuzayedeh, age: 33

** People with first name 'Ahmad'
Person: Ahmad Russell, age: 28
Person: Ahmad Abuzayedeh, age: 33

** Second Person in List
Person: Tom Russell, age: 35
```

Discussion

The final expression in the previous example is a reference to a specific index in a List; .[2] selected the second element in the List supplied to the JXPathContext. Whenever an XPath expression deals with a property, which is a List or an array, a one-based index can be supplied in brackets after the name of the property. If a League object contains a List of Team objects, and a Team object contains a List of Player objects, the third Player object of the fourteenth Team can be selected by using the XPath expression *league/teams[14]/players[3]*.

In the previous example, which filtered a List of Person objects, you might have noticed that the properties age and firstName are referenced as attributes in the XPath predicate expression. A property can be referenced either as an element or an attribute. In XPath terms, when JXPath resolves properties on an object, the *child* and *attribute* axis both reference properties. This means that the expressions *.[@age > 30]* and *.[age > 30]* would return the same results, as age can be addressed as a child element or attribute of the current node.

iterate( ) returns an Iterator that lets you iterate over all nodes that satisfy the given XPath query. getValue( ) returns the first matching result. In the previous example, iterate( ) retrieves two Person objects with an age property greater than 30. If the same expression were evaluated with getValue( ), only one Person object would have been returned: Tom Russell. Use iterate( ) when multiple nodes may match an XPath expression.

See Also

Chapter 5 demonstrates the use of Commons Collections' CollectionUtils to select items in a Collection that satisfy a Predicate. For more information about using Predicate objects to filter collections, refer to Recipe 5.4.

12.4 Applying XPath Queries to Complex Object Graphs

Problem

You need to use XPath expressions to select objects from a complex object graph referencing the contents of a Map and using expressions with variable references.

Solution

Use Jakarta Commons JXPath to select objects from a collection using XPath queries. The following example uses Commons Digester to parse an XML file into an object graph, and selects Planet objects with a radius greater than 5000:

```
import org.apache.commons.digester.Digester;
import org.apache.commons.digester.xmlrules.DigesterLoader;
import org.apache.commons.jxpath.JXPathContext;

List planets = new ArrayList( );

// Parse Planet XML into a List of Planet objects
InputStream input = getClass( ).getResourceAsStream("./planets.xml");
URL rules = getClass( ).getResource("./planet-digester-rules.xml");
Digester digester = DigesterLoader.createDigester(rules);
digester.push(planets);
digester.parse( input );

// Select all planets with a radius greater than 5000
System.out.println( "Planet Name where radius > 5000");
JXPathContext context = JXPathContext.newContext( planets );
Iterator iterator = context.iterate(".[@radius > 5000]/name");
while( iterator.hasNext( ) ) {
    Object o  = (Object) iterator.next( );
    System.out.println( "Object: " + o);
}
```

The Planet objects are filtered and the names of planets with sufficient radii are printed to the console:

```
Planet Name where radius > 5000
Object: Venus
Object: Saturn
```

This object graph was created from an XML document that contains a list of planets and their physical properties including mass, radius, atmospheric composition, lunar population, and orbital distance and period. Commons Digester (from Chapter 6) is used to parse this XML document to a list of Planet objects. The following XML document, *planets.xml*, was parsed in the previous example:

```
<planets>
    <planet name="Venus" mass="4.869e+24" radius="6051.8">
```

```
            <orbit distance="108200000" period="224.701"/>
            <atmosphere meanTemp="482" pressure="92">
                <component symbol="CO2" percentage="96"/>
                <component symbol="N" percentage="3"/>
                <component symbol="Other" percentage="1"/>
            </atmosphere>
        </planet>
        <planet name="Mars" mass="6.421e+23" radius="3397.2">
            <orbit distance="227940000" period="686.98"/>
            <atmosphere meanTemp="-63" pressure="0.007">
                <component symbol="CO2" percentage="95.32"/>
                <component symbol="N2" percentage="2.7"/>
                <component symbol="Ar" percentage="1.6"/>
            </atmosphere>
            <moon>Phobos</moon>
            <moon>Deimos</moon>
        </planet>
        <planet name="Saturn" mass="5.688e+26" radius="60268">
            <orbit distance="1429400000" period="29.458"/>
            <atmosphere meanTemp="-125" pressure="1.4">
                <component symbol="H" percentage="97"/>
                <component symbol="He" percentage="3"/>
            </atmosphere>
            <moon>Pan</moon>
            <moon>Atlas</moon>
            <moon>Prometheus</moon>
            <moon>Pandora</moon>
        <moon>Epimetheus</moon>
        <moon>Janus</moon>
        <moon>Mimas</moon>
    </planet>
</planets>
```

To parse this XML document, the following Digester rules are passed to
DigesterLoader.createDigester( ). This digester rule-set creates a Planet, Orbit, and
Atmosphere object for each planet. Moon objects are created and added to Planet
objects using the addMoon( ) method on Planet. Individual compounds in an atmosphere are added to an Atmosphere's component Map using addComponent( ). The following XML document contains the contents of the *planet-digester-rules.xml* file used in
the previous example:

```
<digester-rules>
    <pattern value="planets/planet">
        <object-create-rule classname="Planet"/>
        <set-properties-rule/>
        <pattern value="orbit">
            <object-create-rule classname=" Orbit"/>
            <set-properties-rule/>
            <set-next-rule methodname="setOrbit" paramtype=" Orbit"/>
        </pattern>
        <pattern value="atmosphere">
            <object-create-rule classname="Atmosphere"/>
            <set-properties-rule/>
```

```
                <pattern value="component">
                        <call-method-rule methodname="addComponent" paramcount="2"
                                        paramtypes="java.lang.String,java.lang.Double"/>
                        <call-param-rule attrname="symbol" paramnumber="0"/>
                        <call-param-rule attrname="percentage" paramnumber="1"/>
                </pattern>
                <set-next-rule methodname="setAtmosphere"
                                        paramtype=" Atmosphere"/>
        </pattern>
        <call-method-rule pattern="moon" methodname="addMoon"
                                paramtypes="java.lang.String" paramcount="0"/>
        <set-next-rule methodname="add" paramtype="java.lang.Object"/>
    </pattern>
</digester-rules>
```

Discussion

XPath expressions can be parameterized by referencing a variable name: *$variable*.
The following example references a variable *$moonName*, which is populated by
calling declareVariable( ) on context.getVariables( ):

```
System.out.println( "Planet Name where a moon is named Deimos");
context.getVariables().declareVariable("moonName", "Deimos");
iterator = context.iterate("./moons[. = $moonName]/../name");
while( iterator.hasNext() ) {
    String name  = (String) iterator.next();
    System.out.println( "Planet Namet: " + name);
}
```

This example selects the name of a planet with a moon named "Deimos." The results
of the previous example are printed below:

```
Planet Name where a moon is named Deimos
Planet Namet: Mars
```

Planet.getAtmosphere().getComponents( ) returns a Map with element symbols as
keys. The following example selects every planet with more than a 2% Helium atmosphere:

```
System.out.println( "Planet where Helium percentage greater than 2");
iterator = context.iterate("./atmosphere/components/He[.>2]/../../..");
while( iterator.hasNext() ) {
    Planet p  = (Planet) iterator.next();
    System.out.println( "Planet: " + p.getName());
}
```

To select every planet with more than a 2% Helium atmosphere, the XPath expression in the previous example references a specific key in the components Map as if it
were a nested element. *components/He[.>2]* will evaluate to true if getComponents( ).
get("He") is a number larger than 2. The previous code determines that Saturn is the
only one of these three planets with more than 2% Helium:

```
Planet where Helium percentage greater than 2
Planet: Saturn
```

The following example prints a list of each moon and the corresponding planet using a reference to a variable in an XPath expression:

```
System.out.println( "All of the Moon Names");
iterator = context.iterate("./moons");
while( iterator.hasNext() ) {
    String moon  = (String) iterator.next();
    context.getVariables().declareVariable("moonName", moon);
    String planet =
        (String) context.getValue("./moons[. = $moonName]/../name");
    System.out.println( "Moon: " + moon + ", \t\t\tPlanet: " + planet);
}
```

The previous example shows that a JXPathContext can be reused. This example iterates through each moon and finds the name of the planet corresponding to each moon using the results of the first expression to populate a variable in the second expression. The XPath expression, *./moons[. = $moonName]/../name*, contains a reference to the variable $moonName, which is set by passing a variable name and value to the declareVariable( ) method on JXPathContext. This example prints each moon and planet to the console as follows:

```
All of the Moon Names
Moon: Phobos,        Planet: Mars
Moon: Deimos,        Planet: Mars
Moon: Pan,           Planet: Saturn
Moon: Atlas,         Planet: Saturn
Moon: Prometheus,    Planet: Saturn
Moon: Pandora,       Planet: Saturn
Moon: Epimetheus,    Planet: Saturn
Moon: Janus,         Planet: Saturn
Moon: Mimas,         Planet: Saturn
```

See Also

There is much more to JXPath including object creation and the ability to set properties using XPath expressions; for more information about using JXPath to access maps, collections, servlet contexts, and DOM/JDOM Documents, see the JXPath User's Guide (*http://jakarta.apache.org/commons/jxpath/users-guide.html*).

12.5   Obtaining Jakarta Lucene

Problem

You need to use Jakarta Lucene to create a searchable index of documents.

Solution

Download Jakarta Lucene 1.4 from *http://jakarta.apache.org/site/binindex.cgi*, and uncompress the distribution archive. Place the *lucene-1.4-final.jar* file in your classpath.

Discussion

Jakarta Lucene is a full-text search engine that can be used to index any information. Lucene maintains an index of Document objects that can contain any number of fields, and this index can be searched using a highly developed query language.

If you have a Maven project that needs to use Jakarta Lucene, add a dependency on Jakarta Lucene 1.4 with the following section in *project.xml*:

```
<dependencies>
  <dependency>
    <id>lucene</id>
    <version>1.4</version>
  </dependency>
  ....other dependencies...
</dependencies>
```

See Also

For more information on the Jakarta Lucene project, see the Jakarta Lucene project page at *http://jakarta.apache.org/lucene*.

12.6   Creating an Index of XML Documents

Problem

You need to quickly search a collection of XML documents, and, to do this, you need to create an index of terms keeping track of the context in which these terms appear.

Solution

Use Jakarta Lucene and Jakarta Digester and create an index of Lucene Document objects for the lowest level of granularity you wish to search. For example, if you are attempting to search for speeches in a Shakespeare play that contain specific terms, create a Lucene Document object for each speech. For the purposes of this recipe, assume that you are attempting to index Shakespeare plays stored in the following XML format:

```
<?xml version="1.0"?>

<PLAY>
  <TITLE>All's Well That Ends Well</TITLE>

  <ACT>
    <TITLE>ACT I</TITLE>

    <SCENE>
      <TITLE>SCENE I.  Rousillon. The COUNT's palace.</TITLE>
```

```
<SPEECH>
  <SPEAKER>COUNTESS</SPEAKER>
  <LINE>In delivering my son from me, I bury a second husband.</LINE>
</SPEECH>

<SPEECH>
  <SPEAKER>BERTRAM</SPEAKER>
  <LINE>And I in going, madam, weep o'er my father's death</LINE>
  <LINE>anew: but I must attend his majesty's command, to</LINE>
  <LINE>whom I am now in ward, evermore in subjection.</LINE>
</SPEECH>
      </SCENE>
    </ACT>
  </PLAY>
```

The following class creates a Lucene index of Shakespeare speeches, reading XML files for each play in the *./data/Shakespeare* directory, and calling the `PlayIndexer` to create Lucene Document objects for every speech. These `Document` objects are then written to a Lucene index using an `IndexWriter`:

```java
import java.io.File;
import java.io.FilenameFilter;

import org.apache.log4j.Logger;
import org.apache.lucene.analysis.standard.StandardAnalyzer;
import org.apache.lucene.index.IndexWriter;
import org.apache.oro.io.GlobFilenameFilter;

File dataDir = new File("./data/shakespeare");
logger.info( "Looking for XML files in "

FilenameFilter xmlFilter = new GlobFilenameFilter( "*.xml" );
File[] xmlFiles = dataDir.listFiles( xmlFilter );

logger.info( "Creating Index");
IndexWriter writer = new IndexWriter("index",
                                     new SimpleAnalyzer( ), true);
PlayIndexer playIndexer = new PlayIndexer( writer );
playIndexer.init( );

for (int i = 0; i < xmlFiles.length; i++) {
    playIndexer.index(xmlFiles[i]);
}

writer.optimize( );
writer.close( );

logger.info( "Parsing Complete, Index Created");
```

The `PlayIndexer` class, shown in Example 12-1, parses each XML file and creates Document objects that are written to an `IndexWriter`. The `PlayIndexer` uses Commons Digester to create a Lucene Document object for every speech. The `init( )` method creates a `Digester` instance designed to interact with an inner class, `DigestContext`, which keeps track of the current context of a speech—play, act, scene, speaker—and the textual contents of a speech. At the end of every speech element, the DigestContext invokes the processSpeech( ) method that creates a Lucene Document for each speech and writes this Document to the Lucene IndexWriter. Because each Document is associated with the specific context of a speech, it will be possible to obtain a specific location for each term or phrase.

Example 12-1. PlayIndexer using Commons Digester and Jakarta Lucene

```java
package com.discursive.jccook.xml.bardsearch;

import java.io.File;
import java.io.IOException;
import java.net.URL;

import org.apache.commons.digester.Digester;
import org.apache.commons.digester.xmlrules.DigesterLoader;
import org.apache.log4j.Logger;
import org.apache.lucene.document.Document;
import org.apache.lucene.document.Field;
import org.apache.lucene.index.IndexWriter;
import org.xml.sax.SAXException;

import com.discursive.jccook.util.LogInit;

public class PlayIndexer {

    private static Logger logger =
        Logger.getLogger( PlayIndexer.class );
    static { LogInit.init( ); }

    private IndexWriter indexWriter;
    private Digester digester;
    private DigestContext context;

    public PlayIndexer(IndexWriter pIndexWriter) {
        indexWriter = pIndexWriter;
    }

    public void init( ) {
        URL playRules =
            PlayIndexer.class.getResource("play-digester-rules.xml");
        digester = DigesterLoader.createDigester( playRules );
    }

    public void index(File playXml) throws IOException, SAXException {
        context = new DigestContext( );
        digester.push( context );
        digester.parse( playXml );
        logger.info( "Parsed: " + playXml.getAbsolutePath( ) );
    }
```

```java
    public void processSpeech( ) {
        Document doc = new Document( );
        doc.add(Field.Text("play", context.playTitle));
        doc.add(Field.Text("act", context.actTitle));
        doc.add(Field.Text("scene", context.sceneTitle));
        doc.add(Field.Text("speaker", context.speaker));
        doc.add(Field.Text("speech",
                            new StringReader( context.speech.toString( ) )));
        try {
            indexWriter.addDocument( doc );
        } catch( IOException ioe ) {
            logger.error( "Unable to add document to index", ioe);
        }
    }

    public class DigestContext {
        File playXmlFile;
        String playTitle, actTitle, sceneTitle, speaker;
        StringBuffer speech = new StringBuffer( );

        public void setActTitle(String string) { actTitle = string; }
        public void setPlayTitle(String string) { playTitle = string; }
        public void setSceneTitle(String string){ sceneTitle = string;}
        public void setSpeaker(String string) { speaker = string; }
        public void appendLine(String pLine) { speech.append( pLine ); }

        public void speechEnd( ) {
            processSpeech( );
            speech.delete( 0, speech.length( ) );
            speaker = "";
        }
    }
}
```

Example 12-1 used a Digester rule set defined in Example 12-2. This set of rules is designed to invoke a series of methods in a set sequence to populate the context variables for each speech. The Digester rules in Example 12-2 never push or pop objects onto the digester stack; instead, the Digester is being used to populate variables and invoke methods on an object that creates Lucene Document objects based on a set of context variables. This example uses the Digester as a shorthand Simple API for XML (SAX) parser; the PlayIndexer contains a series of callback methods, and the Digester rule set simplifies the interaction between the underlying SAX parser and the DigestContext.

Example 12-2. Digester rules for PlayIndexer

```xml
<?xml version="1.0"?>

<digester-rules>
    <pattern value="PLAY">
```

Example 12-2. Digester rules for PlayIndexer (continued)

```
        <bean-property-setter-rule pattern="TITLE"
                              propertyname="playTitle"/>
    <pattern value="ACT">
        <bean-property-setter-rule pattern="TITLE"
                                propertyname="actTitle"/>
          <pattern value="PROLOGUE">
            <bean-property-setter-rule pattern="TITLE"
                                    propertyname="sceneTitle"/>
            <pattern value="SPEECH">
                <bean-property-setter-rule pattern="SPEAKER"
                                        propertyname="speaker"/>
                <call-method-rule pattern="LINE"
                              methodname="appendLine"
                              paramtype="java.lang.String"
                              paramcount="0"/>
                <call-method-rule methodname="speechEnd"
                              paramtype="java.lang.Object"/>
            </pattern>
        </pattern>
        <pattern value="SCENE">
            <bean-property-setter-rule pattern="TITLE"
                                    propertyname="sceneTitle"/>
            <pattern value="SPEECH">
                <bean-property-setter-rule pattern="SPEAKER"
                                        propertyname="speaker"/>
                <call-method-rule pattern="LINE"
                              methodname="appendLine"
                              paramtype="java.lang.String"
                              paramcount="0"/>
                <call-method-rule methodname="speechEnd"
                              paramtype="java.lang.Object"/>
            </pattern>
            </pattern>
        </pattern>
    </pattern>
</digester-rules>
```

Discussion

In this recipe, an `IndexWriter` was created with a `SimpleAnalyzer`. An `Analyzer` takes a series of terms or tokens and creates the terms to be indexed; different `Analyzer` implementations are appropriate for different applications. A `SimpleAnalyzer` will keep every term in a piece of text, discarding nothing. A `StandardAnalyzer` is an `Analyzer` that discards common English words with little semantic value, such as "the," "a," "an," and "for." The `StandardAnalyzer` maintains a list of terms to dis-card—a *stop list*. Cutting down on the number of terms indexed can save time and space in an index, but it can also limit accuracy. For example, if one were to use the `StandardAnalyzer` to index the play *Hamlet*, a search for "to be or not to be" would return zero results, because every term in that phrase is a common English word on `StandardAnalyzer`'s stop list. In this recipe, a `SimpleAnalyzer` is used because it keeps track of the occurrence of every term in a document.

What you end up with after running this example is a directory named *index*, which contains files used by Lucene to associate terms with documents. In this example, a Lucene Document consists of the contextual information fully describing each speech—"play," "act," "scene," "speaker," and "speech." `Field` objects are added to Document objects using Document's `addDoc( )` method. The `processSpeech( )` method in `PlayIndexer` creates Lucene Document objects that contain `Field`s; `Field` objects are created by calling `Text( )`, a static method on `Field`. The first parameter to `Text( )` is the name of the field, and the second parameter is the content to be indexed. Passing a `String` as the second parameter to `Text( )` instructs the `IndexWriter` to store the content of a field in a Lucene index; a `Field` created with a `String` can be displayed in a search result. Passing a `Reader` as the second parameter to `Text( )` instructs the `IndexWriter` not to store the contents of a field, and the contents of a field created with a `Reader` cannot be returned in a search result. In the previous example, the "speech" field is created with a `Reader` to reduce the size of the Lucene index, and every other `Field` is created with a `String` so that our search results can provide a speech's contextual coordinates.

See Also

Sure, you've created a Lucene index, but how would you search it? The index created in this recipe can be searched with Lucene using techniques described in Recipes 12.7 and 12.8.

If you are indexing a huge database of English documents, consider using the `StandardAnalyzer` to discard common English words. If you are indexing documents written in German or Russian, Lucene ships with `GermanAnalyzer` and `RussianAnalyzer`, which both contain stop word lists for these languages. For more information about these two implementations of Analyzer, see the Lucene JavaDoc at *http://jakarta. apache.org/lucene/docs/api/index.html*. Analyzer implementations for French, Dutch, Chinese, and Czech can be found in the Lucene Sandbox (*http://cvs.apache.org/ viewcvs/jakarta-lucene-sandbox/contributions/analyzers/*).

For more information about Jakarta Lucene, see the Lucene project web site at *http:// jakarta.apache.org/lucene*.

This recipe uses the *The Plays of Shakespeare*, compiled by Jon Bosak. To download the complete works of Shakespeare in XML format, see *http://www.ibiblio.org/bosak/*.

12.7   Searching for a Specific Term in a Document Index

Problem

You need to identify which documents in a Lucene index contain specific terms or phrases.

Solution

Use an IndexSearcher to search a Lucene index created with IndexWriter. This recipe assumes that you have created a Lucene index using the techniques shown in the previous recipe. The constructor of IndexSearcher takes the name of a directory that contains a Lucene index. A Query object can be created by passing a String query, a default search field, and an Analyzer to QueryParser.parse( ). The following example searches the Lucene index created in the previous recipe for all speeches containing the term "Ophelia":

```
import org.apache.lucene.analysis.Analyzer;
import org.apache.lucene.analysis.SimpleAnalyzer;
import org.apache.lucene.document.Document;
import org.apache.lucene.queryParser.QueryParser;
import org.apache.lucene.search.Hits;
import org.apache.lucene.search.IndexSearcher;
import org.apache.lucene.search.Query;
import org.apache.lucene.search.Searcher;

logger.info("Searching for Ophelia");
Searcher searcher = new IndexSearcher("index");
Analyzer analyzer = new SimpleAnalyzer( );
Query query = QueryParser.parse("Ophelia", "speech", analyzer);
Hits hits = searcher.search(query);
logger.info( "Searching Done, hit: " + hits.length( ) );

System.out.println( "Score | Play | Act | Scene | Speaker" );

for( int i = 0; i < hits.length( ); i++ ) {
    Document doc = hits.doc(i);
    System.out.print( (int) (hits.score(i) * 100 ) );
    System.out.print( " | " + doc.get("play") );
    System.out.print( " | " + doc.get("act") );
    System.out.print( " | " + doc.get("scene") );
    System.out.print( " | " + doc.get("speaker") + "\n" );
}
```

An IndexSearcher is created by passing in the name of the directory containing the Lucene index to its constructor. Next, an Analyzer is created that will analyze the query String.

It is important at this stage to use the same Anaylzer implementation that was used to create the Lucene index to be searched, and, in this case, a SimpleAnalyzer is used. If you use an Analyzer, which discards the words "to," "be," "or," and "not," and then try to create a Query for "to be or not to be," you are not going to find the appropriate speech in *Hamlet* because the Analyzer you used to parse your query dropped every term.

QueryParser parses the query string and creates a Query object that will search the "speech" field of each Document in the index. The example then calls searcher. search() and iterates through Document objects contained in an instance of Hits. Hits contains a List of Document objects and a relevance score for each result; a relevance score is a number between 1.00 and 0.00 that tells you how strongly a particular Document matches a particular query. The more a term occurs in a speech, the more relevant the speech is, and the closer the relevance score is to 1. The previous example returns every occurrence of the term "Ophelia" in every Shakespeare play, and, from the results, it is clear that Ophelia is a character in *Hamlet*. Every occurrence of Ophelia is listed with the relevance, play, act, scene, and speaker:

```
1   INFO [main] TermSearch      - Searching for Ophelia
321 INFO [main] TermSearch      - Searching Done, hit: 19

Score | Play   | Act     | Scene      | Speaker
100   | Hamlet | ACT IV  | SCENE V    | QUEEN GERTRUDE
100   | Hamlet | ACT IV  | SCENE V    | KING CLAUDIUS
81    | Hamlet | ACT IV  | SCENE V    | QUEEN GERTRUDE
81    | Hamlet | ACT V   | SCENE I    | HAMLET
58    | Hamlet | ACT I   | SCENE III  | LORD POLONIUS
58    | Hamlet | ACT II  | SCENE I    | LORD POLONIUS
50    | Hamlet | ACT I   | SCENE III  | LAERTES
33    | Hamlet | ACT V   | SCENE I    | HAMLET
25    | Hamlet | ACT III | SCENE I    | QUEEN GERTRUDE
24    | Hamlet | ACT III | SCENE I    | LORD POLONIUS
22    | Hamlet | ACT IV  | SCENE VII  | LAERTES
21    | Hamlet | ACT III | SCENE I    | KING CLAUDIUS
17    | Hamlet | ACT IV  | SCENE V    | LAERTES
17    | Hamlet | ACT II  | SCENE II   | LORD POLONIUS
16    | Hamlet | ACT III | SCENE I    | LORD POLONIUS
14    | Hamlet | ACT II  | SCENE II   | LORD POLONIUS
13    | Hamlet | ACT I   | SCENE III  | LORD POLONIUS
11    | Hamlet | ACT I   | SCENE III  | LAERTES
11    | Hamlet | ACT III | SCENE I    | HAMLET
```

A Query can also search for multiple terms in a specific order because a Lucene index keeps track of the order relationships between terms within a Document. Searching for the famous "to be or not to be" returns a single match from Act III, Scene I of *Hamlet*:

```
0 [main] INFO TermSearch  - Searching for 'speech:"to be or not to be"'
354 [main] INFO TermSearch  - Searching Done, hit: 1

Score | Play   | Act     | Scene    | Speaker
100   | Hamlet | ACT III | SCENE I  | HAMLET
```

This search was only possible because the SimpleAnalyzer is used during index creation and query parsing. If a different Analyzer had been used to create the index, the Lucene index would not be storing information about such common words as "to," "be," "or," and "not." It is a common practice for general search engines to discard very common terms such as "the," "a," "an," or "when." Discarding unimportant terms can reduce the size of an index remarkably, but if you need to search for "to be or not to be," you will need to preserve all terms.

Discussion

Both of the previous examples executed queries in about 300 milliseconds on a very cheap 2.0 GHz Celeron eMachine. This search would have taken orders of magnitude longer to execute if every document had to be parsed and searched in response to a query. The only reason a full-text search can be completed in a few hundred milliseconds is the presence of a Lucene index. The Lucene index provides a database of Documents indexed by term, and an IndexSearcher is essentially retrieving objects from this database.

A Lucene query can combine multiple criteria, search for terms matching wildcards, and find documents by multiple fields. A specific field can be searched by prefixing a term with the field name and a colon; for example, to search for documents in a certain play, one would use the query *play:"Hamlet"*. The second parameter to QueryParser.parse( ) is the default field for a query, and, in the previous example, the default field is "speech." This means that a term without a field qualifier will match the "speech" field. Table 12-1 lists some possible Lucene queries and describes the results they would return.

Table 12-1. A survey of Lucene queries

Query	Description
play:"Hamlet"	Returns all documents with a "play" field matching the string "Hamlet"
"to be" AND "not to be"	Returns a document with a "speech" field containing the strings "to be" and "not to be"
play:"Hamlet" AND ("Polonius" OR "Hamlet")	Returns all documents with a "play" field matching "Hamlet" with a "speech" field that contains the terms "Polonius" or "Hamlet"
s*ings	Returns all documents with a "speech" field containing a term that starts with "s" and ends in "ings"; includes terms such as "strings" and "slings"
L?ve	Returns all documents with a "speech" field containing terms such as "Love" or "Live"
"slings" NOT "arrows"	Returns documents with a "speech" field that contains "slings" but not "arrows"

The following Lucene query finds documents containing "Saint Crispin" and "England" or "to be or not to be" and "slings and arrows":

```
("Saint Crispin" AND "England") OR
("to be or not to be" AND ("slings and arrows") )
```

When this query is executed against the Lucene index used in the previous two recipes, two speeches are returned—a rousing battle speech from *Henry V* and Hamlet's existential rant. Running this query would produce the following output:

```
0 [main] INFO TermSearch  - Searching for ("Saint Crispin" AND "England") OR ("to be
or not to be" AND ("slings and arrows") )
406 [main] INFO TermSearch  - Searching Done, hit: 2
Score | Play    | Act     | Scene                          | Speaker
31    | Hamlet  | ACT III | SCENE I.  A room in the castle. | HAMLET
11    | Henry V | ACT IV  | SCENE III.  The English camp.  | KING HENRY V
```

See Also

Lucene is a capable search engine with very rich query syntax supporting fuzzy term matching and searching for terms based on proximity. For more details on Lucene query syntax, see *http://jakarta.apache.org/lucene/docs/queryparsersyntax.html*.

12.8   Finding the Frequency of Terms in an Index

Problem

You need to find the most frequently used terms in a Lucene index.

Solution

Use Jakarta Lucene to index your documents and obtain a TermEnum using an IndexReader. The frequency of a term is defined as the number of documents in which a specific term appears, and a TermEnum object contains the frequency of every term in a set of documents. Example 12-3 iterates over the terms contained in TermEnum returning every term that appears in more than 1,100 speeches.

Example 12-3. TermFreq finding the most frequent terms in an index

```java
package com.discursive.jccook.xml.bardsearch;

import java.util.ArrayList;
import java.util.Collections;
import java.util.Iterator;
import java.util.List;

import org.apache.commons.lang.builder.CompareToBuilder;
import org.apache.log4j.Logger;
import org.apache.lucene.index.IndexReader;
import org.apache.lucene.index.TermEnum;

import com.discursive.jccook.util.LogInit;

public class TermFreq {
    private static Logger logger = Logger.getLogger(TermFreq.class);
    static { LogInit.init(); }
```

Example 12-3. TermFreq finding the most frequent terms in an index (continued)

```
public static void main(String[] pArgs) throws Exception {
    logger.info("Threshold is 1100" );
    Integer threshold = new Integer( 1100 );

    IndexReader reader = IndexReader.open( "index" );
    TermEnum enum = reader.terms( );
    List termList = new ArrayList( );
    while( enum.next( ) ) {
        if( enum.docFreq( ) >= threshold.intValue( ) &&
            enum.term( ).field( ).equals( "speech" ) ) {
            Freq freq = new Freq( enum.term( ).text( ), enum.docFreq( ) );
            termList.add( freq );
        }
    }
    Collections.sort( termList );
    Collections.reverse( termList );

    System.out.println( "Frequency | Term" );
    Iterator iterator = termList.iterator( );
    while( iterator.hasNext( ) ) {
        Freq freq = (Freq) iterator.next( );
        System.out.print( freq.frequency );
        System.out.println( " | " + freq.term );
    }
}

public static class Freq implements Comparable {
    String term;
    int frequency;

    public Freq( String term, int frequency ) {
        this.term = term;
        this.frequency = frequency;
    }

    public int compareTo(Object o) {
        if( o instanceof Freq ) {
            Freq oFreq = (Freq) o;
            return new CompareToBuilder( )
                .append( frequency, oFreq.frequency )
                .append( term, oFreq.term )
                .toComparison( );
        } else {
            return 0;
        }
    }
}
}
```

A Lucene index is opened by passing the name of the *index* directory to IndexReader.
open( ), and a TermEnum is retrieved from the IndexReader with a call to reader.terms( ).
The previous example iterates through every term contained in TermEnum, creating

and populating an instance of the inner class Freq, if a term appears in more than 1,100 documents and the term occurs in the "speech" field. TermEnum contains three methods of interest: next( ), docFreq( ), and term( ). next( ) moves to the next term in the TermEnum, returning false if no more terms are available. docFreq( ) returns the number of documents a term appears in, and term( ) returns a Term object containing the text of the term and the field the term occurs in. The List of Freq objects is sorted by frequency and reversed, and the most frequent terms in a set of Shakespeare plays is printed to the console:

```
0    INFO  [main] TermFreq    - Threshold is 4500
Frequency | Term
2907 | i
2823 | the
2647 | and
2362 | to
2186 | you
1950 | of
1885 | a
1870 | my
1680 | is
1678 | that
1564 | in
1562 | not
1410 | it
1262 | s
1247 | me
1200 | for
1168 | be
1124 | this
1109 | but
```

Discussion

From this list, it appears that the most frequent terms in Shakespeare plays are inconsequential words, such as "the," "a," "of," and "be." The index this example was executed against was created with a SimpleAnalyzer that does not discard any terms. If this index is created with StandardAnalyzer, common articles and pronouns will not be stored as terms in the index, and they will not show up on the most frequent terms list. Running this example against an index created with a StandardAnalyzer and reducing the frequency threshold to 600 documents returns the following results:

```
Frequency | Term
2727 | i
2153 | you
1862 | my
1234 | me
1091 | your
1057 | have
1027 | he
973 | what
```

```
921 | so
893 | his
824 | do
814 | him
693 | all
647 | thou
632 | shall
614 | lord
```

See Also

There is an example of enumerating term frequency in the Jakarta Lucene Sandbox. To see this frequency analysis example, see the "High Frequency Terms" example (*http://jakarta.apache.org/lucene/docs/lucene-sandbox/*).

Index

We'd like to hear your suggestions for improving our indexes. Send email to *index@oreilly.com*.

About the Author

Timothy M. O'Brien is an active committer in the Jakarta Commons, a subproject of the Apache Software Foundation's Jakarta project. As a consultant, Tim tries to encourage the adoption of open source software and nudge organizations to view community participation as an essential strategy. In addition to his professional responsibilities, he is a bass/baritone who sings frequently in the Chicagoland area. Tim discovered programming on a Basic Four, TRS-80, and Commodore 64 in his hometown of Wellesley, Massachusetts; subsequently, he studied Computer Engineering at the University of Virginia.

Colophon

Our look is the result of reader comments, our own experimentation, and feedback from distribution channels. Distinctive covers complement our distinctive approach to technical topics, breathing personality and life into potentially dry subjects.

The animal on the cover of *Jakarta Commons Cookbook* is an aardvark. Native to the grasslands and woodlands of sub-Saharan Africa, the aardvark is the only surviving species in the Orycteropodidae family of mammals. Despite being named for its resemblance to the pig (the word aardvark derives from the Dutch for "earth pig"), the aardvark's appearance is far more similar to that of marsupials, such as the bilby and the bandicoot.

Aardvarks are distinguished by their pig-like torso, arched back, oversized ears, and lengthy snout. They are typically yellow-gray in color, although their tough skin may appear reddish-brown when coated in soil. On average, the adult aadvark is slightly more than three feet long and weighs approximately 90 to 140 pounds. Aardvarks dine almost exclusively on ants and termites, for which their tiny, tubular mouth and long, slender tongue are ideally suited. Upon locating a cache of ants with their keen sense of smell, aardvarks use their strong front legs to dig into the nest and rapidly lap up the insects with their sticky tongue. Scientists have observed aardvarks devouring as many as 50,000 insects in a single night!

By nature, aardvarks tend to be reclusive. They are nocturnal creatures that build elaborate individual burrows of up to 40 feet in length in their home terrain, used to search for food and provide temporary shelter. Mothers make use of burrows as a more permanent home when giving birth to their young.

Currently, aardvarks are not considered an endangered species. However, they are still targeted by hunters for their exquisite cylindrical teeth, which are often used for decorative purposes.

Matt Hutchinson was the production editor for *Jakarta Commons Cookbook*. Octal Publishing, Inc. provided production services. Marlowe Shaeffer, Sarah Sherman, and Darren Kelly provided quality control.

Emma Colby designed the cover of this book, based on a series design by Edie Freedman. The cover image is a 19th-century engraving from *Illustrated Natural History*. Clay Fernald produced the cover layout with QuarkXPress 4.1 using Adobe's ITC Garamond font.

David Futato designed the interior layout. This book was converted by Julie Hawks to FrameMaker 5.5.6 with a format conversion tool created by Erik Ray, Jason McIntosh, Neil Walls, and Mike Sierra that uses Perl and XML technologies. The text font is Linotype Birka; the heading font is Adobe Myriad Condensed; and the code font is LucasFont's TheSans Mono Condensed. The illustrations that appear in the book were produced by Lesley Borash using Macromedia FreeHand MX and Adobe Photoshop CS. The tip and warning icons were drawn by Christopher Bing. This colophon was written by Sanders Kleinfeld.